A Focus on Self-Reflection, Skills Development, and Self-Assessment

Interpersonal Communication and You offers plenty of opportunities for students to apply what they are learning to their own lives:

- Self-Quizzes help students analyze strengths and weaknesses so that they can focus on improving their interpersonal communication.

- Self-Reflections invite students to examine their own experiences and learn the habit of ongoing self-reflection.

- Skills Practices prompt students to put these skills into action with step-by-step instructions.

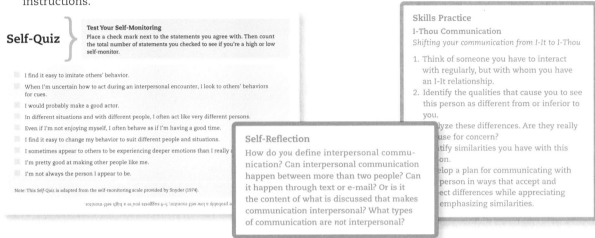

Self-Quiz

Test Your Self-Monitoring

Place a check mark next to the statements you agree with. Then count the total number of statements you checked to see if you're a high or low self-monitor.

- I find it easy to imitate others' behavior.
- When I'm uncertain how to act during an interpersonal encounter, I look to others' behaviors for cues.
- I would probably make a good actor.
- In different situations and with different people, I often act like very different persons.
- Even if I'm not enjoying myself, I often behave as if I'm having a good time.
- I find it easy to change my behavior to suit different people and situations.
- I sometimes appear to others to be experiencing deeper emotions than I really am.
- I'm pretty good at making other people like me.
- I'm not always the person I appear to be.

Note: This *Self-Quiz* is adapted from the self-monitoring scale provided by Snyder (1974).

Self-Reflection

How do *you* define interpersonal communication? Can interpersonal communication happen between more than two people? Can it happen through text or e-mail? Or is it the content of what is discussed that makes communication interpersonal? What types of communication are *not* interpersonal?

Skills Practice

I-Thou Communication

Shifting your communication from I-It to I-Thou

1. Think of someone you have to interact with regularly, but with whom you have an I-It relationship.
2. Identify the qualities that cause you to see this person as different from or inferior to you.
3. Analyze these differences. Are they really cause for concern?
4. Identify similarities you have with this person.
5. Develop a plan for communicating with this person in ways that accept and respect differences while appreciating and emphasizing similarities.

A Current and Comprehensive Overview of the Discipline

An accessible approach draws on the best of classic and cutting-edge scholarship. Topics like online self-presentation and mediated communication competence are integrated with familiar areas such as active listening and intercultural competence.

 **Powerful Multimedia Content Enhances Learning with an Individualized Approach**

LaunchPad is a dynamic new platform that combines the interactive e-book with high-quality multimedia content and activities that give immediate feedback. Featured in LaunchPad:

 More than 70 video activities. Connected to every chapter, these videos help students see theory in action, and the accompanying reflection questions help them apply what they see to their own experiences. Video activities are easily assignable and make excellent journal prompts or discussion starters.

 LearningCurve. This adaptive quizzing program prompts students to test their knowledge while reinforcing their learning. Its reporting tools let instructors see the results and adapt their teaching to student needs.

See the inside back cover for more information about LaunchPad. For more information about *Interpersonal Communication and You*, please visit **macmillanhighered.com/ipcandyou/catalog**.

Interpersonal Communication and You

AN INTRODUCTION

Interpersonal Communication and You

AN INTRODUCTION

Steven McCornack
Michigan State University

Bedford/St. Martin's
Boston • New York

For Bedford/St. Martin's

Vice President, Editorial, Macmillan Higher Education Humanities: Edwin Hill
Publisher for Communication: Erika Gutierrez
Senior Developmental Editor: Julia Bartz
Project Editor: Won McIntosh
Production Manager: Joe Ford
Marketing Manager: Thomas Digiano
Editorial Assistant: Caitlin Crandell
Director of Rights and Permissions: Hilary Newman
Senior Art Director: Anna Palchik
Text Design: Jerilyn Bockorick
Cover Design: William Boardman
Cover Photos: Couple sitting at outdoor table talking. Ruth Jenkinson/Getty Images; Social aid for elderly person. BSIP/UIG/Getty Images; Business executive discussing with her client. ONOKY-Eric Audras/Getty Images; Girl using smartphone in a restaurant. Oscar Wong/Getty Images; Businessman using cell phone in office. Katie Huisman/Getty Images; Co-workers having discussion while standing up. Klaus Vedfelt/Getty Images; Pretty mom talking to toddler girl joyfully. Tang Ming Tung/Getty Images; Teenaged girls socializing at the park. Preappy/Getty Images
Composition: Cenveo Publisher Services
Printing and Binding: RR Donnelley and Sons

Manufactured in the United States of America.

9 8 7 6 5 4
f e d c b a

For information, write: Bedford/St. Martin's, 75 Arlington Street, Boston, MA 02116 (617-399-4000)

ISBN 978-1-4576-6253-9 (Paperback)
ISBN 978-1-4576-9253-6 (Loose-leaf Edition)

Acknowledgments

Test Your Self-Monitoring, p. 17 Copyright © 1974 by the American Psychological Association. Adapted with permission. Snyder, Mark, "Self-monitoring of expressive behavior," *Journal of Personality and Social Psychology*, 1974, Volume 30, Issue 4 (Oct). Adapted with permission.
Figure 1.5 Credo of the National Communication Association, p. 18 The NCA Credo for Ethical Communication is reprinted with permission from the National Communication Association. All rights reserved.
What Kind of Personality Do You Have?, p. 61 Reprinted with permission from Oliver P. John. Source: John, O. P., Naumann, L., & Soto, C. J. (2008). Paradigm shift to the integrative Big Five trait taxonomy: Discovery, measurement, and conceptual issues. In O. P. John, R. W. Robins, & L. A. Pervin (Eds.), *Handbook of personality: Theory and research* (3rd ed., pp. 114–158). New York: Guilford.
Figure 5.1 Power-Distance across Countries, p. 103 Geert Hofstede, Gert Jan Hofstede, and Michael Minkov, "*Cultures and Organizations: Software of the Mind*," 3rd revised edition. McGraw-Hill, 2010 ISBN: 0-07-166418-1. © Geert Hofstede B.V. quoted with permission.

Art acknowledgments and copyrights appear on the same page as the art selections they cover. It is a violation of the law to reproduce these selections by any means whatsoever without the written permission of the copyright holder.

At the time of publication, all Internet URLs published in this text were found to accurately link to their intended Web site. If you do find a broken link, please forward the information to julia.bartz@macmillan.com so that it can be corrected for the next printing.

} Preface

My goal with each new edition of my interpersonal communication text, *Reflect & Relate,* has been to craft a book that is welcoming, friendly, personal, trustworthy, and practical. A book that spotlights the finest of new and classic scholarship on social media, interpersonal relationships, and communication competence; and that gives students a clear sense of our field as a domain of scientific endeavor, not just "common sense." A book that—perhaps most importantly—doesn't just tell students what to do, but teaches them *how* to systemically reason through the various interpersonal communication challenges they face. The resulting success of *Reflect & Relate* has made me confident (and gratified) that due to this text, thousands of students are now empowered to make wise communication decisions.

Of course, the process of writing *Reflect & Relate* has been incredibly instructive to me as well; especially because it has allowed me to receive feedback from instructors and students regarding what approaches to communication—inside the classroom and out—work best for them. As teachers, we realize that there is no one-size-fits-all book for the interpersonal communication course, and that some students benefit from a more streamlined, applied approach. And therein lies the impetus for *Interpersonal Communication and You:* the need for a book that is every bit as authoritative as *Reflect & Relate,* but that focuses even more closely on the practical information students want and need for improving their interpersonal communication and relationships.

Interpersonal Communication and You covers the full spectrum of interpersonal communication content you expect in a text—including information about interpersonal essentials, skills, and relationships—but zeroes in on self-assessment and self-reflection across these topics. Each chapter includes multiple self-assessment quizzes, an enjoyable way for students to be drawn deeply and personally into the material they've just learned. The interaction between reader and content continues with the book's media program: LaunchPad is a powerful (and easy-to-use) learning platform that includes the adaptive quizzing program LearningCurve.

Interpersonal communication students need to know how the skills and knowledge they learn translate to their lives. *Reflect & Relate* has garnered much praise for its powerful ability to show students real-world applications, in the form of engaging and relatable examples. *Interpersonal Communication and You* offers students the same degree of real-life connection, in a more concise package. In addition to examples from my experience, the lives of my students, books, films, current events, and history, *Interpersonal Communication and You* features Self-Reflection boxes throughout each chapter that prompt students to consider their own experiences as they relate to culture, technology, and ethics; Skills Practice boxes that offer students steps for applying new skills; and Self-Quizzes that allow students to test and analyze their own interpersonal communication behavior.

Finally, communication students want to succeed scholastically in their interpersonal communication courses, and *Interpersonal Communication and You* gives them the tools they need to optimize their performance. With its program of self-assessment, self-reflection, and online practice via LaunchPad and LearningCurve, the book allows students to interact and engage with the material and, by emphasizing the application of communication skills, it prepares students to excel both in the course and in their real-life communication. Due to its lower price tag, *Interpersonal Communication and You* is also accessible to students and instructors seeking an affordable option for their classrooms.

Taken as a whole, the focused yet comprehensive pedagogy in *Interpersonal Communication and You*, along with LaunchPad's resources, will make the interpersonal communication course more manageable and easier to understand. I am thrilled that you and your students are using this book, and I hope that it proves to be an invaluable resource in aiding your teaching and their learning!

Features of *Interpersonal Communication and You*: A Closer Look

A current and comprehensive overview of the discipline.

Interpersonal Communication and You draws on the best of cutting-edge and classic scholarship. Topics like online self-presentation and mediated communication competence are integrated with familiar areas such as active listening and intercultural competence.

A focus on student self-reflection, skills development, and self-assessment.

Interpersonal Communication and You is filled with opportunities for students to apply the material to their own lives, while LaunchPad makes it easy for instructors to assign these features and track student progress online. Self-assessment features in the text include the following:

- *Self-Quiz* exercises help students analyze their strengths and weaknesses so they can focus on improving their communication.

- Critical *Self-Reflection* features invite students to examine their own experiences and learn the habit of ongoing self-reflection.

- *Skills Practice* activities prompt students to put their skills into action with step-by-step instructions.

Compelling stories help every student connect to the material.

Drawn from pop culture, current events, and real life, carefully crafted illustrative examples connect students—whether they are conventional undergraduates, nursing students, returning adults, military vets, or communication majors—to the material.

Access to LaunchPad, a dynamic and easy-to-use platform.

LaunchPad makes instructors' lives easier by putting everything in one place, combining the full e-Book with carefully chosen videos, quizzes, activities, instructor's resources, and LearningCurve. LaunchPad—which can be packaged free with *Interpersonal Communication and You* or purchased separately—allows instructors to create reading, video, or quiz assignments in seconds, as well as embed their own videos or custom content. Instructors can also keep an eye on their class's progress throughout the semester by looking at results for individual students and for individual assignments. LaunchPad comes fully loaded with powerful learning tools, including:

- **LearningCurve, an adaptive and personalized quizzing program that puts the concept of "testing to learn" into action.** Chapter call-outs prompt students to tackle the gamelike LearningCurve quizzes to test their knowledge and reinforce learning. Based on cognitive research on how students learn, this adaptive quizzing program motivates students to engage with course materials. The reporting tools let instructors see what students understand so they can adapt their teaching to students' needs.

- **Integrated video clips that extend the book online.** Videos connected to every chapter help students see theory in action, while accompanying reflection questions help students apply concepts to their own experiences. More than 70 video activities are easily assignable and make excellent journal prompts or discussion starters.

- **A host of other assessment materials, activities, and instructor resources,** including interactive quizzes, chapter summaries, classroom activities, the Instructor's Resource Manual, and the Computerized Test Bank.

Digital and Print Formats

For more information on these formats and packaging information, please visit the online catalog at **macmillanhighered.com/ipcandyou/catalog.**

LaunchPad is a dynamic new platform that dramatically enhances teaching and learning. LaunchPad combines the full e-book with carefully chosen videos, quizzes, activities, instructor's resources, and LearningCurve. Offering a student-friendly approach, organized for easy assignability in a simple user interface, LaunchPad also allows instructors to create assignments, embed video or custom content, and track students' progress. LaunchPad can be ordered on its own, or packaged for *free* with *Interpersonal Communication and You.* Learn more at **launchpadworks .com.**

Interpersonal Communication and You **is available as a print text.** To get the most out of the book, package LaunchPad for free with the print text.

The loose-leaf edition of *Interpersonal Communication and You* features the same print text in a convenient, budget-priced format, designed to fit into any three-ring binder. Package LaunchPad with the loose-leaf edition for free.

The Bedford e-book to Go for *Interpersonal Communication and You* includes the same content as the print book, and provides an affordable, tech-savvy PDF e-book option for students. Instructors can customize the e-book by adding their own content and deleting or rearranging chapters. Learn more about custom Bedford e-books to Go at **macmillanhighered.com /ebooks**—where you can also learn more about other e-book versions of *Interpersonal Communication and You* in a variety of formats, including Kindle, CourseSmart, Barnes & Noble NOOK Study, Know, CafeScribe, or Chegg.

Resources for Students

For more information on these resources or to learn about package options, please visit the online catalog at **macmillanhighered.com/ipcandyou/catalog.**

The Essential Guide to Intercultural Communication **by Jennifer Willis-Rivera (University of Wisconsin, River Falls).** This useful guide offers an overview of key communication areas, including perception, verbal and nonverbal communication, interpersonal relationships, and organizations, from a uniquely intercultural perspective. Enhancing the discussion are contemporary and fun examples drawn from real life as well as an entire chapter devoted to intercultural communication in popular culture.

The Essential Guide to Group Communication, **Second Edition, by Dan O'Hair (University of Kentucky) and Mary Wiemann (Santa Barbara City College).** This concise and incisive print text explains the role of group communication within organizations and other settings and contains useful guidelines for acting as an effective leader, avoiding groupthink, and achieving optimal results.

The Essential Guide to Rhetoric **by William M. Keith (University of Wisconsin, Milwaukee) and Christian O. Lundberg (University of North Carolina, Chapel Hill).** This handy guide is a powerful addition to the public speaking portion of the human communication course, providing an accessible and balanced overview of key historical and contemporary rhetorical theories. Written by two leaders in the field, this brief introduction uses concrete, relevant examples and jargon-free language to bring concepts to life.

Media Career Guide: Preparing for Jobs in the 21st Century **by Sherri Hope Culver (Temple University) and James Seguin (Robert Morris University).** Practical and student-friendly, this guide includes a comprehensive directory of media jobs, practical tips, and career guidance for students considering a major in communication studies and mass media.

Resources for Instructors

For more information or to order or download these resources, please visit the online catalog at **macmillanhighered.com/ipcandyou/catalog.**

Instructor's Resource Manual for *Interpersonal Communication and You.* This downloadable manual contains helpful tips and teaching assistance for new and seasoned instructors alike. Content includes learning objectives, lecture outlines, general classroom activities, and review questions as well as suggestions for setting up a syllabus, tips on managing your classroom, and general notes on teaching the course. Also available in LaunchPad.

Computerized Test Bank for *Interpersonal Communication and You.* The Computerized Test Bank includes multiple choice, true/false, short answer, and essay questions keyed to various levels of difficulty. The questions appear in easy-to-use software that allows instructors to add, edit, resequence, and print questions and answers. Instructors can also export questions into a variety of formats, including Blackboard, Desire2Learn, and Moodle. The Computerized Test Bank can be downloaded from the Instructor Resources tab of the book's catalog page, and the content is also loaded in the LaunchPad question bank administrator.

Teaching Interpersonal Communication: A Guidebook, **Second Edition, by Alicia Alexander (Southern Illinois University) and Elizabeth J. Natalle (University of North Carolina-Greensboro)** Written by award-winning instructors, this essential resource provides all the tools instructors need to develop, teach, and manage a successful interpersonal communication course. New and seasoned instructors alike will benefit from the practical advice, scholarly insight, suggestions for integrating research and practice into the classroom—as well as the new chapter dedicated to teaching online.

Coordinating the Communication Course: A Guidebook, **by Deanna Fassett and John Warren.** This guidebook offers the most practical advice on every topic central to the coordinator/director role. Starting with setting a strong foundation, this professional resource continues on with thoughtful guidance, tips, and best practices on crucial topics such as creating community across multiple sections, orchestrating meaningful assessment, hiring and training instructors, and more. Model course materials, recommended readings, and insights from successful coordinators make this resource a must-have for anyone directing a course in communication.

The Interpersonal Communication e-Newsletter is a teaching and research e-newsletter for instructors of the introductory interpersonal communication course. Sign up by e-mailing ipc@bedfordstmartins.com. You can also access an archive of the e-newsletters in the Instructor Resources tab at **macmillanhighered .com/ipcandyou/catalog.**

PowerPoint slides for *Interpersonal Communication and You* provide support for important concepts addressed in each chapter, including graphics of key figures and questions for class discussion. The slides are available for download from the Instructor Resources tab at **macmillanhighered.com/ipcandyou /catalog.** Also available in LaunchPad.

The Bedford/St. Martin's Video Resource Library. A wide selection of interpersonal communication-related movies is available. Qualified instructors are eligible to select videos from the resource library upon adoption of the text. Please contact your local publisher's representative for more information.

Customize *Interpersonal Communication and You*. Add your own content or more of ours. Qualified adopters can create a version of *Interpersonal Communication and You* that exactly matches their specific needs. Learn more about custom options at **macmillanhighered .com/catalog/page/custom-solutions.**

Acknowledgments

I would like to thank everyone at Bedford/St. Martin's and Macmillan Education who was involved in this project and whose support made it possible, especially Denise Wydra, former Vice President, and Director of Production Sue Brown. Thanks to the editorial team who worked with me throughout the process: Publisher Erika Gutierrez; Senior Editors Karen Moore, Noel Hohnstine, and Julia Bartz; and Editorial Assistant Caitlin Crandell. The book also would not have come together without the efforts of Managing Editor Elise Kaiser and Project Editor Won McIntosh, who oversaw the book's tight schedule; and Media Editor Tom Kane; and Associate Editor Alexis Smith, who led the exciting and complex development of the text's LearningCurve. The enthusiasm and support from the marketing team is particularly appreciated: I thank Marketing Manager Tom Digiano and the entire sales force of Bedford/St. Martin's and Macmillan Education.

On a more personal level, I want to thank all those who assisted me personally with the book during its development, and those who collaborated with me in contributing their extraordinary stories to the text: Melissa Seligman, Vy Higginsen, Brenda Villa, Eric Staib, Leigh-Anne Goins, Vivian Derr, and Silvia Amaro. Thanks to my parents, Connie and Bruce McCornack, for raising me to value reading, books, and the unparalleled power of engaging human narrative—both spoken and written. Thanks to my boys—Kyle, Colin, and Conor—who have blessed and enriched my life more than words on a page could ever express. And most of all, I want to thank my unfailing source for relevant and interesting examples, Kelly Morrison. Your exceptional skill in the classroom, and the broad and deep generosity that marks your interactions with others in the world at large, are a constant source of inspiration for me as teacher, spouse, parent, and human being.

Throughout the development of this textbook, hundreds of interpersonal communication instructors voiced their opinion through surveys, focus groups, and reviews of the manuscript, and I thank them all.

ABOUT THE AUTHOR

Dr. Steven McCornack, Michigan State University

"I believe that the most important thing a textbook can teach students is how to make better communication decisions so that they can build happier and healthier interpersonal relationships."

Steven McCornack grew up in Seattle, Washington, in the years before Microsoft and grunge music. For as long as he can remember, he has been fascinated with how people create, maintain, and disband close relationships, especially the challenges confronting romantic couples. As an undergraduate at the University of Washington, he pursued this passion by studying with Malcolm "Mac" Parks, who inspired Steve to devote his life to interpersonal communication teaching and research.

Steve moved to the Midwest in 1984, pursuing his graduate studies under the tutelage of Barbara O'Keefe at the University of Illinois, where he received his master's degree and PhD. Hired in 1988 to teach in the Department of Communication at Michigan State University, Steve has remained there ever since and now serves as associate professor, coordinator of the undergraduate program, and faculty adviser to the Undergraduate Communication Association. He has published dozens of articles in leading communication journals and has received several prestigious awards and fellowships related to undergraduate teaching, including the Lilly Endowment Teaching Fellowship, the Amoco Foundation Excellence-in-Teaching Award, the MSU All-University Teacher/Scholar Award, the Michigan State University Alumni Association Teaching Award, and—most recently—the 2013 NCA Donald H. Ecroyd Award for Outstanding Teaching in Higher Education.

To Steve, his texts (which include this book, *Reflect & Relate,* and *Choices & Connections*) represent the culmination of more than 30 years of devout interest in how best to share knowledge of communication theory and research with undergraduate students. His courses are some of the most popular on campus. Other than his love of teaching, Steve's principal passions are his family (wife Kelly and three redheaded sons, Kyle, Colin, and Conor), his music (he plays drums and piano), his yoga practice, and meditation.

Brief Contents

}Contents

1 Introducing Interpersonal Communication   3

For videos and LearningCurve quizzing within LaunchPad, go to **bedfordstmartins.com/ipcandyou**.

PART ONE   Interpersonal Essentials

For videos and LearningCurve quizzing within LaunchPad, go to **bedfordstmartins.com/ipcandyou**.

4 Experiencing and Expressing Emotions   73

PART TWO   **Interpersonal Skills**

⊙ ✓ For videos and LearningCurve quizzing within LaunchPad, go to
bedfordstmartins.com/ipcandyou.

For videos and LearningCurve quizzing within LaunchPad, go to **bedfordstmartins.com/ipcandyou**.

7 Communicating Verbally   131

For videos and LearningCurve quizzing within LaunchPad, go to **bedfordstmartins.com/ipcandyou**.

8 Communicating Nonverbally 153

For videos and LearningCurve quizzing within LaunchPad, go to **bedfordstmartins.com/ipcandyou.**

9 Managing Conflict and Power 177

⊙ ✔ For videos and LearningCurve quizzing within LaunchPad, go to bedfordstmartins.com/ipcandyou.

PART THREE   Interpersonal Relationships

10 Relationships with Romantic Partners   199

11 Relationships with Family Members   225

12 Relationships with Friends   245

For videos and LearningCurve quizzing within LaunchPad, go to **bedfordstmartins.com/ipcandyou**.

Interpersonal Communication and You

AN INTRODUCTION

☑ Look for **LearningCurve** throughout the chapter to help you review.
bedfordstmartins.com/ipcandyou

1 } Introducing Interpersonal Communication

S he is home with the kids, who are alternating between angry and clingy.[1] She's trying to cook dinner, but the smoke detector keeps blaring, causing the dog to bark. Sure enough, it's at this moment the phone rings. Glancing at the caller ID, she sees it is the caller she hoped for. She answers because, despite the chaos around her, this could be their last conversation. He says, "I've been waiting in line for two hours to talk and I only have ten minutes. I've had a really bad day and miss you all." What should she say? Choice #1: *Lie.* Tell him everything's fine, and mask her frustration with coolness. But he'll sense her aloofness and leave the conversation worrying about why she is distracted. Is she angry with him? Having an affair? Choice #2: *Be honest.* Tell him that things

are chaotic, and ask whether he can talk to the kids for a minute while she clears her head.

Military wife, author, and *New York Times* columnist Melissa Seligman has lived this scene many times during her husband's combat deployments. She has learned to choose the second path because of the inescapable connection between communication choices and relationship outcomes. As she describes, "When a family member is gone for *a year* at a time, how can you sustain closeness? How do you maintain a three-dimensional marriage in a two-dimensional state? The only way is through open, honest, and loving communication."

The Seligmans use multiple media to maintain intimacy, including webcams, and exchanging videos, e-mails, phone calls, and letters. Melissa notes, "This way, we have a rounded communication relationship. We even send care packages of leaves, sand, pine needles, or pieces of fabric with cologne or perfume, to awaken the senses and cement the memories we have of each other." They

---

[1] All information that follows is adapted from a personal interview with the author, July 2011. Published with permission from Melissa Seligman.

◉ **Interpersonal communication is the bridge that connects us to others.**
Photo by Virginia Hagin

also journal, then read each other's writings when they are reunited. The journals "have the dates, circumstances, and what went unsaid in the day-to-day minutiae of our lives. They are our way of staying connected when ripped apart."

Melissa Seligman uses similarly diverse communication in her professional work with military support groups. "In my working life, I am on Facebook, Skype, and Web conference calls all the time. Texting. Instant-messaging. All of these are essential." But she also is mindful of the limits of technology, recognizing the importance of tailoring the medium to the task. "Technology cannot sustain a relationship, and relying on it to do so will create chaos. Rather, choosing the technology that best suits an individual's relationship is the key."

Across years of experience, Melissa Seligman and her family have learned to cope with intense versions of the same challenges we *all* face in our relationships. How can I better manage my anger and frustration? What can I do to maintain closeness with those I love? How can I communicate in a way that's both honest *and* kind? In 2010, she and coauthor Christina Piper released a children's book, *A Heart Apart*, which helps young children cope with the absence of military parents. When she is asked to reflect on the importance of communication, Melissa thinks of the next generation: "Children need to know and understand that anger and sadness go along with missing someone. They must be taught the importance of communication, and how to communicate well. This sets them up for success when their emotions begin to flow. Feelings are not right or wrong—it's what you choose to do with them that counts. Teaching our children to communicate well is the best gift we can give them."

M y life, like yours, is filled with interpersonal communication, in all its varied forms. While I'm sitting in the kitchen, writing on my laptop, the sound of Radiohead's "Lotus Flower" suddenly splits the silence. It's a text from my son Kyle, who's attending a music festival. A few minutes later I get an e-mail alert: it's a Facebook message from Kyle's girlfriend Margot, who's in France visiting relatives. While I'm reading Margot's message, a chat message pops up from Franki, my friend in California: "Check out the photos of my new beagle puppies!" While I'm surfing her puppy photo album, my wife Kelly and sons Colin and Conor walk in to ask if I want to order a pizza.

Interpersonal communication is the bridge that connects us to others. Through interpersonal communication, we build, maintain, and even end relationships with romantic partners, family members, friends, coworkers, and others. We do this through texting, instant-messaging, social networking site posts and chat, e-mail, face-to-face interactions, and phone calls. And we switch back and forth between these various forms fluidly.

But regardless of how we're communicating, or with whom, one fact inescapably binds us: *the communication choices we make determine the personal, interpersonal, and relationship outcomes that follow.* When we communicate well, we create desirable outcomes, such as positive emotions and satisfying relationships. When we communicate poorly, we generate negative outcomes, such as interpersonal conflict or relational dissatisfaction. By studying interpersonal communication, you can acquire knowledge and skills to boost your interpersonal competence. This, in turn, will help you to build and maintain satisfying relationships, and, ultimately, improve your quality of life.

In this chapter, we begin our study of interpersonal communication. You'll learn:

- What communication is and the different models for communication
- The nature of interpersonal communication, the role it plays in relationships, and the needs and goals it helps us fulfill
- How to improve your interpersonal communication competence, both online and off
- Major issues related to the study of interpersonal communication

What Is Communication?

We think about communication constantly. But taking a class on communication is different from personally pondering it. When you're formally educated about communication, you gain knowledge that goes far beyond your intuition, allowing you to broaden and deepen your skills as a communicator. The process of learning about communication begins by answering a basic question: what is communication?

Defining Communication

The National Communication Association, a professional organization representing communication teachers and scholars in the United States, defines **communication** as the process through which people use messages to generate meanings within and across contexts, cultures, channels, and media (NCA, 2002). This definition highlights the five features that characterize communication.

First, communication is a *process* that unfolds over time through a series of interconnected actions carried out by the participants. For example, your

> { **Communication is the process through which people use messages to generate meanings within and across contexts, cultures, channels, and media.** }

◊ **Whether we are watching a movie or starting a new romance, communication plays a significant role in our everyday lives.**

© Fox Searchlight/Courtesy Everett Collection

friend texts you, asking if you want to go to a movie, and you call her back to say yes and to make the arrangements. Because communication is a process, everything you say and do affects what is said and done in the present and the future.

Second, those engaged in communication (*communicators*) use *messages* to convey meaning. A **message** is the "package" of information that is transported during communication. When people exchange a series of messages, whether face-to-face or online, the result is called an **interaction** (Watzlawick, Beavin, & Jackson, 1967).

Third, communication occurs in a seemingly endless variety of **contexts,** or situations. We communicate with others at ball games, while at work, and in household kitchens. In each context, a host of factors influences how we communicate, such as how much time we have, how many people are in the vicinity, and whether the setting is personal or professional.

© Kelly-Mooney Photography/Corbis

◊ The context of an interaction—a formal or casual setting, with a boss or a good friend—will influence how we communicate.

Fourth, people communicate through various *channels*. A **channel** is the sensory dimension along which communicators transmit information. Channels can be auditory (sound), visual (sight), tactile (touch), olfactory (scent), or oral (taste). For example, your manager at work smiles at you and says, "I'm very impressed with your job performance" (visual and auditory channels). A visually impaired friend "reads" a message you left her, touching the Braille letters with her fingertips (tactile). Your romantic partner shows up at your house

exuding an alluring scent and carrying delicious take-out, which you then share together (olfactory and oral).

Fifth, to transmit information, communicators use a broad range of **media**—tools for exchanging messages. Consider the various media used by Melissa Seligman and her husband, described in our chapter opener. Webcams, cell phones, texting, e-mail, letters, face-to-face interaction, all of these media and more, can be used to communicate, often simultaneously. (See **Figure 1.1** for common media forms.)

Understanding Communication Models

Think about all the different ways you communicate each day. You text-message your sister to check in, you give a speech in your communication class to an engaged audience, and you exchange a knowing glance with your best friend at the arrival of someone you mutually dislike. Now reflect on how these forms of communication differ from each other. Sometimes (like when text-messaging), you create messages and send them to receivers, the messages flowing in a single direction from origin to destination. In other instances (like when speaking in front of your class), you present messages to recipients, and the recipients signal to you that

| Text-messaging (SMS) | Face-to-face interaction | Social networking sites | E-mail | Talking on the phone |

◅ **Figure 1.1 Five Most Common Forms of Communication Media Used by College Students**
Source: Dean (2011) and Lenhart, Purcell, Smith, and Zickuhr (2010).

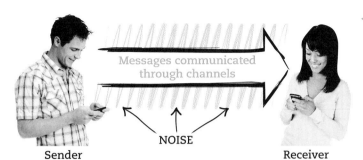

Figure 1.2 **Linear Model of Communication**

Sender   Receiver

they've received and understood them. Still other times (like when you and your best friend exchange a glance), you mutually construct meanings with others, with no one serving as "sender" or "receiver." These different ways of experiencing communication are reflected in three models that have evolved to describe the communication process: the linear model, the interactive model, and the transactional model. As you will see, each of these models has both strengths and weaknesses. Yet each also captures something unique and useful about the ways you communicate in your daily life.

Linear Communication Model

According to the **linear communication model,** communication is an activity in which information flows in one direction, from a starting point to an end point (see Figure 1.2). The linear model contains several compo-

nents (Lasswell, 1948; Shannon & Weaver, 1949). In addition to a *message* and a *channel*, there must be a **sender** (or senders) of the message—the individual(s) who generates the information to be communicated, packages it into a message, and chooses the channel(s) for sending it. There also is **noise**—factors in the environment that impede messages from reaching their destination. Noise includes anything that causes our attention to drift from messages—such as poor reception during a cell-phone call or the smell of fresh coffee nearby. Last, there must be a **receiver:** the person for whom a message is intended and to whom the message is delivered.

Interactive Communication Model

The **interactive communication model** also views communication as a process involving senders and receivers (see Figure 1.3). However, according to this model,

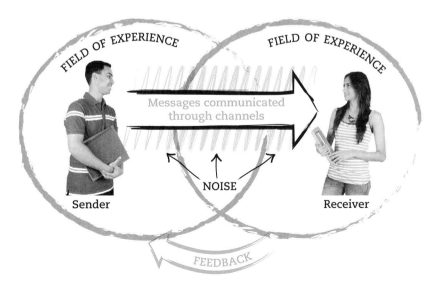

Sender   Receiver

FIELD OF EXPERIENCE   FIELD OF EXPERIENCE

Messages communicated through channels

NOISE

FEEDBACK

Figure 1.3 **Interactive Model of Communication**

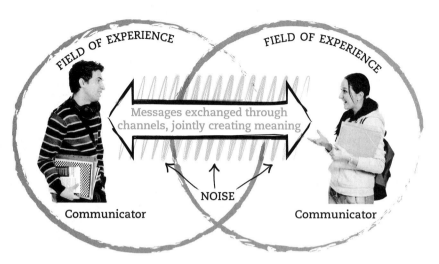

Figure 1.4 **Transactional Model of Communication**

transmission is influenced by two additional factors: feedback and fields of experience (Schramm, 1954). **Feedback** is comprised of the verbal and nonverbal messages (such as eye contact, utterances, or nodding) that recipients convey to indicate their reaction to communication. **Fields of experience** consist of the beliefs, attitudes, values, and experiences that each participant brings to a communication event. People with similar fields of experience are more likely to understand each other while communicating than are individuals with dissimilar fields of experience.

Transactional Communication Model

The **transactional communication model** (see **Figure 1.4**) suggests that communication is fundamentally multidirectional. That is, each participant equally influences the communication behavior of the other participants (Miller & Steinberg, 1975). From the transactional perspective, there are no "senders" or "receivers." Instead, all the parties constantly exchange verbal and nonverbal messages and feedback, *collaboratively* creating meanings (Streek, 1980). This may be something as simple as a shared look between friends, or it may be an animated conversation among family members in which the people involved seem to know what the others are going to say before it's said.

These three models represent an evolution of thought regarding the nature of communication,

from a relatively simplistic depiction of communication as a linear process to the view that communication is a complicated process that is mutually crafted. See **Table 1.1** for more on each model.

LearningCurve
bedfordstmartins.com/ipcandyou

What Is Interpersonal Communication?

When I first took a class on interpersonal communication as an undergraduate, I was amazed at the practical importance of the information we were learning. We talked about how and why people communicate when they are falling in (and out of) love, fighting, forming friendships, and fostering healthy family and workplace relationships. I'd go home after every class and drive my roommates crazy by using material from class to analyze their relationships!

Of course, I'm not the first person to recognize the significance of interpersonal communication; such realization has existed since the dawn of recorded history. In fact, one of the earliest texts ever written—the maxims of the Egyptian sage Ptah Hotep (2200 B.C.E.)—was essentially a guidebook for enhancing interpersonal

Table 1.1 **Communication Models**

Model	Examples	Strength	Weakness
Linear	Text and instant-messaging, e-mail, wall posts, scripted public speeches	Simple and straightforward	Doesn't adequately describe most face-to-face or phone conversations
Interactive	Classroom instruction, group presentations, team/coworker meetings	Captures a broad variety of communication forms	Neglects the active role that receivers often play in constructing meanings
Transactions	Any encounter (most commonly face-to-face) in which you and others jointly create communication meaning	Intuitively captures what most people think of as interpersonal communication	Doesn't apply to many forms of online communication, such as e-mail, Facebook posts, and text-messaging

skills (Horne, 1917). Ptah Hotep encouraged people to be truthful, kind, and tolerant in their communication. He urged active listening and emphasized mindfulness in word choice, noting that "good words are more difficult to find than emeralds."

Defining Interpersonal Communication

Why is learning about interpersonal communication so valuable? Because knowledge of interpersonal skills is essential for maintaining healthy interpersonal *relationships*. For most people, happy relationships with others are of the utmost importance (Myers, 2002).

The link that exists between relationships and interpersonal communication is clearly illustrated by our definition: **interpersonal communication** is a dynamic form of communication between two (or more) people in which the messages exchanged significantly influence their thoughts, emotions, behaviors, and relationships. This definition has four

important implications. First, interpersonal communication differs from some other forms of communication—such as office memos, e-mail spam, and formal lectures or speeches—because it's *dynamic*. That is, interpersonal communication is constantly in motion and changing over time, unlike the carefully planned messages that dominate advertisements, professional journalism, and formal public speeches. For example, consider a Skype interaction you have with a sibling who lives overseas. The first few moments may be awkward or tense as you strive to reconnect with one another. This tension is reflected in long pauses between short sentences. Then one of you cracks a joke, and the whole exchange suddenly feels warmer. Just a few minutes later, the conversation slows, and the mood shifts to sadness and regret, as each of you tries to delay the inevitable disconnection.

Second, most interpersonal communication is *transactional*; both parties contribute to the meaning. For example, you and a romantic partner share an intimate dinner, jointly reminiscing about past times together and exchanging expressions of affection fluidly back and forth. But some interpersonal communication isn't transactional. You know that your sibling is feeling depressed over a breakup, so

{ **Knowledge of interpersonal skills is essential for maintaining healthy interpersonal relationships.** }

you send her a consoling text message in the middle of her workday. You don't expect her to respond, and she doesn't, because she's busy. There's no feedback and no interplay between you and your sister. Instead, there is a sender (you), a message (your expression of support), and a receiver (your sister), making it a linear encounter, albeit an interpersonal one.

Third, interpersonal communication is primarily **dyadic**—it involves pairs of people, or dyads. You chat with your daughter while driving her to school, or you exchange a series of Facebook messages with a friend. Of course, some interpersonal communication may involve more than just two people. For instance, several family members converse at once during dinner, or a group of friends talk while enjoying an evening out. The dyadic nature of interpersonal communication allows us to distinguish it from **intrapersonal communication**—communication involving only one person, in the form of talking out loud to oneself or having a mental "conversation" inside one's head.

Finally, and perhaps most importantly, interpersonal communication creates *impact*: it changes participants' thoughts, emotions, behaviors, and relationships. When we interpersonally communicate, we forge meaningful bonds with others—easing the distance that naturally arises from differences between people. We don't have to agree with everything another person says and does, but to communicate competently with others, we need to approach them with an open mind and welcoming heart, affording them the same attention and respect we expect for ourselves. According to philosopher Martin Buber (1965), we then perceive our relationship with that person as **I-Thou**.

In contrast, when we focus on our differences, refuse to accept or even acknowledge rival viewpoints as legitimate, and communicate in ways that emphasize our own supposed superiority over others, the distance between us and others becomes impenetrable. As a consequence, we increasingly perceive our relationships as **I-It:** we regard other people as "objects which we observe, that are there for our use and exploitation" (Buber, 1965, p. 24). The more we view others as objects, the greater is the likelihood that we'll communicate with them in disrespectful, manipulative, or exploitative ways. When we treat others this way, our relationships deteriorate.

Interpersonal communication contrasts sharply with **impersonal communication**—exchanges that have a negligible perceived impact on our thoughts, emotions, behaviors, and relationships. For example, you're watching TV with your partner, and one of you casually comments on an advertisement that is annoying. Within most close relationships, at least some communication has this impersonal quality. But we can shift to interpersonal at a moment's notice. A while after the ad commentary, you snuggle up to your partner and murmur, "I love you." You're rewarded by warm eye contact, a tender smile, and a gentle hug—all signs that your message has had a significant impact on your partner.

Highlighting the mental, emotional, behavioral, and relational impact of interpersonal communication reinforces the central theme of this text: *the communication choices we make determine the personal, interpersonal, and relationship outcomes that follow.* Through communicating interpersonally with others, you can change your own feelings and thoughts about both yourself and others; alter others' opinions of you; cause heartbreak or happiness; incite hugs or hostility; and create, maintain, or dissolve relationships. This power makes your interpersonal communication choices critically important.

Principles of Interpersonal Communication

Now that we know what interpersonal communication is, we can expand our understanding of how it functions in our daily lives by looking at several principles suggested by scholars, based on decades of research and theory development. These principles are affirmed repeatedly throughout our text, and each one suggests practical insights into how you can improve your interpersonal communication choices, skills, and relationships.

Interpersonal Communication Conveys Both Content and Relationship Information

During every interpersonal encounter, people simultaneously exchange two types of information (Watzlawick et al., 1967). *Content information* is the actual meaning of your words. *Relationship information* consists of signals indicating how each of you views your relationship. These signals may indicate whether you consider yourself superior, equal, or inferior to the other person and whether you see the relationship as intimate, acquainted, or estranged.

You convey content information directly through spoken or written words, but you communicate relationship information primarily through nonverbal cues. These cues can include vocal tone, pitch, and

◊ When we interpersonally communicate, we forge meaningful bonds with others.

Katja Heinemann/Aurora

volume; facial expression and eye contact; hand gestures; position in relation to the listener; and posture. For instance, suppose your housemate hasn't been doing his fair share of kitchen cleanup. One evening, after he leaves his dirty dishes in the sink, you walk into the living room, sit down next to him, smile, and say in a friendly tone of voice, "Do you think you could rinse your dirty dishes off and put them in the dishwasher?" Now imagine the exact same situation—except this time you shout, scowl, and point your finger at him. In both scenarios, the content information is identical—you use exactly the same words—but you communicate very different relationship information. In the first scene, you indicate that you like and respect your housemate, and consider him an equal. In the second, you communicate anger and dislike, and imply that you see yourself as superior or more powerful.

Relationship information strongly influences how people interpret content information (Watzlawick et al., 1967). In the example above, your housemate will look much more to your actions than your words to decide how you feel about him and the relationship. During most interpersonal encounters, however,

⬥ Some only consider an encounter interpersonal if they gain new knowledge, make different decisions, or forge an I-Thou connection. Others consider an encounter interpersonal if information is conveyed.

people aren't consciously aware of the relationship information being delivered. You don't usually sit there thinking, "Gee, what's this person trying to convey to me about how she sees our relationship?" Relationship information becomes most obvious when it's unexpected or when it suggests that the sender's view of the relationship is different from the receiver's. For example, a new acquaintance says something overly intimate to you, or a coworker starts ordering you around as if he's your manager. When such events occur, we often experience annoyance or anxiety. That's why it's important to communicate relationship information in ways that are sensitive to and respectful of others' impressions of the relationship, while staying true to your own relationship feelings.

Interpersonal Communication Can Be Intentional or Unintentional

During interpersonal encounters, people attach meaning to nearly everything you say and do—whether you intend to send a message or not. Scholars express this as the axiom, "One cannot not communicate" (Watzlawick et al., 1967, p. 51.) For example, imagine that you greet a friend of yours, "Hey, how's it going?" She greets you back, "Hi—good to see you!" But then, as your friend tells you about her new boyfriend, your contact lens

Self-Reflection

Consider an instance in which you didn't intend to communicate a message but someone saw your behavior as communication. How did this person misinterpret your behavior? What were the consequences? What did you say and do to correct the individual's misperception?

gets displaced. You sigh loudly in frustration, and move your eyes to try and get it back in position. Your friend, seeing this, thinks you're sighing and rolling your eyes *as a message* about her boyfriend, and gets angry. Whether you like it or not, interpersonal communication *has* occurred, even though it was unintentional. To avoid such misunderstandings, remember that most of what you say and do when interacting with others will be perceived as communication.

Interpersonal Communication Is Irreversible

Every time you communicate interpersonally, you and the other person affect your future communication and the quality of your relationship. Take the way you answer your cell phone when your brother calls. Your warm and enthusiastic "Hi!" or terse "Yeah?" depends on how you feel about him. Your answer also influences how he responds. And his response further affects your next comment.

Self-Reflection

Think of an encounter in which you said something and then immediately regretted it. What effects did your error have on you? On the other person or people involved? On your relationship? How could you have expressed the same information differently to avoid negative outcomes?

This interconnectedness of action makes all interpersonal communication irreversible. By posting a message on someone's Facebook wall, sending a text, leaving a voicemail message, or expressing a thought out loud during a face-to-face encounter, you set in motion the series of outcomes that follow. Simply, once you've said something, you can't take it back. This is why it's important to think carefully *before* you communicate.

Interpersonal Communication Is Dynamic

When you interact with others, your communication and all that influences it—perceptions, thoughts, feelings, and emotions—are constantly in flux. This has several practical implications. First, no two inter-actions with the same person will ever be identical. For example, someone you once felt awkward around may become your closest confidant.

Second, no two moments within the *same* inter-action will ever be identical. The complex combina-tion of perceptions, thoughts, moods, and emotions that fuels our interpersonal communication choices is constantly changing. For instance, you meet your long-distance romantic partner at the airport, and for the first few minutes after reuniting you both feel joyous. But half an hour later, you suddenly find yourselves at a loss for things to talk about. As the minutes pass, the tension increases as you both silently ponder, "What happened?"

> **Self-Reflection**
>
> Recall an interaction that took a sudden turn for the worse. How did each person's communication contribute to the change in the interaction's quality? What did you say or do to deal with the problem?

Motives for Interpersonal Communication

At 19 months of age, Helen Keller fell ill with a severe fever that destroyed her sight and hearing (Dash, 2001). Helen had learned to speak quite early and had a sub-stantial vocabulary (for a toddler), but when she stopped hearing she stopped trying to talk. In the years that

◦ Helen Keller

followed, she created primitive messages through pull-ing, shoving, pinching, and shivering, but she had lost the knowledge of how to *interpersonally* communicate.

With no ability to connect with others through communication, she became filled with hatred and an all-encompassing sense of isolation. She called the resulting sense of self "The Phantom." The Phantom routinely flew into screaming tantrums that ceased only when utter exhaustion set in. In one of her early lessons with Annie Sullivan—the woman who eventu-ally taught Helen how to communicate through hand signals—The Phantom became so enraged that she punched Annie in the mouth, knocking out one of her front teeth.

But when Annie finally taught Helen how to communicate through sign language, The Phantom was slain. As Helen explained years later, "It seemed that something of the mystery of communication was revealed to me . . . and suddenly I felt a misty consciousness as of something remembered—a thrill of returning thought." Helen Keller went on to master sign language, Braille, and spoken language, and graduated magna cum laude from Radcliffe College.

As the Helen Keller story powerfully illustrates, when we communicate interpersonally, we connect with others—fulfilling a profound human need. We also achieve important personal and professional goals. When these outcomes are denied us, we lapse into isolation and loneliness or, worse yet, have a violent "Phantom" emerge from within, as did Helen Keller.

Interpersonal Communication and Human Needs

Psychologist Abraham Maslow (1970) suggested that we seek to fulfill a hierarchy of needs in our daily lives. Only when the most basic needs (at the bottom of the hierarchy) are fulfilled do we turn our attention to pursuing higher-level ones. Interpersonal communication allows us to develop and foster the interactions and relationships that help us fulfill these needs. At the foundational level are *physical needs* such as air, food, water, sleep, and shelter. If we can't satisfy these needs, we prioritize them over all others. Once physical needs are met, we concern ourselves with *safety needs*—such as job stability and protection from violence.

Then we seek to address *social needs*: forming satisfying and healthy emotional bonds with others. Next are *self-esteem needs*, the desire to have others' respect and admiration. We fulfill these needs by contributing something of value to the world. Finally, we strive to satisfy *self-actualization needs* by articulating our unique abilities and giving our best in our work, family, and personal life.

Interpersonal Communication and Specific Goals

In addition to enabling us to meet fundamental needs, interpersonal communication helps us meet three types of goals (Clark & Delia, 1979). During interpersonal interactions, you may pursue one or a combination of these goals. The first—**self-presentation goals**—are desires you have to present yourself in certain ways so that others perceive you as being a particular type of person. For example, you're conversing with a roommate who's just

been fired. You want him to know that you're a supportive friend, so you ask what happened, commiserate, and offer to help him find a new job.

You also have **instrumental goals**—practical aims you want to achieve or tasks you want to accomplish through a particular interpersonal encounter. If you want to borrow your best friend's prized Porsche for the weekend, you might remind her of your solid driving record and your sense of responsibility to persuade her to lend you the car.

Finally, you use interpersonal communication to achieve **relationship goals**—building, maintaining, or terminating bonds with others. For example, if you succeed in borrowing your friend's car for the weekend and accidentally drive it into a nearby lake, you will likely apologize profusely and offer to pay for repairs to save your friendship.

LearningCurve
bedfordstmartins.com/ipcandyou

What Is Interpersonal Communication Competence?

For nine seasons of *South Park*, Jerome "Chef" McElroy was the only adult trusted and respected by the show's central characters: Kyle, Stan, Kenny, and Cartman. In a routine interaction, the boys—while waiting in the school's lunch line—would share their concerns and seek Chef's counsel. He would do his best to provide appropriate, effective, and ethical advice, often bursting into song. Of course, given his reputation as a "ladies' man," the boys frequently asked him for advice regarding relationships and sex. Sometimes Chef would answer in vague and allusive ways, trying to remain child-appropriate, but ending up completely unintelligible. In other instances he'd get carried away, singing about his sexual exploits before remembering his audience. But despite occasional lapses in effectiveness and appropriateness, Chef consistently was the most ethical, kind, and compassionate adult in a show populated by insecure, self-absorbed, and outright offensive characters.

Many of us can think of a Chef character in our own lives—someone who, even if he or she occasionally errs, always *strives* to communicate competently. Often, this person's efforts pay off; competent communicators report more relational satisfaction (including happier marriages), better psychological and physical health, and higher levels of educational and professional achievement than others (Spitzberg & Cupach, 2002).

Although people who communicate competently report positive outcomes, they don't all communicate in the same ways. No one recipe for competence exists. Communicating competently will help you achieve more of your interpersonal goals, but it doesn't guarantee that all of your relationship problems will be solved.

Throughout this text, you will learn the knowledge and skills necessary for strengthening your interpersonal competence. In this chapter, we explore what competence means and how to improve your competence online. Throughout later chapters, we examine how you can communicate more competently across various situations, and within romantic, family, friendship, and workplace relationships.

🔵 Jerome "Chef" McElroy's style may have been unconventional, but he strived for competence in his communication with the boys of *South Park*.

Understanding Competence

Interpersonal communication competence means consistently communicating in ways that are *appropriate* (your communication follows accepted norms), *effective* (your communication enables you to achieve your goals), and *ethical* (your communication treats people fairly) (Spitzberg & Cupach, 1984; Wiemann, 1977). Acquiring knowledge of what it means to communicate competently is the first step in developing interpersonal communication competence (Spitzberg, 1997).

The second step is learning how to translate this knowledge into **communication skills**, repeatable, goal-directed behaviors and behavioral patterns that you routinely practice in your interpersonal encounters and relationships (Spitzberg & Cupach, 2002). Both steps require *motivation* to improve your communication. If you are strongly motivated to improve your interpersonal communication, you can master the knowledge and skills necessary to develop competence.

Appropriateness
The first characteristic of competent interpersonal communication is **appropriateness**—the degree to which your communication matches situational, relational, and cultural expectations regarding how people should communicate. In any interpersonal encounter, norms exist regarding what people should and shouldn't say, and how they should and shouldn't act. Part of developing your communication competence is refining your sensitivity to norms and adapting your communication accordingly. People who fail to do so are perceived by others as incompetent communicators.

> **Although people who communicate competently report positive outcomes, they don't all communicate in the same ways.**

Arthur Schatz/Time Life Pictures/Getty Images

🔹 **Whether speaking with union volunteers or powerful politicians, labor leader César Chávez's interpersonal communication competence allowed him to translate his personal intentions into actions that benefitted America's poorest farm laborers and changed the world.**

We judge how appropriate our communication is through **self-monitoring:** the process of observing our own communication and the norms of the situation in order to make appropriate communication choices. Some individuals closely monitor their own communication to ensure they're acting in accordance with situational expectations (Giles & Street, 1994). Known as *high self-monitors*, they prefer situations in which clear expectations exist regarding how they're supposed to communicate. In contrast, *low self-monitors* don't assess their own communication or the situation. They prefer encounters in which they can "act like themselves" rather than having to abide by norms (Snyder, 1974).

While communicating appropriately is a key part of competence, *overemphasizing* appropriateness can backfire. If you focus exclusively on appropriateness and always adapt your communication to what others want, you may end up forfeiting your freedom of communicative choice to peer pressure or fears of being perceived negatively (Burgoon, 1995).

Effectiveness

The second characteristic of competent interpersonal communication is **effectiveness:** the ability to use communication to accomplish the three types of interpersonal goals discussed earlier (self-presentational, instrumental, and relational). There's rarely a single communicative path for achieving all of these goals, and sometimes you must make trade-offs. For example, a critical part of maintaining satisfying close relationships is the willingness to occasionally sacrifice instrumental goals to achieve important relational goals. Suppose you badly want to see a movie tonight, but your romantic partner needs your emotional support to handle a serious family problem. Would you say, "I'm sorry you're feeling bad—I'll call you after I get home from the movie" (emphasizing your instrumental goals)? Or would you say, "I can see the movie some other time—tonight I'll hang out with you" (emphasizing your relational goals)? The latter approach, which facilitates relationship health and happiness, is obviously more competent.

Ethics

The final defining characteristic of competent interpersonal communication is **ethics,** the set of moral principles that guide our behavior toward others (Spitzberg & Cupach, 2002). At a minimum, we are ethically obligated to avoid intentionally hurting others through our communication. By this standard, communication that's intended to erode a person's self-esteem, that expresses intolerance or hatred, that intimidates or threatens

> **Self-Reflection**
>
> Is the obligation to communicate ethically absolute or situation-dependent? That is, are there circumstances in which it's ethical to communicate in a way that hurts someone else's feelings? Can one be disrespectful or dishonest, and still ethical? If so, when?

Self-Quiz

Test Your Self-Monitoring

Place a check mark next to the statements you agree with. Then count the total number of statements you checked to see if you're a high or low self-monitor.

☐ I find it easy to imitate others' behavior.

☐ When I'm uncertain how to act during an interpersonal encounter, I look to others' behaviors for cues.

☐ I would probably make a good actor.

☐ In different situations and with different people, I often act like very different persons.

☐ Even if I'm not enjoying myself, I often behave as if I'm having a good time.

☐ I find it easy to change my behavior to suit different people and situations.

☐ I sometimes appear to others to be experiencing deeper emotions than I really am.

☐ I'm pretty good at making other people like me.

☐ I'm not always the person I appear to be.

Note: This *Self-Quiz* is adapted from the self-monitoring scale provided by Snyder (1974).

Scoring: 0–4 indicates you're probably a low self-monitor; 5–9 suggests you're a high self-monitor.

others' physical well-being, or that expresses violence is unethical and therefore incompetent (Parks, 1994).

To truly be an ethical communicator, however, we must go beyond simply not doing harm. During every interpersonal encounter, we need to strive to treat others with respect, and communicate with them honestly, kindly, and positively (Englehardt, 2001). For additional guidelines on ethical communication, review the "Credo for Ethical Communication" on the following page.

We all are capable of competence in situations where it's easy to behave appropriately, effectively, and ethically. True competence is developed when we consistently communicate competently across *all* situations that we face, including contexts that are uncertain, complex, and unpleasant. One of the goals of this book is to arm you with the knowledge and skills you need to meet challenges to your competence with confidence.

Improving Your Competence Online

Much of our interpersonal communication is **online communication,** or any interaction by means of social networking sites (such as Facebook), e-mail, text- or instant-messaging, Skype, chatrooms, and even massively multiplayer online video games like *World of Warcraft* (Walther & Parks, 2002). Online communication enables us to meet and form friendships and romances with people we wouldn't encounter otherwise, and it helps us maintain established relationships (Howard, Rainie, & Jones, 2001). It also bolsters our sense of community (Shedletsky & Aitken, 2004).

Credo of the National Communication Association

The National Communication Association (NCA) is the largest professional organization representing communication instructors, researchers, practitioners, and students in the United States. In 1999, the NCA Legislative Council adopted this "Credo for Ethical Communication" (National Communication Association, 1999).

- We advocate truthfulness, accuracy, honesty, and reason as essential to the integrity of communication.

- We endorse freedom of expression, diversity of perspective, and tolerance of dissent to achieve informed and responsible decision making.

- We strive to understand and respect other communicators before evaluating and responding to their messages.

- We promote communication climates of caring and mutual understanding that respect the unique needs and characteristics of individual communicators.

- We condemn communication that degrades people through distortion, intimidation, coercion, and violence, or expression of intolerance and hatred.

- We are committed to the courageous expression of personal convictions in pursuit of fairness and justice.

- We advocate sharing information, opinions, and feelings when facing significant choices while also respecting privacy and confidentiality.

- We accept responsibility for the short- and long-term consequences for our own communication and expect the same of others.

Given how often we use technology to interpersonally communicate, building online competence becomes extremely important. Based on years of research, scholar Malcolm Parks offers five suggestions for improving your online communication competence (see **Table 1.2** on page 19).[2]

1. *Match the gravity of your message to your communication medium.* An essential part of online competence is knowing when to communicate online versus offline. For many interpersonal goals, online communication is more effective. Text-messaging a friend to remind her of a coffee date is probably quicker and less disruptive than calling her. E-mail may be best when dealing with problematic people or certain types of conflicts because you can take time to carefully draft and revise responses before sending them—something that isn't possible during face-to-face interactions.

But online communication is not the best medium for giving in-depth, lengthy, and detailed explanations of professional or personal dilemmas, or for conveying weighty relationship decisions. Despite the ubiquity of online communication, many people still expect important news to be shared in person. Most of us would be surprised if a friend disclosed a cancer relapse through a text message.

2. *Don't assume that online communication is always more efficient.* Matters of relational significance or

[2]Personal communication with author, May 13, 2008. This material was developed specifically for this text and published with permission of Dr. Malcolm Parks; may not be reproduced without written consent of Dr. Parks and the author.

Table 1.2 **Online Communication Competence**

Online Competence Suggestion	Best Practices Suggestion
1. Match the gravity of your message to your communication medium.	*Online* is best for quick reminders, linear messages, or messages that require time and thought to craft. *Offline* is best for important information: engagements, health issues, etc.
2. Don't assume that online communication is always more efficient.	If your message needs a quick decision or answer, a phone call or face-to-face conversation may be best. Use online communication if you want the person to have time to respond.
3. Presume that your posts are public.	If you wouldn't want a message published for public consumption, don't post/send it online.
4. Remember that your posts are permanent.	Even after you delete something, it still exists on servers and may be accessible.
5. Practice the art of creating drafts.	Don't succumb to the pressure to respond to e-mails immediately. Taking your time will result in a more competent message.

issues that evoke strong emotional overtones are more effectively and ethically handled in person or over the phone. But so too are many simple things—like deciding when to meet and where to go to lunch. Many times, a one-minute phone call or quick face-to-face exchange can save several minutes of texting.

3. *Presume that your posts are public.* Your friends may laugh at the funny picture of you drunkenly hugging the houseplant on Facebook. But what about family members, future in-laws, or potential employers who see the picture? That clever joke you made about friend A in an e-mail to friend B—what if B forwards it to C, who then forwards it to A? Even if you have "privacy settings" on your personal page, what's to stop authorized-access friends from downloading your photos and posts and distributing them to others? Keep this rule in mind: anything you've sent or posted online can potentially be seen by anyone.

4. *Remember that your posts are permanent.* The things you say online are like old TV shows: they hang around as reruns forever. Old e-mails, photographs, videos, and blogs may still be accessible years later. As just one example, everything you have ever posted on Facebook is stored on their server, whether you delete it from your profile or not. And Facebook legally reserves the right to sell your content, as long as they delete personally identifying information (such as your name) from it. One of my students learned this the hard way, when he saw a personal family photo he had uploaded to Facebook packaged as the "sample photo" in a gift frame at a local store. Think before you post.

5. *Practice the art of creating drafts.* Get into the habit of saving text and e-mail messages as "drafts," then revisiting them later and editing them as needed for appropriateness, effectiveness, and ethics. Because online communication makes it easy to flame, many of us impetuously fire off messages that we later regret.

Skills Practice

Online Competence

Become a more competent online communicator.

1. Before communicating online, ask yourself: is the information important or complicated; or does it require a negotiated decision? If so, call or communicate face-to-face instead.
2. Don't share content you consider private. Anything you text, e-mail, or post can be exported elsewhere by anyone who has access to it.
3. Save messages as drafts, then revisit them later, checking appropriateness, effectiveness, and ethics.
4. When in doubt, delete, don't send!

LearningCurve
bedfordstmartins.com/ipcandyou

Issues in Interpersonal Communication

As we move through the twenty-first century, scholars and students alike are increasingly appreciating how important interpersonal communication is in our daily lives and relationships. Moreover, they're recognizing the impact of societal changes such as diversity and technological innovation. To ensure that the field stays current with social trends, communication scholars have begun exploring the issues of culture, gender and sexual orientation, online communication, and the dark side of interpersonal relationships.

{ **Scholars are recognizing the impact of society changes such as diversity and technological innovation.** }

Culture

In this text, we define *culture* broadly and inclusively, as an established, coherent set of beliefs, attitudes, values, and practices shared by a large group of people (Keesing, 1974). Culture includes many different types of large-group influences such as nationality, ethnicity, religion, gender, sexual orientation, physical and mental abilities, and even age. We learn our cultural beliefs, attitudes, and values from parents, teachers, religious leaders, peers, and the mass media (Gudykunst & Kim, 2003). As our world gets more diverse, scholars and students must consider cultural differences when discussing interpersonal communication theory and research and how communication skills can be improved.

Throughout this book, and particularly in Chapter 5, we examine differences and similarities across cultures and consider their implications for interpersonal communication. As we cover this material, critically examine the role that culture plays in your own interpersonal communication and relationships.

Gender and Sexual Orientation

Gender consists of social, psychological, and cultural traits generally associated with one sex or the other (Canary, Emmers-Sommer, & Faulkner, 1997). Unlike biological sex, which we're born with, gender is largely learned. Gender influences how people communicate interpersonally, but scholars disagree about how. For example, you may have read in popular magazines or heard on TV that women are more "open" communicators than men, and that men "have difficulty communicating their feelings." But when these beliefs are compared with research and theory on gender and interpersonal communication, it turns out that differences (and similarities) between men and women are more complicated than the popular stereotypes suggest. Throughout this book, we discuss such stereotypes and look at scholarly research on the impact of gender on interpersonal communication.

Each of us also possesses a **sexual orientation:** an enduring emotional, romantic, sexual, or affectionate attraction to others that exists along a

(Clockwise from top left) © Danny Lehman/Corbis; Heiko Meyer/laif/Redux; Kelvin Murray/Getty Images; Carl De Keyzer/Magnum Photos

🜄 Understanding how culture, gender, and sexual orientation can influence interpersonal communication will help you communicate more effectively.

continuum ranging from exclusive homosexuality to exclusive heterosexuality and that includes various forms of bisexuality (APA Online, n.d.). You may have heard that gays and lesbians communicate in ways different from "straights," or that each group builds, maintains, and ends relationships in distinct ways. But, as with common beliefs about gender, research shows that same-gender and opposite-gender relationships are formed, maintained, and dissolved in similar ways. We discuss assumptions about sexual orientation throughout this text.

Online Communication

Radical changes in communication technology have had a profound effect on our ability to interpersonally communicate. Cell phones keep us in almost constant contact with friends, family members, colleagues, and romantic partners. Our ability to communicate easily and frequently, even when separated by geographic distance, is further enhanced through *online communication*. In this book, we treat such technologies as tools for connecting people interpersonally—tools that are now thoroughly integrated into our lives. In every chapter,

🜄 Signs of the social networking times.

you'll find frequent mention of these technologies as they relate to the chapter's specific topics.

The Dark Side of Interpersonal Relationships

Interpersonal communication strongly influences the quality of our interpersonal relationships, and the quality of those relationships in turn affects how we feel about our lives. When our involvements with lovers, family, friends, and coworkers are satisfying and healthy, we typically feel happier in general (Myers, 2002). But the fact that relationships can bring us joy obscures the fact that relationships, and the interpersonal communication that occurs within them, can often be destructive.

In studying interpersonal communication, you can learn much by looking beyond constructive encounters to the types of damaging exchanges that occur all too frequently in life. *The greatest challenges to your interpersonal communication skills lie not in communicating competently when it is easy to do so but in practicing competent interpersonal communication when doing so is difficult.* Throughout the text, we will discuss many of the negative situations that you may experience, as well as recommendations for how to deal with them.

LearningCurve
bedfordstmartins.com/ipcandyou

Postscript }

We began this chapter with a military wife struggling to juggle the competing demands of raising her children and maintaining her marriage. Melissa Seligman uses multiple media to stay connected with her husband during his combat deployments. At the same time, she has learned that computers, phones, and care packages are merely tools. The most important thing is open, honest, and loving communication.

How do you stay close with loved ones who are distant? What tough communication choices have you faced in these relationships?

The story of Melissa Seligman's struggle reminds us of an inescapable truth that forms the foundation for this book. Our close relationships are *the* most important things in our lives, and it's our choices regarding how we communicate that determine whether these relationships survive and thrive, or fade away.

Chapter Review }

KEY TERMS

communication, 5
message, 5
interaction, 5
context, 5
▣ channel, 6
media, 6
▣ linear communication model, 7
sender, 7
▣ noise, 7
receiver, 7
interactive communication
   model, 7

feedback, 8
fields of experience, 8
▣ transactional communication
   model, 8
interpersonal communication, 9
dyadic, 10
intrapersonal communication, 10
I-Thou, 10
I-It, 10
impersonal communication, 10
self-presentation goals, 14
instrumental goals, 14

relationship goals, 14
interpersonal communication
   competence, 15
communication skills, 15
appropriateness, 15
▣ self-monitoring, 16
effectiveness, 16
ethics, 16
online communication, 17
gender, 20
sexual orientation, 20

CHAPTER ACTIVITIES

1. ▣ Watch the videos on **linear communication model, noise,** and **transactional communication model.** Then, write a short paper (no more than 500 words) analyzing how communication models work online based on the videos and the following questions:
   - Why is the linear model often associated with online communication?
   - What experiences have you had with noise, feedback, and jointly creating meaning online?
   - Do you consider these transactional interactions? Why or why not?

2. To illustrate Buber's concept of I-It, go to YouTube and find clips from the TV show *30 Rock* that feature the character Jack Donaghy and his assistant, Jonathan. Over the course of the show, Jack has fired Jonathan "for practice" and has refused to engage in an interpersonal relationship with him. Choose one such scene and discuss Jack's specific communication choices that demonstrate I-It language.

3. Consider a time when you thought "I wish I could take that back" after communicating something you regretted. Discuss with your peers the power of irreversibility. Can apologies help? What makes an apology more, or less, effective?

4. ▣ Watch the video on **self-monitoring** and then find another example of self-monitoring in the media (from an online video, article, etc.). Analyze both examples based on these questions:
   - Do the examples represent high self-monitors or low self-monitors? Why?
   - How competent is the communication in the examples?
   - What could be improved in each?

5. Locate three job descriptions that include "strong communication skills" as a major requirement. What are communication skills? Generate a list of your thoughts in response to this question and write a brief essay on how these skills might impact the career you are currently working toward.

6. Visit the site Lamebook.com, which compiles real, incompetent comments, statuses, and pictures that people have posted on Facebook. Choose three examples that are *appropriate for class discussion in a college setting* and answer the following questions to share with your classmates:
   - Why, specifically, is this status, comment, or photo an example of incompetent communication?
   - Keeping in mind that Facebook posts are permanent, what consequences might this status, comment, or photo have for the individual who shared it? Why?

☑ Look for **LearningCurve** throughout
the chapter to help you review.
bedfordstmartins.com/ipcandyou

2 } Considering Self

A rtist Eric Staib describes his 2002 painting *labeled* (left) as a self-portrait. "It depicts my feelings about how my peers saw me when I was growing up. The hands pointing, words said under people's breath. You can tell what they're thinking: you're an idiot, you're stupid, you're a joke."[1]

By the time Eric was in third grade, he knew he was different. Whereas his classmates progressed rapidly in reading and writing, Eric couldn't make sense of words on the written page. But it wasn't until fifth grade that Eric finally was given a label for his difference: learning disabled, or "LD." The LD label stained Eric's sense of self, making him feel ashamed. His low self-esteem spread outward, constraining his communication and relationships.

---

[1] All information presented regarding artist Eric Staib was provided with his permission, from an interview conducted by the author in February 2005.

"My whole approach was *Don't get noticed!* I'd slouch down in class, hide in my seat. And I would never open up to people. I let nobody in."

Frustrated with the seemingly insurmountable challenges of reading and writing, Eric channeled intense energy into art. By eleventh grade, Eric had the reading and writing abilities of a fifth grader but managed to pass his classes through hard work and artistic ability. He graduated from high school with a D average.

Many of Eric's LD peers turned to substance abuse and dropped out of school, but Eric pursued his education further, taking classes at a local community college. There, something happened that transformed his view of his self, his self-esteem, and the entire course of his life. While taking his first written exam of the semester, Eric knew the answers, but he couldn't write them down. No matter how hard he focused, he couldn't convert the knowledge in his head into written

◖ By deepening your self-understanding, you can begin to clarify your thoughts and feelings about your self.

Photo by Scott Rosenfeld

words. Rather than complete the exam, he wrote the story of his disability on the answer sheet, including his struggles with reading and writing and the pain associated with being labeled LD. He turned in his exam and left. Eric's professor took his exam to the college dean, and the two of them called Eric to the dean's office. They told him, "You need help, and we're going to help you." Their compassion changed Eric's life. Eric's professor arranged for Eric to meet with a learning specialist, who immediately diagnosed him as dyslexic. As Eric explains, "For the first time in my life, I had a label for myself other than 'learning disabled.' To me, the LD label meant I couldn't learn. But dyslexia was different. It could be overcome. The specialist taught me strategies for working with my dyslexia and gave me my most important tool—my Franklin Spellchecker—to check spellings. But most importantly, I was taught that it was okay to be dyslexic."

Armed with an improving sense of self, Eric went from hiding to asserting himself, "from low self-esteem to being comfortable voicing my opinion, from fear to confidence." That confidence led him to transfer to a Big 10 university, where he graduated with a degree in studio arts, percussion, and horticulture. He subsequently earned a postgraduate degree in K–12 art education, graduating with a straight-A average.

Eric Staib is now an art instructor in the Midwest and was a 2006 recipient of the Robert Rauschenberg Foundation Power of Art Award, given to the top arts educators in the country each year. He also teaches instructors how to use art to engage learning-disabled students. What means the most to him is the opportunity to pass down the legacy of his personal transformation. "When I think about my dyslexia, it's really incredible. What was my greatest personal punishment is now the most profound gift I have to offer to others."

E very word you've ever spoken during an encounter, every act of kindness or malevolence you've committed, has the same root source—your self. When you look inward, you are peering into the wellspring from which all of your interpersonal actions flow. But even as your self influences your interpersonal communication, it is shaped by your communication as well. Through communicating with others, we learn who we are, what we're worth, and how we should act. This means that the starting point for improving your communication is to understand your self. In this way, you can begin to clarify your thoughts and feelings about your self; comprehend how these are linked to your interpersonal communication; and develop strategies for enhancing your sense of self, your communication skills, and your interpersonal relationships.

In this chapter, we explore the source of all interpersonal communication: the self. You'll learn:

- The components of self, as well as how critical self-reflection can be used to improve your communication skills and your self-esteem
- The ways in which gender, family, and culture shape your sense of self
- How to present and maintain a positive self when interacting with others
- The importance of online self-presentation
- The challenges of managing selves in relationships, including suggestions for successful self-disclosure.

The Components of Self

At Delphi in ancient Greece, the temple of the sun god Apollo was adorned with the inscription *Gnothi se auton*—"Know thyself." According to legend, when one of the seven sages of Greece, Chilon of Sparta, asked Apollo, "What is best for people?" the deity responded with that simple admonition. More than 2,500 years later, these words still ring true, especially in the realm of interpersonal communication and relationships.

The **self** is an evolving composite of self-awareness, self-concept, and self-esteem. Although each of us experiences the self as singular ("*This* is who I am"), it actually is made up of three distinct, yet integrated, components that evolve continually over time, based on your life experiences.

Self-Awareness

Self-awareness is the ability to view yourself as a unique person distinct from your surrounding environment and to reflect on your thoughts, feelings, and behaviors. According to sociologist George Herbert Mead (1934), self-awareness helps you to have a strong sense of your self because during interpersonal encounters you monitor your own behaviors and form impressions of who you are from such observations. For example, your best friend texts you that she has failed an important exam. You feel bad for her, so you text her a sympathetic response. Your self-awareness of your compassion and your observation of your kind-hearted message lead you to think: "I'm a caring and supportive friend."

As we're watching and evaluating our own actions, we also engage in **social comparison:** observing and assigning meaning to others' behavior and then comparing it against ours. Social comparison has a particularly potent effect on self when we compare ourselves against people we wish to emulate. When we compare favorably against respected others, we think well of ourselves; when we don't compare favorably, we think less of ourselves.

You can greatly enhance your interpersonal communication by practicing a targeted kind of self-awareness known as *critical self-reflection*. To engage in critical self-reflection, ask yourself the following questions:

- What am I thinking and feeling?
- Why am I thinking and feeling the way I am?
- How am I communicating?
- How are my thoughts and feelings affecting my communication?
- How can I improve my thoughts, feelings, and communication?

The ultimate goal of critical self-reflection is embodied in the last question: How can I *improve*? Improving your interpersonal communication is possible only when you accurately understand how your self drives your communication behavior. In the remainder of this chapter, and in the marginal *Self-Reflection* exercises you'll find throughout this book, we help you make links between your self and your communication.

Self-Concept

Self-concept is your overall perception of who you are. Your self-concept is based on the beliefs, attitudes, and values you have about yourself. *Beliefs* are convictions that certain things are true—for example, "I'm an excellent student." *Attitudes* are evaluative appraisals, such as "I'm happy with my appearance." *Values* represent enduring principles that guide your interpersonal actions—for example, "I think it's wrong to . . . ."

Your self-concept is shaped by a host of factors, including your gender, family, friends, and culture (Vallacher, Nowak, Froehlich, & Rockloff, 2002). One of the biggest influences on your self-concept is the labels others put on you. How do others'

{ **The self is an evolving composite of self-awareness, self-concept, and self-esteem.**

Cornell Capa © International Center of Photography/Magnum Photos

💧 Our self-concept is influenced by our beliefs about how others view us.

impressions of you shape your self-concept? Sociologist Charles Horton Cooley (1902) argued that it's like looking at yourself in the "looking glass" (or mirror). When you stand in front of it, you consider your physical appearance through the eyes of others, including lovers, friends, family, and even the media. Do others see you as attractive? Overweight? Too tall or too short? Seeing yourself in this fashion—and

{ **Your self-concept is shaped by a host of factors, including your gender, family, friends, and culture.** }

thinking about how others must see you—has a powerful effect on how you think about your physical self. Cooley noted that the same process shapes our broader self-concept: it is based in part on your beliefs about how others see you, including their perceptions and evaluations of you ("People think I'm talented, and they like me") and your emotional response to those beliefs ("I feel good/bad about how others see me"). Cooley called the idea of defining our self-concepts through thinking about how others see us the **looking-glass self.**

Self-Reflection

Consider your looking-glass self. What kinds of labels do your friends use to describe you? Your family? How do you feel about others' impressions of you? In what ways do these feelings shape your interpersonal communication and relationships?

In considering your self-concept and its impact on your interpersonal communication, keep two implications in mind. First, because your self-concept consists of deeply held beliefs, attitudes, and values, changing it is difficult. Once you've decided you're a compassionate person, for example, you'll likely perceive yourself that way for a long time (Fiske & Taylor, 1991).

Second, our self-concepts often lead us to make **self-fulfilling prophecies,** predictions about future interactions that lead us to behave in ways that ensure the interaction unfolds as we predicted. Some self-fulfilling prophecies set positive events in motion. For instance, you may see yourself as professionally capable, which leads you to predict job interview success. During an interview, your prophecy of success leads you to communicate in a confident fashion, which impresses the interviewers. Other self-fulfilling prophecies set negative events in motion. I once had a friend who believed he was unattractive and undesirable. Whenever we went out to parties, his self-concept would lead him to predict interpersonal failure. He would then spend the entire time in a corner, staring morosely into his drink. Needless to say, no one tried to talk to him. At the end of the evening he'd say, "See, I told you no one would want to talk to me!"

Self-Esteem

Self-esteem is the overall value, positive or negative, that we assign to ourselves. Whereas self-awareness prompts us to ask "Who am I?" and self-concept is the answer to that question, self-esteem is the answer to the follow-up question, "Given who I am, what's my evaluation of my self?" When your overall estimation of self is negative, you'll have a meager sense of self-worth and suffer from low self-esteem. When your evaluation of self is positive, you'll enjoy high self-esteem.

Your self-esteem strongly shapes your interpersonal communication, relationships, and physical and mental health (Pyszczynski, Greenberg, Solomon, Arndt, & Schimel, 2004). People with high self-esteem report greater life satisfaction, communicate more positively with others, experience more happiness in their relationships, and exhibit greater leadership ability, athleticism, and academic performance than do people with low self-esteem (Fox, 1997). High self-esteem also helps insulate people from stress and anxiety. (Pyszczynski et al., 2004). By contrast, low self-esteem can spawn a destructive feedback loop, as depicted in **Figure 2.1**.

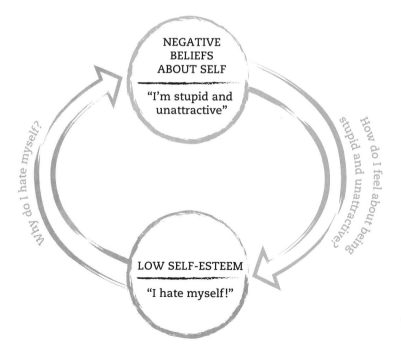

◄ Figure 2.1 **Low Self-Esteem: A Vicious Cycle**

Measuring Up to Your Own Standards

The key to bolstering your self-esteem is understanding its roots. **Self-discrepancy theory** suggests that your self-esteem is determined by how you compare to two mental standards (Higgins, 1987). The first is your *ideal self*, the characteristics (mental, physical, emotional, material, and even spiritual) that you want to possess based on your desires—the "perfect you." The second standard is your *ought self*, the person others wish and expect you to be. This stems from expectations of your family, friends, colleagues, and romantic partners as well as cultural norms. According to self-discrepancy theory, you feel happy and content when your perception of your self matches both your ideal and ought selves (Katz & Farrow, 2000). However, when you perceive your self to be inferior to both your ideal and ought selves, you experience a discrepancy between your self and these standards and are likely to suffer low self-esteem (Veale, Kinderman, Riley, & Lambrou, 2003).

Improving Your Self-Esteem

Your self-esteem can improve only when you reduce discrepancies between your self and your ideal and ought selves. How can you do this? Begin by assessing your self-concept. Make a list of the beliefs, attitudes, and values that make up your self-concept. Be sure to include both positive and negative attributes. Then think about your self-esteem. In reviewing the list you've made, do you see yourself positively or negatively?

Next, analyze your ideal self. Who do you wish you were? Is this ideal attainable, or is it unrealistic? If it is attainable, what would you have to change to become this person? If you made these changes, would you be satisfied with yourself, or would your expectations for yourself simply escalate further?

Third, analyze your ought self. Who do others want you to be? Can you ever become the person others expect? What would you have to do to become this person? If you did all of these things, would others be satisfied with you, or would their expectations escalate?

Fourth, revisit and redefine your standards. This step requires intense, concentrated effort over a long period of time. If you find that your ideal and ought selves are realistic and attainable, move to the final step described below. If you decide that your ideal and ought selves are unrealistic and

(Left to right) © Randy Faris/Corbis; Getty Images

◊ Wondering "Why can't I be the person I want to be?" suggests a discrepancy between someone and their ideal self, while asking "Why can't I be the person others want me to be?" indicates a discrepancy between someone and their ought self.

Self-Quiz

Test Your Self-Esteem

This quiz can help you gauge your self-esteem. Read each statement and assign it a score depending on how much you agree with it. If you strongly agree, give it a 3; if you agree, give it a 2; if you disagree, give it a 1; and if you strongly disagree, give it a 0. Then total your score and see how it compares to the Scoring section below.

On the whole, I am satisfied with myself.

I feel that I have a number of good qualities.

I am able to do things as well as most other people.

I feel that I am a person of worth, at least on an equal plane with others.

I have a positive attitude toward myself.

Note: This *Self-Quiz* is adapted from the self-esteem scale developed by Rosenburg (1965).

Scoring: Scores of 7 and below indicate low self-esteem; scores of 8 and above represent high self-esteem.

unattainable, redefine these standards so that each can be attainable through sustained work. If you find yourself unable to abandon unrealistic and unattainable standards, don't be afraid to consult with a professional therapist or other trusted resource for assistance.

Finally, create an action plan for resolving any self-discrepancies. Map out the specific actions necessary to eventually attain your ideal and ought selves. Frame your new standards as a list of goals, and post them in your planner, cell phone, personal Web page, bedroom, or kitchen to remind yourself of these goals. Since self-esteem can't be changed in a day, a week, or even a month, establish a realistic time line. Then implement this action plan in your daily life, checking your progress as you go.

LearningCurve
bedfordstmartins.com/ipcandyou

The Sources of Self

Imagine for a moment that you wake up in your bed, and although you recognize your surroundings, you have no memory of self. How will you find out who you are?

You might first examine your own body. Knowing whether you are male or female would immediately give you a wealth of useful knowledge about your self, such as which clothes you should wear and how you should talk and act. Second, you would likely talk with family members, gathering as much information from them as you could. You would also watch how they respond to you. Last, you would turn on the computer and surf the Internet, watch TV, or even go for a walk, looking for clues about how people communicate with each other in public, how they dress, and how they behave. From these observations, you might begin to form ideas about where you fit in this culture.

Of course, at the end of the day, you still would have huge holes in your self-knowledge. Biologists and psychologists agree that roughly half of what makes us who we are is determined by our biological

{ **Our selves are shaped by powerful outside forces of gender, family, and culture.** }

heritage (Rothbart, Ahadi, & Evans, 2000). But this doesn't mean that our self-awareness, self-concept, and self-esteem are 50 percent identical to those of our parents and other ancestors. Instead, our selves are shaped by the powerful outside forces of gender, family, and culture.

Gender and Self

Arguably the most profound outside force shaping our sense of self is our *gender*—the composite of social, psychological, and cultural attributes that characterize us as male or female (Canary, Emmers-Sommer, & Faulkner, 1997). Note that scholars distinguish gender, which is largely learned, from *biological sex*, which we're born with. Unlike biological sex, our gender is shaped over time through our interactions with others.

Immediately after birth, we begin a life-long process of gender socialization, learning from others what it means personally, interpersonally, and culturally to be "male" or "female." Girls are typically taught feminine behaviors, such as sensitivity to one's own and others' emotions, nurturance, and compassion (Lippa, 2002). Boys are usually taught masculine behaviors, learning about assertiveness, competitiveness, and independence. As a result of gender socialization, men and women often end up forming comparatively different self-concepts (Cross & Madson, 1997). For example, women are more likely

---

Self-Reflection

What lessons about gender did you learn from your family when you were growing up? From your friends? Based on these lessons, what aspects of your self did you bolster—or bury—given what others deemed appropriate for your gender? How did these lessons affect how you interpersonally communicate?

(Left to right) Nancy Honey/Getty Images; Caroline Penn/Panos Pictures; Digital Vision/Punchstock/Getty Images

🜄 **The sources of self include your gender, your family, and your culture.**

than men to perceive themselves as connected to others and to assess themselves based on the quality of these interpersonal connections. Men are more likely than women to think of themselves as a composite of their individual achievements, abilities, and beliefs—viewing themselves as separate from other people. However, this doesn't mean that all men and all women think of themselves in identical ways. Many men and women appreciate and embrace both feminine and masculine characteristics in their self-concepts.

Family and Self

When we're born, we have no self-awareness, self-concept, or self-esteem. As we mature, we become aware of ourselves as unique and separate from our environments and begin developing self-concepts. Our caregivers play a crucial role in this process, providing us with ready-made sets of beliefs, attitudes, and values from which we construct our fledgling selves. We also forge emotional bonds with our caregivers, and our communication and interactions with them powerfully shape our beliefs regarding the functions, rewards, and dependability of interpersonal relationships (Bowlby, 1969; Domingue & Mollen, 2009).

These beliefs, in turn, help shape two dimensions of our thoughts, feelings, and behavior: attachment anxiety and attachment avoidance (Collins & Feeney, 2004). *Attachment anxiety* is the degree to which a person fears rejection by relationship partners. If you experience high attachment anxiety, you perceive yourself as unlovable and unworthy—thoughts that may result from being ignored or even abused during youth. Consequently, in close relationships you experience chronic fear of abandonment. If you have low attachment anxiety, you feel lovable and worthy of attention—reflections of a supportive and affectionate upbringing. As a result, you feel comfortable and confident in your intimate involvements.

Attachment avoidance is the degree to which someone desires close interpersonal ties. If you have high attachment avoidance, you'll likely experience little interest in intimacy, preferring solitude instead. Such feelings may stem from childhood neglect or an upbringing that encouraged autonomy. If you

experience low attachment avoidance, you seek intimacy and interdependence with others, having learned in youth that such connections are essential for happiness and well-being.

Four attachment styles derive from these two dimensions (Collins & Feeney, 2004; Domingue & Mollen, 2009).

- **Secure attachment** individuals are low in both anxiety and avoidance: they're comfortable with intimacy and seek close ties with others. Secure individuals report warm and supportive relationships, high self-esteem, and confidence in their ability to communicate. When relationship problems arise, they move to resolve them, and are willing to solicit support from others. In addition, they are comfortable with sexual intimacy and unlikely to engage in risky sexual behavior.

- **Preoccupied attachment** adults are high in anxiety and low in avoidance: they desire closeness, but are plagued with fear of rejection. They may use sexual contact to satisfy their compulsive need to feel loved. When faced with relationship challenges, preoccupied individuals react with extreme negative emotion and a lack of trust. These individuals often have difficulty maintaining long-term involvements.

- People with low anxiety but high avoidance have a **dismissive attachment** style. They view close relationships as comparatively unimportant, instead prizing and prioritizing self-reliance. Relationship crises evoke hasty exits, and they are more likely than other attachment styles to engage in casual sexual relationships and to endorse the view that sex without love is positive.

- Finally, **fearful attachment** adults are high in both attachment anxiety *and* avoidance. They fear rejection and tend to shun relationships. Fearful individuals can develop close ties if the relationship seems to guarantee a lack of rejection, such as when a partner is disabled or otherwise dependent on them. But even then, they suffer from a chronic lack of faith in themselves, their partners, and the relationship's viability.

Culture and Self

At the 1968 Summer Olympics, U.S. sprinter Tommie Smith won the men's 200-meter gold medal, and teammate John Carlos won the bronze. During the medal ceremony, as the American flag was raised and "The Star-Spangled Banner" played, both runners closed their eyes, lowered their heads, and raised black-gloved fists. Smith's right fist represented black power, and Carlos' left fist represented black unity (Gettings, 2005). The two fists, raised next to each other, created an arch of black unity and power. Smith wore a black scarf around his neck for black pride, and both men wore black socks with no shoes, representing African American poverty. These

John Dominis/Time & Life Pictures/Getty Images

◊ Tommie Smith's and John Carlos' protest at the 1968 Summer Olympics showed how they identified with the African American culture of the time.

symbols and gestures, taken together, clearly spoke of the runners' allegiance to black culture and their protest of the poor treatment of African Americans in the United States (see the photo at bottom left).

Many Euro-Americans viewed Smith's and Carlos' behavior at the ceremony as a betrayal of "American" culture. Both men were suspended from the U.S. team; they and their families began receiving death threats. Over time, however, people of all American ethnicities began to sympathize with them, and, 30 years later, in 1998, Smith and Carlos were commemorated in an anniversary celebration of their protest.

In addition to gender and family, our culture is a powerful source of self. *Culture* is an established, coherent set of beliefs, attitudes, values, and practices shared by a large group of people (Keesing, 1974). If this strikes you as similar to our definition of self-concept, you're right; culture is like a collective sense of self shared by a large group of people.

Thinking of culture in this way has important implications. First, it includes many different types of large-group influences, including your nationality as well as your ethnicity, religion, gender, sexual orientation, physical abilities, and even age. We learn our cultural beliefs, attitudes, and values from parents, teachers, religious leaders, peers, and the mass media (Gudykunst & Kim, 2003). Most of us belong to more than one culture simultaneously—possessing the beliefs, attitudes, and values of each. Unfortunately, the various cultures to which we belong sometimes clash; when they do, we often have to choose the culture to which we pledge our primary allegiance.

We'll be discussing culture in greater depth in Chapter 5, where we'll consider some of the unique

Self-Reflection

When you consider your own cultural background, to which culture do you "pledge allegiance"? How do you communicate this allegiance to others? Have you ever suffered consequences for openly communicating your allegiance to your culture? If so, how?

(Left to right) West Rock/Getty Images; © Image Source/Alamy; John Elk III/Alamy; © Paul A. Souders/Corbis

◊ Cultural identity is part of a sophisticated definition of self.

{ **In many encounters, our private and public selves mirror each other. At other times, they seem disconnected.** }

variables of culture that help to define us and communicate our selves to others.

Presenting Your Self

Rick Welts is one of the most influential people in professional basketball.[2] He created the NBA All-Star Weekend and is cofounder of the women's professional league, the WNBA. For years he served as the NBA's executive vice president and chief marketing officer, and he now is president of the Phoenix Suns. But throughout his entire sports career he lived a self-described "shadow life," publicly playing the role of a straight male, while privately being gay. In early 2011, following his mother's death, he "came out" publicly. As Welts describes, "I want to pierce the silence that envelops the subject of being gay in men's team sports. I want to mentor gays who harbor doubts about a sports career, whether on the court or in the front office. But most of all, I want to feel whole, authentic."

In addition to our private selves, the composite of our self-awareness, self-concept, and self-esteem, each of us also has a public self— the self we present to others (Fenigstein, Scheier, & Buss, 1975). We actively create our public selves through our interpersonal communication and behavior.

In many encounters, our private and public selves mirror each other. At other times, they seem disconnected. In extreme instances, like that

Photo AP/The Arizona Republic, Michael Chow

◊ Rick Welts was ultimately able to reconcile his private self with his public self. What parts of your private self do you keep hidden from public view?

---

[2]All of the information that follows regarding Welts is adapted from Barry (2011).

of Rick Welts, we may intentionally craft an inauthentic public self to hide something about our private self we don't want others to know. The truth is that most (if not all) of others' impressions of you are based on their appraisals of your public self. Simply, people know and judge the "you" who communicates with them—not the "you" you keep inside. Thus, managing your public self is a crucial part of competent interpersonal communication.

Maintaining Your Public Self

Renowned sociologist Erving Goffman (1955) noted that whenever you communicate with others, you present a public self—your **face**—that you want others to see and know. Your face can be anything you want it to be—"perky and upbeat," "cool and level-headed," or "tough as nails." We create different faces for different moments and relationships in our lives, such as our face as a parent, college student, coworker, or homeless-shelter volunteer.

Sometimes your face is a **mask,** a public self designed to strategically veil your private self (Goffman, 1959). Masks can be dramatic, such as when Rick Welts hid his grief over the loss of his long-time partner before openly acknowledging his sexuality. Or, masks can be subtle—for example, the parent who acts calm in front of an injured child so the youngster doesn't become frightened. Some masks are designed to inflate one's estimation in the eyes of others. One study found that 90 percent of college students surveyed admitted telling at least one lie to impress a person they were romantically interested in (Rowatt, Cunningham, & Druen, 1998). Other masks are crafted so people underestimate us and our abilities (Gibson & Sachau, 2000).

Regardless of the form our face takes—a genuine representation of our private self, or a mask designed to hide this self from others—Goffman argued that we often form a strong emotional attachment to our face because it represents the person we most want others to see when they communicate with and relate to us.

Sometimes after we've created a certain face, information is revealed that contradicts it, causing us to lose face (Goffman, 1955). Losing face provokes feelings of shame, humiliation, and sadness—in a word, **embarrassment.** However, embarrassment is not the only cost. When others see us lose face, they may begin to question whether the public self with which they're familiar is a genuine reflection of our private self. For example, suppose your workplace face is "dedicated, hardworking employee." You ask your boss if there's extra work to be done, help fellow coworkers, show up early, stay late, and so forth. But if you tell your manager that you need your afternoon schedule cleared to work on an urgent report and then she sees you playing World of Warcraft on your computer, she'll undoubtedly view your actions as inconsistent with your communication. Your face as the "hardworking employee" will be called into question, as will your credibility.

Self-Reflection

Recall an embarrassing interpersonal encounter. How did you try to restore your lost face? Were you successful? If you could relive the encounter, what would you say and do differently?

Because losing face can damage others' impressions of you, maintaining face during interpersonal interactions is extremely important. How can you effectively maintain face?[3] Use words and actions consistent with the face you're trying to craft. From one moment to the next and from one behavior to the next, your interpersonal communication and behaviors must complement your face, rather than clash with it. Also, make sure your communication and behaviors mesh with the knowledge that others already have about you. If you say or do things that contradict what others know is true about you, they'll see your face as false.

Finally, for your face to be maintained, your communication and behavior must be reinforced by

---

[3]All of the information that follows regarding how to successfully maintain face is adapted from Goffman (1955).

objects and events in the surrounding environment—things over which you have only limited control. For example, imagine that your romantic partner is overseas for the summer, and you agree to video chat regularly. Your first scheduled chat is Friday at 5 p.m, but when 5 p.m. Friday rolls around, your Internet connection is down. By the time it's up again, your partner has already signed off, leaving a perplexed message regarding your "neglect." To restore face, you'll need to explain what happened.

Of course, all of us fall from grace on occasion, whether it's getting caught gaming when we should be working, or failing to be available when we've promised. In such cases, promptly acknowledge that the event happened, admit responsibility for any of your actions that contributed to the event, apologize for your actions and for disappointing others, and move to maintain your face again. Apologizing is a fairly successful method for reducing people's negative impressions and anger—especially when such apologies avoid excuses that contradict what people know really happened (Ohbuchi & Sato, 1994). People who deny their inconsistencies or who blame others for their lapses are judged much more harshly than those who admit their mistakes.

Skills Practice

Apologizing

Creating a skillful apology

1. Watch for instances in which you offend or disappoint someone.
2. Face-to-face (if possible) or by phone, acknowledge the incident and admit your responsibility.
3. Apologize for any harm you have caused.
4. Avoid pseudo-apologies that minimize the event or shift accountability, like "I'm sorry you overreacted" or "I'm sorry you think I'm to blame."
5. If the person accepts your apology, express gratitude for their understanding.

The Importance of Online Self-Presentation

One of the most powerful vehicles for presenting your self online is your profile photo. Whether it's on Facebook, LinkedIn, Google, Tumblr, Flickr, Foursquare, or any other site, this image, more than any other, represents who you are to others. When I first built my Facebook profile, the photo I chose was one taken at a club, right before my band went onstage. For me, it depicted the "melancholy artist" that I consider part of my self-concept. But presenting my self online in this fashion was a disaster. Within hours of posting it, I was flooded with messages from students, colleagues, and even long-lost friends: "Are you OK?" I quickly pulled the photo and replaced it with a more positive one—a sunny image of me and my boys taken atop a mountain near Sun Valley. Now I use the melancholy photo only rarely, as accompaniment to a sad or angry status update.

Presenting the Self Online

Online communication provides us with unique benefits and challenges for self-presentation. When you talk with others face-to-face, people judge your public self on your words as well as what you look like—your age, gender, clothing, facial expressions, and so forth. Similarly, during a phone call, vocal cues such as tone, pitch, and volume help you and your conversation partner draw conclusions about each other. But during online interactions, the amount of information communicated—visual, verbal, and nonverbal—is radically restricted and more easily controlled. We carefully choose our photos and edit our text messages, e-mail, instant messages, and profile descriptions. We selectively self-present in ways that make us look good, without having to worry about verbal slipups, uncontrollable nervous habits, or physical disabilities that might make people judge us (Parks, 2007).

People routinely present themselves online (through photos and written descriptions) in ways that amplify positive personality characteristics such as warmth, friendliness, and extraversion

Courtesy of Facebook Inc.

Courtesy of Facebook Inc.

Courtesy of Facebook Inc.

Steve McCornack

💧 The freedom to create an online identity can cause discord if people think this identity doesn't match your offline persona.

(Vazire & Gosling, 2004). For instance, photos posted on social networking sites typically show groups of friends, fostering the impression that the person in the profile is likable, fun, and popular (Ellison, Steinfield, & Lampe, 2007). These positive and highly selective depictions of self generally work as intended. Viewers of online profiles tend to form impressions of a profile's subject that match the subject's intended self-presentation (Gosling, Gaddis, & Vazire, 2007).

The freedom that online communication allows us in flexibly crafting our selves comes with an associated cost: unless you have met someone in person, you will have difficulty determining whether their online self is authentic or a mask. Through misleading profile descriptions, fake photos, and phony screen names, people communicating online can assume identities that would be impossible for them to maintain in offline encounters (Rintel & Pittam, 1997). For example, scholars suggest that you should never presume the gender of someone you interact with online if you haven't met the person face-to-face, even if he or she has provided photos (Savicki, Kelley, & Oesterreich, 1999).

Self-Reflection

Have you ever distorted your self-presentation online to make yourself appear more attractive and appealing? If so, was this ethical? What were the consequences—for yourself and others—of creating this online mask?

Evaluating the Self Online

Because of the pervasiveness of online masks, people often question the truthfulness of online self-presentations, especially overly positive or flattering ones. *Warranting theory* (Walther & Parks, 2002) suggests that, when assessing someone's online self-descriptions, we consider the **warranting value** of the information presented—that is, the degree to which the information is supported by other people and outside evidence (Walther, Van Der Heide, Hamel, & Schulman, 2008). Information that was obviously crafted by the person, that isn't supported by others, and that can't be verified offline has *low warranting value*, and most people wouldn't trust it. Information that's created or supported by others and that can be readily verified through alternative sources on- and offline has *high warranting value*, and consequently is perceived as valid. So, for example, news about a professional accomplishment that you post on your Facebook page will have low warranting value. But if the same information is also featured on your employer's Web site, its warranting value will increase (Walther et al., 2008).

Not surprisingly, the warranting value of online self-descriptions plummets when they are directly contradicted by others. Imagine that Jane, a student in your communication class, friends you on Facebook. Though you don't know her especially well, you accept and, later, check out her page. In the content that Jane has provided, she presents herself as quiet, thoughtful, and reserved. But messages from her friends on her Facebook wall contradict this, saying things like: "You were a MANIAC last night!" and "U R A wild child!" Based on this information, you'll likely disregard Jane's online self-presentation and judge her instead as sociable and outgoing, perhaps even "crazy" and "wild."

Research shows that when friends, family members, coworkers, or romantic partners post information on your page, their messages shape others' perceptions of you more powerfully than your own postings do—especially when their postings contradict your self-description (Walther et al., 2008). This holds true not just for personality characteristics such as extraversion (how "outgoing" you are), but also physical attractiveness. One study of Facebook profiles found that when friends posted things like "If only I was as hot as you" or (alternatively) "Don't pay any attention to those jerks at the bar last night; beauty is on the inside," such comments influenced others' perceptions of the person's attractiveness more than the person's own description of his or her physical appeal (Walther et al., 2008).

Improving Your Online Self-Presentation

Taken as a whole, the research and theory about online self-presentation suggests three practices for improving your online self-presentation. First, keep in mind that online communication is dominated by visual information such as text, photos, and videos. Make wise choices in the words and images you select to present yourself to others. For example, many female managers know they're more likely than their male peers to be judged solely on appearance, so they post photos of themselves that convey professionalism (Miller & Arnold, 2001).

Skills Practice

Your Online Self
Maintaining your desired online face

1. Describe your desired online face (e.g., "I want to be seen as popular, adventurous, and attractive").
2. Critically compare this description with your profiles, photos, and posts. Do they match?
3. Revise or delete content that doesn't match your desired face.
4. Repeat this process for friends' postings on your personal pages.
5. In your future online communication—texting, e-mailing, and posting—present yourself only in ways that mesh with your desired face.

Second, always remember the important role that warranting value plays in shaping others' impressions of you. The simple rule is *what others say about you online is more important than what you say about yourself*. Consequently, be wary of allowing messages and wall postings on your personal Web pages that contradict the self you want to present, or that cast you in a negative light—even if you think such messages and postings are cute, funny, or provocative.

Finally, subject your online self-presentation to what I call *the interview test*: ask yourself, "Would I feel comfortable sharing all elements of this presentation—photos, personal profiles, videos, blogs—in a job interview?" If your answer is no, modify your current online self-presentation immediately. In a survey of 1,200 human resources professionals and recruiters, 78 percent reported using search engines to screen candidates, while 63 percent reported perusing social networking sites (Balderrama, 2010).

LearningCurve
bedfordstmartins.com/ipcandyou

The Relational Self

One of the reasons we carefully craft the presentation of our self is to create interpersonal relationships. We present our self to acquaintances, coworkers, friends, family members, and romantic partners, and through our interpersonal communication, relationships are fostered, maintained, and sometimes ended. Within each of these relationships, how close we feel to one another is defined largely by how much of our self we reveal to others and vice versa.

Managing the self in interpersonal relationships isn't easy. Exposing our self to others can make us

DREAMWORKS LLC/The Kobal Collection/Art Resource

feel vulnerable, provoking tension between how much to reveal versus how much to veil. Even in the closest of relationships, certain aspects of the self remain hidden, from our partners as well as ourselves.

Opening Your Self to Others

In the movie *Shrek*, the ogre Shrek forges a friendship with a likable but occasionally irksome donkey (Adamson & Jenson, 2001). As their acquaintance deepens to friendship, Shrek tries to explain the nature of his inner self to his companion: "For your information, there's a lot more to ogres than people think! . . . Ogres . . . are like onions. . . . Onions have layers—OGRES have layers! Onions have layers! You get it!? We both have layers!"

Shrek was not the first to use the onion as a metaphor for self. In fact, the idea that revealing the self to others involves peeling back or penetrating layers was first suggested by psychologists Irwin Altman and Dalmas Taylor (1973) in their **social penetration theory.** Like Shrek, Altman and Taylor envisioned the self as an "onion-skin structure," consisting of sets of layers.[4]

At the *outermost, peripheral layers* of your self are demographic characteristics such as birthplace, age, gender, and ethnicity (see Figure 2.2). Discussion of these characteristics dominates first conversations with new acquaintances: "What's your name? Where are you from?" In the *intermediate layers* reside your attitudes and opinions about music, politics, food, entertainment, and other such matters. Deep within the "onion" are the *central layers* of your self—core characteristics such as self-awareness, self-concept, self-esteem, personal values, fears, and distinctive personality traits. We'll discuss these in more detail in Chapter 3.

---

[4]Although Altman and Taylor use *personality* to describe the self, they define personality in terms of self-concept and self-esteem, and use the terms *personality* and *self* interchangeably throughout their text (for example, see 1973, pp. 17–19).

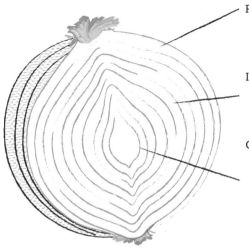

◀○ Figure 2.2 The Layers of Self

PERIPHERAL LAYERS
- Age
- College major
- Hometown

INTERMEDIATE LAYERS
- Musical tastes
- Political beliefs
- Leisure interests

CENTRAL LAYERS
- Values, traits, fears
- Self-awareness
- Self-concept
- Self-esteem

The notion of layers of self helps explain the development of interpersonal relationships, as well as how we distinguish between casual and close involvements. As relationships progress, partners communicate increasingly personal information to each other. This allows them to mutually penetrate one another's peripheral, then intermediate, and finally central selves. Relationship development, therefore, is like slowly pushing a pin into an onion: it proceeds layer by layer, without skipping layers.

The revealing of selves that occurs during relationship development involves both breadth and depth. *Breadth* is the number of different aspects of self each partner reveals at each layer—the insertion of more and more pins into the onion, so to speak. *Depth* involves how deeply into the other's self the partners have penetrated: have you revealed only your peripheral self, or have you given the other person access into your intermediate or central selves as well?

Although social penetration occurs in all relationships, the rate at which it occurs isn't consistent. For example, some people let others in quickly, while others never grant access to certain elements of their selves, no matter how long they know a person. The speed with which people grant one another access to the broader and deeper aspects of their selves depends on a variety of factors, including the attachment styles discussed earlier in the chapter. But, in all relationships, depth and breadth of social penetration is intertwined with **intimacy:** the feeling of closeness and "union" that exists between us and our partners (Mashek & Aron, 2004). The deeper and broader we

Cathy Yeulet/123RF.com

◊ The ability to share our selves with someone else feels like a rare experience, but when the opportunity arises, information flows more freely, and greater relational intimacy develops.

penetrate into each other's selves, the more intimacy we feel; the more intimacy we feel, the more we allow each other access to broad and deep aspects of our selves (Shelton, Trail, West, & Bergsieker, 2010).

Your Hidden and Revealed Selves

The image of self and relationship development offered by social penetration theory suggests a relatively straightforward evolution of intimacy, with partners gradually penetrating broadly and deeply into each other's selves over time. But in thinking about our selves and our relationships with others, two important questions arise: First, are we really aware of all aspects of ourselves? Second, are we willing to grant others access to all aspects of ourselves?

We can explore possible answers to these questions by looking at the model of the relational self called the Johari Window (see Figure 2.3 on page 43), which suggests that some "quadrants" of our selves are open to self-reflection and sharing with other people, while others remain hidden—to both ourselves and others (Luft, 1970).

During the early stages of an interpersonal relationship, and especially during first encounters, our *public area* of self is much smaller than our *hidden area*. As relationships progress, partners gain access to broader and deeper information about their selves; consequently, the public area expands and the hidden area diminishes. The Johari Window thus provides us with a useful alternative metaphor to social penetration. As relationships develop, we don't just let people "penetrate inward" to our central selves; we let them "peer into" more parts of our selves by revealing information that we previously hid from them.

Importantly, as our interpersonal relationships develop and we increasingly share previously hidden information with our partners, our *unknown* and *blind* quadrants remain fairly stable. By their very nature, our unknown areas remain unknown throughout much of our lives. And for most of us,

the blind area remains imperceptible. That's because our blind areas are defined by our deepest-rooted beliefs about ourselves—those beliefs that make up our self-concepts. Consequently, when others challenge us to open our eyes to our blind areas, we resist.

To improve our interpersonal communication, we must be able to see into our blind areas and then change the aspects within them that lead to incompetent communication and relationship challenges. But this isn't easy. After all, how can you correct misperceptions about yourself that you don't even know exist or flaws that you consider your greatest strengths? Delving into your blind area means challenging fundamental beliefs about yourself—subjecting your self-concept to hard scrutiny. Your goal is to overturn your most treasured personal misconceptions. Most people accomplish this only over a long period of time and with the assistance of trustworthy and willing relationship partners.

Self-Reflection

Consider your "blind area" of self. What strengths might you possess that you don't recognize? What character flaws might exist that don't mesh with your self-concept? How can you capitalize on these strengths and mend your flaws so that your interpersonal communication and relationships improve?

Disclosing Your Self to Others

We all can think of situations in which we've revealed private information about ourselves to others. This is known as **self-disclosure** (Wheeless, 1978), and it plays a critical role in interpersonal communication and relationship development. According to the **interpersonal process model of intimacy,** the closeness we feel toward others in our relationships is created through two things:

QUADRANT I	QUADRANT II
Public Area Aspects of your self that you and others are aware of. Includes everything you openly disclose—from music and food preferences to religious beliefs and moral values.	*Blind Area* Facets of your self that are readily apparent to others through your interpersonal communication but that you're not aware of. Includes strengths that you may not see in yourself or character flaws that don't mesh with your self-concept.
QUADRANT III	QUADRANT IV
Hidden Area Parts of your self that you're aware of but that you hide from most others. These include destructive thoughts, impulses, and fantasies, and disturbing life experiences that don't fit comfortably with your public self or your own self-concept.	*Unknown Area* Aspects of your self that you and others aren't aware of, such as unconscious motives and impulses that strongly influence your interpersonal communication and relationships. While you can't gain access to your unknown area through critical self-reflection, you can indirectly infer aspects of your unknown area by observing consistent patterns in your own behavior.

◄◦ Figure 2.3 **The Johari Window**

self-disclosure and responsiveness of listeners to disclosure (Reis & Patrick, 1996). Relationships are intimate when both partners share private information with each other *and* each partner responds to the other's disclosures with understanding, caring, and support (Reis & Shaver, 1988). One practical implication of this is *just because you share your thoughts and feelings with someone doesn't mean that you have an intimate relationship*. For example, if you regularly chat with a classmate, both online and off, and tell her all of your secrets—but she never does the same in return—your relationship isn't intimate, it's one-sided.

On the other hand, when listeners are nonsupportive in response to disclosures, or people disclose information that's perceived as problematic, intimacy can be undermined. Think about an instance in which you shared something deeply personal with a friend, but he or she responded by ridiculing or judging you. How did this reaction make you feel? Chances are, it widened, rather than narrowed, the emotional distance between you and your friend. Research suggests that one of the most damaging events that can happen in interpersonal relationships is a partner's sharing information that the other person finds inappropriate and perplexing (Planalp & Honeycutt, 1985). This is especially true in relationships where the partners are already struggling with challenging problems or experiencing painful transitions. For example, during divorce proceedings, parents commonly disclose negative and demeaning information about each other to their children. The parents may see this sharing as stress relieving or "cathartic" (Afifi, McManus, Hutchinson, & Baker, 2007), but these disclosures only intensify the children's mental and physical distress and make them feel caught between the two parents (Koerner, Wallace, Lehman, & Raymond, 2002).

Differences in Disclosure

Researchers have conducted thousands of self-disclosure studies over the past 40 years (Tardy & Dindia, 1997). These studies suggest five important facts regarding how people self-disclose.

1. In any culture, people vary widely in the degree to which they self-disclose. Some people are naturally transparent, others are more opaque (Jourard, 1964).

2. People across cultures differ in their self-disclosure. For instance, people of Asian descent tend to disclose less than do people of European ancestry; Japanese disclose substantially less than Americans in both friendships and romantic relationships, and view self-disclosure as a less important aspect of intimacy development than do Americans (Barnlund, 1975).

3. People disclose more quickly, broadly, and deeply when interacting online than face-to-face. One reason for this is that during online encounters, people can't see those with whom they are interacting, and so the consequences of such disclosure seem less noticeable (Joinson, 2001).

4. Self-disclosure appears to promote mental health and relieve stress (Tardy, 2000). Especially when the information is troubling, keeping it inside can escalate your stress levels substantially, resulting in problematic mental and physical symptoms and ailments (Kelly & McKillop, 1996; Pennebaker, 1997).

5. Little evidence exists that supports the stereotype that men can't disclose their feelings in relationships. In close same-sex friendships, for example, both men and women disclose deeply and broadly (Shelton et al., 2010). And in cross-sex romantic involvements, men often disclose at levels equal to or greater than their female partners (Canary et al., 1997). At the same time, however, both men and women feel more comfortable disclosing to female than to male recipients (Dindia & Allen, 1992). Teenagers are more likely to disclose to mothers and best female friends than to fathers and best male friends—suggesting that adolescents may perceive females as more empathic and understanding than males (Garcia & Geisler, 1988).

Self-Reflection

During your childhood, to which family member did you feel most comfortable disclosing? Why? Of your friends and family right now, do you disclose more to women or men, or is there no difference? What does this tell you about how gender has guided your disclosure decisions?

Competently Disclosing Your Self

Based on all we know about self-disclosure, how can you improve your disclosure skills? Consider these recommendations for competent self-disclosure:

- **Follow the advice of Apollo: know your self.** Before disclosing, make sure that the aspects of your self you reveal to others are aspects that you want to reveal and that you feel certain about. This is especially important when disclosing intimate feelings, such as romantic interest. When you disclose feelings about others directly to them, you affect their lives and relationship decisions. Consequently, you're ethically obligated to be certain about the truth of your own feelings before sharing them with others.

- **Know your audience.** Whether it's a wall post or an intimate conversation with a friend, think carefully about how others will perceive your disclosure and how it will impact their thoughts and feelings about you. If you're unsure of the appropriateness of a disclosure, don't disclose. This holds equally true for online and face-to-face encounters.

- **Don't force others to self-disclose.** We often presume it's good for people to "open up" and share their secrets, particularly those that are troubling them. Although it's perfectly appropriate to let someone know you're available to listen, it's unethical and destructive to force or cajole others into sharing information against their will. People have reasons for not wanting to tell you things—just as you have reasons for protecting your own privacy.

- **Don't presume gender preferences.** Don't fall into the trap of thinking that because someone is a woman, she will disclose freely; or that because he's a man, he's incapable of discussing his feelings. At the same time, be mindful of the tendency to feel more comfortable disclosing to women. Don't presume that because you're talking with a woman it's appropriate for you to freely disclose.

- **Be sensitive to cultural differences.** When interacting with people from different backgrounds, disclose gradually. As with gender, don't presume disclosure patterns based on ethnicity. Just because someone is Asian doesn't mean he or she will be comparatively

⬥ Ted and Robin of *How I Met Your Mother* sometimes experience discomfort and distance in their relationship due to conflicting ideas of self-disclosure.

more reluctant to disclose than someone of European descent.

- **Go slowly.** Share intermediate and central aspects of your self gradually and only after thorough discussion of peripheral information. Moving too quickly to discussion of your deepest fears, self-esteem concerns, and personal values not only increases your sense of vulnerability, but it may make others uncomfortable enough to avoid you.

LearningCurve
bedfordstmartins.com/ipcandyou

Postscript }

Look again at the painting *labeled*. Note that this work of art isn't simply a portrait of the pain and isolation felt by one artist suffering from dyslexia. It embraces all of us. We've all had fingers pointed and names hurled at us.

What metaphorical fingers point at you? Are some of those fingers your own? What names go with them? How do these shape the ways in which you communicate with others and make choices in your relationships?

This chapter began with a self-portrait of suffering—an artist stigmatized in youth by labels. But we can all draw inspiration from Eric Staib's story. Each of us possesses the uniquely human capacity to turn our personal punishments into profound gifts, just as Eric did.

Chapter Review

KEY TERMS

self, 27
self-awareness, 27
⊙ social comparison, 27
self-concept, 27
looking-glass self, 28
⊙ self-fulfilling
  prophecies, 28
self-esteem, 29

self-discrepancy theory, 30
secure attachment, 33
preoccupied attachment, 33
dismissive attachment, 33
fearful attachment, 33
⊙ face, 36
⊙ mask, 36
embarrassment, 36

warranting value, 38
social penetration
  theory, 40
intimacy, 41
⊙ self-disclosure, 42
interpersonal process model
  of intimacy, 42

CHAPTER ACTIVITIES

1. Brainstorm a list of socioeconomic expectations you have for people in specific age groups (e.g., career decisions, marital status, income, living arrangements, etc., for 18- to 25- or 40- to 50-year-olds). Then answer the following questions: How are these expectations generated? What role do the media play in shaping these expectations? How do these expectations shape self-esteem?

2. ⊙ Watch the video on **self-fulfilling prophecies,** then write a journal entry or short paper about a self-fulfilling prophecy you have experienced, and answer the following: What impact does your self-fulfilling prophecy have on your interactions? How has it affected your relationships? What have you done (or can you do) to reduce the impact of your self-fulfilling prophecy?

3. One way to examine the media's influence on self-esteem is to explore how various media campaigns portray beauty and success. For example, Dove's "Real Beauty" ads encourage women to reject the notion that beauty is only for the young and thin. Find several examples of commercials, ads, and clips that focus on appearance. In small groups, discuss which campaigns are helpful for improving self-esteem and which are damaging.

4. ⊙ Watch the video on **mask** and then analyze the video by looking at the interaction from each person's perspective. Address the following: What type(s) of masks would you present if you were the

loser in this situation? The winner? When have you displayed such a mask? Why? Groups can share their findings with the class.

5. Generate a list of the faces you present; basically, how do you want others to see and know you (e.g., "I want to be generous and loving")? Then create another list of the faces someone close to you maintains (i.e., best friend, girlfriend, father). Think about a time when you had a conflict with that person because of a face issue. What makes "face conflicts" difficult to resolve? Why is face so important in close relationships?

6. View your own and others' online dating profiles or Facebook pages and examine the ways in which self is presented online. Answer the following questions in a journal or essay: What strategies of self-presentation (photos and written descriptions) seem appropriate or inappropriate? What techniques are used to represent positive personality characteristics? How accurate are these representations? To what extent do you or others create a mask for your online interactions?

7. Consider a scene from a film or television show in which a character discloses information with others that is too personal and creates negative impressions. In a brief essay, analyze how and why you sense that the disclosure is inappropriate. What, if any, effect does it have on interpersonal relationships among characters in the film?

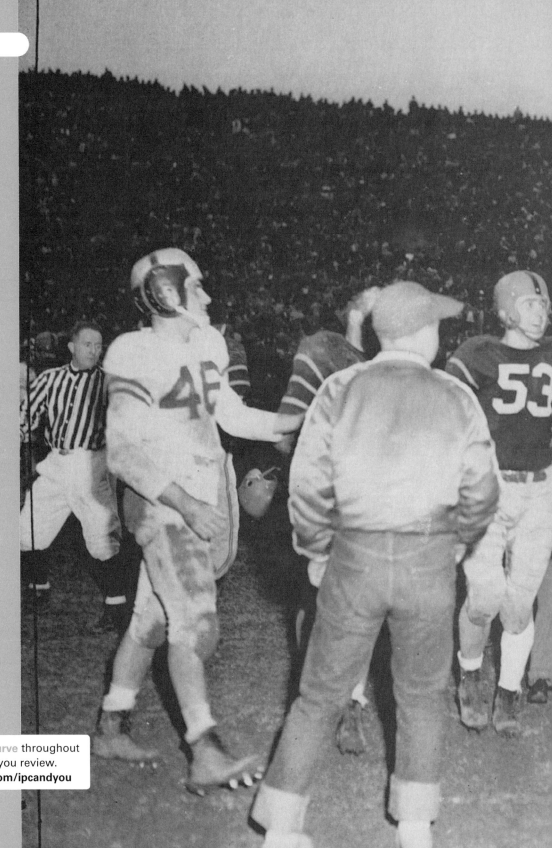

✓ Look for **LearningCurve** throughout the chapter to help you review.
bedfordstmartins.com/ipcandyou

3 } Perceiving Others

I n November 1951, the Dartmouth College football team traveled to Princeton University to play the final game of the season.[1] For Princeton, the contest had special significance: it was the farewell performance of their all-American quarterback, Heisman Trophy winner Dick Kazmaier. Princeton had an 18–1 record at home during Kazmaier's tenure, and they walked onto their turf that day undefeated for the season.

From the opening kickoff, it was a brutal affair. Kazmaier suffered a late hit in the second quarter that broke his nose, caused a concussion, and forced him from the field. In retaliation, Princeton defenders knocked two consecutive Dartmouth quarterbacks out of the game, one of them with a broken leg. Several fights erupted, and referees' flags filled the afternoon air, most of them signaling

"roughing." Although Princeton prevailed, both sides left the stadium bitter about the on-field violence.

In the days that followed, perceptions of the game diverged wildly, depending on scholastic allegiance. Princeton supporters denounced Dartmouth's "dirty play," and the *Daily Princetonian* decried Dartmouth for "deliberately attempting to cripple Kazmaier." The Dartmouth student paper countered, accusing Princeton's coach of urging his players to "get" the Dartmouth quarterbacks.

Perceptual differences weren't limited to players and attendees. A Dartmouth alumnus in the Midwest heard reports of his team's "disgusting" play and requested a copy of the game film. After viewing it, he sent a telegram to the university: "Viewing of the film indicates considerable cutting of important parts. Please airmail the missing excerpts." Why did he believe that the film had been edited? Because when he watched it, he didn't perceive *any* cheap shots by his team.

[1]The information that follows is adapted from Hastorf & Cantril (1954) and Palmer Stadium (2008).

◆ We rely on perception constantly to make sense of everything and everyone in our environment.

AP Photo/Wide World

Intrigued by the perceptual gulf between Princeton and Dartmouth devotees, two psychologists—Albert Hastorf from Dartmouth and Hadley Cantril from Princeton—teamed up to study reactions to the game. What they found was striking. After viewing the game film, students from both schools were asked, "Who instigated the rough play?" Princeton students overwhelmingly blamed Dartmouth, while Dartmouth students attributed the violence to both sides. When questioned about whether Dartmouth had intentionally injured Kazmaier, Princeton students said yes; Dartmouth students said no. And when asked about penalties, Dartmouth students perceived both teams as committing the same number. Princeton students said Dartmouth committed twice as many as Princeton. Though the two groups saw the same film, they perceived two very different games.

Although Hastorf and Cantril examined rival perceptions of a historic college football game, their results tell us much about the challenges we face in responsibly perceiving other people. Each of us perceives the "games," "cheap shots," and "fights" that fill our lives in ways skewed to match our own beliefs and desires. All too often we fail to consider that others feel just as strongly about the "truth" of their viewpoints as we do about ours. Every time we perceive our own behavior as beyond reproach and others' as deficient, see others as exclusively to blame for conflicts, or neglect to consider alternative perspectives and feelings, we are exactly like the Dartmouth and Princeton fans who could perceive only the transgressions of the *other* team.

But competent interpersonal communication and healthy relationships are not built upon belief in perceptual infallibility. Instead, they are founded upon recognition of our perceptual limitations, constant striving to correct perceptual errors, and sincere effort invested in considering others' viewpoints.

P erception is our window to the world. Everything we experience while interacting with others is filtered through our perception. While information seems to enter our conscious minds without bias, our perception is not an objective lens. Instead, it's a product of our own mental creation. When we perceive, we actively create the meanings we assign to people, their communication, and our relationships, and we look to our perception—not reality itself—to guide our interpersonal communication and relationship decisions. This is why it's essential to understand how perception works. By honing our awareness of the perception process, we can improve our interpersonal communication and forge better relationships.

In this chapter, we explore how you can improve your perception to become a better interpersonal communicator. You'll learn:

- How the perception process unfolds and which perceptual errors you need to watch for
- The influence that culture, gender, and personality have in shaping your perception of others and your interpersonal communication
- How you form impressions of others, and the benefits and limitations of the methods you use
- Strategies for improving your perceptual accuracy

Perception as a Process

In the movie *Inception*, Dom Cobb—played by Leonardo DiCaprio—enters others' unconscious minds while they're asleep and steals their thoughts. Since living inside others' dreams can lead one to confuse dream states with reality, Cobb has a "totem" that he keeps

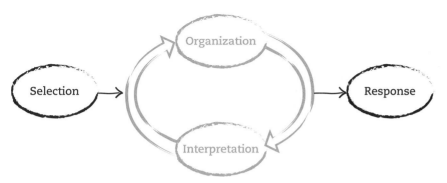

◐ Figure 3.1 The Process of Perception

> **We rely on perception constantly to make sense of everything and everyone in our environment.**

with him always, a simple tool that allows him to tell quickly whether he's dreaming or awake.

Like Dom Cobb, each of us has a totem we trust to tell us what's real and what isn't: *our perception.* **Perception** is the process of selecting, organizing, and interpreting information from our senses. We rely on perception constantly to make sense of everything and everyone in our environment. Perception begins when we select information on which to focus our attention. We then organize the information into an understandable pattern inside our minds and interpret its meaning. Each activity influences the other: our mental organization of information shapes how we interpret it, and our interpretation of information influences how we mentally organize it. (See **Figure 3.1** above.) Let's take a closer look at the perception process.

Selecting Information

It's finals week, and you're in your room studying for a difficult exam. Exhausted, you decide to take a break and listen to some music. You don your headphones and close your eyes. Suddenly you hear a noise. Startled, you open your eyes and remove your headphones to find that your housemate has just yanked open your bedroom door. "I've been yelling at you to pick up your phone for the last five minutes," she snaps. "What's going on?!"

The first step of perception, **selection,** involves focusing attention on certain sights, sounds, tastes, touches, or smells in our environment. Consider the housemate example. Once you hear her enter, you would likely select her communication as the focus of your attention. The degree to which particular people or aspects of their communication attract our attention is known as **salience** (Fiske & Taylor, 1991). When something is salient, it seems especially noticeable and significant. We view aspects of interpersonal communication as salient under three conditions (Fiske &

◐ In the movie *Inception*, Dom Cobb's totem helps him to distinguish what is real and what is not.

Stephen Vaughan/© Warner Bros./Courtesy Everett Collection

Taylor, 1991). First, communication is salient if the communicator behaves in a visually and audibly stimulating fashion. A yelling and energetically gesturing housemate is more salient than a quiet and still housemate. Second, communication becomes salient if our goals or expectations lead us to view it as significant. Even a housemate's softly spoken phone announcement will command our attention if we are anticipating an important call. Last, communication that deviates from our expectations is salient. An unexpected verbal attack will always be more salient than an expected one.

Organizing the Information You've Selected

Once you've selected something as the focus of your attention, you take that information and structure it into a coherent pattern inside your mind, a phase of the perception process known as **organization** (Fiske & Taylor, 1991). For example, imagine that a cousin is telling you about a recent visit to your hometown. As she speaks, you select certain bits of her narrative on which to focus your attention based on salience, such as a mutual friend she visited or a favorite old hangout she saw. You then organize your own representation of her story inside your head.

During organization, you engage in **punctuation,** structuring the information you've selected into a chronological sequence that matches how you experienced the order of events (Watzlawick, Beavin, & Jackson, 1967). To illustrate punctuation, think about how you might punctuate the sequence of events in

our housemate example. You hear a noise, open your eyes, see your housemate in your room, and then hear her yelling at you. But two people involved in the same interpersonal encounter may punctuate it in very different ways. Your housemate might punctuate the same incident by noting that your ringing cell phone in the common area was disrupting her studying and, despite her efforts to get your attention, you never responded.

If you and another person organize and punctuate information from an encounter differently, the two of you may well feel frustrated with one another. Disagreements about punctuation, and especially disputes about who "started" unpleasant encounters, are a common source of interpersonal conflict (Watzlawick et al., 1967). For example, your housemate may contend that "you started it" because she told you to get your phone but you ignored her. You may believe that "she started it" because she barged into your room without knocking.

> ### Self-Reflection
> Recall a conflict in which you and a friend disagreed about "who started it." How did you punctuate the encounter? How did your friend punctuate it? If each of you punctuated differently, how did those differences contribute to the conflict? If you could revisit the situation, what might you say or do differently to resolve the dispute?

We can avoid perceptual misunderstandings that lead to conflict by understanding how our organization and punctuation of information differ from those of other people. One helpful way to forestall such conflicts is to practice asking others to share their views of encounters. You might say, "Here's what I saw, but that's just my perspective. What do *you* think happened?"

Interpreting the Information

As we organize information we have selected into a coherent mental model, we also engage in **interpretation,** assigning meaning to that information. We call to mind familiar information that's relevant to the current encounter, and we use that information to make sense of what we're hearing and seeing. We also create explanations for why things are happening as they are.

Using Familiar Information

We make sense of others' communication in part by comparing what we currently perceive with knowledge that we already possess. For example, I proposed to my wife by surprising her after class. I had decorated her apartment with flowers and donned my best (and only!) suit. When she opened the door, and I asked her to marry me, she immediately interpreted my communication correctly. But how, given that she never had been proposed to before? Because she knew from friends, family members, movies, and television shows what a marriage proposal looks and sounds like.

The knowledge we draw on when interpreting interpersonal communication resides in **schemata,** mental structures that contain information defining the characteristics of various concepts, as well as how those characteristics are related to each other (Macrae & Bodenhausen, 2001). Each of us develops schemata for individual people, groups of people, places, events, objects, and relationships. In the example above, my wife had a schemata for "marriage proposal," and that enabled her to correctly interpret my actions.

Because we use familiar information to make sense of current interactions, our interpretations reflect what we presume to be true. For example, suppose you're interviewing for a job with a manager who has been at the company for 18 years. You'll likely interpret everything she says in light of your knowledge about "long-term employees." This knowledge includes your assumption that "company veterans generally know insider information." So, when your interviewer talks in glowing terms about the company's future, you'll probably interpret her comments as credible. Now imagine you receive the same information from someone who has been with the company only a few weeks. Based on your perception of him as "new employee," and on the information you have in your "new employee" schema, you may interpret his message as naïve speculation rather than "expert commentary"—even if his statements are accurate.

(Left to right) anyamay/Shutterstock; Steve Cukrov/Shutterstock; © Royalty-Free/Corbis; Syda Production/Shutterstock

Together, a bunch of roses, a nice suit, and a diamond ring form a schema suggesting a marriage proposal.

Table 3.1 **Internal versus External Attributions**

Communication Event	Internal Attribution	External Attribution
Your romantic partner doesn't reply after you send a flirtatious text message.	"My partner doesn't care about me."	"My partner is probably too busy to respond."
Your unfriendly coworker greets you warmly.	"My coworker is friendlier than I thought."	"Something unusual must have happened to make my coworker act so friendly."
Your friend ridicules your taste in music.	"My friend has an unpredictable mean streak."	"My friend must be having a really bad day."

Creating Explanations

In addition to drawing on our schemata to interpret information from interpersonal encounters, we create explanations for others' comments or behaviors, known as **attributions.** Attributions are our answers to the "why" questions we ask every day. "Why didn't my partner return my text message?" "Why did my best friend post that embarrassing photo of me on Facebook?"

Consider an example shared with me by a friend of mine, Sarah. She had finished teaching for the semester and was out of town and offline for a week. When she returned and logged onto her e-mail, she found a week-old note from a student "Janet," who failed her course, asking Sarah if there was anything she could do to improve her grade. Janet sent a curt follow-up e-mail a few days later accusing Sarah of ignoring her by failing to respond to the original request promptly.[2] Put yourself in Janet's shoes for a moment. What attributions did Janet make about Sarah's failure to respond? How did these attributions shape Janet's communication in her second e-mail? Now consider this situation from Sarah's perspective. If you were in her shoes, what attributions would you make about Janet, and how would they shape how you interpreted her e-mail?

Attributions take two forms, internal and external (see Table 3.1). *Internal attributions* presume that a person's communication or behavior stems from internal causes, such as character or personality. For example, "My professor didn't respond to my e-mail because she doesn't care," or "Janet sent this message because she's rude." *External attributions* hold that a person's communication is caused by factors unrelated to personal qualities: "My professor didn't respond to my e-mail because she hasn't checked her messages yet," or "Janet sent this message because I didn't respond to her first message."

Like schemata, the attributions we make influence how we interpret and respond to others' communication. For example, if you think Janet's e-mail was caused by her having a terrible day, you'll likely interpret her message as an understandable venting of frustration. If you think her message was caused by her personal rudeness, you'll probably interpret the e-mail as inappropriate and offensive.

Given the dozens of people with whom we communicate each day, it's not surprising that we often form invalid attributions. One common mistake is the **fundamental attribution error,** the tendency to attribute others' behaviors solely to internal causes (the kind of person they are) rather than the social or environmental forces affecting them (Heider, 1958). For example, communication scholar Alan Sillars and his colleagues found that during conflicts between parents

---

[2]This is an example e-mail contributed to the author by a professional colleague, with all identifying information removed to protect the identity of the student in question.

and teens, both parties fall prey to the fundamental attribution error (Sillars, Smith, & Koerner, 2010). Parents commonly attribute teens' communication to "lack of responsibility" and "desire to avoid the issue" whereas teens attribute parents' communication to "desire to control my life." These errors make it harder for teens and parents to constructively resolve their conflicts, something we discuss more in Chapter 9.

The fundamental attribution error is especially common during online interactions (Shedletsky & Aitken, 2004). Because we aren't privy to the rich array of environmental factors that may be shaping our communication partners' messages—all we perceive is words on a screen—we're more likely to interpret others' communication as stemming solely from internal causes (Wallace, 1999). As a consequence, when a text message, Facebook wall post, e-mail, or instant message is even slightly negative in tone, we're very likely to blame that negativity on bad character or personality flaws.

Skills Practice
Improving Online Attributions
Improving your attributions while communicating online

1. Identify a negative text, e-mail, IM, or Web posting you've received.
2. Consider why the person sent the message.
3. Write a response based on this attribution, and save it as a draft.
4. Think of and list other possible, external causes for the person's message.
5. Keeping these alternative attributions in mind, revisit and reevaluate your message draft, editing it as necessary to ensure competence before you send or post it.

Self-Reflection
Recall a fight you've had with parents or other family members. Why did they behave as they did? What presumptions did they make about you and your behavior? When you assess both your and their attributions, are they internal or external? What does this tell you about the power and prevalence of the fundamental attribution error?

A related error is the **actor-observer effect,** the tendency of people to make external attributions regarding their own behaviors (Fiske & Taylor, 1991). Because our mental focus during interpersonal encounters is on factors external to us—especially the person with whom we're interacting—we tend to credit these factors as causing our own communication. This is particularly prevalent during unpleasant interactions. Our own impolite remarks during family conflicts are viewed as "reactions to their hurtful communication" rather than "messages caused by our own insensitivity."

However, we don't always make external attributions regarding our own behaviors. In cases where our actions result in noteworthy success, we typically take credit by making an internal attribution, a tendency known as the **self-serving bias** (Fiske & Taylor, 1991). Suppose, for example, you've successfully persuaded a friend to lend you her car for the weekend. In this case, you will probably attribute this success to your charm and persuasive skill rather than to luck or your friend's generosity. The self-serving bias is driven by *ego protection*: by crediting ourselves for our life successes, we can feel happier about who we are.

Clearly, attributions play a powerful role in how we interpret communication. For this reason, it's important to consider the attributions you make while you're interacting with others. Check your attributions frequently, watching for the fundamental attribution error, the actor-observer effect, and the self-serving bias. If you think someone has spoken to you in an offensive way, ask yourself if it's possible that outside forces—including *your own behavior*—could have caused the problem. Also keep in mind that communication (like other forms of human behavior) rarely stems from *only* external *or* internal causes. It's caused by a combination of both (Langdridge & Butt, 2004).

Finally, when you can, check the accuracy of your attributions by asking people for the reasons behind their behavior. When you've made attribution errors that lead you to criticize or lose your patience with someone else, apologize and explain your mistake to the person. After Janet learned that Sarah hadn't responded because she had been out-of-town, Janet apologized. She also explained why her message was so terse: she thought Sarah was intentionally ignoring her. Upon receiving Janet's apology, Sarah apologized also. She realized that she, too, had succumbed to the fundamental attribution error by wrongly presuming that Janet was a rude person.

Reducing Uncertainty

When intercultural communication scholar Patricia Covarrubias (2000) was a young girl, she and her family immigrated to the United States from Mexico. On her first day of school in her adoptive country, Patricia's third-grade teacher, Mrs. Williams, led her to the front of the classroom to introduce her to her new classmates. She expected Mrs. Williams to introduce her as "Patricia Covarrubias," or perhaps "Patricia." Instead, Mrs. Williams turned to the class and said, "Class, this is Pat." Patricia was dumbfounded. In her entire life, she had never been "Pat," nor could she understand why someone would call her "Pat." As she explains, "In one unexpected moment, all that I was and had been was abridged into three-letter, bottom-line efficiency" (Covarrubias, 2000, pp. 10–11). The encounter bolstered her feeling that she was an outsider in an uncertain environment.

In most interpersonal interactions, the perception process unfolds in a rapid, straightforward manner. But sometimes we find ourselves in situations where people communicate in perplexing ways. In such contexts, we experience *uncertainty*, the anxious feeling that comes when we can't predict or explain someone else's communication.

Uncertainty is common during first encounters with new acquaintances, when we don't know much about the people with whom we're communicating.

According to **Uncertainty Reduction Theory,** our primary compulsion during initial interactions is to reduce uncertainty about our communication partners by gathering enough information about them so their communication becomes predictable and explainable (Berger & Calabrese, 1975). When we reduce uncertainty, we're inclined to perceive people as attractive and likable, talk further, and consider forming relationships with them (Burgoon & Hoobler, 2002).

Uncertainty can be reduced in several ways, each of which has advantages and disadvantages (Berger & Bradac, 1982). First, you can observe how someone interacts with others. Known as *passive strategies*, these approaches can help you predict how he or she may behave when interacting with you. Examples include observing someone hanging out with friends at a party or checking out someone's Facebook page. Second, you can try *active strategies* by asking other people questions about someone you're interested in. You might find someone who knows the person you're assessing and then get him or her to disclose as much information as possible about that individual. Be aware, though, that this poses risks: the target person may find out that you've been asking questions. That could embarrass you—and upset the target. In addition, third-party information may not be accurate. Third, and perhaps most effective, are *interactive strategies*: starting a direct interaction with the person you're interested in. Inquire where the person is from, what he or she does for a living, and what interests he or she has. You should also disclose personal information about yourself. This enables you to test the other person's reactions to you. Is the person intrigued or bored? That information can help you reduce your uncertainty about how to communicate further.

> ### Self-Reflection
> When do you use passive strategies to reduce your uncertainty? Active strategies? Interactive? Which do you prefer and why? What ethical concerns influence your own use of passive and active strategies?

Cindy Charles/PhotoEdit

Jonas Ingerstedt/Getty Images

David Grossman/The Image Works

When we are uncertain about other people's behavior, we can learn more about them by observing them, by asking their friends about them, or even by interacting with them directly.

LearningCurve
bedfordstmartins.com/ipcandyou

Influences on Perception

A sense of directness dominates the perceptual process. Someone says something to us, and with lightning speed we focus our attention, organize information, and interpret its meaning. Although this process seems unmediated, powerful forces outside of our conscious awareness shape our perception during every encounter, whether we're communicating with colleagues, friends, family members, or lovers. Three of the most powerful influences on perception are culture, gender, and personality.

Perception and Culture

Your cultural background influences your perception in at least two ways. Recall that culture is an established, coherent set of beliefs, attitudes, values, and practices shared by a large group of people. Whenever you interact with others, you interpret their communication in part by drawing on information from your schemata, which are filled with the beliefs, attitudes, and values you learned in your own culture (Gudykunst & Kim, 2003). Consequently, people raised in different cultures have different knowledge in their schemata, so they interpret one another's communication in very different ways. Competent interpersonal communicators recognize this fact. When necessary and appropriate, they check the accuracy of their interpretation by asking questions such as "I'm sorry, could you clarify what you just said?"

Second, culture affects whether you perceive others as similar to or different from yourself. When you grow up valuing certain cultural beliefs, attitudes, and values as your own, you naturally perceive those who share these with you as fundamentally similar to yourself—people you consider **ingroupers** (Allport, 1954). You may consider individuals from many different groups as your ingroupers as long as they share substantial points of cultural commonality with you, such as nationality, religious beliefs, ethnicity,

> { **Perceiving others as ingroupers or outgroupers is one of the most important perceptual distinctions you make.** }

socioeconomic class, or political views (Turner, Hogg, Oakes, Reicher, & Wetherell, 1987). In contrast, you may perceive people who aren't similar to yourself as **outgroupers.**

Perceiving others as ingroupers or outgroupers is one of the most important perceptual distinctions you make. You often feel passionately connected to your ingroups, especially when they are tied to central aspects of your self-concept such as sexual orientation, religious beliefs, or ethnic heritage. Consequently, you are more likely to give valued resources such as money, time, and effort to those who are perceived as ingroupers versus those who are outgroupers (Castelli, Tomelleri, & Zogmaister, 2008).

You also are more likely to form positive interpersonal impressions of people you perceive as ingroupers (Giannakakis & Fritsche, 2011). One study of 30 different ethnic groups in East Africa found that members of each group perceived ingroupers' communication as substantially more trustworthy, friendly, and honest than outgroupers' communication (Brewer & Campbell, 1976). And in cases where people communicate in rude or inappropriate ways, you're substantially more inclined to make negative, internal attributions if you perceive them as outgroupers (Brewer, 1999).

While categorizing people as ingroupers or outgroupers, it's easy to make mistakes. For example, even if people dress differently than you do, they may hold beliefs, attitudes, and values similar to your own. If you assume they're outgroupers based on surface-level differences, you may communicate with them in ways that prevent the two of you from getting to know each other better. You may never discover that you share other important qualities, and you lose an opportunity to make a friend, gain a new colleague, or forge a romantic bond.

◊ Ingroupers or outgroupers? It depends on your point of view.

Self-Reflection

Consider people in your life who you view as outgroupers. What points of difference lead you to see them that way? How does their outgrouper status shape your communication toward them? Is there anything you could learn about them that would lead you to judge them as ingroupers?

Perception and Gender

Get your family or friends talking about gender differences, and chances are you'll hear most of them claim that men and women perceive interpersonal communication differently. They may insist that "men are cool and logical" while "women see everything emotionally." But the relationship between gender and perception is much more complex, as evidenced by the rich—and sometimes conflicting—research produced by scholars of interpersonal communication, psychology, biology, and a variety of other academic fields of study.

For example, linguist Deborah Tannen (1990) argues that men and women perceive and produce communication in vastly different ways. She suggests that when problems arise, men focus on solutions, and women offer emotional support. Consequently, women perceive men's solutions as unsympathetic, and men perceive women's needs for emotional support as unreasonable. In contrast, researchers from communication and psychology argue that men and women are actually more similar than different in how they interpersonally communicate (Hall, Carter, & Horgan, 2000). Researchers Dan Canary, Tara Emmers-Sommer, and Sandra Faulkner (1997) reviewed data from over 1,000 gender studies and found that if you consider all of the factors that influence our communication and compare their impact, only about 1 percent of people's communication behavior is caused by gender. They concluded that when it comes to interpersonal communication, "men and women respond in a similar manner 99% of the time" (p. 9).

Despite the debate over differences, we know one thing about gender and perception for certain: people are socialized to *believe* that men and women communicate differently. For example, people believe that women talk more about their feelings than men, talk about "less important" issues than men (women "gossip," whereas men "discuss"), and generally talk more than men (Spender, 1984). But in one of the best-known studies of this phenomenon, researchers found that this was more a matter of perception than real difference (Mulac, Incontro, & James, 1985). Two groups of participants were given the same speech. One group was told that a man had authored and presented the speech, while the other was told that a woman had written and given it. Participants who thought the speech was a woman's perceived it as having more "artistic quality." Those who believed it was a man's saw the speech as having more "dynamism." Participants also described the "man's" language as strong, active, and aggressive,

◊ Despite popular beliefs, most researchers argue that men and women are more similar than different in how they interpersonally communicate.

and the "woman's" language as pleasing, sweet, and beautiful, despite the fact that the speeches were identical.

Given our tendency to presume broad gender differences in communication, can we improve the accuracy of our perception? Yes—if we challenge the assumptions we make about gender and if we remind ourselves that both genders' approaches to communication are more similar than different. The next time you find yourself thinking, "Oh, she said that because she's a woman," or "He sees things that way because he is a man," question your perception. Are these people really communicating differently because of their gender, or are you simply perceiving them as different based on *your* beliefs about their gender?

Personality

When you think about the star of a hit television show, a cartoon aardvark isn't usually the first thing to come to mind. But, as any one of the 10 million weekly viewers of PBS's *Arthur* will tell you, the appeal of the show is more than just the title character.

It is the breadth of personalities displayed across the entire cast, allowing us to link each of them to people in our own lives. Sue Ellen loves art, music, and world culture, while the Brain is studious, meticulous, and responsible. Francine loves interacting with people, especially while playing sports, and Buster is laid-back, warm, and friendly to just about everyone. D.W. drives Arthur crazy with her moods, obsessions, and tantrums; while Arthur—at the center of it all—combines all of these traits into one appealing, complicated package.

In the show *Arthur*, we see embodied in animated form the various dispositions that populate our real-world interpersonal lives. And when we think of these people and their personalities, visceral reactions are commonly evoked. We like, loathe, or even love people based on our perception of their personalities and how their personalities mesh with our own.

Clearly, personality shapes how we perceive others, but what exactly is it? **Personality** is an individual's characteristic way of thinking, feeling, and acting, based on the traits—enduring motives and impulses—that he or she possesses (McCrae & Costa, 2001). Contemporary psychologists argue that, although thousands of different personalities exist, each is composed of only five primary traits, referred to as the "Big Five" (John, 1990). These are openness, conscientiousness, extraversion, agreeableness, and neuroticism (see Table 3.2). A simple way to remember them is the acronym *OCEAN*. The degree to which a person possesses each of the Big Five traits determines his or her personality (McCrae, 2001).

Table 3.2 The Big Five Personality Traits (OCEAN)

Personality Trait	Description
Openness	The degree to which a person is willing to consider new ideas and take an interest in culture. People high in openness are more imaginative, creative, and interested in seeking out new experiences than those low in openness.
Conscientiousness	The degree to which a person is organized and persistent in pursuing goals. People high in conscientiousness are methodical, well organized, and dutiful; those low in conscientiousness are less careful, less focused, and more easily distracted. Also known as *dependability*.
Extraversion	The degree to which a person is interested in interacting regularly with others and actively seeks out interpersonal encounters. People high in extraversion are outgoing and sociable; those low in extraversion are quiet and reserved.
Agreeableness	The degree to which a person is trusting, friendly, and cooperative. People low in agreeableness are aggressive, suspicious, and uncooperative. Also known as *friendliness*.
Neuroticism	The degree to which a person experiences negative thoughts about oneself. People high in neuroticism are prone to insecurity and emotional distress; people low in neuroticism are relaxed, less emotional, and less prone to distress. Also known as *emotional stability*.

Self-Quiz

What Kind of Personality Do You Have?

For each of the five personality traits, check the descriptions that accurately describe your personality. Then total up the number of check marks for each category. Use the Scoring key below to determine whether you're low, moderate, or high in each category.

I see myself as someone who . . .

Openness

- is curious about many different things
- has an active imagination
- values artistic, aesthetic experiences
- is sophisticated in art, music, or literature
- likes to reflect, play with ideas

Conscientiousness

- does a thorough job
- is a reliable worker
- perseveres until the task is finished
- does things efficiently
- makes plans and follows through with them

Extraversion

- is talkative
- is full of energy
- generates a lot of enthusiasm

- has an assertive personality
- is outgoing, sociable

Agreeableness

- is helpful and unselfish with others
- has a forgiving nature
- is generally trusting
- is considerate and kind to almost everyone
- likes to cooperate with others

Neuroticism

- is depressed, blue
- can be tense
- worries a lot
- can be moody
- gets nervous easily

Source: John, O. P., Naumann, L., & Soto, C. J. (2008). Paradigm Shift to the Integrative Big Five Trait Taxonomy, in *Handbook of personality: Theory and research* (3rd ed., pp. 114–158).

Scoring: 0–1, low; 2–3, moderate; 4–5, high

Prioritizing Our Own Traits When Perceiving Others

Our perception of others is strongly guided by the personality traits we see in ourselves and how we evaluate these traits. If you're an extravert, for example, another person's extraversion becomes salient to you when you're communicating with him or her. Likewise, if you pride yourself on being friendly, other people's friendliness becomes your perceptual focus.

But it's not just a matter of focusing on certain traits to the exclusion of others. We evaluate people positively or negatively in accordance with how we feel about our own traits. We typically like in others the same traits we like in ourselves, and we dislike in others the traits that we dislike in ourselves.

Self-Reflection

What personality traits do you like in yourself? When you see these traits in others, how does that impact your communication toward them? How do you perceive people who possess traits you don't like in yourself? How do these perceptions affect your relationships with them?

To avoid this preoccupation with your own traits, carefully observe how you focus on other people's traits and how your evaluation of these traits reflects your own feelings about yourself. Strive to perceive people broadly, taking into consideration all of their traits and not just the positive or negative ones that you share. Then evaluate them and communicate with them independently of your own positive and negative self-evaluations.

Generalizing from the Traits We Know

Another effect that personality has on perception is the presumption that because a person is high or low in a certain trait, he or she must be high or low in other traits. For example, say that I introduce you to a friend of mine, Shoshanna. Within the first minute of interaction you perceive her as highly friendly. Based on your perception of her high friendliness, you'll likely also presume that she is highly extraverted, simply because high friendliness and high extraversion intuitively seem to "go together." If people you've known in the past who were highly friendly and extraverted also were highly open, you may go further, perceiving Shoshanna as highly open as well.

Your perception of Shoshanna was created using **implicit personality theories,** personal beliefs about different types of personalities and the ways in which traits cluster together (Bruner & Taguiri, 1954). When we meet people for the first time, we use implicit personality theories to perceive just a little about an individual's personality and then presume a great deal more, making us feel that we know the person and helping to reduce uncertainty. At the same time, making presumptions about people's personalities is risky. For example, if you presume that Shoshanna is high in openness, you might mistakenly presume she has certain political or cultural beliefs, leading you to say things to her that cut directly against her actual values.

LearningCurve
bedfordstmartins.com/ipcandyou

Forming Impressions of Others

When we use perception to size up other people, we form **interpersonal impressions**—mental pictures of who people are and how we feel about them. All aspects of the perception process shape our interpersonal impressions: the information we select as the focus of our attention, the way we organize this information, the interpretations we make based on knowledge in our schemata and our attributions, and even our uncertainty.

Given the complexity of the perception process, it's not surprising that impressions vary widely. Some impressions come quickly into focus. We meet a person and immediately like or dislike him. Other impressions form slowly, over a series of encounters. Some impressions are intensely positive, others neutral, and still others negative. But regardless of their form, interpersonal impressions exert a profound impact on our communication and relationship choices. To illustrate this impact, imagine yourself in the following situation.

You're at a lake, hanging out with friends. As you lie on the beach, the man pictured in the photo on page 63 approaches you and introduces himself as "Ted." He tells you that he's waiting for some friends who were supposed to help him load his sailboat onto his car. He's easy to talk to, friendly, and has a nice smile. His left arm is in a sling, and he casually mentions that he injured it playing racquetball. Because his arm is hurting, and his friends are missing, he asks if you would help him with his boat. You say, "Sure." You walk with him to the parking lot, but when you get to Ted's car, you don't see a boat. When you ask him where his boat is, he says, "Oh! It's at my folks' house, just up the hill. Do you mind going with me? It'll just take a couple of minutes." You tell him you can't go with him because your friends will wonder where you are. "That's OK," Ted says cheerily, "I should have told you it wasn't in the parking lot. Thanks for bothering anyways." He's polite and strikes you as sincere.

Think about your encounter with Ted, and all that you've perceived. What's your impression of him? What do you predict would have happened if you had gone with him to his folks' house to help

> Interpersonal impressions exert a profound impact on our communication and relationship choices.

load the boat? Would you want to play racquetball with him? Would he make a good friend?

The scenario you've read actually happened. The above description is drawn from the police testimony of Janice Graham, who was approached by Ted at Lake Sammamish Park, near Seattle, Washington, in 1974 (Michaud & Aynesworth, 1989). Graham's decision not to accompany Ted saved her life. Two other women—Janice Ott and Denise Naslund—were not so fortunate. Each of them went with Ted, who raped and murdered them. Friendly, handsome, and polite Ted was none other than Ted Bundy, one of the most notorious serial killers in U.S. history.

Thankfully, most of the interpersonal impressions we form don't have life-or-death consequences. But all impressions do exert a powerful impact on how we communicate with others and whether we pursue relationships with them. For this reason, it's important to understand how we can flexibly adapt our impressions to create more accurate and reliable conceptions of others.

Constructing Gestalts

One way we form impressions of others is to construct a **Gestalt**, a general sense of a person that's either positive or negative. We discern a few traits, and, drawing upon information in our schemata, we arrive at a judgment based on these traits. The result is an impression of the person as a whole rather than as the sum of individual parts (Asch, 1946). For example, suppose you strike up a conversation with the person sitting next to you at lunch. The person is funny, friendly, and attractive—characteristics associated with positive information in your schemata. You immediately construct an overall positive impression ("I like this person!") rather than spending additional time weighing the significance of his or her separate traits.

© Bettmann/Corbis

Gestalts form rapidly. This is one reason why people consider "first impressions" so consequential. Gestalts require relatively little mental or communicative effort. Thus, they're useful for encounters in which we must render quick judgments about others with only limited information. Gestalts also are useful for interactions involving casual relationships (contacts with acquaintances or service providers) and contexts in which we are meeting and talking with a large number of people in a small amount of time (business conferences or parties). During such exchanges, it isn't possible to carefully scrutinize every piece of information we perceive about others. Instead, we quickly form broad impressions and then mentally walk away from the interactions. But this also means that Gestalts have significant shortcomings.

The Positivity Bias

In 1913, author E. H. Porter published a novel titled *Pollyanna*, about a young child who was happy nearly all of the time. Even when faced with horrible tragedies, Pollyanna saw the positive side of things. Research on human perception suggests that some Pollyanna exists inside each of us (Matlin & Stang, 1978). Examples of *Pollyanna effects* include people believing pleasant events as more likely to happen than unpleasant ones or most people deeming their lives "happy" and describing themselves as "optimists" (Matlin & Stang, 1978; Silvera, Krull, & Sassler, 2002).

Pollyanna effects come into play when we form Gestalts. When Gestalts are formed, they are more likely to be positive than negative, an effect known as the **positivity bias.** Let's say you're at a party for the company where you just started working. During the party, you meet six new coworkers for the first time and talk with each of them for a few minutes. You form a Gestalt for each. Owing to the positivity bias, most or all of the Gestalts you form are likely to be positive. Although the positivity bias is helpful in initiating relationships, it also can lead us to make bad interpersonal decisions, such as when we pursue relationships with people who turn out to be unethical or even abusive.

The Negativity Effect

When we create Gestalts, we don't treat all information that we learn about people as equally important. Instead, we place emphasis on the negative information we learn about others, a pattern known as the **negativity effect.** Across cultures, people perceive negative information as more informative about someone's "true" character than positive information (Kellermann, 1989). Though you may be wondering whether the negativity effect contradicts Pollyanna effects, it actually derives from them. People tend to believe that positive events, information, and personal characteristics are more commonplace than negative events, information, and characteristics. So when we learn something negative about another person, we see it as "unusual." Consequently, that information becomes more salient, and we judge it as more truly representative of a person's character than positive information (Kellermann, 1989).

Sometimes the negativity effect leads us to accurate perceptions of people. One of the women who rejected Ted Bundy's request for assistance reported that she had seen him "stalking" other women before he approached her. This information led her to form a negative Gestalt before he even talked with her—an impression that saved her life. But just as often, the negativity effect leads us away from accurate perception. Accurate perception is rooted in carefully and critically assessing everything we learn about people, then flexibly adapting our impressions to match these data. When we

Self-Reflection

Think of someone for whom you have a negative Gestalt. How did the negativity effect shape your impression? Now call to mind personal flaws or embarrassing events from your past. If someone learned of this information and formed a negative Gestalt of you, would his or her impression be accurate? Fair?

weight negative information more heavily than positive, we perceive only a small part of people, aspects that may or may not represent who they are and how they normally communicate.

Halos and Horns

Once we form a Gestalt about a person, it influences how we interpret that person's subsequent communication and the attributions we make regarding that individual. For example, think about someone for whom you've formed a strongly positive Gestalt. Now imagine that this person discloses a dark secret: he or she lied to a lover or cheated on exams. Because of your positive Gestalt, you may dismiss the significance of this behavior, telling yourself instead that the person "had no choice" or "wasn't acting normally." This tendency to positively interpret what someone says or does because we have a positive Gestalt of them is known as the **halo effect.**

The counterpart of the halo effect is the **horn effect,** the tendency to negatively interpret the communication and behavior of people for whom we have negative Gestalts. Call to mind someone you can't stand. Imagine that this person discloses the same secret as the individual described above. Although the information in both cases is the same, you would likely chalk up this individual's unethical behavior to bad character or lack of values.

Calculating Algebraic Impressions

A second way we form interpersonal impressions is to develop **algebraic impressions** by carefully evaluating each new thing we learn about a person (Anderson, 1981). Algebraic impressions involve comparing and assessing the positive and negative things we learn about a person in order to calculate an overall impression, then modifying this impression as we learn new information. It's similar to solving an algebra equation, in which we add and subtract different values from each side to compute a final result.

Consider how you might form an algebraic impression of Ted Bundy from our earlier example.

At the outset, his warmth, humor, and ability to chat easily strike you as "friendly" and "extraverted." These traits, when added together, lead you to calculate a positive impression: friendly + extraverted = positive impression. But when you accompany Bundy to the parking lot and realize his boat isn't there, you perceive this information as deceptive. This new information—Ted is a liar—immediately causes you to revise your computation: friendly + extraverted + potential liar = negative impression.

When we form algebraic impressions, we don't place an equal value on every piece of information in the equation. Instead, we weigh some pieces of information more heavily than others, depending on the information's *importance* and its *positivity* or *negativity*. For example, your perception of potential romantic partners' physical attractiveness, intelligence, and personal values likely will carry more weight when

---

Skills Practice

Algebraic Impressions
Strengthen your ability to use algebraic impressions.

1. When you next meet a new acquaintance, resist forming a general positive or negative Gestalt.
2. Instead, observe and learn everything you can about the person.
3. Then make a list of his or her positive and negative traits and weigh each trait's importance.
4. Form an algebraic impression based on your assessment, keeping in mind that this impression may change over time.
5. Across future interactions, flexibly adapt your impression as you learn new information.

calculating your impression than their favorite color or breakfast cereal.

As this discussion illustrates, algebraic impressions are more flexible and accurate than Gestalts. For encounters in which we have the time and energy to ponder someone's traits and how they add up, algebraic impressions offer us the opportunity to form refined impressions of people. We can also flexibly change them every time we receive new information about people. But since algebraic impressions require a fair amount of mental effort, they aren't as efficient as Gestalts. In unexpected encounters or casual conversations, such mental calculations are unnecessary and may even work to our disadvantage, especially if we need to render rapid judgments and act on them.

Using Stereotypes

A final way we form impressions is to categorize people into social groups and then evaluate them based on information we have in our schemata related to these groups (Bodenhausen, Macrae, & Sherman, 1999). This is known as **stereotyping,** a term first coined by journalist Walter Lippmann (1922) to describe overly simplistic interpersonal impressions. When we stereotype others, we replace the subtle complexities that make people unique with blanket assumptions about their character and worth based solely on their social group affiliation.

We stereotype because doing so streamlines the perception process. Once we've categorized a person as a member of a particular group, we can apply all of the information we have about that group to form a quick impression (Bodenhausen et al., 1999). For example, suppose a friend introduces you to Conor, an Irish transfer student. Once you perceive Conor as "Irish," beliefs that you might hold about Irish people could come to mind: they love to tell exaggerated stories (the blarney), have bad tempers, like to drink, and are passionate about soccer. Mind you, none of these assumptions may be accurate about Irish people or relevant to Conor. But if this is what you *believe* about the Irish, you'll keep it in mind during your conversation with Conor and look for ways to confirm your beliefs.

Stereotyping frequently leads us to form flawed impressions of others. One study of workplace perception found that male supervisors who stereotyped women as "the weaker sex" perceived female employees' work performance as deficient and gave women low job evaluations—regardless of the women's actual job performances (Cleveland, Stockdale, & Murphy, 2000). A separate study examining college students' perceptions of professors found a similar biasing effect for ethnic stereotypes. Euro-American students who stereotyped Hispanics as "laid-back" and "relaxed" perceived Hispanic professors who set high expectations for classroom performance as "colder" and "more unprofessional" than Euro-American professors who set identical standards (Smith & Anderson, 2005).

However, stereotyping doesn't automatically lead to negative outcomes. Communication scholars Valerie Manusov and Radha Hegde (1993) found that during encounters between American and Indian students, the Americans who held positive or negative stereotypes about Indians were more inquisitive and actively engaged during the interaction than those who lacked stereotypes. As this study suggests, stereotyping can create an opportunity for communication, but the quality of the communication will depend on the nature of the stereotype.

Stereotyping is almost impossible to avoid. Researchers have documented that categorizing people in terms of their social group affiliation is the most common way we form impressions (Bodenhausen et al., 1999). Why? Social group categories such as race and gender are among the first things we notice about others upon meeting them. As a consequence, we often perceive people in terms of their social group membership before any other impression is even possible (Devine, 1989). The Internet provides no escape from this tendency. Without many of the nonverbal cues and additional information that can distinguish a person as a unique individual, people communicating online are even more likely than those communicating face-to-face to form stereotypical impressions when meeting others for the first time (Spears, Postmes, Lea, & Watt, 2001).

Time Life Pictures/Getty Images

Self-Reflection

Think of an instance in which you perceived someone stereotypically based on the information the person posted online (photos, profile information, tweets). How did the information affect your overall impression of him or her? Your communication with the person? What stereotypes might others form of you, based on *your* online postings?

Most of us presume that our beliefs about groups are valid. As a consequence, we have a high degree of confidence in the legitimacy of our stereotypical impressions, despite the fact that such impressions are frequently flawed (Brewer, 1993). We also continue to believe in stereotypes even when members of a stereotyped group repeatedly behave in ways that contradict the stereotype. In fact, contradictory behavior may actually *strengthen* stereotypes. For example, if you think of Buddhists as quiet and contemplative and meet a talkative and funny Buddhist, you may dismiss his or her behavior as atypical and not worthy of your attention (Seta & Seta, 1993). You'll then actively seek examples of behavior that confirm the stereotype to compensate for the uncertainty that the unexpected behavior aroused (Seta & Seta, 1993). As a result, the stereotype is reinforced.

You can overcome stereotypes by critically assessing your beliefs about various groups, especially those you dislike. Then educate yourself about these groups. Pick several groups you feel positively or negatively about. Read a variety of materials about these groups' histories, beliefs, attitudes, values, and behaviors. Look for similarities and differences between people affiliated with these groups and yourself. Finally, when interacting with members of these groups, keep in mind that just because someone belongs to a certain group, it doesn't necessarily mean that all of the defining characteristics of that group apply to that person.

💧 When you look at Tupac Shakur, do you see a famous rapper? A tattooed gangster who died young in a hail of gunfire? Or, a man named after an Inca chief who studied ballet and acting, and read the *New York Times* as a boy because his mother wanted him to?

LearningCurve
bedfordstmartins.com/ipcandyou

Improving Your Perception of Others

Malcolm X is most remembered for his fiery rhetoric denouncing white racism and his rejection of nonviolent protest as a means for dealing with

(Left to right) AP/Wide World Photos; © Bettmann/Corbis

💧 After 1964, Malcolm X's perception changed as his belief shifted to a view "recognizing every human being as a human being, neither white, black, brown, nor red."

oppression. Less well known is the marked change in his perception and communication that occurred following his visit to Saudi Arabia. Malcolm traveled to Mecca for a traditional Muslim hajj, or pilgrimage. During his visit, he worshipped, ate, socialized, and slept in the same room with white Muslims. In doing so, he was shocked to discover that despite their differences in skin color, they all shared similar degrees of religious devotion. The experience was a revelation, and led him to reassess his longstanding belief in an unbridgeable racial divide between whites and blacks.

Malcolm's transformation suggests important lessons for everyone interested in improving his or her own perception and communication. He came to appreciate others' perspectives and feel a strong emotional kinship with those he previously disparaged. He accepted others' beliefs as legitimate and deserving of respect. He also freely called into question his own perceptual accuracy by critically assessing his prior judgments. These changes reveal two ways we can improve our perception and interpersonal communication: offering empathy and checking our perception.

Offering Empathy

When we experience **empathy,** we "feel into" others' thoughts and emotions, making an attempt to understand their perspectives and be aware of their feelings in order to identify with them (Kuhn, 2001). Empathy is one of our most valuable tools for communicating competently with others (Campbell & Babrow, 2004).

Empathy consists of two components. The first is *perspective-taking*—the ability to see things from someone else's vantage point without necessarily experiencing that person's emotions (Duan & Hill, 1996). The second is *empathic concern*—becoming aware of how the other person is feeling, experiencing a sense of compassion regarding the other person's emotional state, and perhaps even experiencing some of his or her emotions (Stiff, Dillard, Somera, Kim, & Sleight, 1988).

But experiencing empathy isn't sufficient in itself to improve your interpersonal communication

{ **Empathy is one of our most valuable tools for communicating competently with others.** }

and relationships. You also must convey your empathy to others. To competently communicate the perspective-taking part of empathy, let others know that you're genuinely interested in hearing their viewpoints ("I'd love to get your impression"), and tell them that you think their views are important and understandable ("Seeing it from your side makes a lot of sense"). To communicate empathic concern, disclose to others that you care about them and their feelings ("I hope you're doing OK"). Share with them your own emotions regarding their situation ("I feel terrible that you're going through this").

Importantly, avoid using "I know" messages ("I know just how you feel" or "I know just what you're going through"). Even if you make such comments with kind intentions, others will likely view you as presumptuous and perhaps even patronizing, especially if they suspect that you don't or can't feel as they do. For example, when people suffer a great loss—such as the death of a loved one—many don't believe that anyone else could feel the depth of anguish they're experiencing. Saying "I know how you feel" isn't helpful under these conditions.

Skills Practice

Enhancing Empathy

Improving your ability to experience and express empathy

1. Identify a challenging interpersonal encounter.
2. As the encounter unfolds, consider how the other person is viewing you and the interaction.
3. Think about the emotions he or she is feeling.
4. Communicate perspective-taking, avoiding "I know" messages.
5. Express empathic concern, letting the person know you value his or her feelings.
6. Disclose your own feelings.

Checking Your Perception

Another way to improve your perception is through **perception-checking,** a five-step process in which you apply all that you've learned in this chapter to your perception of others.

1. *Check your punctuation.* People punctuate encounters in different ways, often disagreeing on "who/what started it" or "who/what ended it." This kind of disagreement is common during interpersonal conflicts. When you experience a conflict, be aware of your own punctuation and keep in mind that other people may see things differently. Remember to ask others to share their punctuation with you.

2. *Check your knowledge.* Your perception of others is only as accurate as the information you have in your schemata. Never presume that you know the "truth" about what others "really" mean or what they're "really" like. When in doubt, ask others to explain their meaning to you.

3. *Check your attributions.* Avoid the common temptation to attribute others' communication and behavior exclusively to internal causes such as character or personality. Question any internal attributions you make. Remember that all behavior—including interpersonal communication—stems from a complex combination of internal and external forces.

4. *Check perceptual influences.* Reflect on how culture, gender, and personality are shaping your perception of others. Are you perceiving others as ingroupers or outgroupers? If so, on what basis? How is this perception affecting your communication? Your relationships?

5. *Check your impressions.* Reflect on your impressions as you're forming them. If you find yourself making Gestalts, realize that your Gestalts may bias your perception of subsequent information you learn about a person. Resist stereotyping but also realize that it's difficult to avoid, given the natural human tendency to categorize people into groups upon first meeting. Strive to

create flexible impressions, thoughtfully weighing new information you learn about a person and reshaping your overall impression based on new data.

Perception-checking is an intense mental exercise. Mastering it takes time and effort, but the ability to critically check your own perception goes, as Malcolm X wrote, "hand in hand with every form of intelligent search for truth," whether the truth is personal, interpersonal, or universal. When you routinely perception-check, errors are corrected and perception becomes more accurate, balanced, and objective. As a result, you will make fewer communication blunders, you will be able to tailor your communication to people as they really are, and others will likely see you as a competent communicator.

LearningCurve
bedfordstmartins.com/ipcandyou

Postscript }

We began this chapter with an account of a football game marked by brutality and accusations of unfair play and an examination of its perceptual aftermath. Following the Dartmouth-Princeton game, fans from both sides felt the opposition had played dirty and that their own team had behaved honorably. Although there was only one game, fans perceived two radically different contests.

When you observe the "game film" of your own life, how often do you perceive others as instigating all of the rough play and penalties you've suffered while seeing yourself as blameless? Do you widen the perceptual gulf between yourself and those who see things differently? Or do you seek to bridge that divide by practicing and communicating empathy?

More than 60 years ago, two teams met on a field of play. Decades later, that game—and people's reactions to it—reminds us of our own perceptual limitations and the importance of overcoming them. Although we'll never agree with everyone about everything that goes on around us, we can strive to understand one another's viewpoints much of the time. In doing so, we build lives that connect us to others rather than divide us from them.

Chapter Review

Visit LaunchPad for *Interpersonal Communication and You* to watch brief, illustrative videos of these terms and to access LearningCurve. **bedfordstmartins.com/ipcandyou**

KEY TERMS

perception, 51
selection, 51
salience, 51
organization, 52
punctuation, 52
interpretation, 53
schemata, 53
attributions, 54
fundamental attribution error, 54
actor-observer effect, 55
self-serving bias, 55
Uncertainty Reduction Theory, 56
ingroupers, 57
outgroupers, 58
personality, 60
implicit personality theories, 62
interpersonal impressions, 62
Gestalt, 63
positivity bias, 64
negativity effect, 64
halo effect, 65
horn effect, 65
algebraic impressions, 65
stereotyping, 66
empathy, 68
perception-checking, 69

CHAPTER ACTIVITIES

1. Gather physical or virtual images of people you do not know (for example, use magazine images or photos of friends of friends that appear in your Facebook feed). Based on your observations of these individuals, describe their marital status, occupation, political affiliation, likability, intelligence, and so on. Describe how and why you made these judgments based on a photo. What information was salient to you? How did you use existing knowledge to interpret information?
2. Watch the video on **punctuation** and write out your own original scenario in which punctuation is perceived differently among the people involved, leading to problematic interactions. At the end of your scenario, write two to three paragraphs on how your situation could have been avoided or improved.
3. Write a brief synopsis of a recent time someone was rude to you. Identify the possible internal and external attributions that could be made for your own and the other person's behavior. Name potential attribution errors that may have contributed to this situation (e.g., the fundamental attribution error, actor-observer effect, self-serving bias, etc.).
4. Fill in the blanks: "Craig is smart, funny, and ____." Alison is "kind, fun-loving, and _____." Then create your own phrase for a significant other and challenge your class (or a small group) to fill in the blank. Discuss how presuming specific personality traits can lead to communicating in inappropriate and ineffective ways.
5. Watch the videos on **halo effect** and **horn effect** and then find another example of either from a media source. (YouTube or movieclips.com are always good options.) Analyze your example based on these questions: What effects (positive or negative) does the halo effect or horn effect have on the relationships in the example? How could the communication and relationships be improved?

Look for **LearningCurve** throughout the chapter to help you review.
bedfordstmartins.com/ipcandyou

4 { Experiencing and Expressing Emotions

When radio personality and producer Vy Higginsen created the nonprofit Gospel for Teens program, her mission was to teach teens gospel music.[1] Higginsen and a group of volunteer instructors met weekly with kids ages 13 to 19, honing their vocal skills and sharing with them the history of gospel. As Higginsen notes, "The lyrics of gospel songs provide courage, inner strength, and hope for a better life in the future." But she quickly found that her program wouldn't only be about introducing gospel to a generation more versed in rap and hip-hop. Instead, Gospel for Teens would become a powerful vehicle for helping teens manage intense and challenging emotions.

Higginsen originally instituted a simple rule governing emotions and program participation:

leave the baggage at the door. As she describes, "The teen years are a vulnerable time in kids' lives, and they are dealing with shyness, anxiety, trauma, and family dysfunction. Many students are uncomfortable about their physical appearance and self-esteem based on the peers around them. Some are overcome with anxiety from their home life, school, and thoughts of their futures." To keep difficult emotions from hindering performances, Higginsen started each singing session by having participants stand up and shake their hands, arms, legs, and feet, physically purging themselves of emotional constraints. As she instructed, "Any worry, any pain, any problem with your mother, your father, your sister, your brother, the boyfriend, the girlfriend, I want that out now of your consciousness. That's your baggage; leave the bags outside because *this* time is for you!"

But Higginsen's "no baggage" policy was abandoned when the cousin of one of her most talented students was shot and killed. Higginsen realized that many program participants had suffered similar

[1]The information that follows is adapted from a personal interview with the author, October 2011, and www.mamafoundation.org, retrieved October 12, 2011. Interview content published with permission from Vy Higginsen.

◖ **Emotion fills our lives with meaning.**
Photo by G.N. Miller/MaMa Foundation Gospel for Teens

tragedies, and that her class could provide a forum within which students could safely share their stories, their pain, and their grief with one another—working together to begin healing. As she describes, "Our teens are living a very adult life—their friends and family are getting murdered, dying from diseases and drugs—and it's leaving emotional scars on them. They need something uplifting in their lives. So I decided to allow the students to bring their baggage in. I invited the students to share what was happening in their worlds. I wasn't trying to fix their situations because I couldn't—but their being heard was a profound step in their being healed. It made our choir realize we are not alone in our experience. We made a connection, emotionally, personally, and interpersonally."

Whereas Higginsen once encouraged students to leave their emotions at the door, she now realizes that the experience of singing—and sharing the experience of singing with others—provides students with a powerful vehicle for managing negative emotions in positive ways. "I would like the teens to take away the idea that we have emotions yet we are not our emotions. We can recover and thrive by changing our mind and rechanneling our energy through music, art, service, acceptance, meditation, and practice. In simple terms, we can rechannel the negative to the positive and use this as an opportunity for excellence. Gospel music has the power to empower and transform. More than anything, I want my students to know that joy, hope, faith, and goodness are possible."

E motion fills our lives with meaning (Berscheid & Peplau, 2002). To experience emotion is to feel "alive," and to lack emotion is to view life itself as colorless and meaningless (Frijda, 2005). Because emotion is so important, we feel compelled to express our emotional experiences to others through communication. And when we share our emotions with others, they transition from private and personal to profoundly interpersonal. It's at this point that choice becomes relevant. We may not be able to select our emotions before they arise, but we can choose how to handle and convey them after they occur. When we intelligently manage and competently communicate emotional experiences, our relationship satisfaction and overall life happiness increase. When we don't, our relationships suffer, and these lapses are reflected in relationships and lives torn by anger and sadness.

In this chapter, we examine the most personal and interpersonal of human experiences—emotion. You'll learn:

- The important differences between emotions, feelings, and moods, as well as the best approaches to managing negative moods
- Ways in which gender, personality, and culture influence emotion
- Why improving your emotional intelligence can help you more competently manage your experience and expression of emotion
- How to deal with emotional challenges such as communicating empathy online, fading romantic passion, managing anger, and suffering grief.

The Nature of Emotion

Take a moment and recall the most recent "emotion" you felt. What comes to mind? For most people, it's a "hot" emotion—that is, a physically and mentally intense experience like joy, anger, or grief, during which your palms sweated, your mouth felt dry, and your heart pounded (Berscheid & Regan, 2005).

{ **Understanding what emotions are and how they differ from feelings and moods are the first steps in better managing our emotions.** }

Understanding what emotions are and how they differ from feelings and moods are the first steps in better managing our emotions.

Defining Emotion

Scholarly definitions of emotion mirror our everyday experiences. **Emotion** is an intense reaction to an event that involves interpreting event meaning, becoming physiologically aroused, labeling the experience as emotional, managing reactions, and communicating through emotional displays and disclosures (Gross, Richards, & John, 2006). This definition highlights the five key features of emotion. First, emotion is reactive, triggered by our perception of outside events (Cacioppo, Klein, Berntson, & Hatfield, 1993). A friend telling you that her cancer is in remission leads you to experience joy. Receiving a scolding text message from a parent triggers both your surprise and your anger.

A second feature of emotion is that it involves physiological arousal in the form of increased heart rate, blood pressure, and adrenaline release. Many researchers consider arousal *the* defining feature of emotion, a belief mirrored in most people's descriptions of emotion as "intense" and "hot" (Berscheid, 2002).

Third, to experience emotion, you must become aware of your interpretation and arousal as "an emotion"—that is, you must consciously label them as such (Berscheid, 2002). For example, imagine that a friend shares an embarrassing photo of you on Facebook—an image that he promised you he wouldn't post. The moment you see it, you know your trust has been betrayed. Your face grows hot, your breathing quickens, and you become consciously aware of these physical sensations. This awareness, combined with your assessment of the situation, causes you to label your experience as the emotion "anger."

Fourth, how we each experience and express our emotions is constrained by historical, cultural, relational, and situational norms governing what is and isn't appropriate (Metts & Planalp, 2002). As a consequence, once we become aware that we're experiencing an emotion, we try to manage that experience and express that emotion in ways we consider acceptable. We may allow our emotion to dominate our thoughts

RAUL ARBOLEDA/AFP/Getty Images

◌ Emotions are not just internally felt but are also expressed through body language, gestures, facial expressions, and other physical behaviors.

Self-Reflection

Recall an emotional event in a close relationship. What specific action triggered your emotion? How did you interpret the triggering event? What physical sensations resulted? What does this tell you about the link between events, mind, and body that is the basis of emotional experience?

and communication, try to channel it in constructive ways, or suppress our emotion completely. Emotion management results from the recognition that the totally unrestrained experience and expression of emotion will lead to negative consequences.

Finally, when emotion occurs, the choices you make regarding emotion management are reflected outward in your verbal and nonverbal displays, in the form of word choices, exclamations or expletives, facial expressions, body posture, gestures (Mauss, Levenson, McCarter, Wilhelm, & Gross, 2005), and even in the emoticons that accompany your text and e-mail messages.

Another way in which emotion is communicative is that we talk about our emotional experiences with others, a form of communication known as **emotion-sharing.** Much of interpersonal communication consists of emotion-sharing—disclosing emotions, talking about them, and pondering them. Studies on emotion-sharing suggest that people share between 75 and 95 percent of their emotional experiences with at least one other person, usually a spouse, parent, or friend (Frijda, 2005). The people with whom we share our emotions generally enjoy being confided in. Often, they share the incident with others, weaving a socially intimate network of emotion-sharing.

Sometimes emotion-sharing leads to **emotional contagion,** when the experience of the same emotion rapidly spreads from one person to others. Emotional contagion can be positive, such as when the joy you experience over an unexpected job promotion spreads to your family members as you tell them about it. At other times, emotional contagion can be negative, such as when fear moves quickly from person to person in a large crowd.

Self-Reflection

With whom do you share your **emotional experiences?** Does such sharing always have a positive impact on your relationships, or does it cause problems at times? What ethical boundaries govern emotion-sharing?

Feelings and Moods

We often talk about emotions, feelings, and moods as if they are the same thing. But they're not. **Feelings** are short-term emotional reactions to events that generate only limited arousal; they typically do not trigger attempts to manage their experience or expression (Berscheid, 2002). We experience dozens, if not hundreds, of feelings daily—most of them lasting only a few seconds or minutes. For example, a friend texts you unexpectedly when you're trying to study, making you feel briefly annoyed. Feelings are like "small emotions." Common feelings include gratitude, concern, pleasure, relief, and resentment.

Whereas emotions occur occasionally in response to substantial events, and feelings arise frequently in response to everyday incidents, moods are different. **Moods** are low-intensity states—such as boredom, contentment, grouchiness, or serenity—that are not caused by particular events and typically last longer than feelings or emotions (Parkinson, Totterdell, Briner, & Reynolds, 1996). Positive or negative, moods are the slow-flowing emotional currents in our everyday lives. We can think of our frequent, fleeting feelings and occasional intense emotions as riding on top of these currents, as displayed in **Figure 4.1**.

Moods powerfully influence our perception and interpersonal communication. People who describe their moods as "good" are more likely to form positive impressions of others than those who report being in "bad" moods (Forgas & Bower, 1987). Similarly, people in good moods are more likely than those in bad moods to perceive new acquaintances as sociable, honest, giving, and creative (Fiedler, Pampe, & Scherf, 1986). Our moods also influence how we talk with partners in close relationships (Cunningham, 1988). People in good moods are significantly more likely to disclose relationship thoughts and concerns to close friends, family members, and romantic partners. People in bad moods typically prefer to sit and think, to be left alone, and to avoid social and leisure activities (Cunningham, 1988).

Your mood's profound effect on your perception and interpersonal communication suggests

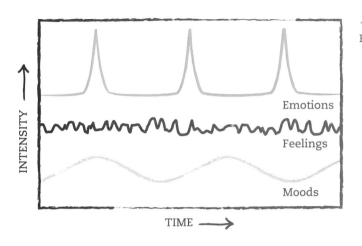

○ Figure 4.1 The Flow of Emotions, Feelings, and Moods

that it's important to learn how to shake yourself out of a bad mood (Thayer, Newman, & McClain, 1994). Effective strategies for elevating mood are active ones, especially strategies that combine relaxation, stress management, mental focus and energy, and exercise. The most effective strategy of all appears to be rigorous physical exercise (Thayer et al., 1994). Sexual activity does not seem to consistently elevate mood.

> **Self-Reflection**
>
> How do you behave toward others when you're in a bad mood? What strategies do you use to better your mood? Are these practices effective in elevating your mood and improving your communication in the long run, or do they merely provide a temporary escape or distraction?

○ It can be tempting to improve bad moods by drinking alcohol or caffeinated beverages, taking recreational drugs, or eating. However, studies show that one of the best ways to feel better is through physical exercise.

AP Photo/Pat Sullivan

Types of Emotions

Take a moment and look at the emotions communicated by the people in the photos on the following page. How can you discern the emotion expressed in each picture? One way to distinguish between different types of emotions is to examine consistent patterns of facial expressions, hand gestures, and body postures that characterize specific emotions. By considering these patterns, scholars have identified six emotions they consider **primary emotions**—emotions that involve unique and consistent behavioral displays across cultures (Ekman, 1972). The six primary emotions are surprise, joy, disgust, anger, fear, and sadness.

Table 4.1 **Intense Primary Emotions**

Primary Emotion	High-Intensity Counterpart
Surprise	Amazement
Joy	Ecstasy
Disgust	Loathing
Anger	Rage
Fear	Terror
Sadness	Grief

Some situations, like receiving an unexpected gift from a romantic partner or experiencing the death of a close relative, provoke especially intense primary emotions. In such cases, we often use different words to describe the emotion, even though what we're experiencing is simply a more intense version of the same primary emotion (Plutchik, 1980). For instance, receiving a gift from a romantic partner may cause intense joy that we think of as "ecstasy," just as the passing of a close relative likely will trigger intense sadness that we label as "grief" (see Table 4.1).

In other situations, an event may trigger two or more primary emotions simultaneously, resulting in an experience known as **blended emotions** (Plutchik, 1993). For example, if you encounter your romantic partner flirting with someone else, you might experience jealousy, a blended emotion because it combines the primary emotions anger, fear, and sadness (Guerrero & Andersen, 1998): in this case, *anger* at your partner, *fear* that your relationship may be threatened, and *sadness* at the thought of potentially losing your partner to a rival. Other examples of blended emotions include contempt (anger and disgust), remorse (disgust and sadness), and awe (surprise and fear) (Plutchik, 1993).

While North Americans often identify six primary emotions—surprise, joy, love, anger, fear, and sadness

(Left to right) © Lisa B./Corbis; Digital Vision/Getty Images; © Randy Faris/Corbis; © David Leeson/Dallas Morning News/Sygma/Corbis

💧 According to studies performed by psychologist Paul Ekman (1972), people around the world associate the same facial expressions with particular feelings. Can you identify the ones in each of these photographs?

(Shaver, Wu, & Schwartz, 1992)—some cultural variation exists. For example, in traditional Chinese culture, shame and sad love (an emotion concerning attachment to former lovers) are primary emotions. Traditional Hindu philosophy suggests nine primary emotions: sexual passion, amusement, sorrow, anger, fear, perseverance, disgust, wonder, and serenity (Shweder, 1993).

LearningCurve
bedfordstmartins.com/ipcandyou

Forces Shaping Emotion

What I remember most about the morning of September 11, 2001, besides its absolute normalcy, was the beauty of the late-summer day. Driving my boys to school before heading to the university, I was listening to my favorite radio station when the DJ joked about how "some idiot has apparently managed to fly his plane into the Twin Towers." Within minutes, however, the truth of that day filled the television and radio airwaves. As rage and grief surged within me, I felt an almost primal compulsion to communicate with my closest intimates.

Arriving in the lecture hall an hour later, I found a classroom full of students equally eager to share their emotions, from shocked disgust to silent sadness. Whereas most of the women in my class expressed grief over the loss of life, the men felt furious. Personality also seemed to make a difference. For example, my less agreeable students vocalized their anger and insisted that the attacks confirmed "the innate evil of human nature." As you can see, my students and I (as well as people around the globe) were united in a newly forged bond of anger and sadness over the loss of so many innocent lives, but divided along lines of gender and personality as to how we each experienced this bitter bond.

Gender

Across cultures, women report experiencing more sadness, fear, shame, and guilt than men, while men report feeling more anger and other hostile emotions (Fischer, Rodriguez Mosquera, van Vianen, & Manstead, 2004). In Western cultures, gender differences in emotion derive in part from differences in how men and women orient to interpersonal relationships (Brody & Hall, 2000). Women are more likely than men to express emotions that support relationships and suppress emotions that assert their own interests over another's (Zahn-Waxler, 2001). As a consequence, women may feel sadness more often than men because sadness, unlike anger, isn't directed outward at another person; thus, it doesn't threaten relationships. Sadness communicates personal vulnerability and signals the need for comforting from others. It therefore reflects a willingness to submit oneself to the care of another. By contrast, anger conveys a motivation to achieve one's own goals or to take satisfaction in one's success over another's (Chaplin, Cole, & Zahn-Waxler, 2005).

Though men and women may experience emotions with different frequency and express these emotions differently, when they experience the same emotions, there is no difference in the intensity of the emotion experienced (Fischer et al., 2004). Whether it's anger, sadness, joy, or disgust, men *and* women experience these emotions with equal intensity.

Personality

Like culture and gender, personality exerts a pronounced impact on our emotions. Recall the Big Five personality traits described in Chapter 3—openness, conscientiousness, extraversion, agreeableness, and neuroticism (or OCEAN). Of these five, three strongly influence our experience and communication of emotion (Pervin, 1993). The first is *extraversion*, the degree to which one is outgoing and sociable versus quiet and reserved. High-extraversion people experience positive emotions more frequently than low-extraversion people, because high-extraversion people seem to "look for happiness" in their everyday lives, focusing their attention more on positive events than on negative (Larsen & Ketelaar, 1991). High-extraversion people also rate themselves as better able to cope with stress and more skilled at managing their emotional communication than do low-extraversion people (Lopes, Salovey, Cote, & Beers, 2005).

Justin Lane/AFP/Getty Images

◌ A father who lost his son in the 9/11 attack has an emotional response upon seeing his son's name at the north pole of the 9/11 Memorial in New York City.

Another personality trait that influences emotion is *agreeableness*. People high in agreeableness—those who are trusting, friendly, and cooperative—report being happier in general, better able to manage stress, and more skilled at managing their emotional communication than low-agreeable people. High-agreeable people also score substantially higher on measures of emotion management and are rated by their peers as having superior emotion management skills (Lopes et al., 2005).

The tendency to think negative thoughts about oneself, known as *neuroticism*, also affects emotional experience and expression. High-neurotic people focus their attention primarily on negative events (Larsen & Ketelaar, 1991). Consequently, they report more frequent negative emotions than do low-neurotic people and rate themselves as less happy overall. They also describe themselves as less skilled at emotional communication, and they test lower on scientific measures of emotion management than do low-neurotic people (Lopes et al., 2005).

Clearly, your degree of extraversion, agreeableness, and especially neuroticism influences how

often you experience positive and negative emotions and how effectively you manage and communicate these emotions. At the same time, keep in mind that personality is merely one of many pieces that make up the complex puzzle that is emotion. Part of becoming a competent emotional communicator is learning how your personality traits shade your emotional experience and expression and learning how to treat personality-based emotion differences in others with sensitivity and understanding.

LearningCurve
bedfordstmartins.com/ipcandyou

Managing Your Emotional Experience and Expression

It's arguably the most well-known psychology experiment.[2] Over a six-year period, Stanford psychologist Walter Mischel brought 653 young children from the university's Bing Nursery School into a room and offered them a tasty treat of their choice: marshmallow, Oreo cookie, or pretzel stick. But he also presented them with a dilemma. If they could resist eating the treat while he stepped out for several minutes, they would get a second treat as a reward. The children were then left alone. The experiment was a simple test of impulse control: the ability to manage one's emotional arousal, excitement, and desire. Most of the kids gave in and ate the treat, usually in less than three minutes. But about 30 percent held out. Years later, Mischel gathered more data from the same children—who were then in high school. He was stunned to learn that their choices in the experiment predicted a broad range of outcomes. Children who had waited were more socially skilled, better able to cope with stress, less likely to have emotional outbursts when frustrated, and better able to deal with temptations, and had closer, more stable friendships than those who hadn't waited. They also had substantially higher SAT scores. Why was "the

[2]The information that follows is adapted from Goleman (2007b); Lehrer (2009); and Shoda, Mischel, and Peake (1990).

marshmallow test" such a powerful predictor of long-term personal and interpersonal outcomes? Because it taps a critical skill: the ability to constructively manage emotions.

Emotional Intelligence

Managing your emotions is part of **emotional intelligence**: the ability to interpret emotions accurately and to use this information to manage emotions, communicate them competently, and solve relationship problems (Gross & John, 2002). People with high degrees of emotional intelligence typically possess four skills:

1. Acute understanding of their own emotions
2. Ability to see things from others' perspectives and have a sense of compassion regarding others' emotional states—that is, *empathy*
3. Aptitude for constructively managing their own emotions
4. Capacity for harnessing their emotional states in ways that create competent decision making, communication, and relationship problem solving (Kotzé & Venter, 2011)

Given that emotional intelligence (EI) involves understanding emotions coupled with the ability to manage them in ways that optimize interpersonal competence, it's not surprising that people with high EI experience a broad range of positive outcomes. For example, within leadership positions, people with high EI are more likely than low-EI people to garner trust, inspire followers, and be perceived as having integrity (Kotzé & Venter, 2011). High-EI individuals are less likely than low-EI people to bully people, or use violence to get what they want (Mayer, Salovey, & Caruso, 2004). High-EI people even find it easier to forgive relational partners who have wronged them, because of their strong empathy and skill at emotion management (Hodgson & Wertheim, 2007).

> { **People with high emotional intelligence experience a broad range of positive outcomes.** }

◊ Can you recall a time when you had to resist an emotional impulse or desire, like in the marshmallow study? What was the outcome of this event?

Of the skills comprising emotional intelligence, emotion management is arguably the most important one to improve because—as demonstrated by Mischel's research—it directly influences your communication choices and the outcomes that result (Lopes et al., 2005). **Emotion management** involves attempts to influence which emotions you have, when you have them, and how you experience and express them (Gross et al., 2006). Emotions naturally trigger attempts to manage them. Consequently, the practical issue is not whether you will manage your emotions, but how you can do so in ways that improve your interpersonal communication and relationships.

Managing Your Emotions after They Occur

One strategy for managing emotions is to try to modify or control them after we become aware of them (Gross et al., 2006). An event triggers arousal, interpretation, and awareness of an emotion. We then consciously try to modify our internal experience and outward communication of that emotion.

The two most common ways people manage emotions after they have been triggered are suppression and venting. **Suppression** involves inhibiting thoughts, arousal, and outward behavioral displays of emotion (Richards, Butler, & Gross, 2003). For example, you might hide your happiness and surprise after receiving a good grade on an exam if your roommate received a poor grade on the same test. The desire to suppress stems from the recognition that feeling, thinking, and openly communicating certain emotions would be relationally, socially, or culturally inappropriate. Although people sometimes suppress positive emotion, suppression occurs most commonly with negative emotions, especially anger and sadness (Gross et al., 2006). This is because displays of pleasant emotions elicit favorable responses from others, whereas the expression of negative emotions often drives other people away (Argyle & Lu, 1990; Furr & Funder, 1998).

The inverse of suppression is **venting:** allowing emotions to dominate our thoughts and explosively expressing them (Fuendeling, 1998; Kostiuk & Fouts, 2002). Venting may be positive, such as when we jump up and shout for joy after learning we got the job we wanted. At other times, we vent negative emotions, such as when we "blow up" at a spouse or other family member who has been pestering us repeatedly.

Self-Reflection

Consider your own use of suppression and venting. What leads you to choose one or the other strategy? Are there limits to how often you vent or how long you suppress? What ethical considerations arise related to each strategy?

Preventing Emotions

An alternative to managing emotions after they occur is to prevent unwanted emotions from happening in the first place. Four strategies are commonly used for preventing emotions (Gross et al., 2006), the first of which is **encounter avoidance:** staying away from people, places, or activities that you know will provoke emotions you don't want to experience. For example, you might purposely avoid a particular class that your ex signed up for because seeing him or her always provokes intense and unpleasant emotions within you.

A second preventive strategy is **encounter structuring:** intentionally avoiding specific topics that you know will provoke unwanted emotions during encounters with others. For example, I love my in-laws (honestly!), but my political attitudes are very different from theirs. Early in our acquaintanceship, my father-in-law and I would both get angry whenever we discussed politics. After a few such battles, we agreed to avoid this topic and now structure our encounters so politics isn't discussed.

A third preventive strategy is **attention focus:** intentionally devoting your attention only to aspects of an event or encounter that you know will not provoke an undesired emotion. For example, you might choose to pay attention to your instructor's lecture rather than your two classmates giggling annoyingly behind you.

A fourth way to preventively manage emotion is **deactivation:** systematically desensitizing yourself to emotional experience (Fuendeling, 1998). Some people, especially after experiencing a traumatic emotional event, decide that they no longer want to feel anything. The result is an overall deadening of emotion. Though the desire to use this strategy is understandable, deactivation can trigger deep depression.

Reappraising Your Emotions

Imagine that you (like me) occasionally receive friendly Facebook messages from former romantic partners. You feel ethically obligated to share these messages with your current partner, but you also know that, when you do, he or she will respond with nasty remarks about your ex that anger you. How can you best manage the emotions that will arise?

The most fruitful strategy for engaging difficult and unavoidable emotions is **reappraisal:** actively changing how you think about the meaning of emotion-eliciting situations so that their emotional impact is changed (Jackson, Malmstadt, Larson, & Davidson, 2000). To use reappraisal in the previous example, you might think vividly about your partner's positive aspects, your mutual love for one another, and your future together (Richards et al., 2003). As a result, you'll be more likely to communicate positively, with empathy.

Reappraisal is effective because you employ it *before* a full-blown emotional reaction commences. This strategy requires little effort compared to trying to suppress or control your emotions after they've occurred. In addition, reappraisal produces interpersonal communication that is partner-focused and perceived as engaged and emotionally responsive (Gross et al., 2006). Across studies, people who are most effective at managing their emotional communication report reappraisal as their primary strategy (John & Gross, 2004).

Reappraisal is accomplished in two steps. First, before or during an encounter that you suspect will trigger an undesired emotion in yourself, *call to mind the positive aspects of the encounter.* If you truly can't think of anything positive about the other person, your relationship, or the situation, focus on seeing yourself as the kind of person who can constructively communicate even during unpleasant encounters. Second, *consider the short- and long-term consequences of your actions.* Think about how communicating positively in the here-and-now will shape future outcomes in constructive ways.

Skills Practice

Using Reappraisal
Managing difficult emotions through reappraisal

1. Identify a recurring behavior or event that triggers emotions you'd like to manage more effectively.
2. When the behavior or event happens, focus your thoughts on positive aspects of yourself, the other person, your relationship, and the situation.
3. Consider ways to communicate that will foster positive outcomes.
4. Communicate in those ways.
5. Observe how your positive thoughts and constructive communication affect the relationship.

You can use reappraisal to effectively manage problematic positive emotions as well. Imagine again that you've received a good grade on an exam that your roommate failed. Jumping for joy will not help to maintain your relationship with him or her. In this case, reappraisal allows you to focus on your roommate's

feelings and perspective; you might respond with "I did well on the exam, but I'm really sorry to hear that you weren't happy with your grade. I'm sure you'll do much better on the next exam now that you have a better sense of what Dr. Rodriguez is looking for."

LearningCurve
bedfordstmartins.com/ipcandyou

Emotional Challenges

Each day we face personal trials that trigger difficult-to-manage emotions affecting our communication, relationships, and the quality of our lives. For example, romantic jealousy—which we discuss in Chapter 10—is toxic to interpersonal communication and must be managed effectively for relationships to survive (Guerrero & Andersen, 1998). Likewise, fear—of emotional investment, vulnerability, or long-term commitment—can prevent us from forming intimate connections with others (Mickelson, Kessler, & Shaver, 1997). In the remainder of this chapter, we focus on four such challenges that occur all too frequently in our daily lives: lack of empathy online, anger, passion, and grief.

Online Communication and Empathy Deficits

After giving a lecture about stereotypes, I received an e-mail from a student: "Stereotypes are DEMEANING!! People should DENOUNCE them, not TEACH them!!! WHY LECTURE ABOUT STEREOTYPES???" Noting the lack of greeting, capped letters, and excessive punctuation, I interpreted the message as angry. Irritated, I popped back a flippant response, "Uhhhh . . . because people often wrongly believe that stereotypes are true?" Hours later, I received a caustic reply: "I think it's really disrespectful of you to treat my question so rudely!! I'M PAYING YOU TO TEACH, NOT MOCK!!!"

You have probably had similar experiences—online encounters in which anger or other emotions were expressed inappropriately, triggering a destructive exchange. In most of these interactions, the messages traded back and forth would never have been expressed face-to-face.

Why are we more likely to inappropriately express our emotions online? Two features of online interaction—asynchronicity and invisibility—help explain this phenomenon (Suler, 2004). Much of our online communication is *asynchronous*. That is, we don't interact with others in real time but instead exchange messages (such as text, e-mail, or Facebook postings) that are read and responded to at later points. When communicating asynchronously, it's almost as if time is magically suspended (Suler, 2004). We know that there likely *will* be responses to our messages, but we choose when (and if) we view those responses. This predisposes us to openly express emotions that we might otherwise conceal if we knew the response would be immediate.

Online communication also provides us with a sense of *invisibility*. Without sharing a physical context with the people with whom we're communicating, we feel as if we're "not really there"—that is, people can't really see or hear us. Consequently, we feel distant from the consequences of our messages.

Recent brain research suggests that our sense of invisibility when communicating online may have a neurological basis. Recall from Chapter 1 that *feedback* consists of the verbal and nonverbal messages recipients convey to indicate their reaction to communication. Now remember our definition of *empathy* from Chapter 3: the ability to experience others' thoughts and emotions. Research documents that the same part of the brain that controls empathy—the

orbitofrontal cortex—also monitors feedback (Goleman, 2006). This means that our ability to experience empathy is neurologically tied to our ability to perceive feedback (Beer, John, Scabini, & Knight, 2006). During face-to-face and phone encounters, we constantly track the feedback of others, watching and listening to their nonverbal communication. This enables us to feel empathy for them, to consider what they're thinking and feeling about our communication. When we see or hear people react negatively to something we're saying, we can instantly modify our messages in ways that avoid negative consequences.

Now consider what happens when we lack feedback—such as when we're communicating online. Without the ability to perceive others' immediate responses to our communication, it's difficult for us to experience empathy and to adjust our communication in ways that maintain appropriateness (Goleman, 2007a). We're less able to *perspective-take* (see the situation and our communication from our partner's point of view) and to feel *empathic concern* (experience his or her emotions and feelings). Consequently, we're more likely to express negative emotions—especially anger—in blunt, tactless, and inappropriate ways. Complicating matters further, people on the receiving end of our communication have the same deficit. Their online messages are less sensitive, less tactful, and maybe even more offensive than their offline messages.

(Left to right) © Steve Hix/Somos Images/Corbis; © Michael Doolittle/Alamy

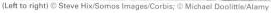 When we communicate face-to-face, we have the advantage of communicating in real time and having feedback from the person with whom we are interacting. Online communication can cause empathy deficits that we may need to compensate for.

What can you do to experience and express emotions more competently online? First, compensate for the online empathy deficit by investing intense effort into perspective-taking and empathic concern.

Second, communicate these aspects of empathy directly to your online partners, following suggestions from Chapter 3. Integrate into your online messages questions that seek the other person's perspectives, such as "What's your view on this situation?" Validate their views when they provide them: "You make a lot of sense." Communicate empathic concern by saying things like, "I hope you're doing OK." If you receive what looks like an angry message, convey that you recognize the other person is angry and that you feel bad about it: "I feel really terrible that you're so upset."

Self-Reflection

Recall an online encounter in which you inappropriately expressed emotion. How did lack of empathy shape your behavior? Would you have communicated the same way face-to-face? What does this tell you about the relationship between feedback, empathy, and emotional expression?

Third, expect and be tolerant of any aggressive messages you receive, accepting that such behavior is a natural outcome of the online environment, rather than evidence that other people are "mean" or "rude." Finally, avoid crafting and sending angry online messages in the heat of the moment. You might craft a response, wait 24 hours to cool off, revisit it, assess it in terms of empathy, and then modify or even delete it if it's inappropriate.

> **Anger is almost always triggered by someone or something external to us, and is driven by our perception that the interruption is "unfair."**

Anger

Anger is a negative primary emotion that occurs when you are blocked or interrupted from attaining an important goal by what you see as the improper action of an external agent (Berkowitz & Harmon-Jones, 2004). As this definition suggests, anger is almost always triggered by someone or something external to us, and is driven by our perception that the interruption is "unfair" (Scherer, 2001).

Skills Practice

Managing Anger Online
Responding competently during an online encounter in which you're angry

1. Identify a message or post that triggers anger.
2. Before responding, manage your anger.
3. Practice perspective-taking and empathic concern toward the message source.
4. Craft a response that expresses empathy, and save it as a draft.
5. Later, review your message, revise it as necessary, and then send it.

Anger is commonplace: the average person is mildly to moderately angry anywhere from several times a day to several times a week (Berkowitz & Harmon-Jones, 2004). Perhaps because of its frequency, we commonly underestimate anger's destructive potential. We wrongly presume that we can either suppress it or openly express it and that the damage will be minimal. But anger is our most intense and potentially destructive emotion. For example, anger causes perceptual errors that enhance the likelihood we will respond with verbal or physical violence toward others (Lemerise & Dodge, 1993). Both men and women report the desire to punch, smash, kick, bite, or take similar violent actions toward others when they are angry (Carlson & Hatfield, 1992). The impact of anger on interpersonal communication is also devastating. Angry people are more likely to argue, make accusations, yell, swear, and make hurtful and abusive remarks (Knobloch, 2005). Additionally, passive-aggressive communication such as ignoring others, pulling away, giving people dirty looks, and using the "silent treatment" are all more likely to happen when you're angry (Knobloch, 2005).

The most frequently used strategy for managing anger is suppression. You "bottle it up" inside rather than let it out. Occasional suppression can be constructive, such as when open communication of anger would be unprofessional, or when anger has been triggered by mistaken perceptions or attributions. But *always* suppressing anger can cause physical and mental problems: you put yourself in a near-constant state of arousal and negative thinking known as **chronic hostility.** People suffering from chronic hostility spend most of their waking hours simmering in a thinly veiled state of suppressed rage. They are more likely than others to believe that human nature is innately evil and that most people are immoral, selfish, exploitative, and manipulative. Ironically, because chronically hostile people believe the worst about others, they tend to be difficult, self-involved, demanding, and ungenerous (Tavris, 1989).

A second common anger management strategy is *venting*: explosively disclosing all of your angry thoughts to whomever triggered them. Many people view venting as helpful and healthy; it "gets the anger out." The assumption that venting will rid you of anger is rooted in the concept of **catharsis,** which holds that openly expressing your emotions enables you to purge them. But in contrast to popular belief, research suggests that venting actually *boosts* anger. One field study of engineers and technicians who were fired from their jobs found that the more individuals vented their anger about the company, the angrier they became (Ebbeson, Duncan, & Konecni, 1975).

To manage your anger, it's better to use strategies such as encounter avoidance, encounter structuring, and reappraisal. In cases where something or someone has already triggered anger within you, consider using the **Jefferson strategy,** named after the third president of the United States. When a person says or does something that makes you angry, count slowly to 10 before you speak or act (Tavris, 1989). If you are very angry, count slowly to 100; then speak or act. Thomas Jefferson adopted this simple strategy for reducing his own anger during interpersonal encounters.

Although the Jefferson strategy may seem silly, it's effective because it creates a delay between the event that triggered your anger, the accompanying arousal

(Left to right) © Richard Schulman/Corbis; Phil Schermeister/Getty Images; Justin Guariglia/NGS/Getty Images

🔹 Anger is our most intense and potentially destructive emotion. Both men and women report the desire to react to anger in similar ways through verbal or physical violence.

Self-Quiz

Test Your Chronic Hostility

Place a check mark next to the statements with which you agree. Count up all your check marks, and then use the Scoring key below to interpret your score.

- People are always trying to use me for their own selfish purposes.
- It's human nature to be immoral and exploitative.
- I can't help but feel angry when I consider the rudeness of others.
- People seem to enjoy behaving in ways that annoy and provoke me.
- It's hard to not blow up at people, given how they're always screwing up.
- I get furious just thinking about how inconsiderate most people are.
- Most people are manipulative and they truly sicken me.

Scoring: A score of 0–2 means low hostility. If you've scored in this range, you likely experience anger on an occasional basis; triggered in the normal way by events that you perceive negatively. A score of 3–4 means moderate hostility. If you fall into this range, anger may be an issue of concern in your interpersonal relationships. A score of 5–7 means high hostility. You likely experience anger frequently, and your interpersonal relationships are probably strongly and detrimentally affected by your anger.

and awareness, and your communication response. The delay between your internal physical and mental reactions and your outward communication allows your arousal to diminish somewhat, including lowering your adrenaline, blood pressure, and heart rate. Therefore, you communicate in a less extreme (and possibly less inappropriate) way than if you had not "counted to 10." A delay also gives you time for critical self-reflection, perception-checking, and empathy. These three skills can help you identify errors in your assessment of the event or person and plan a competent response.

Passion

When Bella first meets Edward in the book *Twilight*, she is confused, bewildered, and even angered by him and his unpredictable behavior. Over time, however, his ability to surprise her in pleasing ways, and his stunningly handsome appearance, feed a deepening attraction. Eventually, she learns that the passion she feels is mutually shared.

Passion is a blended emotion, a combination of surprise and joy coupled with a number of positive feelings such as excitement, amazement, and sexual attraction. Akin to Bella's response to Edward, people

who elicit passion in us are those who communicate in ways that deviate from what we expect (triggering surprise and amazement), whom we interpret positively (generating joy and excitement), and whom we perceive as physically pleasing (leading to sexual attraction).

Because passion stems in large part from surprise, the longer and better you know someone, the less passion you will experience toward that person on a daily basis (Berscheid, 2002). In the early stages of romantic involvements, our partners communicate in ways that are novel and positive. The first time our lovers invite us on a date, kiss us, or disclose their love are all surprising events and intensely passionate. But as partners become increasingly familiar with each other, their communication and behavior do, too. Things that once were perceived as unique become predictable. Partners who have known each other intimately for years may be familiar with almost all of the communication behaviors in each other's repertoires (Berscheid, 2002). Consequently, the capacity to surprise partners in dramatic, positive, and unanticipated ways is diminished (Hatfield, Traupmann, & Sprecher, 1984).

Because passion derives from what we perceive as surprising, you can't engineer a passionate evening

🔹 **Kristen Stewart and Robert Pattinson's on-screen romance as Bella and Edward in the *Twilight* films was mirrored by a romantic relationship offscreen.**

Self-Reflection

How has passion changed over time in your romantic relationships? What have you and your partners done to deal with these changes? Is passion a necessary component of romance, or is it possible to be in love without passion?

---

by carefully negotiating a dinner or romantic rendezvous. You or your partner might experience passion if an event is truly unexpected, but jointly planning and then acting out a romantic candlelight dinner together or spending a weekend in seclusion cannot recapture passion for both you and your partner. When it comes to passion, the best you can hope for in long-term romantic relationships is a warm afterglow (Berscheid, 2002). However, this is not to say that you can't maintain a happy *and* long-term romance; maintaining this kind of relationship requires strategies that we discuss in Chapter 10.

Grief

The intense sadness that follows a substantial loss, known as **grief,** is something each of us will experience. We cannot maintain long-term, intimate involvements with other mortal beings without at some point losing loved ones to death. But grief isn't only about mortality. You're likely to experience grief in response to *any* type of major loss. This may include parental (or personal) divorce, physical disability due to injury, romantic relationship breakup, loss of a much-loved job, or even the destruction or misplacing of a valued object such as an engagement ring or treasured family heirloom.

Managing grief is enormously and uniquely taxing. Unlike other negative emotions such as anger, which is typically triggered by a onetime, short-lived event, grief stays with us for a long time—triggered repeatedly by experiences linked with the loss.

Managing Your Grief

No magic pill can erase the suffering associated with a grievous loss. It seems ludicrous to think of applying strategies such as reappraisal, encounter structuring, or the Jefferson strategy to such pain. Grief is a unique emotional experience, and none of the emotion management strategies discussed in this chapter so far can help you.

Instead, you must use *emotion-sharing*: talking about your grief with others who are experiencing or have experienced similar pain, or people who are skilled at providing you with much-needed emotional support and comfort. Participating in a support group for people who have suffered similar losses can encourage you to share your emotions. When you share your grief, you feel powerfully connected with others—and this sense of connection can be a source of comfort. You also gain affirmation that the grief process you're experiencing is normal. For example, a fellow support-group participant who also lost his mother to cancer might tell you that he, too, finds Mother's Day a particularly painful time. Finally, other participants in a support group can help you remember that grief does get gradually more bearable over time.

For those of us without ready access to face-to-face support groups, online support offers a viable alternative. Besides not requiring transportation and allowing access to written records of any "missed" meetings,

© Arko Datta/Reuters/Corbis

◔ This photograph, taken by Arko Datta, shows a woman mourning a relative who was killed in the 2004 tsunami in South Asia. It won the World Press Photo Foundation Spot News award in 2005.

online support groups also provide a certain degree of anonymity for people who feel shy or uncomfortable within traditional group settings (Weinberg, Schmale, Uken, & Wessel, 1995). You can interact in a way that preserves some degree of privacy. This is an important advantage, as many people find it easier to "discuss" sensitive topics online than face-to-face, where they'd run the risk of embarrassment (Furger, 1996).

Comforting Others

The challenges you face in helping others manage their grief are compounded by the popular tendency to use suppression for managing sadness. The decision to use suppression derives from the widespread belief that it's important to maintain a stoic bearing, a "stiff upper lip," during personal tragedies (Beach, 2002). However, a person who uses suppression to manage grief can end up experiencing stress-related disorders such as chronic anxiety or depression. Also, the decision to suppress can lead even normally open and communicative people to stop talking about their feelings. This places you in the awkward position of trying to help others

{ **Grief stays with us for a long time—triggered repeatedly by experiences linked with the loss.** }

manage emotions that they themselves are unwilling to admit they are experiencing.

The best way you can help others manage their grief is to engage in **supportive communication**—sharing messages that express emotional support and that offer personal assistance (Burleson & MacGeorge, 2002). Competent support messages convey sincere expressions of sympathy and condolence, concern for the other person, and encouragement to express emotions. Incompetent support messages tell a person how he or she *should* feel or indicate that the individual is somehow inadequate or blameworthy. Communication scholar and social support expert Amanda Holmstrom offers seven suggestions for improving your supportive communication.[3]

1. *Make sure the person is ready to talk.* You may have amazing support skills, but if the person is too upset to talk, don't push it. Instead, make it clear that you care and want to help, and that you'll be there to listen when he or she needs you.

2. *Find the right place and time.* Once a person is ready, find a place and a time conducive to quiet conversation. Avoid distracting settings such as parties, where you won't be able to focus, and find a time of the day where neither of you has other pressing obligations.

3. *Ask good questions.* Start with open-ended queries such as "How are you feeling?" or "What's on your mind?" Then follow up with more targeted questions based on the response, such as "Are you eating and sleeping OK?" (if not, a potential indicator of depression), or "Have you connected with a support group?" (essential to emotion-sharing). Don't assume that because you've been in a similar situation, you know what someone is going through. Importantly, *if you suspect a person is contemplating suicide, ask him or her directly about it.* Say, "Have you been thinking about killing yourself?" or "Has suicide crossed your mind?" People often mistakenly think that direct questions such as these will "push

---

[3]Content that follows was provided to the author by Dr. Amanda Holmstrom, and published with permission. The author thanks Dr. Holmstrom for her contribution.

someone over the edge," but in fact it's the opposite. Research suggests that someone considering suicide *wants* to talk about it, but believes that no one cares. If you ask direct questions, a suicidal person typically *won't* be offended or lie but instead will open up to you. Then you can encourage the person to seek counseling. Someone not considering suicide will express surprise at the question, often laughing it off with a "What? No way!"

4. *Legitimize, don't minimize.* Don't dismiss the problem or the significance of the person's feelings by saying things such as "It could have been worse," or "Why are you so upset?!" Research shows these comments are unhelpful. Instead, let the person know that it's normal and OK to feel as they do.

5. *Listen actively.* Show the person that you are interested in what is being said. Engage in good eye contact, lean toward him or her, and say "Uh-huh" and "Yeah" when appropriate.

6. *Offer advice cautiously.* We want to help someone who is suffering. So we often jump right in and offer advice. But many times that's not helpful or even wanted. Advice is best when it's asked for, when the advice giver has relevant expertise or experience (e.g., a relationship counselor), or when it advocates actions the person can actually do. Advice is hurtful when it implies that the person is to blame or can't solve his or her own problems. When in doubt, ask if advice would be appreciated—or just hold back.

7. *Show concern and give praise.* Let the person know you genuinely care and are concerned about his or her well-being ("I am so sorry for your loss; you're really important to me"). Build the person up by praising his or her strength in handling this challenge. Showing care and concern helps connect you to someone, while praise will help a person feel better.

Skills Practice

Supportive Communication
Skillfully providing emotional support

1. Let the person know you're available to talk, but don't force an encounter.
2. Find a quiet, private space.
3. Start with general questions, and work toward more specific. If you think he or she might be suicidal, ask directly.
4. Assure the person that his or her feelings are normal.
5. Show that you're attending closely to what is being said.
6. Ask before offering advice.
7. Let the person know you care!

 LearningCurve
bedfordstmartins.com/ipcandyou

Postscript }

We began this chapter with the story of a woman committed to transforming the lives of teenagers. Vy Higginsen founded Gospel for Teens in part to create a musical refuge for young people to escape their emotional turmoil. But she quickly learned that her students' emotions couldn't be suppressed, and that through sharing their emotions with one another they could more quickly heal their wounds of anger and grief.

How do you manage the emotional challenges of your life? Do you leave your baggage at the door, burying your emotions? Or do you bring your baggage in, sharing your emotions with others?

The story of Vy Higginsen and her students reminds us that, although we have emotions, we are not our emotions. It's our capacity to constructively manage the emotions we experience, and communicate them in positive ways, that makes hope and goodness in our lives possible.

Chapter Review }

Visit LaunchPad for *Interpersonal Communication and You* to watch brief, illustrative ⊙ videos of these terms and to access ✓ LearningCurve. **bedfordstmartins.com/ipcandyou**

KEY TERMS

emotion, 75
emotion-sharing, 76
⊙ emotional contagion, 76
feelings, 76
moods, 76
primary emotions, 77
⊙ blended emotions, 78
emotional intelligence, 81

emotion management, 81
suppression, 81
venting, 82
⊙ encounter avoidance, 82
⊙ encounter structuring, 82
attention focus, 82
deactivation, 82
⊙ reappraisal, 82

anger, 85
chronic hostility, 86
catharsis, 86
Jefferson strategy, 86
passion, 87
grief, 88
⊙ supportive communication, 89

CHAPTER ACTIVITIES

1. Create a list of significant others such as parents, siblings, boyfriend/girlfriend, spouse, roommate, and so forth. Then, indicate on a scale of 1 = "least likely" to 5 = "most likely" your likelihood of sharing your emotional experiences with each person on your list. How does the relationship type affect your likelihood of sharing? Does relational history have an impact? What other factors influence emotion-sharing?

2. ⊙ Watch the video on **emotional contagion** and work in groups with your classmates to create role-plays showing positive emotional contagion (e.g., joy, excitement) as well as negative emotional contagion (e.g., disappointment, anger). Discuss with your group members the potential relational outcomes for different types of emotional contagion.

3. Write a short response paper based on the following questions: Of two of the forces that shape emotions—gender and personality—which has the most impact on how you express your emotions? Why? Do you agree or disagree that both forces are interconnected?

4. In small groups, discuss the ways in which you believe you will manage your emotions in your current or future career. What types of occupations require more suppression than others? What challenges can arise when suppressing your emotions at work? What types of jobs allow for more venting than others?

5. Try the Jefferson strategy the next time you become angry, and write a brief paper about the experience. Describe the scenario and any outcomes: Did the Jefferson strategy work? Did it diffuse your arousal? Did it allow you time for self-reflection, perception-checking, and empathy? How did it help you identify errors in your assessment of your partner or the situation?

6. Comforting individuals experiencing grief is extremely challenging. Reflect on some sort of grief you have experienced in your lifetime and discuss these questions: What are some examples of incompetent support communication people provided during your grief? Did they include such sayings as "everything happens for a reason" or "it could be worse"? How did this communication make you feel? What would have been more effective?

 Look for LearningCurve throughout
the chapter to help you review.
bedfordstmartins.com/ipcandyou

5 } Understanding Culture

H elen Torres was born in Puerto Rico but spent her early childhood in a diverse Detroit neighborhood of Polish, Hispanic, Lebanese, and Euro-American families. The summer before she entered third grade, her family moved. Now in a suburb populated mostly by white families, the Torreses were the only Hispanic family in the area.[1] Helen's mother was excited about the change and immediately volunteered to help out with activities at Helen's school, including fundraising and school parties.

Soon an incident occurred that changed Helen's view of interpersonal communication and culture forever. A parent called Helen's mother and asked her to bake cupcakes for an upcoming school event. Helen's mother, a bilingual but a dominant Spanish speaker, didn't know what "cupcakes" were. Why would anyone in their right mind want a *cup*-sized cake? Concluding that the caller must be confused, Helen's mom baked a beautiful full-sized cake, and brought it to school. Seeing the cake, the other kids teased Helen. "I shut them up," Helen explains. "I said, 'My mom can speak two languages. *Can yours*?'"

The cupcake incident quickly faded from Helen's classmates' memories, but for Helen's mother it fostered a sense of insurmountable difference between her and the other mothers. She stopped volunteering for school functions, afraid of embarrassing her daughters. For Helen, the misunderstanding inspired an intense curiosity about interpersonal communication

---

[1] All information that follows was provided to the authors by Helen Torres in a personal interview, December 5, 2012. Published with the permission of Helen Torres.

◦ **Understanding culture and communicating competently with people from other cultural communities is an essential skill.**
Courtesy of Helen Torres

and cultural difference. This curiosity would eventually lead her to earn a bachelor's and master's degree in communication, and to become a national activist on behalf of Hispanic civil rights.

Years later, Helen hosted a roundtable for a federal agency looking to expand its reach and service to underrepresented communities. One participant was a woman who ran a nonprofit organization helping victims of Eastern European war crimes to establish themselves in the United States. She spoke slowly and nervously, with a thick accent. Helen immediately sensed that the other group members were getting irritated with how long the woman was taking to express herself. As Helen describes, "I kept imagining my mother and the cupcake. So I told the other group members to be patient with her, and allow her extra time to speak. She had great

ideas, and the fact that she was willing to share these with us meant that we should support her."

Today, Helen Torres is Executive Director and CEO of Hispanas Organized for Political Equality (HOPE), an influential nonprofit committed to achieving political and economic equality for Latinas through leadership, advocacy, and education. But she still recalls the cupcake incident and its impact on her life. "Some may think it's a silly story, but it illustrates a profound point: communicating competently with people from other cultural communities is an essential skill. We must be able to bridge cultural divides through our interpersonal communication, to ensure that *all* people have their voices heard, understood, respected, and valued; and that no one feels the sense of alienation that my mother once did."

 ost of us can think of situations where, like Helen's mother, we wanted to connect with others but felt distant from them because of cultural differences. But regardless of the setting or the particular differences, interpersonal communication is your tool for bridging these divides. By improving your ability to communicate with people from other cultures, you can build more positive and mutually satisfying interpersonal connections with them. In this chapter, you'll learn:

- The defining characteristics of culture
- What co-cultures are and their role in interpersonal communication
- The impact of prejudice on interpersonal communication

- Ways cultural differences influence how people communicate
- How to improve your intercultural communication competence

What Is Culture?

As our world gets more diverse, understanding culture and cultural differences in interpersonal communication becomes increasingly important. Consider, for example, cultural diversity in the United States. In 2011, more than 50 percent of all births in the United States were nonwhite—including Latino, Asian, African American, and mixed-raced children (U.S. Census Bureau, 2012). International student enrollments in the United States are also on the rise (Institute of International Education, 2011). This

(Clockwise from top left) NARINDER NANU/AFP/Getty Images; Asia Images Group/Getty Images; Robert McGouey/Getty Images; Mario Tama/Getty Images

💧 Culture is often so fused into your everyday life, it is easy to overlook how something like where you live can inform everything you see, hear, and believe. How do the activities and images shown relate to your culture or not? What other aspects of your culture make you *you*?

means that your classmates are just as likely to be from Seoul as Seattle. Plus, with all the smartphones and tablet computers available, we have easy access to people around the world. This enables us to interact with others and create interpersonal relationships on a global level in a way never possible before. As our daily encounters increasingly cross cultural lines—making us more aware of diversity—the question arises, what exactly is culture?

Culture Defined

As explained in Chapter 1, I take a broad and inclusive view of **culture**, defining it as an established,

{ **What makes a culture a culture is that it is widely shared.** }

coherent set of beliefs, attitudes, values, and practices shared by a large group of people (Keesing, 1974). Culture includes many types of influences, such as your nationality, ethnicity, religion, gender, sexual orientation, physical abilities, and even age. But, really, what makes a culture a culture is that it is widely shared. This happens because our cultures are learned, communicated, layered, and lived.

Culture Is Learned

You learn your cultural beliefs, attitudes, and values from many sources, including your parents, teachers, religious leaders, peers, and the mass media (Gudykunst & Kim, 2003). This process begins at birth, through customs such as choosing a newborn's name, taking part in religious ceremonies, and selecting "godparents" or special guardians. As you mature, you learn deeper aspects of your culture, including the history behind certain traditions. For example, when I was young, Halloween was all about trick-or-treating and competing with my brother to see who could get the most candy. But as I aged, my parents shared with me the rich history behind such practices, and how they date back to ancient Celtic celebrations of the New Year. You also learn how to participate in cultural rituals—everything from blowing out the candles on a birthday cake to lighting candles on a menorah. In most societies, teaching children to understand, respect, and practice their culture is considered an essential part of childrearing. Consequently, when I raised my three

boys, I shared with them the history behind Halloween just as my parents had done with me.

Culture Is Communicated

Each culture has its own practices regarding how to communicate (Whorf, 1952). Imagine you're part of a group project and the other members decide to do the project in a particular way. If you grew up in Singapore, you'd be expected to support the group's decision even if you thought another approach would be better. Withholding your dissenting opinion would be considered competent communication because the culture in Singapore emphasizes group harmony over personal preferences. American culture, however, stresses the importance of individual expression. So, if you grew up in the United States, you'd probably feel that it's perfectly acceptable—and perhaps even your duty—to voice your concerns about the group's decision.

Culture Is Layered

Many people belong to more than one culture simultaneously. As a result, there are multiple "layers" of culture—various traditions, heritages, and practices that are important to people. My wife's Uncle Rick, for example, is originally from Canada but is now an American citizen. Rick is passionately American in many ways: he played hockey for a U.S. collegiate team, is deeply patriotic, sings the national anthem at ball games, and celebrates the fourth of July. But every four years, when the Winter Olympics roll around, his Canadian cultural allegiance comes to the forefront, and he cheers the Canadians over and above everyone else—especially when it comes to hockey!

Culture Is Lived

Culture affects everything about how you live your life. It influences the neighborhoods you live in; the means of transportation you use; the way you think, dress, talk, and even eat. Its impact runs so deep that it is often taken for granted. At the same time, culture is often a great source of personal pride. Many people consciously live in ways that celebrate their cultural heritage—through behaviors like wearing a Muslim hijab, placing a Mexican flag decal on their car, or greeting others with the Thai gesture of the Wai (hands joined in prayer, head bowed).

> **Self-Reflection**
>
> What is your earliest memory of "learning" your culture? Do you believe that event or instance had a significant impact on your understanding of culture? Why or why not?

Co-Cultures

As societies become more culturally diverse, there is also an increased awareness of how various cultures, and groups of people within them, interact. In any society, there's usually a group of people who have more **power** than others, that is, the ability to influence or control people and events (Donohue & Kolt, 1992). Having more power in a society comes from controlling major societal institutions, such as banks, businesses, the government, and legal and educational systems. According to **Co-Cultural Communication Theory**, the people who have more power within a society determine the *dominant culture* because they get to decide the prevailing views, values, and traditions of the society (Orbe, 1998). Consider the United States. Throughout its history, Euro-American, wealthy men have been in power. When the United States was first founded, the only people allowed to vote were land-owning males of European ancestry. Now, more than 200 years later, Euro-American men still comprise the vast majority of U.S. members of Congress and Fortune 500 CEOs. As a consequence, what is thought of as "American culture" is tilted toward emphasizing the interests, activities, and accomplishments of these men.

Members of a society who don't conform to the dominant culture—by way of language, values, life style, or even physical appearance—often form what are called **co-cultures**: that is, they have their own cultures that *co-exist* within a dominant cultural sphere (Orbe, 1998). Co-cultures may be based on age, gender, social class, ethnicity, religion, mental and physical ability, sexual orientation, and other unifying elements, depending on the society (Orbe, 1998). U.S. residents who are not members of the dominant culture—people of color, women, members of the LGBTQ community, and so forth—exist as distinct co-cultures, with their own political lobbying groups, Web sites, magazines, and television networks (such as Lifetime, BET, Telemundo, and HERE TV).

Because members of co-cultures are (by definition) different from the dominant culture, they develop and use numerous communication practices that help them interact with people in the culturally

> **Self-Reflection**
>
> Each of us belongs to several co-cultures, though we may strongly identify with some co-cultures more than others. Which of your co-cultures comes to the forefront of your identity? Which identifications seem less powerful? (For example, you may identify strongly as a Latina but not identify as strongly as a Catholic.) How might your answers affect your communication with others?

dominant group (Ramirez-Sanchez, 2008). These range from denial of co-cultural identity to conformity with negative stereotypes associated with the co-culture. For example, they might:

- Use overly polite language with individuals from the dominant culture

- Suppress reactions when members of the dominant culture make offensive comments

- Try to excel in all aspects of their professional and personal lives to counteract negative stereotypes about their co-culture

- Conform to negative stereotypes in an exaggerated way in order to meet the expectations of members from the dominant culture or to shock and scare them

- Act, look, and talk as much as possible like members of the dominant culture

- Openly disparage their own co-culture

- Quietly but clearly express their co-cultural identity through appearance, actions, and words

How might these communication practices work in real life? Imagine an African American couple moves to a largely Euro-American suburb. They socialize primarily with their white neighbors—never displaying any indication of their African American heritage other than their skin color. Meanwhile, their

(Left to right) © Bob Sacha/Corbis; © Kevin R. Morris/Corbis

🜄 Would you classify the people and activities shown above as ingroupers or outgroupers? What specific aspects in each image make someone seem similar or dissimilar to you? How does this classification influence your communication?

son dresses in sagging pants, wears a do-rag, and blasts gangsta rap through Beats headphones. Through these behaviors, he actively strives to conform to stereotypes about young black males. Despite their differences, all these behaviors have the same goal: managing the tension between African American co-culture and the dominant Euro-American culture.

As discussed in Chapter 3, our perceptions of shared attitudes, beliefs, and values based on cultural and co-cultural affiliations can lead us to classify those who are similar to us as *ingroupers* and those who are different as *outgroupers*. This, however, can be a dangerous trap. Just because someone shares a particular co-culture with you (say, your race or sexual orientation), it doesn't mean that you are truly "the same." For example, you and a classmate might both be "white" (the same race), but you may be Irish-Catholic and she may be Russian-Jewish, with a host of different ethnic and religious factors that affect your interpersonal communication. In fact, you may be more similar to an Asian American classmate who shares your religious dedication and your socioeconomic background.

Prejudice

Because people often shy away from interacting with outgroupers, they may rely on stereotypes to form judgments about them. As you learned in chapter 3, *stereotypes* are a way to categorize people into a social group and then evaluate them based on information you have related to this group. Stereotypes play a big part in how you form impressions about others during the perception process. This is especially true for racial and gender characteristics since they are among the things you notice first when encountering others. But when stereotypes reflect rigid attitudes toward groups and their members, they become **prejudice** (Ramasubramanian, 2010).

Because prejudice is rooted in stereotypes, it can vary depending on whether those stereotypes are positive or negative. According to the **Stereotype Content Model** (Fiske, Cuddy, Glick, & Xu, 2002), prejudice centers on two judgments made about

{ **When stereotypes reflect rigid attitudes toward groups and their members, they become prejudice.** }

> **Skills Practice**
>
> **Addressing Prejudice**
>
> *Become a less prejudiced communicator.*
>
> 1. Recognize that we all have prejudices, even if they seem innocuous (as in "Men who watch football are lazy" or "Droves of teenagers at the mall are dangerous").
> 2. Commit to having an open mind about groups about which you hold prejudiced beliefs.
> 3. Seek interpersonal communication encounters with members of these groups. Get to know individuals and don't be afraid to ask questions!
> 4. Evaluate your own communication. Do you communicate with group members in ways that set them up to confirm your prejudiced beliefs?

others: how warm and friendly they are, and how competent they are. These judgments create two possible kinds of prejudice: *benevolent* and *hostile*.

Benevolent prejudice occurs when people think of a particular group as inferior but also friendly and competent. For instance, someone judges members of a group as "primitive," "helpless," and "ignorant" but attributes their "inferiority" to forces beyond their control, such as lack of education, technology, or wealth (Ramasubramanian, 2010). Thus, although the group is thought of negatively, they also trigger feelings of sympathy (Fiske et al., 2002). If you ever find yourself thinking about a group of people that you consider "inferior" but that you also think could improve themselves "if only they knew better," you're engaging in benevolent prejudice.

Hostile prejudice happens when people have negative attitudes toward a group of individuals that they see as unfriendly and incompetent (Fiske et al., 2002). Someone demonstrating hostile prejudice might interpret the group's supposed incompetence as intrinsic: "They're naturally lazy," "They're all crazy zealots," or "They're mean and violent." People

exhibiting hostile prejudice often believe that the group has received many opportunities to improve ("They've been given so much") but that their innate limitations hold them back ("They've done nothing but waste every break that's been given to them").

Prejudice, no matter what form, is destructive and unethical. Benevolent prejudice leads you to communicate in condescending and disrespectful ways with others. Hostile prejudice is the root of every exclusionary "ism": racism, sexism, ageism, classism, ableism, and so on.

However, even if you don't treat people in a prejudiced way, that doesn't mean you're not prejudiced. Prejudice is based on deeply held negative beliefs about particular groups (Ramasubramanian, 2010). If you think you have prejudiced beliefs, you must confront—and permanently give up—those beliefs. How? Learn about the cultures and groups you have prejudiced beliefs about. Ask members of these groups questions about themselves, listen actively to the answers, and interact with them as much as you can. This will ease the uncertainty and anxiety you may feel around others who are culturally different from you (Berger & Calabrese, 1975).

○ In April 2013, the students of Wilcox County High School took matters into their own hands and organized the school's first integrated prom, overcoming the prejudice that had previously resulted in years of racially segregated celebrations.

✓ LearningCurve
bedfordstmartins.com/ipcandyou

{ **The real-world communication distinctions between cultures can be profound.** }

Cultural Influences on Communication

The hit TV show *Modern Family* focuses on a California clan whose members have different cultural backgrounds. Euro-American patriarch Jay is married to the (much younger) Gloria, who is originally from Colombia. In addition to their child together, Jay serves as stepfather to Gloria's son Manny. Jay's children from a previous marriage also have families of their own. His son Mitchell and his partner Cam have an adopted daughter from Vietnam, while Jay's daughter Claire and her goofy husband Phil have three children. Given this diversity, interpersonal exchanges between the characters routinely cross lines of age, gender, ethnicity, and sexual orientation—sometimes at the same time! Not surprisingly, there's

a lot of miscommunication stemming from these differences. For example, Gloria speaks with a Colombian accent and often tangles up her English words. On Halloween, she tells Jay he's "going to be a gargle." Manny chimes in to clarify, "She means 'gargoyle.'" Later, when a box of Jesus figurines is mysteriously delivered to their house, Jay realizes the error: he had told Gloria to call his secretary and order a box of baby *cheeses*.

Shows like *Modern Family* poke lighthearted fun at cultural differences. However, the real-world communication distinctions between cultures can be profound. Scholars suggest that seven cultural characteristics shape our interpersonal communication: individualism versus collectivism, high and low context, uncertainty avoidance, emotion displays, power distance, masculinity versus femininity, and views of time. To improve your cross-cultural interpersonal communication skills, you need to understand these differences.

Individualism versus Collectivism

In **individualistic cultures,** people tend to value independence and personal achievement. Members of these cultures are encouraged to focus on themselves and their immediate family (Hofstede, 2001), and individual achievement is praised as the highest good (Waterman, 1984). Individualistic countries include the United States, Canada, New Zealand, and Sweden (Hofstede, 2001).

By contrast, in **collectivistic cultures** people emphasize group identity ("we" rather than "me"), interpersonal harmony, and the well-being of ingroups (Park & Guan, 2006). If you were raised in a collectivistic culture, you were probably taught that it's important to belong to groups or "collectives" that look after you in exchange for your loyalty. In collectivistic cultures, people emphasize the goals, needs, and views of

ABC/Photofest

◊ Gloria Delgado-Pritchett, played by Sofia Vergara, is a Colombian woman whose cultural norms often, and hilariously, conflict with those of her American-born family members. How do you navigate situations where culture blurs the line of understanding between yourself and others?

groups over those of individuals and define the highest good as cooperation with others rather than individual achievement. Collectivistic countries include Guatemala, Pakistan, Taiwan, and Japan (Hofstede, 2001).

Differences between individualistic and collectivistic cultures can powerfully influence people's behaviors—including which social networking sites they use and how they use them. For instance, people in collectivistic cultures tend to use sites that emphasize group connectedness; whereas individualistic culture members use sites that focus on self-expression (Barker & Ota, 2011). American Facebook users devote most of their time on the site describing their own actions and viewpoints as well as events that are personally important to them. They also post controversial status updates and express their personal opinions—even if these trigger debate. Japanese users of Mixi, meanwhile, carefully edit their profiles so they won't offend anyone (Barker & Ota, 2011). While American Facebook users often post photos of themselves alone doing various activities, Mixi users tend to write in diaries that are shared with their closest friends, boosting ingroup solidarity (Barker & Ota, 2011).

> **Self-Reflection**
>
> Examine your own presence on social media (if you have one). For example, does your Facebook profile tend to reveal an individualistic or collectivistic orientation? Why?

High and Low Context

Cultures can also be described as *high* or *low context*. In **high-context cultures**, such as in China, Korea, and Japan, people use relatively vague and ambiguous language and even silence to convey important meanings. (High-context cultures are often collectivistic as well.) People in such cultures often talk indirectly (using hints or suggestions) because they presume that members of their ingroup will know what they're trying to say. As a result, they don't feel

a need to provide a lot of explicit information. For example, if you ask a friend who grew up in Japan to drive you to the airport, she might say, "That might be difficult," instead of outright refusing your request.

In **low-context cultures**, people tend *not* to presume that others share their beliefs, attitudes, and values. So they strive to be informative, clear, and direct in their communication (Hall & Hall, 1987). Many low-context cultures are also individualistic; as a result, people openly express their views and try to persuade others to accept them (Hall, 1976, 1997a). Within such cultures, which include Germany, Scandinavia, Canada, and the United States, people work to make important information obvious, rather than hinting or implying. For example, during a small-group discussion, a Canadian classmate might directly state, "Here's my thinking on this topic. . . ."

Uncertainty Avoidance

Cultures vary in how much they tolerate and accept unpredictability, known as **uncertainty avoidance**. As scholar Geert Hofstede explains, "The fundamental issue here is how a society deals with the fact that the future can never be known: should we try to control the future or just let it happen?"[2] In *high-uncertainty-avoidance cultures*, people place a lot of value on control. They define rigid rules and conventions to guide all beliefs and behaviors, and they feel uncomfortable with unusual or innovative ideas. People from such cultures want structure in their organizations, institutions, relationships, and everyday lives (Hofstede, 2001). For example, a coworker raised in a high-uncertainty-avoidance culture (such as Greece, Portugal, or Germany) would expect everyone assigned to a project to have clear roles and responsibilities, including a designated leader. In his research on organizations, Hofstede found that in high-uncertainty-avoidance cultures, people commit to organizations for long periods of time, they expect their job responsibilities to be clearly defined, and they strongly believe that organizational rules should not be broken (2001, p. 149). Children raised in such cultures are taught to

---

[2]http://geert-hofstede.com/dimensions.html

believe in cultural traditions and practices without ever questioning them.

In *low-uncertainty-avoidance cultures*, people put more emphasis on "letting the future happen," without trying to control it (Hofstede, 2001). They care less about rules, they tolerate diverse viewpoints and beliefs, and they welcome innovation and change. They also feel free to question and challenge authority. In addition, they teach their children to think critically about the beliefs and traditions they're exposed to, rather than automatically following them. Examples of low-uncertainty-avoidance cultures include Singapore, Jamaica, and Denmark.

Emotion Displays

All cultures have norms regarding which forms of emotional expression are socially desirable and appropriate, and which are not. These are called **display rules:** guidelines for when, where, and how to appropriately express emotion (Ekman & Friesen, 1975).

These rules vary across cultures, however (Soto, Levenson, & Ebling, 2005). Take the two fastest-growing ethnic groups in the United States—Mexican Americans and Chinese Americans (Buriel & De Ment, 1997). In traditional Chinese culture, people prioritize emotional control and moderation; intense emotions are considered dangerous and are even thought to cause illness (Wu & Tseng, 1985). This belief even shapes communication in close relationships. Chinese American couples don't openly express positive emotions toward each other as often as Euro-American couples do (Tsai & Levenson, 1997). Meanwhile, in traditional Mexican culture, people openly express emotion, even more so than those from Euro-American cultures (Soto et al., 2005). For people of Mexican descent, the experience, expression, and deep discussion of emotions provide some of life's greatest rewards and satisfactions.

When families emigrate to a new society, the move often provokes tension over which display rules they should follow. People more closely oriented to their cultures of origin continue to communicate their emotions in traditional ways. Others—usually the first generation of children born in the new society—may move away from traditional forms of emotional expression (Soto et al., 2005). For example, Chinese Americans who adhere strongly to traditional Chinese culture openly display fewer negative emotions than those who are Americanized (Soto et al., 2005). Similarly, Mexican Americans with strong ties to traditional Mexican culture express intense negative emotion more openly than "Americanized" Mexican Americans.

It's important to be aware of these differences when communicating with others. An emotional expression—such as a loud shout of intense joy—might be considered shocking and inappropriate in some cultures but perfectly normal and natural in others. At the same time, don't presume that all people from the same culture necessarily share the same expectations. As much as possible, adjust your expression of emotion to match the style of the individuals with whom you're interacting.

Power Distance

The degree to which people in a particular culture view the unequal distribution of power as acceptable is known as **power distance** (Hofstede, 1991, 2001). In *high-power-distance cultures*, it's considered normal and even desirable for people of different social and professional status to have different levels of power (Ting-Toomey, 2005). In such cultures, people give privileged treatment and extreme respect to those in high-status positions (Ting-Toomey, 1999). They also expect individuals of lesser status to behave humbly, especially around people of higher status, who are expected to act superior.

In *low-power-distance cultures*, people in high-status positions try to minimize the differences between themselves and lower-status persons by interacting with them in informal ways and treating them as equals (Oetzel et al., 2001). For instance, a high-level marketing executive might chat with the cleaning service workers in her office and invite them to join her for a coffee break. See **Figure 5.1** for examples of high-, moderate-, and low-power-distance cultures.

Power distance also affects how people deal with conflict. In low-power-distance cultures, people with little power still may choose to engage in conflict with high-power people. For instance, employees may question management decisions, or townspeople may attend a meeting and argue with the mayor.

HIGH- POWER-DISTANCE COUNTRIES	MODERATE- POWER-DISTANCE COUNTRIES	LOW- POWER-DISTANCE COUNTRIES
Russia	Spain	Norway
Panama	Pakistan	Sweden
Guatemala	Italy	Ireland
Philippines	South Africa	New Zealand
Mexico	Hungary	Denmark
Venezuela	Jamaica	Israel
China	United States	Australia

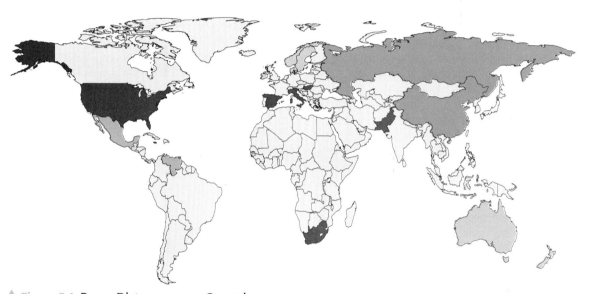

○ Figure 5.1 **Power Distance across Countries**
Source: Hofstede (2009). Retrieved May 16th, 2011, from: http://www.geert-hofstede.com/index.shtml.

These behaviors are less common in high-power-distance cultures (Bochner & Hesketh, 1994).

Power distance also influences how people communicate in close relationships, especially families.

In traditional Mexican culture, for instance, the value of *respeto* emphasizes power distance between younger people and their elders (Delgado-Gaitan, 1993). As part of *respeto*, children are expected to defer to elders' authority and to avoid openly disagreeing with them. In contrast, many Euro-Americans believe that, once children reach adulthood, power in family relationships should be balanced—with children and their elders treating one another as equals (Kagawa & McCornack, 2004).

Masculinity versus Femininity

Another way that cultures differ from one another is the degree to which masculine versus feminine values are emphasized (Hofstede, 2009). **Masculine cultures**

> **Self-Reflection**
>
> Consider your own comfort with power distance. Are you comfortable communicating with individuals who are better educated or more established than you are? (e.g., Can you chat openly with a professor you admire?) What cultural or co-cultural factors help to determine your response?

place importance upon personal ambition, competition, assertiveness, and material gain as core values. Examples of masculine cultures include Japan, Austria, and Italy. In contrast, **feminine cultures** emphasize personal connections to others, relationship health, quality of life, and concern for the poor and elderly. Feminine cultures include Norway, Sweden, and the Netherlands. The United States and Canada are both moderately masculine.

Importantly, whether a culture is masculine, feminine, or somewhere in-between impacts both men *and* women, by teaching what they learn to be "the most important values in life." Within more masculine cultures, people of both sexes come to view competition and "getting ahead" as admirable; whereas within feminine cultures, people are expected to be other-centered and compassionate. As just one example, feminine cultures typically offer lengthy unpaid leaves from work following the birth or adoption of a child—in some cases, for as long as a *year*—whereas within masculine cultures, such extended leaves would be unimaginable. The masculinity or femininity of a culture also shapes very specific aspects of communication. For example, managers in masculine cultures are expected to be decisive and authoritarian; whereas feminine culture managers are expected to focus more on the process of decision making and the achievement of consensus between involved parties.

Views of Time

A final difference between cultures that impacts interpersonal communication is views of time. Scholar Edward Hall distinguished between two time orientations: monochronic (*M-time*) and polychronic (*P-time*) (Hall, 1997b). People who have a **monochronic time orientation** view time as a precious resource. It can be saved, spent, wasted, lost, or made up, and it can even run out. If you're an M-time person, "spending time" with someone or "making time" in your schedule to share activities with him or her sends the message that you consider that person—and your relationship—important (Hall, 1983). You may view time as a gift you give others to show your affection, or as a tool for punishing someone ("I no longer have time for you").

People who have a **polychronic time orientation** don't view time as a resource to be spent, saved, or guarded. They don't consider time of day (what time it is) as especially important or relevant to daily activities. Instead, they're flexible when it comes to time, and they believe that harmonious interaction with others is more important than "being on time" or sticking to a schedule.

Differences in time orientation can create problems when people from different cultures make appointments with each other (Hall, 1983). For example, those with an M-time orientation, such as many Americans, often find it frustrating if P-time people show up for a meeting after the scheduled start time. In P-time cultures, such as those in Arab, African,

---

Skills Practice

Understanding Time Orientation

Become more mindful of the way you and your communication partners communicate with time.

1. Learn about different time orientations. Perhaps your roommate isn't just a stickler about her bedtime; she may simply be on M-time!
2. Be mindful. While being true to your own beliefs and communication style, try to accommodate others. Don't rush your P-time grandmother off the phone when she's telling you about her week. Call her when your schedule allows for a leisurely conversation.
3. Avoid criticizing others. Remember, time is just one dimension of intercultural communication. It's possible that your high- or low-context or individualistic or collectivistic communication style confuses someone as much as you're frustrated by another's time orientation.
4. Be willing to accept others as they are and adapt to them. Your relational partners might just do the same for you!

Self-Quiz

Are You an M-Time or a P-Time Person?

Read the questions below and choose the answer that most closely reflects your view of time. When you're done, review your answers and see what they suggest about your personal time orientation: Are you an M-time person or a P-time person?

1. Do you have a personal planner or smartphone in which you carefully keep track of your daily schedule and appointments?

    (a) Of course! How could I survive without one?

    (b) What exactly do I need to plan?

2. Do you often check the time during the day to see if you're "on schedule"?

    (a) All the time. I also make sure that my watch is synchronized with my cell phone, and I program my cell to issue alarm reminders for key appointments

    (b) Never. I don't even own a watch.

3. Do you get stressed out about not having enough time to do the things you're supposed to?

    (a) Not having enough time to do what I'm supposed to do is the number-one source of stress in my life.

    (b) What exactly are "the things we're supposed to do," other than share life with those we love and be happy?

4. Your best friend calls you at work, says that she has been dumped by her romantic partner, and badly needs to talk with you. You

    (a) check your schedule to see if there's an opening at some point later in the day.

    (b) arrange to leave work to go comfort your friend.

5. You have to renew your driver's license because it expires tomorrow. You use your lunch hour to do so, but there are only two people working the counter at the registry of motor vehicles, and the line is long. You

    (a) check your watch and feel your stress increase as the hour passes and you're still not at the head of the line. Finally, you cut to the front and ask, "Is there any way I can go next? I've been waiting for an hour!"

    (b) take the opportunity to chat with other people who are waiting, making new acquaintances.

Note: Examples in this *Self-Quiz* were gathered by the author from undergraduate volunteers.

Caribbean, and Latin American countries, people think that arriving 30 minutes or more after a meeting's scheduled start is perfectly acceptable and that it's okay to change important plans at the last minute.

You can improve your interpersonal communication by understanding other people's views of time. Learn about the time orientation of a destination or country before you travel there. For example, before my family and I traveled to St. Martin in the French West Indies, we learned that it was a P-time culture. Thus, at the end of our trip, I planned accordingly. When we needed a cab to pick us up at the hotel at 10:30 in the morning, I told the cab driver to be there by 9:45. Sure enough, at around 10:25 he rolled up—almost exactly the amount of lateness that I had anticipated! Also, respect others' time orientation. If you're an M-time person interacting with a P-time individual, don't suddenly dash off to your next appointment because you feel you have to stick to your schedule. Your communication partner will likely think you're rude. If you're a P-time person interacting with an M-time partner, realize that he or she may get impatient with a long, leisurely conversation or see a late arrival to a meeting as inconsiderate. In addition, avoid criticizing or complaining about behaviors that stem from other people's time orientations. Instead, accept the fact that people view time differently, and be willing to adapt your own expectations and behaviors accordingly.

LearningCurve
bedfordstmartins.com/ipcandyou

Creating Intercultural Communication Competence

In the award-winning movie *Gran Torino*, Clint Eastwood plays Walt, a bitter, racist widower who lives alone, estranged from his sons. Despite his bigoted attitudes, Walt strikes up a friendship with two Hmong teens who live next door—Sue and Thao—after he saves Thao from a gang beating. To help Walt communicate more effectively with the Hmong, Sue teaches him some simple interpersonal rules: Never touch a Hmong on the head, because they believe that the soul resides there. Don't look a Hmong straight in the eye; they consider it rude. Don't be surprised if a Hmong smiles when he or she is embarrassed; that's how they handle that emotion. In return, Walt teaches Thao how to interpersonally communicate during a job interview with an American construction foreman: "Look him straight in the eye, and give a firm handshake!" He even instructs

> **Intercultural competence is the ability to interpersonally communicate in an appropriate, effective, and ethical fashion with people from diverse backgrounds.**

Thao on the art of trading teasing insults with American male friends. As these unlikely friendships deepen, Walt (to his astonishment) realizes he has more in common with his neighbors than with his own family.

Like Walt, Thao, and Sue, you will likely form lasting bonds with people who come from cultures vastly different from your own. The gateway to such connections is **intercultural communication competence**, the ability to interpersonally communicate in an appropriate, effective, and ethical fashion with people from diverse backgrounds. You can strengthen your intercultural communication competence by applying the following practices: world-mindedness, attributional complexity, and communication accommodation.

World-Mindedness

When you possess **world-mindedness**, you demonstrate acceptance and respect toward other cultures' beliefs, values, and customs (Hammer, Bennett, & Wiseman, 2003). You can practice world-mindedness in three ways. First, accept others' expression of their culture or co-culture as a natural element in their interpersonal communication, just as your communication reflects your cultural background (Chen & Starosta, 2005). Second, avoid any temptation to judge others' cultural beliefs, attitudes, and values as "better" or "worse" than your own. Third, treat people from all cultures with respect.

This can be especially challenging when differences seem impossible to bridge or when the other person's beliefs, attitudes, and values conflict with your own. But practicing world-mindedness means more than just tolerating cultural differences you find perplexing or problematic. Instead, treat all people with respect by being kind and courteous in your interpersonal communication. You can also preserve others'

Suzanne Hanover/© Sony
Pictures/Courtesy Everett Collection

💧 In the film *Gran Torino*, Walt realizes his previous beliefs were racist only when he allows himself to experience his neighbor's culture. How has learning about someone's culture changed or enhanced your impressions for the better?

personal dignity by actively listening to and asking questions about viewpoints that may differ from yours.

World-mindedness is the opposite of **ethnocentrism**, the belief that one's own cultural beliefs, attitudes, values, and practices are superior to others'. Ethnocentric people view their own culture or co-culture as the standard against which all other cultures should be judged (Neulip & McCroskey, 1997). Such people tend to see their own interpersonal communication as competent and that of people from other cultures as incompetent.

Attributional Complexity

When you recognize **attributional complexity**, you acknowledge that other people's behaviors have complex causes. To develop this practice, observe others' behavior and analyze the various forces influencing it. For example, rather than deciding that a classmate's reserved demeanor or limited eye contact means she's unfriendly, consider the possibility that these behaviors might reflect cultural differences.

Also, learn as much as you can about different cultures and co-cultures, so you can better understand why people from those cultures communicate as they do. Experiencing other cultures through observation, travel, or interaction is a great way to sharpen your intercultural communication competence (Arasaratnam, 2006).

In addition, routinely use *perception-checking* (a practice discussed in Chapter 3) to avoid attributional errors, and regularly demonstrate empathy. In situations where the cultural gaps between you and others seem impossibly wide, try to see things from others' perspectives and consider the motivations behind their communication. Examine how people from diverse backgrounds make decisions, and compare their approaches to yours. Finally, ask others to explain the reasons for their behavior, and then accept and validate their explanations ("That makes sense to me") rather than challenging them ("You've got to be kidding!"). Avoid making statements like "I know that people like you act this way because you think that. . . ." You'll only come across as presumptuous.

> **Self-Reflection**
>
> Describe a situation in which you failed to engage in perception-checking in an intercultural communication situation. What was the outcome? What are specific actions you might have taken to improve that situation and outcome?

Communication Accommodation

A final way to enhance your intercultural communication competence is to adjust your interpersonal communication to mesh with the behaviors of people from other cultures. According to **Communication Accommodation Theory**, people are especially motivated to adapt their communication when they seek social approval, when they wish to establish relationships with others, and when they view others' language usage as appropriate (Giles, Coupland, & Coupland, 1991). In

{ **Research suggests that people who use communication accommodation are perceived as more competent.** }

Table 5.1 **Creating Intercultural Communication Competence**

1. Understand the many factors that create people's cultural and co-cultural identities.

2. Be aware of the different cultural influences on communication: individualism and collectivism, high- and low-context, uncertainty avoidance, emotional displays, power distance, masculinity and femininity, and views on time.

3. Embrace world-mindedness to genuinely accept and respect others' cultures.

4. Acknowledge attributional complexity to consider the possible cultural influences on your and others' communication.

5. Use communication accommodation when building and maintaining relationships with people from different cultural backgrounds.

contrast, people tend to accentuate differences between their communication and others' when they wish to convey emotional distance and disassociate themselves from others. Research suggests that people who use communication accommodation are perceived as more competent (Coupland, Giles, & Wiemann, 1991; Giles et al., 1991).

How does this work in practice? Try adapting to other people's communication preferences (Bianconi, 2002). During interactions, notice how long a turn people take when speaking, how quickly they speak, how direct they are, and how much they appear to want to talk compared to you. You may also need to learn and practice cultural norms for nonverbal behaviors, including eye contact, head touching, and hand shaking, such as those Sue taught Walt in *Gran Torino*.

For an overview of ways to create intercultural communication competence, see Table 5.1.

LearningCurve
bedfordstmartins.com/ipcandyou

Postscript }

We began this chapter with a Latina CEO and a cake bigger than a cup. When Helen Torres' mother misinterpreted a request from another parent, a chain of events was set in motion that led Helen to study interpersonal communication, earn undergraduate and graduate degrees, and eventually create one of the most powerful Latina leadership organizations on the West Coast. Helen's interpersonal communication education, coupled with her real-world experiences interacting with diverse others, has provided her with the knowledge and skills necessary to collaborate with powerful people on behalf of individuals in need.

What challenges have you faced in communicating across cultures? How might those challenges have been surmounted? Armed with interpersonal communication knowledge and skills, you need never again view cultural differences as barriers to connection, but instead as opportunities to build bridges with others who are as unique as you are.

Chapter Review

Visit LaunchPad for *Interpersonal Communication and You* to watch brief, illustrative videos of these terms and to access ✓ LearningCurve. **bedfordstmartins.com/ipcandyou**

KEY TERMS

culture, 95
power, 97
Co-Cultural Communication
 Theory, 97
co-cultures, 97
prejudice, 98
Stereotype Content Model, 98
individualistic cultures, 100
collectivistic cultures, 100

high-context cultures, 101
low-context cultures, 101
uncertainty avoidance, 101
display rules, 102
power distance, 102
masculine cultures, 103
feminine cultures, 104
monochronic time
 orientation, 104

polychronic time
 orientation, 104
intercultural communication
 competence, 106
world-mindedness, 106
ethnocentrism, 107
attributional complexity, 107
Communication Accommodation
 Theory, 107

CHAPTER ACTIVITIES

1. To better understand cultural influences on your communication, make a list of the cultural factors that influence communication described on pages 100–104 and explain where you fall on each spectrum. For example, are you from a high- or low-power-distance culture? Have an M-time or P-time orientation? From a masculine or feminine culture? Include an example of a recent event that reflects each cultural influence. Then, partner with a classmate and exchange lists. What cultural influences do you share? Where are you different? Would you have communicated in the same way for each example? Why or why not? Consider how these influences illustrate the saying "it's not bad, it's not wrong, it's just different!"

2. Many TV shows and movies base their jokes on stereotypical communication problems between men and women or between people from different cultures. For example, think about how shows like *New Girl* or movies like *The Hangover* trilogy get a lot of their laughs. With a partner, find an example from the media that uses culture and communication in this way. Discuss how the example embodies or violates principles discussed in this chapter. How could the media better represent communication between people from different cultures?

3. Watch the video for **display rules** and think about the appropriateness of the emotions displayed. Then, write a one-page reflection paper that answers these questions:
 - In what contexts are public displays of affection appropriate? Inappropriate?
 - How do cultures differ in their display rules regarding public affection?
 - What other emotional displays are considered taboo in various contexts?

4. Go to the site understandingprejudice.org and access the Ambivalent Sexism quiz. (There is a link in the right-hand column of the home page.) Take the quiz, answering as honestly as you can, and submit your results. What was your "hostile sexism" score? What about your "benevolent sexism" score? How do you compare to other people in the country you currently live in? How about any other country you've lived in? What do these comparisons tell you about your own potential for sexism and how might you improve your communication in the future?

✓ Look for LearningCurve throughout the chapter to help you review.
bedfordstmartins.com/ipcandyou

6 } Listening Actively

F red McFeely Rogers began each day by swimming laps in a local pool.[1] A nonsmoking, nondrinking vegetarian, he was happily married for close to 50 years and helped raise two sons. He also was the most awarded person in television history: he received two Peabody Awards, numerous Emmys, the Presidential Medal of Freedom, and a star on the Hollywood Walk of Fame. But Rogers saw himself primarily as a minister who believed in the power of listening. From his perspective, the greatest communicative gift people could give was attentive silence that encouraged others to openly express their deepest emotions.

Although he eventually would receive honorary degrees from more than 40 different institutions—including Yale, Carnegie Mellon, and Boston University—Rogers' first degree was in music composition from Rollins College in Florida. Rogers planned on entering the seminary after graduation but was sidetracked by the chance to help establish the first public television station, WQED in Pittsburgh. As he later explained, "I got into television because I hated it so, and I thought there's some way of using this fabulous instrument to nurture those who would watch and listen" (Stimson, 1998). While working at the station, Rogers attended classes at Pittsburgh Theological Seminary. Ordained in 1963, he decided to minister to children and their families by creating *Mister Rogers' Neighborhood*, a TV program emphasizing affirmation, acceptance, and, most of all, listening. In Rogers' words, "being a good listener is a vital part of ministry, especially ministry with children. . . . I cultivated my own listening skills in part by integrating silence into my life as a part of my

---

[1] All information regarding Fred Rogers was obtained from Millman (1999), Stimson (1998), and Mister Rogers (n.d.).

◥ **Listening is our most primal and primary communication skill.**
AP/Wide World Photos

daily spiritual discipline." By providing children with an adult who would listen to their concerns, Rogers' show helped youngsters express their emotions in healthy ways. During the Gulf War, for example, Rogers dedicated a series of episodes to parents and children with close relatives fighting in Desert Storm. He encouraged parents to discuss life and death openly with their children rather than lying to them or avoiding their questions.

Rogers' renowned listening ability matched a talent for speaking powerfully in ways that made *others* listen. In the late 1960s, a congressional committee headed by notoriously gruff Senator John Pastore was considering halving public broadcasting's funding. Rogers testified before the committee, describing the importance of providing children with a compassionate adult listener on television. After hearing Rogers' testimony, Pastore remarked, "I'm supposed to be a pretty tough guy, but this is the first time I've had goose bumps in the last two days." The committee then voted to approve full funding for public broadcasting.

Mister Rogers' Neighborhood became the longest-running show in television history. During a 33-year span, Rogers welcomed guests as diverse as the Harlem Boys Choir, chef Julia Child, and cellist Yo-Yo Ma. The show became so well known that it remains a cultural icon—many people still remember the opening song, the gentle lilt of Rogers' voice, and his famous cardigan sweaters. Rogers was lampooned by everyone from comedian Eddie Murphy to the writers of the animated series *Family Guy*. But through it all, he remained committed to the central message of his subtle, nondenominational television ministry: listen to others and offer them love, respect, and kindness. Even after his death in 2003, the words he shared at the end of each episode still linger: "I'll be back when the day is new, and I'll have more ideas for you. And you'll have things you'll want to talk about. I will too."

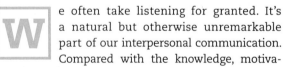

We often take listening for granted. It's a natural but otherwise unremarkable part of our interpersonal communication. Compared with the knowledge, motivation, and skill that competent speaking requires, listening seems to just happen. But if we view listening as secondary to speaking, we miss two truths about it. First, listening is our most primal and primary communication skill. As children, we develop the ability to listen long before we learn how to speak, read, or write. As adults, we spend more time listening than we do in any other type of communication activity (Wolvin & Coakley, 1996). Second, we each have the potential to develop our listening into something far more profound than passive action. When we practice *active listening*, we transcend our own thoughts, ideas, and beliefs and begin to directly experience the words and worlds of other people (McNaughton, Hamlin, McCarthy, Head-Reeves, & Schreiner, 2007). By focusing our attention, tailoring our listening to the situation, and letting others know we understand them, we move beyond the personal and create the *interpersonal*. The result is improved relationships (Bunkers, 2010).

In this chapter, we discuss how to build your active listening skills. You'll learn:

- The five stages of the listening process and strategies for improving your listening skills
- The many functions of listening

- The advantages and disadvantages of different listening styles
- Ways to avoid common forms of incompetent listening

{ **The process of listening unfolds over time, rather than instantaneously.** }

Listening: A Five-Step Process

Whether it's the *Paranormal Activity* series, *Insidious*, or *The Conjuring*, the scares in horror movies almost always begin with sounds: rustling in the darkness, whispering voices, moaning and clanking noises. As we sit in the comfort of movie theaters or living rooms—feeling our blood pressure rising—we too listen intently to these sounds, trying to understand them, and imagining how we would respond if we were in similar situations.

Horror screenwriters use sounds to trigger fear because they know the powerful role that listening plays in our lives. But what the writers, and we, often forget is that listening is a complex process. Specifically, **listening** involves receiving, attending to, understanding, responding to, and recalling sounds and visual images (Wolvin & Coakley, 1996). When you're listening to someone, you draw on both auditory and visual cues. In addition to spoken messages, behaviors such as head nodding, smiling, gestures, and eye contact affect how you listen to others and interpret their communication. The process of listening also unfolds over time, rather than instantaneously, through the five steps discussed here.

Receiving

While walking to class, you run into a friend and stop to chat with her. As she talks, you listen to her words as well as observe her behavior. But how does this process happen? As you observe your friend, light reflects off her skin, clothes, and hair and travels through the lens of your eye to your retina, which contains optic nerves. These nerves become stimulated, sending information to your brain, which translates the information into visual images such as your friend smiling or shaking her head, an effect called *seeing*. At the same time, sound waves generated

◊ In *Insidious*, Dalton's mother listens intently to the strange whispers coming from her son's baby monitor, causing an emotional response of fear but also prompting her to investigate. Whenever we hear sounds or listen to others, we go through a process to help us figure out what we heard and how to respond.

Self-Reflection

Think of the most recent instance in which you were truly frightened. What triggered your fear? Was it a noise you heard, or something someone told you? Or was it something you only saw? What does this tell you about the primacy of listening in shaping intense emotions?

by her voice enter your inner ear, causing your eardrum to vibrate. These vibrations travel along acoustic nerves to your brain, which interprets them as your friend's words and voice tone, an effect known as **hearing**.

Together, seeing and hearing constitute **receiving**, the first step in the listening process. Receiving is critical to listening—you can't listen if you don't "see" or hear the other person. Unfortunately, our ability to receive is often hampered by *noise pollution*, sound in the surrounding environment that obscures or distracts our attention from auditory input. Sources of noise pollution include crowds, road and air traffic, construction equipment, and music.

You can enhance your ability to receive—and improve your listening as a result—by becoming aware of noise pollution and adjusting your interactions accordingly. Practice monitoring the noise level in your environment during your interpersonal encounters, and notice how it impedes your listening. When possible, avoid interactions in loud and noisy environments, or move to quieter locations when you wish to exchange important information with others.

Attending

When Cleveland rapper Colson Baker (aka "Machine Gun Kelly") tweeted his fans: "Today we flash mob NO MATTER WHAT! 5pm at SouthPark mall in the food court," hundreds of fans showed up (as did police who had heard about the tweet). What makes such flash mobs possible? The fact that we pay attention to the messages that interest us the most.

Attending, the second step in the listening process, involves devoting attention to the information you've received. If you don't attend to information, you can't go on to interpret and understand it, or respond to it (Kahneman, 1973). The extent to which you attend to received information is determined largely by its *salience*—the degree to which it seems especially noticeable and significant. In the Colson Baker case, fans attended to his Twitter post in part because he used caps (visually stimulating), and because it was unexpected (Baker hadn't made any public appearances in Ohio since he had signed a major record deal). But the main reason they attended to his invite—and showed up at the mall—was because he was important to them: he was a local boy who had made it big.

We have only limited control over salience; whether people communicate in stimulating, unexpected, or important ways is largely determined by them, not us. However, we do control our attention level. To improve your attention, consider trying two things: limiting your multitasking and elevating your attention.

Michael Putland/Getty Images

⬥ Repeated exposure to intense levels of noise pollution can result in hearing impairment. Guitarist Pete Townshend of the Who, after years of exposure to his own noise pollution, can no longer hear spoken words during normal conversations.

Limiting Multitasking Online

One way to improve attention is to limit the amount of time you spend each day *multitasking online*— that is, using multiple forms of technology at once, each of which feeds you unrelated streams of information (Ophir, Nass, & Wagner, 2012). An example of such multitasking is writing a class paper on your computer while also Facebook chatting with several friends, watching TV, playing an online game, and texting family members. Stanford psychologist Clifford Nass has found that habitual multitaskers are extremely confident in their ability to perform at peak levels on the tasks they simultaneously juggle (Glenn, 2010). However, their confidence is misplaced. Multitaskers perform substantially worse on tasks compared with individuals who focus their attention on only one task at a time (Ophir et al., 2012).

Why is limiting multitasking online important for improving attention? Because multitasking erodes your capacity for sustaining focused attention (Jackson, 2008). Cognitive scientists have discovered that our brains adapt to the tasks we regularly perform during our waking hours, an effect known as *brain plasticity* (Carr, 2010). People who spend much of their time shifting attention rapidly between multiple forms of technology train their brains to only be able to focus attention in brief bursts. The consequence is that they lose ability to focus attention for long periods of time on just one task (Jackson, 2008). Not surprisingly, habitual multitaskers have grave difficulty listening, as listening requires extended attention (Carr, 2010). Limiting your multitasking, and spending at least some time each day focused on just one task, without technological distractions, helps train your brain to be able to sustain attention. To gauge the degree to which multitasking has impacted your attention, take the *Self-Quiz* "Multitasking and Attention" on page 116.

Elevating Attention

The second thing you can try to improve your attention is to elevate it, by following these steps (Marzano & Arredondo, 1996). First, develop awareness of your attention level. During interpersonal interactions, monitor how your attention naturally waxes and wanes. Notice how various factors such as fatigue, stress, or hunger influence your attention. Second, take note of encounters in which you *should* listen carefully, but that seem to trigger low levels of attention. These might include interactions with parents, teachers, or work managers, or situations such as family get-togethers, classrooms, or work meetings. Third, consider the optimal level of attention required for adequate listening during these encounters. Fourth, compare the level of attention you observed in yourself versus the level of attention that is required, identifying the "attention gap" that needs to be bridged for you to improve your attention.

Finally, and most important, elevate your level of attention to the point necessary to take in the auditory and visual information you're receiving. You can do this in several ways. Before and during an encounter, boost the salience of the exchange by reminding yourself of how it will impact your life and relationships. Take active control of the factors that may diminish your attention. When possible, avoid important encounters when you are overly

> **Skills Practice**
>
> **Elevating Attention**
>
> *Focusing your attention during interpersonal encounters*
>
> 1. Identify an important person to whom you find it difficult to listen.
> 2. List factors—fatigue, time pressure—that impede your attention when you're interacting with this person.
> 3. Before your next encounter with the individual, address factors you can control.
> 4. During the encounter, increase the person's salience by reminding yourself of his or her importance to you.
> 5. As the encounter unfolds, practice mental bracketing to stay focused on your partner's communication.

Self-Quiz }

Multitasking and Attention

This quiz gauges how multitasking between various forms of technology can divide your attention and how your ability to focus may suffer as a result. Read each statement below and mark the ones with which you agree. Use your score to assess the degree to which your attention is divided.

1. At any one time, I typically have multiple forms of technology turned on, including my phone and computer.

2. If I focus my attention on just one task, I find that my mind quickly starts drifting to other stuff, such as who is messaging me, or what is happening online.

3. Even during class or while I'm at work, I stay connected to and communicate with others through text, e-mail, cell phone, or the Internet.

4. When I spend too much time doing any one thing, I get bored.

5. Text messages, cell-phone calls, e-mail, and online posts frequently interrupt activities I am trying to focus upon and perform.

6. I spend much of my day switching rapidly between multiple activities and apps, including Facebook, text, e-mail, games, schoolwork, and Web surfing.

7. I feel that I am more easily distracted now than I was just a few years ago.

Note: Adapted from Bane (2010).

Scoring: Total up the number of items with which you agree. If you agree with 0–2 of these, your attention is not divided by multitasking, and you likely find it easy to concentrate on one thing for extended periods of time. If you agree with 3–4 of these, you have moderately divided attention and may be experiencing challenges with focusing attention. If you agree with 5–7 of these items, you spend much of your time multitasking and likely find it challenging to focus your attention on just one thing.

stressed, hungry, ill, fatigued, or under the influence of alcohol—such factors substantially impair attention. If you have higher energy levels in the morning or early in the week, try to schedule attention-demanding activities and encounters during those times. If you find your attention wandering, practice **mental bracketing**, systematically putting aside thoughts that aren't relevant to the interaction at hand. When irrelevant thoughts arise, let them pass through your conscious awareness and drift away without allowing them to occupy your attention fully.

Understanding

While serving with her National Guard unit in Iraq, Army Specialist Claudia Carreon suffered a traumatic brain injury (TBI)[2] that wiped her memory clean. She could no longer remember major events or people from her past, including her husband and her 2-year-old daughter. However, because she seemed physically

---

[2]The information that follows is adapted from http://www.braininjurymn.org/library/archive/NewWarsHallmarkInjury.pdf, retrieved October 12, 2011.

"normal," her TBI went unnoticed and she returned to duty. A few weeks later, Carreon received an order from a commanding officer, but she couldn't understand it and shortly afterward forgot it. She subsequently was demoted for "failure to follow an order." When Army doctors realized that she wasn't being willfully disobedient—but instead simply couldn't understand or remember orders—her rank was restored, and Carreon was rushed to the Army's Polytrauma Center in Palo Alto, California. Now Carreon carries with her captioned photos of loved ones and a special handheld personal computer to help her remember people and make sense of everyday conversations.

The challenges faced by Claudia Carreon illustrate the essential role that memory plays in shaping the third stage of listening. **Understanding** involves interpreting the meaning of another person's communication by comparing newly received information against our past knowledge (Macrae & Bodenhausen, 2001). Whenever you receive and attend to new information you place it in your **short-term memory**, the part of your mind that temporarily houses the information while you seek to understand its meaning. While the new information sits in your short-term memory, you call up relevant knowledge from your **long-term memory**, the part of your mind devoted to permanent information storage. You then compare relevant prior knowledge from your long-term memory with the new information in your short-term memory to create understanding.

Responding

You're spending the afternoon at your apartment discussing your wedding plans with two friends, John and Sarah. You want them to help you with ideas for

{ **When you actively listen, you do more than simply attend and understand.** }

◊ Claudia Carreon now relies on captioned photos to supplement her damaged long-term memory. Without this help, she can't compare new information with previous knowledge, prohibiting her from fully understanding any message she may receive.

Disabled American Veterans (DAV) • www.dav.org

your rehearsal dinner, ceremony, and reception. As you talk, John looks directly at you, smiles, nods his head, and leans forward. He also asks questions and makes comments periodically during the discussion. Sarah, in contrast, seems completely uninterested. She alternates between looking at the people strolling by your living-room window and texting on her phone. She also sits with her body half-turned away from you and leans back in her chair. You become frustrated because it's obvious that John is listening closely and Sarah isn't listening at all.

What leads you to conclude that John is listening and Sarah isn't? It's the way your friends are **responding**—communicating their attention and understanding to you. When you actively listen, you do more than simply attend and understand. You also convey your attention and understanding to others by clearly and constructively responding through positive feedback, paraphrasing, and clarifying (McNaughton et al., 2007).

Feedback

Critical to active listening is using verbal and nonverbal behaviors known as **feedback** to communicate attention and understanding *while* others are talking. Scholars distinguish between two kinds of feedback, positive and negative (Wolvin & Coakley, 1996). When you use positive feedback, like John in our earlier example, you look directly at the person speaking, smile, position your body so that you're facing him or her, and lean forward. You may also offer **back-channel cues**, verbal and nonverbal behaviors such as nodding and making comments—like "Uh-huh," "Yes," and "That makes sense"—that signal you've paid attention to and understood specific comments (Duncan & Fiske, 1977). All of these behaviors combine to show speakers that you're actively listening. In contrast, people who use negative feedback, like Sarah in our example, send a very different message to speakers. Behaviors that convey negative feedback include avoiding eye contact, turning your body away, looking bored or distracted, and not using back-channel cues.

To effectively display positive feedback during interpersonal encounters, try four simple suggestions (Barker, 1971; Daly, 1975). First, make your feedback obvious. As communication scholar John Daly notes, no matter how actively you listen, unless others perceive your feedback, they won't view you as actively listening. Second, make your feedback appropriate. Different situations, speakers, and messages require more or less intensity of positive feedback. Third, make your feedback clear by avoiding behaviors that might be mistaken as negative feedback. For example, something as simple as innocently stealing a glance at your phone to see what

time it is might unintentionally suggest that you're bored or wish the person would stop speaking. Finally, always provide feedback quickly in response to what the speaker has just said.

Paraphrasing and Clarifying

Active listeners also communicate attention and understanding through saying things after their conversational partners have finished their turns—things that make it clear they were listening. One way to do this is by **paraphrasing**, summarizing others' comments after they have finished ("My read on your message is that . . ." or "You seem to be saying that . . ."). This practice can help you check the accuracy of your understanding during both face-to-face and online encounters. Paraphrasing should be used judiciously, however. Some conversational partners may find paraphrasing annoying if you use it a lot or they view it as contrived. Paraphrasing can also lead to conversational lapses, silences of three seconds or longer that participants perceive as awkward (McLaughlin & Cody, 1982). One reason for such awkward lapses is that paraphrasing does little to

---

Self-Reflection

Recall an encounter in which you were saying something important but the other person gave you negative feedback. How did the feedback affect your communication? Your relationship? Is negative feedback ever appropriate? If so, under which circumstances?

Skills Practice

Responding Online
Responding effectively during online encounters

1. Identify an online interaction that's important.
2. During the exchange, provide your conversational partner with immediate, positive feedback to his or her messages, sending short responses like "I agree!" and attaching positive emoticons.
3. Check your understanding by paraphrasing your partner's longer messages ("My read on your last message is . . .").
4. Seek clarification regarding messages you don't understand ("I'm having trouble understanding— would you mind explaining that a bit more?").

usefully advance the conversational topic forward in new and interesting ways (Heritage & Watson, 1979). To avoid this problem, always couple your paraphrasing with additional comments or questions that usefully build on the previous topic or take the conversation in new directions.

Of course, on some occasions, we simply don't understand what others have said. In such instances, it's perfectly appropriate to respond by seeking clarification rather than paraphrasing, saying, "I'm sorry, but could you explain that again? I want to make sure I understood you correctly." This technique not only helps you clarify the meaning of what you're hearing, it also enables you to communicate your desire to understand the other person.

Recalling

The fifth stage of listening is **recalling**, remembering information after you've received, attended to, understood, and responded to it. As researchers L. Todd Thomas and Timothy Levine (1994) note, recalling is a crucial part of the listening process because we judge the effectiveness of listening based on our ability to accurately recall information after we've listened to it. Indeed, practically every scientific measure of listening uses recall accuracy as evidence of listening effectiveness (Janusik, 2007).

Your recall accuracy varies depending on the situation. When people have no task other than simple memorization, recall accuracy is high (Freides, 1974). But when people are engaged in activities more complicated than straight memorization, recall accuracy plummets. That's because in such cases, we're receiving a lot of information, which

increases the likelihood of perceptual and recall errors. Research on the recall accuracy of criminal eyewitnesses, for instance, has found that people frequently err in their recall of crimes, something most jurors and even the eyewitnesses themselves don't realize (Wells, Lindsay, & Tousignant, 1980). Our recall of interpersonal and relational encounters is not exempt from error. Especially for negative and unpleasant interactions, such as conflicts, we tend to recall our own behavior as positive and constructive and the behavior of others as comparatively negative, regardless of what actually happened (Sillars, Smith, & Koerner, 2010).

How can you enhance your recall ability? One way is to use **mnemonics**, devices that aid memory. For example, when I was an undergraduate at the University of Washington, I delivered pizzas. Many of my deliveries went to the Wallingford neighborhood, a residential area west of campus. Wallingford was different from other neighborhoods because the streets had names instead of numbers: Eastern, Sunnyside, Corliss, Bagley, Meridian, Burke, Wallingford, Densmore, Woodlawn, and Ashworth. No matter how many times my supervisor told me, "No, Woodlawn is *between* Densmore and Ashworth!" I couldn't recall the street order when I was out on a run. So I created a mnemonic. I took the first syllable of each street name, in order from east to west, and created a simple phrase, "Eas-Sun Cor-Bag Mer-Bur Wal-Den Wood-Ash." The phrase was so distinct that it stuck in my mind, and from then on I had no problem locating the streets. The mnemonic was so powerful that even now, nearly 30 years later, I can recall it, even though I live thousands of miles from Seattle and the pizza restaurant for which I delivered no longer exists.

Several other practices can also help you boost your recall ability. Because listening is rooted in both visual and auditory information and memory is enhanced by using all five senses, try bolstering your memory of an interpersonal communication encounter by linking information you've listened to with pleasant or even silly visuals, scents, or sounds. To create visual images of an interpersonal encounter, you could write

> We tend to recall our own behavior as positive and constructive and the behavior of others as comparatively negative, regardless of what actually happened.

Self-Reflection

What's an example of a mnemonic you've created? How did you go about constructing it? Has it helped you more effectively recall important information? If not, what could be done to improve its usefulness?

detailed notes or draw diagrams documenting the contents of a conversation. You could also link a new acquaintance's name with a unique physical feature characterizing him or her. Finally, when you develop mnemonics or notes, review them repeatedly, including reciting them out loud, because repetition aides memory.

LearningCurve
bedfordstmartins.com/ipcandyou

◊ Fashion gurus Stacy London and Clinton Kelly used a variety of listening styles on their show *What Not to Wear.* While it may seem like they listened only to analyze, one of their strengths was their ability to adjust their listening styles depending on the situation.

The Five Functions of Listening

When style gurus Stacy London and Clinton Kelly gave a makeover to a hapless fashion victim on their former hit TLC show, *What Not to Wear*, they didn't just dole out advice. Instead, they spent a lot of time listening. Upon first meeting a new participant, they listened carefully to her story so they could better comprehend where she was coming from. When they thought someone was lying to them, or hiding important fears or feelings, they listened carefully to her tone of voice and wording, trying to discern her inner states. When a participant argumentatively defended a fashion faux pas, Stacy and Clinton listened analytically, looking for ways to attack her reasoning and move her in a different direction. When a guest joyously described her experience, they listened appreciatively—sharing in her happiness. Finally, given the emotional intensity of deconstructing someone's appearance, Stacy and Clinton often listened supportively when a participant broke down in tears.

The different reasons for listening displayed on *What Not to Wear* mirror the **listening functions**, or purposes for listening, we experience daily. Akin to Stacy and Clinton's interactions with participants, our interpersonal encounters are characterized by five common listening functions: to comprehend, to discern, to analyze, to appreciate, and to support.

Listening to Comprehend

Think for a minute about your interpersonal communication class—the course for which this text was assigned. When you're attending class, *why* do you listen to your professor? The answer is so obvious it's silly: you listen so that you can comprehend the information he or she is presenting to you. When you listen for this purpose, you work to accurately interpret and store the information you receive, so you can correctly recall it later. Additional examples of this type of listening include listening to a coworker explain how to use a software application and listening to a prospective landlord explain your contractual obligations if you sign a lease on an apartment.

Listening to Discern

When you listen to discern, you focus on distinguishing specific sounds from each other. The most common form is to listen carefully to someone's vocal tone to assess mood and stress level. For example, if you're concerned that your romantic partner is angry with you, you might listen carefully to the sound of his or her voice rather than the actual words to gauge how upset he or she is.

Listening to Analyze

When you listen to analyze, you carefully evaluate the message you're receiving, and you judge it. For instance, you might analyze your father's neutral comments about his recent medical checkup, listening for signs of worry so you can determine whether he's hiding serious health problems.

Listening to Appreciate

When you listen to appreciate, your goal is simply to enjoy the sounds you're experiencing and then to respond by expressing your appreciation. Common examples include listening to your child excitedly share the story of his Little League home run or listening while a close friend tells a funny story.

Listening to Support

You're making lunch in your apartment one afternoon, when your best friend calls you. You answer only to hear him sobbing uncontrollably. He tells you that he and his girlfriend just broke up because she cheated on him. He says he needs someone to talk to.

Providing comfort to a conversational partner is another common purpose for listening. To provide support through listening, you must suspend judgment—taking in what someone else says without evaluating it, and openly expressing empathy. Examples include comforting a relative after the death of a spouse or responding with a kind e-mail to

> { **An essential part of active listening is skillfully and flexibly adapting your listening purposes to the changing demands of interpersonal encounters.** }

a coworker who sends you a message complaining that her boss just criticized her at a team meeting.

Adapting Your Listening Purpose

The five functions that listening commonly serves are not mutually exclusive. We change between them frequently and fluidly. You might change your purpose for listening even within the same encounter. For example, you're listening with appreciation at a concert when suddenly you realize one of the musicians is out of tune. You might shift to discerning listening (trying to isolate that particular instrument from the others) and ultimately to listening to analyze (trying to assess whether you are in fact correct about its being out of tune). If the musician happens to be a friend of yours, you might even switch to supportive listening following the event, as she openly laments her disastrous performance!

An essential part of active listening is skillfully and flexibly adapting your listening purposes to the changing demands of interpersonal encounters (Bunkers, 2010). To strengthen your ability to adapt your listening purpose, heighten your awareness of the various possible listening functions during your interpersonal encounters. Routinely ask yourself,

---

Self-Reflection

Recall a situation in which you listened the wrong way. For instance, a friend needed you to listen supportively, but you listened to analyze. What led you to make this error? What consequences ensued from your mistake? What can you do in the future to avoid such listening mishaps?

"What is my primary purpose for listening at this moment, in this situation? Do I want to comprehend, discern, analyze, appreciate, or support?" Then adjust your listening accordingly. As you do this, keep in mind that, for some situations, certain approaches to listening may be inappropriate or even unethical, like listening to analyze when a relational partner is seeking emotional support.

> **Your listening style is your habitual pattern of listening behaviors, which reflects your attitudes, beliefs, and predispositions regarding the listening process.**

LearningCurve
bedfordstmartins.com/ipcandyou

Understanding Listening Styles

When Fred Rogers first began hosting his children's show, he intentionally adopted a nonthreatening listening style that put children at ease and helped them feel safe. His listening style reflected his religious practice of contemplative silence, which emphasizes responding empathically to others. While Rogers' trademark listening style has earned ridicule from some quarters of our popular culture, it proved extremely effective in the context of his show and with his chosen audience.

Four Listening Styles

Your **listening style** is your habitual pattern of listening behaviors, which reflects your attitudes, beliefs, and predispositions regarding the listening process (Watson, Barker, & Weaver, 1995). Four different primary listening styles exist (Bodie & Worthington, 2010). **Action-oriented listeners** want brief, to-the-point, and accurate messages from others—information they can then use to make decisions or initiate courses of action. Action-oriented listeners can grow impatient when communicating with people they perceive as disorganized, long-winded, or imprecise in their talk. For example, when faced with an upset spouse, an action-oriented listener wants information

(Left to right) Scott Olson/Getty Images; Blend Images – LWA/Dann Tardif/Getty Images

🜄 Active listeners understand that different situations require different listening styles. For example, what type(s) of listening style(s) would be appropriate in these images? Why?

about what caused the problem, so a solution can be generated. He or she is less interested in hearing elaborate details of the spouse's feelings.

Time-oriented listeners prefer brief and concise encounters. They tend to let others know in advance exactly how much time they have available for each conversation. Time-oriented listeners want to stick to their allotted schedules and often look at clocks, watches, or phones to ensure this is the case (Bodie & Worthington, 2010).

In contrast, **people-oriented listeners** view listening as an opportunity to establish commonalities between themselves and others. When asked to identify the most important part of effective listening, people-oriented listeners cite concern for other people's emotions. Like Fred Rogers, they strive to demonstrate empathy when listening by using positive feedback and offering supportive responses.

Content-oriented listeners prefer to be intellectually challenged by the messages they receive during interpersonal encounters. They often take time to carefully evaluate facts and details before forming an opinion about information they've heard. Of the four listening styles, content-oriented listeners are the most likely to ask speakers clarifying or challenging questions (Bodie & Worthington, 2010).

Most of us use only one or two listening styles in all of our interpersonal interactions (Chesebro, 1999). One study found that 36.1 percent of people reported exclusively using a single listening style across all of their interpersonal encounters; an additional 24.8 percent reported that they never use more than two different styles (Watson et al., 1995). We also resist attempts to switch from our dominant styles, even when those styles are ill-suited to the situation at hand. This can cause others to perceive us as insensitive, inflexible, and even incompetent communicators.

To be an active listener, you have to use all four styles, so you can strategically deploy each of them as needed. For example, in situations where your primary listening function is to provide emotional support—when friends, family members, or romantic partners obviously want to discuss feelings or turn to you for comfort—you should quickly adopt a people-oriented listening style (Barker & Watson, 2000). Studies document that use of a people-oriented listening style substantially boosts others' perceptions of your interpersonal sensitivity (Chesebro, 1999). In such encounters, use of a content-, time-, or action-oriented style would likely be perceived as incompetent. By contrast, if your dominant listening function is to comprehend—for instance, during a training session at work—you'll need to use a content-oriented listening style. Similarly, if you're talking with someone who is running late for an appointment or who has to make a decision quickly, you should use a more time- or action-oriented style. For additional tips on how to improve your active listening, see Table 6.1.

Table 6.1 Active Listening

To be a more active listener, try these strategies:

1. Concentrate on important aspects of encounters and control factors that impede your attention.

2. Communicate your understanding to others in competent and timely ways by providing polite, obvious, appropriate, clear, and quick feedback.

3. Improve your recall abilities by using mnemonics or linking new information to other senses, visuals, or features.

4. Develop an awareness of your primary listening functions in various situations.

5. Practice shifting your listening style quickly, depending on the demands of the encounter.

🔹 Natalie Portman talks with director Darren Aronofsky during the filming of *Black Swan*. Using a content-oriented listening style can be very effective in work situations where your primary goal is to comprehend.

Gender Differences in Listening Styles

Studies have found that women and men differ in their listening-style preferences and practices (Watson et al., 1995). Women are more likely than men to use people-oriented and content-oriented listening styles, and men are more likely to use time-oriented and action-oriented styles. These findings have led researchers to conclude that men (in general) tend to have a task-oriented and hurried approach to listening whereas women perceive listening as an intellectual, emotional, and ultimately relational activity.

Keeping these differences in mind during interpersonal encounters is an important part of active listening. When interacting with men, observe the listening styles they display and adapt your style to match theirs. Don't be surprised if time- or action-oriented styles emerge the most. When conversing with women, follow the same pattern, carefully watching their listening styles and adjusting your style accordingly. Be prepared to quickly shift to more people- or content-oriented styles if needed. But don't automatically assume that just because a person is female or male means that she or he will always listen—or expect you to listen—in certain ways. Take your cue from the actual person you are talking with.

> **Self-Reflection**
>
> Do your preferred listening styles match research on male–female differences? How have your listening styles affected your communication with people of the same gender? The opposite gender?

Culture and Listening Styles

Culture powerfully shapes the use and perception of listening styles. What's considered effective listening by one culture is often perceived as ineffective by others, something you should always keep in mind when communicating with people from other cultures. For example, in individualistic cultures such as the United States and Canada (and particularly in the American workplace), time-oriented and action-oriented listening styles dominate. People often approach conversations with an emphasis on time limits ("I have only 10 minutes to talk"). Many people also feel and express frustration if others don't communicate their ideas efficiently ("Just say it!").

The value that people from individualistic cultures put on time and efficiency—as discussed in Chapter 5—frequently places them at odds with people from other cultures. In collectivistic cultures, people- and content-oriented listening is emphasized. In many East Asian countries, for example, Confucian teachings admonish followers to pay close attention when listening, display sensitivity to others' feelings, and be prepared to assimilate complex information—hallmarks of people- and content-oriented listening styles (Chen & Chung, 1997). Studies have found that students from outside the

United States view Americans as less willing and patient listeners than individuals who come from Africa, Asia, South America, and southern Europe—regions that emphasize people-oriented listening (Wolvin, 1987).

LearningCurve
bedfordstmartins.com/ipcandyou

Preventing Incompetent Listening

No one is a perfect active listener all the time. At one time or another we all make errors during the listening process, fail to identify the right purpose for listening during an interpersonal encounter, or neglect to use the appropriate listening style. In previous sections of this chapter, we discussed ways to avoid such errors. But being an active listener also means systematically avoiding five notoriously incompetent types of listening.

Selective Listening

A colleague stops by your office to chat and shares exciting news: a coworker to whom you're romantically attracted is similarly interested in you. As your thoughts become riveted upon this revelation, the remainder of what he says fades from your awareness, including important information he shares with you about an upcoming project deadline.

Perhaps the greatest challenge to active listening is overcoming **selective listening**, taking in only those bits and pieces of information that are immediately salient during an interpersonal encounter and dismissing the rest. When we selectively listen, we rob ourselves of the opportunity to learn

> **No one is a perfect active listener all the time.**

information from others that may affect important personal or professional outcomes, such as a project deadline.

Selective listening is difficult to avoid because it is the natural result of fluctuating attention and salience. To overcome selective listening, you shouldn't strive to learn how to listen to everything all at once. Instead, seek to slowly and steadily broaden the range of information you can actively attend to during your encounters with others. The best way to do this is by improving your overall level of attention, through practicing the techniques for enhancing attention discussed earlier in this chapter. Through these means, you boost your chances of noticing information that has important short- and long-term consequences for your personal and professional relationships.

> **Self-Reflection**
>
> What personal and professional consequences have you suffered because of your selective listening? What factors led you to selectively listen in those situations? How could you have overcome those factors to listen more actively?

Eavesdropping

In *Wuthering Heights*, Emily Brontë's classic tale of romance and vengeance, a major turning point occurs when Heathcliff eavesdrops on a conversation between his lover Catherine and Nelly, the story's narrator. Heathcliff's interpretation of Catherine's comments cause him to abandon her, setting in motion a tragic series of events that lead to Catherine's death (Brontë, 1995).

We often assume that our conversations occur in isolation and that the people standing, sitting, or walking around us can't hear the exchange. But they can. As sociologist Erving Goffman (1979) noted, the presence of other individuals within the auditory and visual range of a conversation should be considered

NBC/Photofest

⬧ On the television show *30 Rock*, ineffective listening styles are often the cause of frustration for the characters and laughter for the audience. Network executive Jack Donaghy, for example, occasionally becomes so preoccupied with his own ideas that he misses important details when he only selectively listens to Liz Lemon and his other coworkers.

the rule and not the exception. This is the case even with phone conversations, e-mail, and texting. Most cell-phone conversations occur with others in the immediate proximity, and e-mail and texting are no more secure than a postcard.

When people intentionally and systematically set up situations so they can listen to private conversations, they are **eavesdropping** (Goffman, 1979). People eavesdrop for a host of reasons: desire to find out if someone is sharing personally, professionally, or legally incriminating information; suspicion that

others are talking behind their backs; or even simple curiosity. Eavesdropping is both inappropriate and unethical (hence, incompetent) because it robs others of their right to privacy and it disrespects their decision to not share certain information with you. Perhaps not surprisingly, the social norms governing this behavior are powerful. If people believe that you eavesdropped on a conversation, they typically will be upset and angry, and they may threaten reprisals. Eavesdropping can be personally damaging as well. People occasionally say spiteful or hurtful things that they don't really mean, simply to impress others, fit in, or draw attention to themselves. The lesson is clear: don't eavesdrop, no matter how tempting it might be.

Pseudo-Listening

You stayed up late the night before to finish a report, and, when you finally got to bed, one of your kids got sick and kept you up the rest of the night. Now it's the afternoon and you're sitting in a warm and cozy coffeehouse, listening to your friend tell you a story she's already shared with you several times previously. Try as you might, you find yourself fading. But you don't want to embarrass yourself or your friend, so you do your best to play the part of an active listener—maintaining good eye contact, nodding your head, and contributing appropriate responses when needed.

You're engaging in **pseudo-listening**, behaving as if you're paying attention though you're really not. Pseudo-listening is obviously an ineffective way to listen because it prevents us from attending to or understanding information coming from the other person. Thus, we can't recall the encounter later. Pseudo-listening is also somewhat unethical because it's deceptive. To be sure, occasional instances of pseudo-listening to veil fatigue or protect a friend's feelings (such as in our example) are understandable. But if you continually engage in pseudo-listening during your encounters with others, eventually they will realize what's going on and conclude that you're dishonest or disrespectful. Consequently, pseudo-listening should be avoided.

Aggressive Listening

People who engage in **aggressive listening** (also called *ambushing*) attend to what others say solely to find an opportunity to attack their conversational partners. For example, your friend may routinely ask for your opinions regarding fashion and music, but she then disparages your tastes whenever you share them with her.

The personal, interpersonal, and relational costs of aggressive listening are substantial. People who consistently use listening to ambush others typically think less favorably about themselves (Infante & Wigley, 1986), experience lower marital satisfaction (Payne & Sabourin, 1990), and may experience more physical violence in their relationships (Infante, Chandler, & Rudd, 1989).

Some people engage in aggressive listening online. People known as **provocateurs** post messages designed solely as "trolls" (from the fishing technique of trolling) to annoy others. They wait for people to post responses, and then they attack the responses. If the attacks of a provocateur are sophisticated enough, naïve group members may side with him or her against participants who seek to oust the instigator from the group. The result can be a flame war that prompts the site manager to shut down the discussion group—the ultimate "victory" for a provocateur.

If you find yourself habitually listening in an aggressive fashion, combat this type of incompetent listening by discovering and dealing with the root causes of your aggression. Oftentimes, external pressures such as job stress, relationship challenges, or family problems can play a role, so be careful to consider all possible causes and solutions for your behavior. Don't hesitate to seek professional assistance if you feel that it would be helpful. If you're in a personal or professional relationship with someone who uses aggressive listening against you, deal with that person by following the recommendations for addressing verbal aggression outlined in Chapter 7. Limit your interactions when possible, be polite and respectful, and use a people-oriented listening style. Avoid retaliating by using aggressive listening yourself because it will only escalate the aggression.

⬦ The good cop/bad cop scenario is something we have all seen on television and in movies. The "bad cop" succeeds only if the "good cop" listens well enough to draw information out of the intimidated person both are interrogating. The bad cop's aggressive listening style is unlikely to work on its own.

Narcissistic Listening

In Greek mythology, the beautiful nymph Echo falls in love with Narcissus immediately upon seeing him (Bulfinch, 1985). But when she approaches and moves to throw her arms around him, he recoils, telling her that he would rather die than be with her. Heartbroken, Echo flees to the mountains and plots her revenge. She casts a spell on Narcissus, making him fall in love with his own reflected image in a pool. Upon seeing the enchanted image, Narcissus can't tear himself away. He abandons all thought of food and rest and gazes, entranced, at himself—until he finally dies of starvation.

Like its namesake in Greek mythology, **narcissistic listening** is self-absorbed listening: the perpetrator ignores what others have to say and redirects the conversation to him- or herself and his or her own interests. People who engage in narcissistic listening provide positive feedback as long as they are the center of conversational attention, but the moment the topic switches to something other than them, they give negative feedback. In some cases,

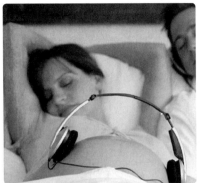  

(Left to right) Bernd Opitz/Getty Images; © Lucidio Studio Inc./Corbis; Somos/Punchstock/Getty Images

🜄 The ability to listen begins to develop well before we are born and serves us throughout our lives.

the negative feedback may be extreme—narcissistic listeners may pout, whine, or even throw tantrums when the conversation switches away from them and onto the other person (Bushman & Baumeister, 1998). To avoid narcissistic listening, allow the conversation to focus on topics other than you and your own interests and offer positive feedback when such topics are discussed.

LearningCurve
bedfordstmartins.com/ipcandyou

Postscript }

We began this chapter with the story of a man who dedicated his life to active listening. Fred Rogers brought his ministerial values of compassion and kindness to the small screen, and through television he touched the lives of millions of children. In addition to establishing the longest-running show in history, he created a safe space in which children felt simultaneously entertained, educated, and affirmed by an adult who genuinely listened to them.

How do you use listening in *your* life? What values underlie your listening? Do you create metaphorical "neighborhoods" through your listening—places in which people feel welcomed and valued? Or, as Eddie Murphy once quipped, do you create places where whenever you "move in, everyone else moves away"?

The PBS soundstage Fred Rogers once strolled through lies abandoned now, just as his famous cardigan hangs empty in a Smithsonian display case. He'll never again "be back when the day is new." Yet the values he espoused will endure as long as people actively, compassionately, and respectfully listen to one another.

Chapter Review

Visit LaunchPad for *Interpersonal Communication and You* to watch brief, illustrative ▣ videos of these terms and to access ☑ LearningCurve. **bedfordstmartins.com/ipcandyou**

KEY TERMS

listening, 113
hearing, 114
receiving, 114
attending, 114
mental bracketing, 116
understanding, 117
short-term memory, 117
long-term memory, 117
responding, 117

feedback, 117
back-channel cues, 118
paraphrasing, 118
recalling, 119
mnemonics, 119
listening functions, 120
listening style, 122
▣ action-oriented listeners, 122
▣ time-oriented listeners, 123

people-oriented listeners, 123
▣ content-oriented listeners, 123
▣ selective listening, 125
eavesdropping, 126
pseudo-listening, 126
▣ aggressive listening, 127
provocateurs, 127
▣ narcissistic listening, 127

CHAPTER ACTIVITIES

1. Generate a list of distractions or "noise" you often face when trying to listen in a variety of situations, such as following instructions, getting directions, listening to a friend complain about his job, and so forth. Then, develop one or two strategies for overcoming each. Together with a small group (or your entire class), discuss more effective ways of attending to messages.

2. On the show *Parks and Recreation* (season three, episode six, "Indianapolis") nurse Ann Perkins misunderstands a conversation with her boyfriend and doesn't realize she was dumped. As her friend Leslie explains, "Here is what happened. Sweet and beautiful Ann has never been dumped before. And Chris is such a positive person that when he broke up with her she just didn't realize it." Write a brief essay on how not having a reference for something (like a breakup) can lead to misunderstandings.

3. In class, work in pairs with someone from a different hometown. Spend about three minutes describing your hometown (i.e., size, population, attractions, unique features, and other details) and then switch with your partner. Do not take notes during the process, but use other means (discussed in the chapter) to remember all the details. When you get home, write down as many of the details as you can recall. Compare notes with your

partner the next class period. As a class, discuss your recall abilities.

4. ▣ Watch the three videos on **action-oriented listeners**, **time-oriented listeners**, and **content-oriented listeners** while reading about listening styles on pages 122–123. Then, write a one-page paper on the listening style that best fits your behavior, answering the following: What style do you use the most? Please provide specific examples to illustrate your understanding of the style. How could you improve your listening skills?

5. During the 2007 Miss Teen USA pageant, Miss Teen South Carolina became a victim of her own selective listening. As she became anxious during her interview, she inappropriately selected information from her stockpile of knowledge and rehearsed answers. (You can see a video of this on YouTube.) In a brief essay or with a small group, share your experiences with selective listening. How has this caused you to communicate inappropriately or to make incorrect decisions?

6. ▣ Watch the three videos on incompetent listening: **narcissistic listening**, **aggressive listening**, and **selective listening**. Then work in groups to create role plays (or your own videos) of eavesdropping and pseudo-listening. Discuss strategies for dealing with all five incompetent listening styles and ways for developing improved active listening skills.

✓ Look for LearningCurve throughout the chapter to help you review.
bedfordstmartins.com/ipcandyou

7 } Communicating Verbally

T he game is pretty near up," George Washington wrote his cousin in 1776.[1] His army had suffered several devastating defeats, and the British had taken New York City. With only 3,000 of his original 20,000 troops remaining, Washington retreated to the Delaware River. There, his troops hunkered down in the snow, sick and fatigued. Ten miles upstream, on the opposing shore, lay the city of Trenton—and a British garrison filled with German "Hessian" mercenaries.

The morning of Christmas Eve, Congressman Benjamin Rush paid Washington a visit, hoping to lift his spirits. During their conversation, Washington furiously scribbled on scraps of paper. Seeing one fall to the floor—and thinking

perhaps they were notes to loved ones—Rush picked it up. He was surprised to see only three words: "Victory or Death." It was Washington's password to his officers for an assault on Trenton.

Washington's plan was audacious and unprecedented: he would launch a surprise attack on Christmas Day. The risks were enormous. With so few men left, if the ploy failed, the war would be lost, and with it, the dream of a free and independent "United States." The odds of success were minimal. Washington's troops would have to navigate the turbulent, ice-packed river with horses, equipment, and weapons, at night, then hike 10 miles through the snow to attack a heavily fortified encampment filled with highly trained troops.

But Washington had a secret motivational weapon. Five days earlier, intellectual and revolutionary Thomas Paine had penned "The

---

[1]Information in this section is adapted from Randall (1998) and Rothbard (1999).

⟡ **Verbal communication opens doorways to shared understanding, intimacy, and enduring relationships.**

Washington Crossing the Delaware River, 25th December 1776, 1851 (oil on canvas) (copy of an original painted in 1848), Leutze, Emanuel Gottlieb (1816–68)/Metropolitan Museum of Art, New York, USA/The Bridgeman Art Library

American Crisis," an essay that opened with the following words:

> These are the times that try men's souls. The summer soldier and the sunshine patriot will, in this crisis, shrink from the service of their country; but he that stands it now, deserves the love and thanks of man and woman. Tyranny, like hell, is not easily conquered; yet we have this consolation with us: the harder the conflict, the more glorious the triumph!

Sensing his soldiers' low morale, and realizing the power of the spoken word to inspire, Washington ordered officers along the riverbank to read Paine's passage out loud to their troops before they embarked. It worked. Uplifted by the impassioned words, the troops braved the crossing without incurring any losses, despite the giant chunks of ice that surged down the river and rammed their boats.

By 4 a.m. the crossing was complete, and the troops began their cold, treacherous journey to Trenton. It took four hours to march the 10 miles.

But when they arrived, they immediately attacked—and caught the sleeping Hessians and their British officers unawares. As they stormed the town, Washington's sleet- and mud-covered troops shouted, "These are the times that try men's souls!"

The battle ended quickly. The Americans suffered only four casualties, whereas 100 Hessians were killed or wounded, over 900 were taken prisoner, and the garrison and all of its weapons and supplies were confiscated. More importantly, a stunning psychological blow had been landed against the British: the "upstart colonists" could fight—and win—after all. In the months that followed, Washington prevailed in a series of similar clashes, ultimately winning the war itself and ensuring the survival of the fledgling nation.

On Christmas Day 1776, a beleaguered general put his faith in the power of verbal communication to motivate forlorn troops to cross an impassable river and attack an impregnable fortress. Centuries later, millions of people live, learn, and love in a country that exists because of those words.

O ur first spoken word is a first we don't even remember. But it's celebrated by the people around us, who recognize in that fleeting moment the dawning of a life filled with language. By age 6, we learn more than 15 new words a day, and our vocabularies have grown to anywhere between 8,000 and 14,000 words (Cole & Cole, 1989). As we master our native tongues, we discover the power of verbal communication. Through exchanging words with others via text, online, over the phone, and face-to-face, we share ideas, influence others, and make relationship choices. We also learn that language can serve both constructive and destructive ends. Used constructively, verbal communication opens doorways to shared understanding, intimacy, and enduring relationships. Used destructively, verbal communication can mislead and injure others and damage our relationships.

In this chapter, we examine the nature and role of verbal communication in our lives. You'll learn:

- The defining characteristics of language
- The important functions that verbal communication serves in our interpersonal encounters and relationships

- Principles you can apply to use verbal communication more cooperatively
- The behaviors and actions that undermine cooperative verbal communication—and what can be done about them

Characteristics of Verbal Communication

When we think of what it means to communicate, what often leaps to mind is the exchange of spoken or written language with others during interactions, known as **verbal communication**. Across any given day, we use words to communicate in various face-to-face or mediated contexts. During each of these encounters, we tailor our language in creative ways, depending on whom we're speaking with. We shift grammar, word choices, and sometimes even the entire language itself—for example, firing off a Spanish text message to one friend and an English text to another.

Because verbal communication is defined by our use of language, the first step toward improving our verbal communication is to deepen our understanding of language.

> **Self-Reflection**
>
> How is the language that you use different when talking with professors, versus when talking to your best friend or romantic partner? Which type of language makes you feel more comfortable or close? What does this tell you about the relationship between language and intimacy?

Language Is Symbolic

Take a quick look around you. You'll likely see a wealth of images: from this book to, perhaps, your roommate or romantic partner. You might experience thoughts and emotions related to what you're seeing—memories of your roommate asking to borrow

Bloomberg via Getty Images

💧 **Whether face-to-face or online, we exchange verbal communication daily in our interactions with others.**

your car or feelings of love toward your partner. Now imagine communicating all of this to others. To do so, you need words to represent these things: *roommate*, *borrow*, *car*, *love*, and so forth. Whenever we use items to represent other things, they are considered **symbols**. In verbal communication, words are the primary symbols that we use to represent people, objects, events, and ideas (Foss, Foss, & Trapp, 1991).

All languages are basically collections of symbols in the form of words that allow us to communicate with one another. When we agree with others on the meanings of words, we communicate easily. Your friend probably knows exactly what you mean by the word *roommate*, so when you use it, misunderstanding is unlikely. But some words have several possible meanings, making confusion possible. For instance, in English, the word *table* might mean a piece of furniture, an element in a textbook, or a verb referring to the need to end talk ("Let's table this discussion until our next meeting"). For words that have multiple meanings, we rely on the surrounding context to help clarify meaning. If you're in a classroom and the

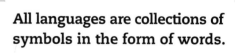

{ **All languages are collections of symbols in the form of words.** }

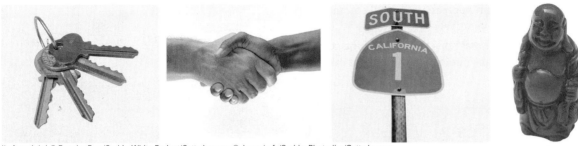

(Left to right) © Royalty-Free/Corbis; White Packert/Getty Images; © Joson/zefa/Corbis; Photodisc/Getty Images

💧 We use words as symbols to represent objects, actions, people, places, and ideas.

professor says, "Turn to Table 3 on page 47," you aren't likely to search the room for furniture.

Language Is Governed by Rules

When we use language, we follow rules. Rules govern the meaning of words, the way we arrange words into phrases and sentences, and the order in which we exchange words with others during conversations. **Constitutive rules** define word meaning: they tell us which words represent which objects (Searle, 1965). For example, a constitutive rule in the English language is: "The word *dog* refers to a domestic canine." Whenever you learn the vocabulary of a language—words and their corresponding meanings—you're learning the constitutive rules for that language.

Regulative rules govern how we use language when we verbally communicate. They're the traffic laws controlling language use. Regulative rules guide everything from spelling ("i before e except after c") to sentence structure ("The article *the* or *a* must come before the noun *dog*") to conversation ("If someone asks you a question, you should answer").

To communicate competently, you must understand and follow the constitutive and regulative rules governing the language you're using. If you don't know which words represent which meanings (constitutive rules), you can't send clear messages to others or understand messages delivered by others. Likewise, without knowing how to form a grammatically correct sentence and when to say particular things (regulative rules), you can't communicate clearly with others or accurately interpret their messages to you.

Language Is Flexible

Although all languages have constitutive and regulative rules, people often bend those rules. Partners in close relationships, for example, often create **personal idioms**—words and phrases that have unique meanings to them (Bell, Buerkel-Rothfuss, & Gore, 1987). One study found that the average romantic couple had created more than a half dozen idioms, the most common being nicknames such as "Honeybear" or "Pookie." When large groups of people share creative variations on language rules, those variations are called **dialects** (Gleason, 1989). A dialect may include unique phrases, words, and pronunciations (what we call *accents*). Dialects can be shared by people living in a certain region, people with a common socioeconomic status, or people of similar ethnic or religious ancestry (Chen & Starosta, 2005).

Most people prefer their own dialect. Communication scholar Jesse Delia (1972) conducted a study that asked people to form impressions of others based solely on voice recordings of dialects. Listeners formed positive impressions of persons who used dialects similar to their own, and more negative impressions of those with dissimilar dialects. Since dialects powerfully influence our perceptions of others, you should be aware of how they may affect your own communication. Resist making negative or stereotypical judgments about others who speak with dialects different from your own.

Language Is Cultural

Languages and cultures are fused in fundamental ways. Language is the set of symbols that members of a

Self-Quiz

Test Your Knowledge of American Dialects
Each of the following phrases is common to a specific U.S. dialect.
See if you know what each one means and where it is from.

1. "Are you packing a card?"

2. "Check out the second growth."

3. "Mind if I use your commode?"

4. "Hey, that guy just budged!"

5. "Is there a bubbler nearby?"

6. "You're blocking my dooryard."

7. "He's just a leafer."

8. "Let's sit in the parlor."

9. "It's in the locker."

Note: Information in this *Self-Quiz* was obtained from "Regional vocabularies of American English" (n.d.).

Answers: (1) Union membership, Pacific Northwest. (2) Timber that has grown back on a previously harvested area, **Pacific Northwest**. (3) Bathroom, Deep South. (4) Cut in line, eastern Wisconsin and Minnesota. (5) Drinking fountain, eastern Wisconsin. (6) Driveway, Maine and northern New England. (7) Tourist traveling to see the seasonal foliage, northern New England. (8) Living room, Delaware Valley. (9) Closet, New Orleans.

culture create to communicate their thoughts, beliefs, attitudes, and values with one another. Once created, a language is used to bolster a sense of cultural identity and connectedness (Whorf, 1952). Thus, languages both reflect the cultures that created them and enable people to perpetuate those cultures, while also sustaining a sense of collective identity—for example, "We are Japanese" or "We are Kenyans."

Moreover, people use language differently depending on the extent to which they assume that others share their cultural beliefs, attitudes, and values. Recall from Chapter 5 that some cultures are *high-context cultures*, in which people presume that listeners share extensive knowledge in common with them. As a result, they don't feel a need to provide a lot of explicit information to gain listeners' understanding. In contrast, in *low-context cultures*, people tend *not* to presume that listeners share their beliefs, attitudes,

> **Self-Reflection**
> What language do you consider your native tongue? In what ways does this language connect you culturally to those who share it? How does it distance you from those who don't speak it?

and values, so they tailor their verbal communication to be informative, clear, and direct (Hall & Hall, 1987). Consider how this dichotomy affected a friend of mine, communication professor Naomi Kagawa, when she first came to the United States from Japan. In Japan (a high-context culture), when undesirable requests are received, respondents often reject them using words equivalent to "OK" or "sure," accompanied by subtle vocal tones that *imply* "no." Requesters and rejecters—informed by their shared knowledge of Japanese customs—recognize that such seeming assents are actually rejections. In the United States (a low-context culture), people typically don't presume that others share similar knowledge and beliefs, so they "spell things

> **Once created, a language is used to bolster a sense of cultural identity and connectedness.**

out" much more explicitly. When people reject requests, they may come right out and say "no," then provide an explanation of why they can't grant the request. Needless to say, Naomi—and those with whom she interacted upon first arriving in the States—experienced much confusion. She rejected unwanted requests by saying "OK," only to find that people thought she was consenting rather than refusing!

Language Evolves

Each year, the American Dialect Society selects a "Word of the Year." Recent winners include *tweet*, a "short, timely message sent via the Twitter.com service," and *app*, "an abbreviated form of application, a software program for a computer or phone operating system." Even the *Oxford English Dictionary*—the resource that defines the English language—annually announces what new terms have officially been added to the English vocabulary.

Many people view language as fixed. But in fact, language constantly changes. A particular language's constitutive rules—which define the meanings of words—may shift. As time passes and technology changes, people add new words to their language and discard old ones. Sometimes people create new phrases, such as *helicopter parent*, that eventually see wide use. Other times, speakers of a language borrow

🔹 As technology changes, we add new words to our vocabulary, such as *iPad* and *app*. Meanwhile, other words, such as *tablet* and *tweet*, may become associated with new meanings.

words and phrases from other languages and incorporate them into their own.

A language's regulative rules also change. When you learned to speak and write English, for example, you probably were taught that *they* is inappropriate as a singular pronoun. But before the 1850s, people commonly used *they* as the singular pronoun for individuals whose gender was unknown—for example, "the owner went out to the stables, where *they* fed the horses" (Spender, 1990). In 1850, male grammarians petitioned the British Parliament to pass a law declaring that all gender-indeterminate references be labeled *he* instead of *they* (Spender, 1990). Since that time, teachers of English worldwide have taught their students that *they* used as a singular pronoun is "not proper."

LearningCurve
bedfordstmartins.com/ipcandyou

Functions of Verbal Communication

He was crowned "Sportsman of the Century" by *Sports Illustrated*, and "Sports Personality of the Century" by the BBC.[2] He is considered by many to be the greatest boxer of all time, a fact reflected in his nickname, "The Greatest." He certainly was the most verbal. Muhammad Ali made a name for himself early in his career by poetically boasting about his abilities and trash-talking his opponents. "Ali was just as verbal outside of the boxing ring. Early in his professional career, he embraced Islam, and subsequently abandoned his birth name of Cassius Clay because the surname came from his ancestors' slave owners. Years before public sentiment joined him, Ali spoke out repeatedly against the Vietnam War. His refusal to participate in the military draft cost him both his world title and his boxing license (both of which were eventually reinstated). Years later, he continues to be outspoken—on behalf of humanitarian causes. His

---

[2]The information that follows is adapted from Hauser (2006).

work with UN hunger relief organizations has helped feed tens of millions of people; he was a UN Messenger of Peace and a recipient of the Presidential Medal of Freedom. Whether in the boxing ring or on a charity mission, he has used his prowess with verbal communication to achieve his goals and dreams.

Similar to Muhammad Ali, we all use verbal communication to serve many different functions in our daily lives. Let's examine six of the most important of these, all of which strongly influence our interpersonal communication and relationships.

Sharing Meaning

The most obvious function verbal communication serves is enabling us to share meanings with others during interpersonal encounters. When you use language to verbally communicate, you share two kinds of meanings. The first is the literal meaning of your words, as agreed on by members of your culture, known as **denotative meaning**. Denotative meaning is what you find in dictionaries—for example, the word *bear* means "any of a family (Ursidae of the order Carnivora) of large heavy mammals of America and Eurasia that have long shaggy hair" (*Merriam-Webster Dictionary*, 2011).

But when we verbally communicate, we also exchange **connotative meaning**: additional understandings of a word's meaning based on the situation and the knowledge we and our communication partners share. Connotative meaning is implied, suggested, or hinted at by the words you choose while communicating with others. Say, for example, that your romantic partner has a large stuffed teddy bear that, despite its weathered and worn appearance, is your partner's most prized childhood possession. To convey your love and adoration for your partner, you might say, "You're *my* big ugly bear." In doing so, you

> **Connotative meaning is implied, suggested, or hinted at by the words you choose while communicating with others.**

◊ Muhammad Ali's verbal communication skills have served important functions throughout his life, whether intimidating opponents or attracting supporters to his causes.

AP Photo/Phil Sandlin

certainly don't mean that your lover is big, ugly, or bearlike in appearance! Instead, you rely on your partner understanding your implied link to his or her treasured object (the connotative meaning). Relationship intimacy plays a major role in shaping how we use and interpret connotative meanings while communicating with others (Hall, 1997a): people who know each other extremely well can convey connotative meanings accurately to one another.

Shaping Thought

In addition to enabling us to share meaning during interpersonal encounters, verbal communication also shapes our thoughts and perceptions of reality. Consider an encounter I had at a family gathering. My 6-year-old niece told me that a female neighbor of hers had helped several children escape a house fire. When I commended the neighbor's heroism, my niece corrected me. "Girls can't be *heroes*," she scolded. "Only boys can be *heroes*!" In talking with her further, I discovered she knew of no word representing "brave woman." Her only exposure to *heroine* was through her mother's romantic novels. Not knowing a word for "female bravery," she considered the concept unfathomable: "The neighbor lady wasn't a hero, she just saved the kids."

The idea that language shapes how we think about things was first suggested by researcher Edward Sapir, who conducted an intensive study of Native American languages in the early 1900s. Sapir argued that, because language is our primary means of sharing meaning with others, it powerfully affects how we perceive others and our relationships with them (Gumperz & Levinson, 1996). Almost 50 years later, Benjamin Lee Whorf expanded on Sapir's ideas in what has become known as the Sapir-Whorf Hypothesis. Whorf argued that we cannot conceive of that for which we lack a vocabulary—that language quite literally defines the boundaries of our thinking. This view is known as **linguistic determinism**. As contemporary scholars note, linguistic determinism suggests that our ability to think is "at the mercy" of language (Gumperz & Levinson, 1996). We are mentally "constrained" by language to only think certain thoughts, and we cannot interpret the world in neutral ways because we always see the world through the lens of our languages.

Both Sapir and Whorf also recognized the dramatic impact that culture has on language. Because language determines our thoughts, and different people from different cultures use different languages, Sapir and Whorf agreed that people from different cultures would perceive and think about the world in very different ways, an effect known as **linguistic relativity**.

> ### Self-Reflection
>
> Think about the vocabulary you inherited from your culture for thinking and talking about relationships. What terms exist for describing serious romantic involvements, casual relationships that are sexual, and relationships that are purely platonic? How do these various terms shape your thinking about these relationships?

Naming

A third important function of verbal communication is **naming**—that is, creating linguistic symbols for objects. The process of naming is one of humankind's most profound and unique abilities (Spender, 1984). When we name people, places, objects, and ideas, we create symbols that represent them. We then use these symbols during our interactions with others to communicate meaning about these things. Because of the powerful impact language exerts on our thoughts, the decisions we make about what to name things ultimately determine not just the meanings we exchange but also our perceptions of the people, places, and objects we communicate about. This was why Muhammad Ali decided to abandon his birth name of Cassius Clay. He recognized that our names are *the* most powerful symbols that define who we are throughout our lives, and he wanted a name that represented his Islamic faith while also renouncing the surname of someone who had, years earlier, enslaved his forebears.

As the Ali example suggests, the issue of naming is especially potent for people who face historical and cultural prejudice, given that others outside the group often label them with derogatory names. Consider the case of gays and lesbians. For many years, gays and lesbians were referred to as "homosexual." But, as scholar Julia Wood (1998) notes, many people shortened "homosexual" to "homo" and used the new term as an insult. In response, lesbian and gay activists in the 1960s renamed themselves "gay." This move also triggered disputes, however. Antigay activists protested the use of a term that traditionally meant "joyous and lively." Some lesbian activists argued that "gay" meant only men and was therefore exclusionary to women. Many straight people began using "gay" as an insult in the same manner as earlier epithets. In the 2000s, the inclusive label of "LGBTQ" (lesbian, gay, bisexual, transgendered, queer) was created to embrace the entire community. But this name still doesn't adequately represent many people's self-impressions. One study identified over a dozen different names that individuals chose for their sexual orientation and gender identity, including "pansexual," "omnisexual," and "same-gender loving/SGL" (Morrison & McCornack, 2011). Given the way positive names have been turned to negative in the past, some people reject names for nonstraight sexual orientations altogether. As one study respondent put it, "I don't use labels—I'm not a can of soup!" (Morrison & McCornack, 2011).

⬧ We see the world through the lens of our language.

⬧ Yet different people from different cultures use different languages.

Performing Actions

A fourth function of verbal communication is that it enables us to take action. We make requests, issue invitations, deliver commands, or even taunt—as Ali did to his competitors. We also try to influence others' behaviors. We want our listeners to grant our requests, accept our invitations, obey our commands, or suffer from our curses. The actions that we perform with language are called **speech acts** (Searle, 1969). (See Table 7.1 on page 140 for types of speech acts.)

During interpersonal encounters, the structure of our back-and-forth exchange is based on the speech acts we perform (Jacobs, 1994; Levinson, 1985). When your professor asks you a question, how do you know what to do next? You recognize that the words she has spoken constitute a "question," and you realize that an "answer" is expected as the relevant response. Similarly, when your best friend text-messages you and inquires, "Can I borrow your car tonight?" you immediately recognize his message as a "request." You also understand that two speech acts are possible as relevant responses: "granting" his request ("no problem") or "rejecting" it ("I don't think so").

Crafting Conversations

A fifth function served by language is that it allows us to craft conversations. Language meanings, thoughts, names, and acts don't happen in the abstract; they occur within conversations. Although each of us intuitively knows what a conversation is, scholars suggest four characteristics fundamental to conversation (Nofsinger, 1999). First, conversations are *interactive*. At least two people must participate in the exchange for it to count as a conversation, and participants must take turns exchanging messages.

Second, conversations are locally managed. *Local management* means that we make decisions regarding who gets to speak when, and for how long, each time we exchange turns. This makes conversation different from other verbal exchanges such as debate, in which the order and length of turns are decided before the event begins, and drama, in which people speak words that have been written down in advance.

Third, conversation is *universal*. Conversation forms the foundation for most forms of interpersonal communication and for social organization generally. Our relationships and our places in society are created and maintained through conversations.

Fourth, conversations often adhere to *scripts*—rigidly structured patterns of talk. This is especially true in first encounters, when you are trying to reduce other people's uncertainty. Communication researcher Kathy Kellermann (1991) conducted several studies looking at the first conversations of college students and found that 95 percent of the topic changes

Table 7.1 **Types of Speech Acts**

Act	Function	Forms	Example
Representative	Commits the speaker to the truth of what has been said	Assertions, Conclusions	"It sure is a beautiful day."
Directive	Attempts to get listeners to do things	Questions, Requests, Commands	"Can you loan me five dollars?"
Commissive	Commits speakers to future action	Promises, Threats	"I will always love you, no matter what happens."
Expressive	Conveys a psychological or emotional state that the speaker is experiencing	Thanks, Apologies, Congratulations	"Thank you so much for the wonderful gift!"
Declarative	Produces dramatic, observable effects	Marriage Pronouncements, Firing Declarations	"From this point onward, you are no longer an employee of this organization."

Note: The information in this table is adapted from Searle (1976).

followed the same pattern regardless of gender, age, race, or geographic region. This suggests that a critical aspect of appropriately constructing conversations is grasping and following relevant conversational scripts.

Does the fact that we frequently use scripts to guide our conversations mean this type of communication is inauthentic? If you expect more from an exchange than a prepackaged response, scripted communication may strike you as such. However, communication scripts allow us to relevantly *and* efficiently exchange greetings, respond to simple questions and answers, trade pleasantries, and get to know people in a preliminary fashion without putting much active thought into our communication. This saves us from mental exertion and allows us to focus our energy on more involved or important interpersonal encounters.

Managing Relationships

Verbal communication's final, and arguably most profound, function in our lives is to help us manage our relationships. We use language to create relationships by declaring powerful, intimate feelings to others: "You are beautiful!" or "You are the best friend I could ever have." Verbal communication is the principal means through which we maintain our ongoing relationships with lovers, family members, friends, and coworkers (Stafford, 2011). For example, romantic partners who verbally communicate frequently with each other, and with their partners' friends and families, experience less uncertainty in their relationships and are not as likely to break up as those who verbally communicate less often (Parks, 2007). Finally, most of the heartbreaks we'll experience in our lives are preceded by verbal messages that state, in one form or another, "It's over." We'll discuss more about how we forge, maintain, and end our relationships in Chapters 10 through 12.

LearningCurve
bedfordstmartins.com/ipcandyou

Cooperative Verbal Communication

Eager to connect with your teenage son, you ask him how his day was when he arrives home from school. But you get only a grunted "Fine" in return, as he

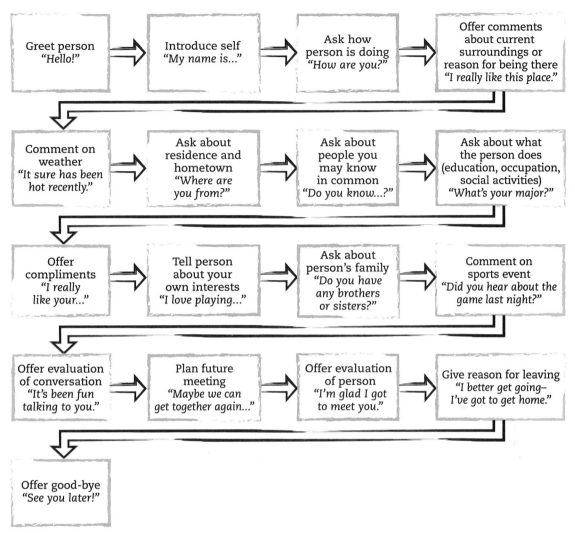

⬥ Figure 7.1 **Conversational Pattern**

quickly disappears into his room to play video games. You invite your romantic partner over for dinner, excited to demonstrate a new recipe. But when you query your partner's opinion of the dish, the response is "It's interesting." You text your best friend, asking for her feedback on an in-class presentation you gave earlier that day. She responds, "You talked way too fast!"

Although these examples seem widely disparate, they share an underlying commonality: people failing to verbally communicate in a fully cooperative fashion. To understand how these messages are

uncooperative, consider their cooperative counterparts. Your son tells you, "It was all right—I didn't do as well on my chem test as I wanted, but I got an A on my history report." Your partner says, "It's good, but I think it'd be even better with a little more salt." Your friend's text message reads, "It went well, but I thought it could have been presented a little slower."

When you use **cooperative verbal communication**, you produce messages that have three characteristics. First, you speak in ways that others can easily understand, using language that is informative, honest,

◌ Oral storytelling is an ancient art, one that creates and passes histories and mythologies down from generation to generation. Through blogs and podcasts, this tradition continues to take on new forms.

relevant, and clear. Second, you take active ownership for what you're saying by using "I" language. Third, you make others feel included rather than excluded—for example, through the use of "we."

Understandable Messages

In his exploration of language and meaning, philosopher Paul Grice noted that cooperative interactions rest on our ability to tailor our verbal communication so others can understand us. To produce understandable messages, we have to abide by the **Cooperative Principle**: making our conversational contributions as *informative, honest, relevant*, and *clear* as is required, given the purposes of the encounters in which we're involved (Grice, 1989).

Being aware of situational characteristics is critical to applying the Cooperative Principle. For example, while we're ethically bound to share important information with others, this doesn't mean we

{ **Cooperative interactions rest on our ability to tailor our verbal communication so that others can understand us.** }

always should. Suppose a friend discloses a confidential secret to you and your sibling later asks you to reveal it. In this case, it would be unethical to share this information without your friend's permission.

Being Informative

According to Grice (1989), being informative during interpersonal encounters means two things. First, you should present all of the information that is relevant and appropriate to share, given the situation. When a coworker passes you in the hallway and greets you with a quick "How's it going?" the situation requires that you provide little information in return—"Great! How are you?" The same question asked by a concerned friend during a personal crisis creates very different demands; your friend likely wants a detailed accounting of your thoughts and feelings.

Second, you want to avoid being *too* informative—that is, disclosing information that isn't appropriate or important in a particular situation. A detailed description of your personal woes ("I haven't been sleeping well lately, and my cat is sick . . .") in response to your colleague's quick "How's it going?" query would likely be perceived as inappropriate and even strange.

The responsibility to be informative overlaps with the responsibility to be ethical. To be a cooperative

◌ Practicing the Cooperative Principle is important in our relationships with coworkers, with whom information often needs to be shared in a timely and professional manner. This is especially relevant when communicating via e-mail, where nonverbal cues, such as vocal tone and gestures, are not possible.

verbal communicator, you must share information with others that has important personal and relational implications for them. To illustrate, if you discover that your friend's spouse is having an affair, you're ethically obligated to disclose this information if your friend asks you about it.

Self-Reflection

Recall an encounter where you possessed important information but knew that disclosing it would be personally or relationally problematic. What did you do? How did your decision impact your relationship? Was your choice ethical? Based on your experience, is it always cooperative to disclose important information?

Being Honest

Honesty is the single most important characteristic of cooperative verbal communication because other people count on the fact that the information you share with them is truthful (Grice, 1989). Honesty means not sharing information that you're uncertain about and not disclosing information that you know is false. When you are dishonest in your verbal communication, you violate standards for ethical behavior, and you lead others to believe false things (Jacobs, Dawson, & Brashers, 1996). For example, if you assure your romantic partner that your feelings haven't changed when in fact they have, you give your partner false hope about your future together. You also lay the groundwork for your partner to make continued investments in a relationship that you know is already doomed.

Being Relevant

Relevance means making your conversational contributions responsive to what others have said. When people ask you questions, you provide answers. When they make requests, you grant or reject their requests. When certain topics arise in the conversation, you tie your contributions to that topic. During conversations, you stick with relevant topics and avoid those that aren't. Dodging questions or abruptly changing topics

is uncooperative, and in some instances, others may see it as an attempt at deception—especially if you change topics to avoid discussing something you want to keep hidden (McCornack, 2008).

Being Clear

Using clear language means presenting information in a straightforward fashion rather than framing it in obscure or ambiguous terms. For example, telling a partner that you like a recipe but that it needs more salt is easier to understand than veiling your meaning by vaguely saying, "It's interesting." But note that using clear language doesn't mean being brutally frank or dumping offensive and hurtful information on others. Competent interpersonal communicators always consider others' feelings when designing their messages. When information is important and relevant to disclose, choose your words carefully to be both respectful *and* clear, so that others won't misconstrue your intended meaning.

Dealing with Misunderstanding

Of course, just because you use informative, honest, relevant, and clear language doesn't guarantee that you will be understood by others. When one person misperceives another's verbally expressed thoughts, feelings, or beliefs, **misunderstanding** occurs. Misunderstanding most commonly results from a failure to actively listen. Recall, for example, our discussion of action-oriented listeners in Chapter 6. Action-oriented listeners often become impatient with others while listening and frequently jump ahead to finish other people's (presumed) points (Watson, Barker, & Weaver, 1995). This listening style can lead them to misunderstand others' messages. To overcome this source of misunderstanding, practice the active listening skills described in Chapter 6.

Misunderstanding occurs frequently online, owing to the lack of nonverbal cues to help clarify meaning. One study found that 27.2 percent of respondents agreed that e-mail is likely to result in miscommunication of intent, and 53.6 percent agreed that it is relatively easy to misinterpret an e-mail message (Rainey, 2000). The tendency to misunderstand communication online is so prevalent that

Brand X Pictures/Punchstock/Getty Images

⬥ One downside of our frequent online communication is that it is easy to misunderstand others' messages, often mistaking them as ruder or less clear than intended. If you need a message to be error-free, considering delivering it in person or over the phone.

scholars suggest the following practices: *If a particular message absolutely must be error-free or if its content is controversial, don't use e-mail or text messaging to communicate it.* Whenever possible, conduct high-stakes encounters face-to-face. Finally, never use e-mails, posts, or texts for sensitive actions such as professional reprimands or dismissals, or relationship breakups (Rainey, 2000).

> ### Self-Reflection
> Recall an online encounter in which you thought you understood someone's e-mail, text message, or post, then later found out you were wrong. How did you discover that your impression was mistaken? What could you have done differently to avoid the misunderstanding?

Using "I" Language

It's the biggest intramural basketball game of the year, and your team is down by a point with five seconds left when your teammate is fouled. Stepping to the line for two free throws and a chance to win the game, she misses both, and your team loses. As you leave the court, you angrily snap at her, "You really let us down!"

The second key to cooperative verbal communication is taking ownership of the things you say to others, especially in situations where you're expressing negative feelings or criticism. You can do this by avoiding **"you" language**, phrases that place the focus of attention and blame on other people, such as "*You let us down.*" Instead, rearrange your statements so that you use **"I" language**, phrases that emphasize ownership of your feelings, opinions, and beliefs (see Table 7.2). The difference between "I" and "you" may strike you as minor, but it actually has powerful effects: "I" language is less likely to trigger defensiveness on the part of your listeners than "you" language (Kubany, Richard, Bauer, & Muraoka, 1992). "I" language creates a clearer impression on listeners that you're responsible for what you're saying and that you're expressing your own perceptions rather than stating unquestionable truths.

Using "We" Language

It's Thursday night, and you're standing in line waiting to get into a club. In front of you are two couples, and you can't help but overhear their conversations. As you listen, you notice an interesting difference in their verbal communication. One couple expresses everything in terms of "I" and "you"—"What do you want to do later tonight?" "I don't know, but I'm hungry, so I'll probably get something to eat." The other couple consistently uses "we"—"What should we do later?" "Why don't we get something to eat?"

What effect does this simple difference in pronoun usage have on your impressions of the two couples? If you perceive the couple using "we" as being closer than the couple using "I" and "you," you would be right. "We" is a common way people signal their closeness (Dreyer, Dreyer, & Davis, 1987). Couples who use **"we" language**—wordings that emphasize inclusion—tend to be more satisfied with their relationships than those who routinely rely on "I" and "you" messages (Honeycutt, 1999).

Table 7.2 "You" Language versus "I" Language

"You" Language	"I" Language
You make me so angry!	I'm feeling so angry!
You totally messed things up.	I feel like things are totally messed up.
You need to do a better job.	I think this job needs to be done better.
You really hurt my feelings.	I'm feeling really hurt.
You never pay any attention to me.	I feel like I never get any attention.

An important part of cooperative verbal communication is using "we" language to express your connection to others; "we" language helps us bolster feelings of connection and similarity with not only romantic partners but also anyone to whom we want to signal a collaborative relationship. When I went through my training to become a certified yoga instructor, part of the instruction was to replace the use of "you" with "we" and "let's" during in-class verbal cueing of moves. Rather than saying, "You should lunge forward with your left leg" or "I want you to step forward left," we were taught to say, "*Let's* step forward with *our* left legs." After I implemented "we" language in my yoga classes, my students repeatedly commented on how they liked the "more personal" and "inclusive" nature of my verbal cueing.

Gender and Cooperative Verbal Communication

Powerful stereotypes exist regarding what men and women value in verbal communication. These stereotypes suggest that men appreciate informative, honest, relevant, and clear language more than women do. In Western cultures, many people believe that men communicate in a clear and straightforward fashion and that women are more indirect and wordy (Tannen, 1990). These stereotypes are reinforced powerfully through television, in programs in which female characters often use more polite language than men ("I'm *sorry* to bother you . . ."), more uncertain phrases ("I *suppose* . . ."), and more flowery adjectives ("that's *silly*," "oh, how *beautiful*"), and male characters fill their language with action verbs ("let's *get a move on!*") (Mulac, Bradac, & Mann, 1985).

Skills Practice

Cooperative Language Online

Using cooperative language during an important online interaction

1. Identify an important online encounter.
2. Create a rough draft of the message you wish to send.
3. Check that the language you've used is fully informative, honest, relevant, and clear.
4. Use "I" language for all comments that are negative or critical.
5. Use "we" language throughout the message, where appropriate.
6. Send the message.

Richard Foreman/© FOX/Courtesy Everett Collection

◊ On the television show *Bones*, Dr. Temperance Brennan (Emily Deschanel) is so direct and concise, she often accidentally offends those around her. Dr. Lance Sweets (John Francis Daley), in contrast, uses more indirect language and questions so that people must infer his actual meaning. How do these differences compare to common stereotypes about the ways in which men and women communicate?

But research suggests that when it comes to language, men and women are more similar than different. For example, data from 165 studies involving nearly a million and a half subjects found that women do not use more vague and wordy verbal communication than men (Canary & Hause, 1993). The primary determinant of whether people's language is clear and concise or vague and wordy is not gender but whether the encounter is competitive or collaborative (Fisher, 1983). Both women and men use clear and concise language in competitive interpersonal encounters, such as when arguing with a family member or debating a project proposal in a work meeting. Additionally, they use comparatively vaguer and wordier language during collaborative encounters, such as eating lunch with a friend or relaxing in the evening with a spouse.

LearningCurve
bedfordstmartins.com/ipcandyou

Barriers to Cooperative Verbal Communication

When used cooperatively, language can clarify understandings, build relationships, and bring us closer to others. But language also has the capacity to create divisions and damage relationships. Some people use verbal communication to defensively lash out at others, or intentionally deceive them. Others are filled with fear and anxiety about interacting and therefore do not speak at all. In this section, we explore the darker side of verbal communication by looking at four common barriers to cooperative verbal communication: communication apprehension, defensive communication, verbal aggression, and deception.

Communication Apprehension

Some people experience **communication apprehension**, fear or anxiety associated with interaction that keeps them from being able to communicate cooperatively (Daly, McCroskey, Ayres, Hopf, & Ayres, 2004). People with high levels of communication apprehension experience intense discomfort while talking with others and therefore have difficulty forging productive relationships. Such individuals also commonly experience physical symptoms such as nervous stomach, dry mouth, sweating, increased blood pressure and heart rate, mental disorganization, and shakiness (McCroskey & Richmond, 1987).

Most of us experience communication apprehension at some points in our lives. The key to overcoming it is to develop **communication plans**—mental maps that describe exactly how communication encounters will unfold—*prior* to interacting in the situations or with the people or types of people that cause your apprehension. Communication plans have two elements. The first is *plan actions*, the "moves" you think you'll perform in an encounter that causes you anxiety. Here, you map out in advance the topics you will talk about, the messages

{ **Language also has the capacity to create divisions and damage relationships.** }

you will say in relation to these topics, and the physical behaviors you'll demonstrate.

The second part of a communication plan is *plan contingencies*, the messages you think your communication partner or partners will say during the encounter and how you will respond. To develop plan contingencies, think about the topics your partner will likely talk about, the messages he or she will likely present, his or her reaction to your communication, and your response to your partner's messages and behaviors.

Skills Practice

Overcoming Apprehension
Creating communication plans to overcome communication apprehension

1. Think of a situation or person that triggers communication apprehension.
2. Envision yourself interacting in this situation or with this person.
3. List plan actions: topics you will discuss and messages you will present.
4. List plan contingencies: events that might happen during the encounter, things the other person will likely say and do, and your responses.
5. Implement your plan the next time you communicate in that situation or with that person.

When you implement your communication plan during an encounter that causes you apprehension, the experience is akin to playing chess. While you're communicating, envision your next two, three, or four possible moves—your plan actions. Try to anticipate how the other person will respond to those moves and how you will respond in turn. The goal of this process is to interact with enough confidence and certainty to reduce the anxiety and fear you normally feel during such encounters.

Defensive Communication

A second barrier to cooperative verbal communication is **defensive communication** (or *defensiveness*), impolite messages delivered in response to suggestions, criticism, or perceived slights. For example, at work, you suggest an alternative approach to a coworker, but she snaps, "We've *always* done it this way." You broach the topic of relationship concerns with your romantic partner, but he or she shuts you down, telling you to "Just drop it!" People who communicate defensively dismiss the validity of what another person has said. They also refuse to make internal attributions about their own behavior, especially when they are at fault. Instead, they focus their responses away from themselves and on the other person.

Four types of defensive communication are common (Waldron, Turner, Alexander, & Barton, 1993). Through *dogmatic messages*, a person dismisses suggestions for improvement or constructive criticism, refuses to consider other views, and continues to believe that his or her behaviors are acceptable. With *superiority messages*, the speaker suggests that he or she possesses special knowledge, ability, or status far beyond that of the other individual. In using *indifference messages*, a person implies that the suggestion or criticism being offered is irrelevant, uninteresting, or unimportant. Through *control messages*, a person seeks to squelch criticism by controlling the other individual or the encounter (see Table 7.3).

Defensive communication is *interpersonally incompetent* because it violates norms for appropriate behavior, rarely succeeds in effectively achieving interpersonal goals, and treats others with disrespect (Waldron et al., 1993). People who communicate in a chronically defensive fashion suffer a host of negative consequences, including high rates of conflict and lower satisfaction in their personal and professional relationships (Infante, Myers, & Burkel, 1994). Yet even highly competent communicators behave defensively on occasion. Defensiveness is an almost instinctive reaction to behavior that makes us angry—communication we perceive as inappropriate, unfair, or unduly harsh. Consequently, the key to overcoming it is to control its triggering factors. For example, if a certain person or situation invariably provokes defensiveness in you, practice preventive anger management strategies such as encounter avoidance or encounter restructuring (see Chapter 4). If you can't avoid the person or situation, use

Table 7.3 **Examples of Defensive Communication**

Message Type	Example
Dogmatic message	"Why would I change? I've always done it like this!"
Superiority message	"I have more experience and have been doing this longer than you."
Indifference message	"*This* is supposed to interest me?"
Control message	"There's no point to further discussion; I consider this matter closed."

techniques such as reappraisal and the Jefferson Strategy (also in Chapter 4). Given that defensiveness frequently stems from attributional errors—thinking the other person is "absolutely wrong" and you're "absolutely right"—perception-checking (see Chapter 3) can also help you reduce your defensiveness.

> ### Self-Reflection
> Recall a situation in which you were offered a suggestion, advice, or criticism, and you reacted defensively. What caused your reaction? What were the outcomes of your defensive communication? How could you have prevented a defensive response?

To prevent others from communicating defensively with you, use "I" and "we" language appropriately, and offer empathy and support when communicating suggestions, advice, or criticism. At the same time, realize that using cooperative language is not a panacea for curing chronic defensiveness in another person. Some people are so deeply entrenched in their defensiveness that any language you use, no matter how cooperative, will still trigger a defensive response. In such situations, the best you can do is strive to maintain ethical communication by treating the person with respect. You might also consider removing yourself from the encounter before it can escalate into intense conflict.

Verbal Aggression

The tendency to attack others' self-concepts rather than their positions on topics of conversation is known as **verbal aggression** (Infante & Wigley, 1986). Verbally aggressive people denigrate others' character, abilities, or physical appearance rather than constructively discussing different points of view. Verbal aggression can be expressed not only through speech but also through behaviors, such as physically mocking another's appearance or displaying rude gestures (Sabourin, Infante, & Rudd, 1993).

Why are some people verbally aggressive? At times, such aggression stems from a temporary mental state. Most of us have found ourselves in situations at one time or another where various factors—stress, exhaustion, frustration or anger, relationship difficulties—converge. As a result, we "lose our heads" and spontaneously "go off" on another person. Some people who are verbally aggressive suffer from chronic hostility (see Chapter 4). Others are frequently aggressive because it helps them achieve short-term interpersonal goals (Infante & Wigley, 1986). For example, people who want to cut in front of you in line, win an argument, or steal your parking spot may believe that they stand a better chance of achieving these objectives if they use insults, profanity, and threats. Unfortunately, their past experiences may bolster this belief because many people give in to verbal aggression, which encourages the aggressor to use the technique again.

If you find yourself consistently communicating in a verbally aggressive fashion, identify and address the root causes behind your aggression. Has external stress (job pressure, a troubled relationship, a family

💧 When dealing with a verbally aggressive person, sometimes it is better to leave the encounter than to allow it to escalate into a conflict.

conflict) triggered your aggression? Do you suffer from chronic hostility? If you find that anger management strategies don't help you reduce your aggression, seek professional assistance.

Communicating with others who are verbally aggressive is also a daunting challenge. Dominic Infante (1995), a leading aggression researcher, offers three tips. First, avoid communication behaviors such as teasing, baiting, or insulting that may trigger verbal aggression in others. Second, if you know someone who is chronically verbally aggressive, avoid or minimize contact with that person. For better or worse, the most practical solution for dealing with such individuals is to not interact with them at all. Third, if you can't avoid interacting with a verbally aggressive person, remain polite and respectful during your encounters with him or her. Allow the individual to speak without interruption. Stay calm, and express empathy (when possible). Avoid retaliating with personal attacks of your own; they will only further escalate the aggression. Finally, end interactions when someone becomes aggressive, explaining gently but firmly, "I'm sorry, but I don't feel comfortable continuing this conversation."

Deception

A student of mine, Taryn, had finished her junior year and was doing a summer internship. One night at a club, a handsome but obviously underage boy approached her and introduced himself as "Paul." After exchanging pleasantries, he told her, "I'm a pilot with United Airlines." *So that's how you want to play it!* Taryn thought. She returned the lie, saying, "I'm an account exec with Chase." Banter completed, their conversation progressed, and—somewhat to Taryn's surprise—attraction kindled. Before parting ways, she gave Paul her number. The next day he called, and once again they felt a passionate connection. He asked her to dinner, and when he picked her up, she was dumbfounded to see him driving a Porsche.

Paul was a 27-year-old pilot. At dinner, Taryn joked about his "baby face" and told him how she thought he had lied about his job. She was setting the stage for confessing her own lie about being an account executive at Chase. But when he replied, "I wouldn't lie—I value honesty above all else," she held off.

In the weeks that followed, they fell in love. Taryn kept looking for chances to tell him the truth but couldn't find them. By August, she was an emotional wreck. The week before she had to leave for school, she came clean. It was Paul's turn to be dumbfounded. He said, "All summer you've kept this from me? I have no idea who you are, or what kind of game you're playing. But I want no part of it—or you." And he left. He ignored her texts, e-mails, and calls. It was over. Taryn returned to school, devastated.

When most of us think of deception, we think of situations like Taryn's, in which one person communicates false information to another. But people deceive in any number of ways, only some of which involve saying untruthful things. **Deception** occurs when people deliberately use uninformative, untruthful, irrelevant, or vague language for the purpose of misleading others. The most common form of deception doesn't involve saying anything false at all: studies document that *concealment*—leaving important and relevant information out of messages—is practiced more frequently than all other forms of deception combined (McCornack, 2008).

As noted in previous chapters, deception is commonplace during online encounters. People communicating on online dating sites, posting on social networking sites, and sending messages via e-mail and text distort and hide whatever information they want, providing little opportunity for the recipients of their messages to check accuracy. Some people provide false information about their backgrounds, professions, appearances, and gender online to amuse themselves, to form alternative relationships unavailable to them offline, or to take advantage of others through online scams (Rainey, 2000).

Deception is uncooperative, unethical, impractical, and destructive. It exploits the belief on the part of listeners that speakers are communicating cooperatively—"tricking" listeners into thinking that the messages received are informative, honest, relevant, and clear when they're *not* (McCornack, 2008). Deception is unethical because, when you deceive others, you deny them information that may be relevant to their continued participation in a relationship, and, in so doing, you fail to treat them with respect (LaFollette & Graham, 1986). Deception is also impractical. Although at times it may seem easier to deceive than to tell the truth (McCornack, 2008), deception typically calls for additional deception. In Taryn's case, she had to conceal her internship from Paul throughout the summer. Finally, deception is destructive: it creates intensely unpleasant personal,

interpersonal, and relational consequences. As occurred with Taryn and Paul, the discovery of deception typically causes intense disappointment, anger, and other negative emotions and frequently leads to relationship breakups (McCornack & Levine, 1990).

At the same time, keep in mind that people who mislead you may not be doing so out of malicious intent. Many cultures view ambiguous and indirect language as hallmarks of cooperative verbal communication. In addition, sometimes people intentionally veil information out of kindness and desire to maintain the relationship, such as when you tell a close friend that her awful new hairstyle looks great because you know she'd be agonizingly self-conscious if she knew how bad it really looked (McCornack, 1997; Metts & Chronis, 1986). For me, this was the most haunting aspect of Taryn's story: she sincerely loved Paul and wanted to build a life with him, but she was doomed by a seemingly small lie told during playful bar banter.

LearningCurve
bedfordstmartins.com/ipcandyou

Postscript }

At the time that General George Washington ordered his officers to read aloud the words of Thomas Paine to their troops, the war to create the United States appeared lost. Washington, along with his officers and soldiers, seemed doomed to certain death. But as they stood on the icy shore of the Delaware River, this simple act of verbal communication—"These are the times that try men's souls . . ."—transformed the mood of the moment. Fatigued men's spirits were uplifted, and the soldiers set out across a seemingly impassable river to triumph in a mission that just a few hours earlier had seemed hopeless.

What words have helped you to ford the raging rivers of your life? How have you used verbal communication to inspire others to face their own daunting personal and interpersonal challenges?

More than 200 years ago, a disheartened general borrowed the words of a patriot to raise his soldiers' spirits. In so doing, he created the first link in a chain of events that led to the creation of a country. Now, centuries later, the power of verbal communication to inspire, uplift, embolden, and create is still available to each of us.

Chapter Review

}

Visit LaunchPad for *Interpersonal Communication and You* to watch brief, illustrative ⊙ videos of these terms and to access ✔ LearningCurve. **bedfordstmartins.com/ipcandyou**

KEY TERMS

verbal communication, 133
symbols, 133
constitutive rules, 134
regulative rules, 134
personal idioms, 134
dialects, 134
⊙ denotative meaning, 137
⊙ connotative meaning, 137
linguistic determinism, 138

linguistic relativity, 138
naming, 138
speech acts, 139
cooperative verbal
   communication, 141
Cooperative Principle, 142
honesty, 143
misunderstanding, 143
⊙ "you" language, 144

⊙ "I" language, 144
⊙ "we" language, 144
communication apprehension,
   146
communication plans, 146
⊙ defensive communication,
   147
verbal aggression, 148
deception, 149

CHAPTER ACTIVITIES

1. A common regional variance in the United States is the word used for soft drinks (e.g., *Coke, pop,* and *soda*). View the map from http://popvssoda .com/countystats/total-county.html and discuss with your classmates their preferred variations of this word. Expand the discussion by offering other experiences you have had with dialects while traveling or living in different places. What are your thoughts on such differences? Did you associate any stereotypes with language variances? Why?

2. In addition to adding new words to its dictionary each year, Merriam-Webster hosts an "open dictionary" where anyone can submit a new word: http://nws.merriam-webster.com/opendictionary /newword_display_recent.php. Spend a few minutes checking out some recent submissions. Have you heard of these new words? Do you understand and agree on the meaning for each? How do new words come about and how do they spread through society? Write a brief one- to two-paragraph response addressing these questions.

3. In small groups or in a brief response paper, discuss the implications of gendered communication such as *fireman* vs. *firefighter*. Which term do you prefer: *policeman, policewoman,* or *police officer*? How often do you use phrasing such as "male nurse" or "female professor" when the added

gender descriptor is unnecessary? What do you notice about others' use (or nonuse) of such terms? How does such gendered communication affect our interactions?

4. Identify specific scripts you frequently use with acquaintances, friends, family members, and so on. Then, for an out-of-class experiment, deviate from your usual scripts and report back to the class on others' reactions to your behavior. For example, you could hang up at the end of a phone conversation without saying, "Bye, I love you," or launch into a detailed story when a classmate passes in the hall and says, "Hi. How are you?"

5. ⊙ Watch the video on **defensive communication** and write a short point-of-view analysis. Consider the teacher's and the parent's perspectives on the interaction. What does each person hear in the video? How does each person perceive the interaction? What could each person do to improve the interaction? Ask students to discuss times when they have been in similar situations.

6. Work in groups and discuss the definitions of and differences between half-truths, lies of omission (concealment), and little white lies. Do you and your classmates view all of these concepts as deception? When are these acceptable or unacceptable in relationships? Provide examples and a rationale for each.

Look for **LearningCurve** throughout the chapter to help you review.
bedfordstmartins.com/ipcandyou

8 } Communicating Nonverbally

C losely examine this photograph. As you do, try to recall other images of Native Americans from the late 1800s or early 1900s that you've seen. What is different, unique, or interesting about this photo? How does the picture make you feel? What's your impression of the people in it?

I first came upon this image in poster form in my son's preschool classroom, and I was stunned. Intuitively, I found the picture perplexing and provocative, but I couldn't put my finger on precisely why. Seeing me staring at it, the teacher approached me. "Pretty neat, isn't it?" she said. "Yes," I said, "but something about it strikes me as unusual. Do you know what it is?" "Of course," she replied. "They're *smiling*."

By the late 1800s, stereotypical images of Native Americans were being sold as tourist postcards and magazine illustrations (Silversides, 1994). These images depicted Native peoples in full ceremonial dress, astride their horses or posed in front of teepees, scowling fearsomely.

As Cambridge University professor Maria Tippett (1994) notes, "The image one gets throughout this seventy year period is of a blank-faced, stiff, and unengaged people" (p. 2). When I surveyed more than 5,000 photos from this era, I found not a single image portraying Native Americans with smiles—except for this family photo.[1]

In contrast, this rare portrait, taken by amateur photographer Mary Schaffer (1861–1939), shows people who, rather than staring blankly into the camera, "communicate with the eyes

_____
[1] Author review of 5,000 photos in the Curtis Archives, http://curtis.library.northwestern.edu/toc.cgi.

👁 **Nonverbal communication powerfully shapes others' perceptions of you.**
The Beaver Family, 1907. Whyte Museum of the Canadian Rockies, #V527, by Mary Schaffer, Photographer.

behind it" (Tippett, 1994). The image has an intriguing history. Schaffer, with her friend Mollie Adams and two guides, were exploring the headwaters of the Saskatchewan and Athabasca Rivers in Canada in late 1907, where they met a band of Stoney Indians who befriended them. Among them were Samson Beaver, his wife Leah, and their young daughter Frances, who invited Mary to dinner. After the meal, Mary asked them if she could take their picture, and they agreed.

The Beaver family photo provides a literal and metaphorical snapshot of an interpersonal encounter: the postures, faces, dress, and use of space during a family meeting with a new friend late one sunny afternoon. You can almost feel the fellowship that must have infused the conversation, communicated through Samson's smile, his forward lean, and his direct gaze—all cues conveying intimacy and closeness. If you feel an immediate connection and empathy with Samson, you're not alone. This is a typical human reaction to the sight of a smiling person. A scowling face has quite the opposite effect.

The Beaver family photo reminds us of the universal and transcendent nature of human nonverbal expression and of its powerful role in shaping our impressions of others. A hundred years ago, a family joined new friends to share a meal and something of themselves with one another. Although they're all long since dead, the image of their encounter serves as an enduring reminder of the power of human nonverbal expression to shape our interpersonal communication and relationships.

L earning to manage your nonverbal communication is both important and challenging. It's important because most of the meaning we exchange during interpersonal encounters comes from our nonverbal expressions (Burgoon & Hoobler, 2002). What's more, nonverbal skill is associated with a host of positive outcomes, from high self-esteem to relationship satisfaction (Hodgins & Belch, 2000). It's challenging because nonverbal communication involves many different aspects of behavior, all of which must be considered and controlled simultaneously. When you communicate nonverbally, you manipulate your bodily movements, your voice, and the way you touch others. You also decide how to occupy space, craft your appearance, and use time. To do so competently requires knowledge of the various means of nonverbal communication, the ability to shape and adapt nonverbal expression, and the motivation to do so.

In this chapter, we discuss nonverbal communication and offer guidelines for strengthening your skills. You'll learn:

- How nonverbal communication differs from verbal communication

- How culture and gender affect our nonverbal communication

- What the eight codes of nonverbal communication are, and how you can more skillfully use them when interacting with others

- What purposes nonverbal communication serves in our everyday lives

Principles of Nonverbal Communication

In this book, we define **nonverbal communication** as the intentional or unintentional transmission of meaning through an individual's nonspoken physical and behavioral cues (Patterson, 1995). This definition embraces both intentional and unintentional nonverbal behaviors as communication. Sometimes we do things like yawn, sigh, or grimace and mean nothing by them. But others may interpret these behaviors as acts of communication, and this perception may lead others to respond in ways that affect us, our interpersonal communication, and our relationships. A boss who catches you yawning may express concern that you're "not paying attention," even though you're closely attending to your work. At other times, we intentionally craft nonverbal behaviors to communicate information to others. We add frowning emoticons to texts to show family members we're sad, or we look at coworkers to signal we're ready for meetings. We touch other people to signal sympathy or affection and move closer or farther away from them to indicate intimacy or emotional distance. We arrange and light our offices and homes to convey power or peacefulness, dress and groom ourselves to communicate casualness or formality, and don

artifacts such as jewelry and watches to display status and wealth.

As you might have gathered, nonverbal communication differs greatly from verbal communication. Let's take a closer look at the key distinctions between nonverbal and verbal forms of expression.

Nonverbal Communication Uses Multiple Channels

In contrast with verbal communication, our nonverbal messages are expressed through multiple channels simultaneously—such as auditory, visual, and tactile. When you talk with a good friend, for example, you simultaneously listen to your friend's tone of voice (auditory); watch your friend's facial expressions, use of eye contact, and hand gestures (visual); and perhaps even touch and receive touch from your friend (tactile). What's more, you do this while also listening to and making sense of your friend's verbal communication.

Nonverbal Communication Is More Ambiguous

Nonverbal meanings are more flexible and ambiguous than verbal meanings. A smile can express comfort or contempt, just as a shared glance can convey intimacy or warning—depending on the situation. The ambiguity of nonverbal messages can pose difficulties

(Left to right) JoJo Whilden/©Paramount Pictures/Courtesy Everett Collection; Jonathan Wenk/©TriStar Pictures/Courtesy Everett Collection; Screen Gems/Photofest; ph: Claudette Barius/©Warner Bros/Courtesy Everett Collection

What comes to mind when you think about nonverbal communication? Is it as subtle as the look in your partner's eyes when you've said something funny? Is it as dramatic as an image from a movie that sticks in your memory?

{ **Nonverbal meanings are more flexible and ambiguous than verbal meanings.** }

for interpersonal communication and relationships. For instance, suppose a friend you suspect of harboring romantic feelings for you gives you an extra-long hug. Is he or she just being friendly or signaling romantic interest?

Nonverbal Communication Has Fewer Rules

Nonverbal communication is more ambiguous than verbal communication because it is governed by fewer rules. As you saw in Chapter 7, you learn thousands of constitutive and regulative rules regarding grammar, spelling, pronunciation, and meaning as you master your first and any additional languages. But consider how rarely you've been instructed in the use of nonverbal communication. To be sure, nonverbal rules do exist, but most of these rules are informal norms—for instance, "It's not polite to stare at people."

Nonverbal Communication Has More Meaning

When we interact with others, we often deduce more meaning from people's nonverbal communication

than from their verbal, and we convey more meaning to them through our nonverbal than through our verbal. This is particularly true during first encounters, when nonverbal communication has a tremendous impact on our overall impressions of others' attractiveness (Zuckerman, Miyake, & Hodgins, 1991).

Our reliance on nonverbal communication escalates even higher when people display **mixed messages**, verbal and nonverbal behaviors that convey contradictory meanings (Burgoon & Hoobler, 2002). A friend says she "isn't sad," but her slumped shoulders and downturned mouth suggest otherwise. In such cases, we almost always trust the nonverbal messages over the verbal ones. In contrast, when verbal and nonverbal messages align ("Yes, I'm sad" coupled with slumped shoulders and frown), the amount of attention we pay to verbal communication rises (Burgoon & Hoobler, 2002).

Self-Reflection

When you receive mixed messages from someone, which do you put more faith in, the verbal or the nonverbal communication? Why? Is it ethical to deliberately send mixed messages to someone?

Nonverbal Communication Is Influenced by Culture

You're at a dinner party, and an Iranian student named Amid introduces himself. Amid approaches you very closely—standing so close that his face is only about 12 inches from yours. You think, "Close talker," and you back up, but he closes the distance again. The two of you end up repeating this little "distance dance" throughout your conversation, with both of you feeling uncertain and uncomfortable.

This "hypothetical" example happened to me when I was in college. Although Amid and I went on to become close friends, our initial conversation

© Barbara Peacock/Corbis

◊ Whether you intend it or not, your nonverbal communication will transmit meaning to others.

was awkward because of our competing cultural views regarding the appropriate amount of distance that should exist during first encounters. North Americans may feel that people from North Africa and the northern and western Middle East intrude on their personal space. Likewise, people from those cultures (such as Amid) may judge North Americans' desire for larger distance as off-putting (Chen & Starosta, 2005).

As my encounter illustrates, nonverbal communication and culture are inextricably linked. You can wrinkle your brow, use a hand gesture, or speak loudly to make a point, but if people in the culture surrounding you don't understand your behavior, you haven't communicated your message. Consider cultural differences in the meaning of eye contact, for example (Chen & Starosta, 2005). In the United States and Canada, it's considered impolite or even offensive for men to gaze openly at women, but in Italy, people view it as perfectly appropriate. Middle Easterners view gazing as a sign of respect during conversation, but Cambodians see direct eye contact as insulting and an invasion of privacy. Euro-Americans use more eye contact when they're listening than when they're talking, but for African Americans, the opposite often is true.

The tight link between culture and nonverbal communication makes cross-cultural communication difficult to master. Sure, the nonverbal symbols used in different cultures are easy enough to learn. But familiarity with the full tapestry of cues—use of personal space, attitudes toward time, perception of touch, appropriateness of gaze, facial expressions—takes much longer. Most people need many years of immersion in a culture before they fully understand the meanings of that culture's nonverbal communication (Chen & Starosta, 2005).

> The tight link between culture and nonverbal communication makes cross-cultural communication difficult to master.

Nonverbal Communication Is Influenced by Gender

Try Googling "men and women's body language," and see what pops up.[2] You'll receive *millions* of results. Most are self-help or advice sites that focus on how to tell whether men and women are romantically attracted to you. If you skim through these, you'll see a theme about gender repeatedly expressed: women are better at nonverbal communication than men.

Although online content regarding interpersonal communication and relationships often is inaccurate and stereotypical, in the case of gender and nonverbal communication some posts on popular Web sites are derived from research. Psychologist Judith Hall has examined data from hundreds of gender studies (Hall, Carter, & Horgan, 2000). Her findings suggest four consistent patterns, the first of which matches common wisdom: women *are* better than men at both sending and receiving nonverbal messages. Women surpass men at nonverbally communicating in ways receivers can correctly interpret, and women are more accurate than men in their interpretations of others' nonverbal expressions.

Second, women show greater facial expressiveness than men, and they smile more. The difference in smiling stems in part from cultural expectations that women should exhibit only positive and pleasant nonverbal expressions (Spender, 1990). Third, women gaze more at others during interpersonal interactions. This is especially apparent within same-sex conversations, where mutual gaze occurs much more often between females than between males.

Finally, men are more territorial than women. Men maintain more physical space between themselves and others during encounters. Women tolerate more intrusion into their personal space, give way to others more frequently if space is scarce, and try to take up less space than do men. Women also adopt closer conversational distances during same-sex encounters than do men, prefer side-by-side

---

[2]The information that follows is adapted from DeAngelo (2011) and Talbot (2008).

Ian Berry/Magnum Photos

💧 We often deduce more meaning from people's nonverbal communication than from their verbal communication.

seating more than men, and perceive crowded situations more favorably.

You can use your knowledge of these differences to improve your nonverbal skills. When interacting with men, be aware that they may prefer greater conversational distance and a less direct gaze than women, and take pains to convey nonverbal messages as clearly as possible. During encounters with women, don't be surprised if they adopt a closer conversational distance, and be sensitive to their likely preference for a more direct gaze and more frequent eye contact. Failing to recognize these differences may result in frustration or misunderstandings.

Nonverbal Communication Is Liberated through Technology

When I walked into the kitchen and found my two youngest sons giggling, I knew they'd been up to something. "What were you doing?" I asked. "Come see!" they gleefully invited. Walking over, I found them watching themselves on YouTube. They had posted a music video of their own creation. The clip was almost entirely nonverbal: it showed them dancing wildly, waving their hands in the air, making funny faces, and pretending (badly) to sing. When I asked them why they had created the video, they said, "Because we want our friends who are gone for the summer to be able to see us!" Sure enough, the rest of the evening was spent checking the number of "views" they had received and texting their vacationing friends regarding the video.

As recently as 20 years ago, our ability to communicate nonverbally was radically restricted by technology. Phone calls limited us to vocal cues, and communicating on the computer meant seeing words on a screen—nothing else. Only one option existed for experiencing the full tapestry of nonverbal communication: face-to-face interaction. But now, nonverbal communication has been liberated through technology. We can upload and download photos and video clips on our devices. We can podcast, stream videos, and post clips of ourselves—then alert all our friends via e-mail, Twitter, texts, and Facebook that our content is available for viewing. As of 2012, over four billion videos are viewed *daily* on YouTube ("YouTube Statistics," n.d.).

This shift from technological restriction to liberation has created two notable outcomes. First, whereas we used to have just two communication modes—face-to-face interaction or methods with limited nonverbal content (such as phone calls or e-mails)—now we can choose various media that let us hear *and* see others when interacting. Second, we can use these media to better maintain intimate, long-distance relationships. Like my sons and their YouTube video, friends and loved ones separated by distance—through summer vacations or unanticipated relocations—can also maintain intimate connections through frequent sharing of video clips and photos.

💧 When you text or post photos for your friends and loved ones, you're engaging in nonverbal communication. How else do you communicate nonverbally via technology?

> ### Skills Practice
>
> **Maintaining Online Friendship**
> *Using nonverbal communication online to maintain a friendship*
>
> 1. Identify a long-distance friend with whom you haven't communicated recently.
> 2. Think of a story or an update that you want to share with that friend.
> 3. Compose a message explaining your story that uses nonverbal cues such as photos or video of yourself.
> 4. Before sending, review your facial expressions, eye contact, body movement, voice, and appearance; make sure they communicate positively what you want to express.
> 5. E-mail or post the footage, and see how your friend responds.

Nonverbal and Verbal Combine to Create Communication

Despite the differences between verbal and nonverbal forms of expression, and the weight we give nonverbal communication when sending and receiving information, both forms are essential. When we interact with others, our verbal and nonverbal behaviors combine to create meaning (Jones & LeBaron, 2002). In everyday encounters, verbal and nonverbal communication are not experienced or expressed separately but are used jointly to create interpersonal communication (Birdwhistell, 1970). Keep this in mind: your skill as a nonverbal communicator goes hand in hand with your skill as a verbal communicator, so you need *both* to communicate competently.

LearningCurve
bedfordstmartins.com/ipcandyou

Nonverbal Communication Codes

One reason nonverbal communication contains such rich information is that, during interpersonal encounters, we use many different aspects of our behavior, appearance, and surrounding environment simultaneously to communicate meaning. You can greatly strengthen your nonverbal communication skills by understanding **nonverbal communication codes**, the different means used for transmitting information nonverbally (Burgoon & Hoobler, 2002). Scholars distinguish eight different nonverbal communication codes, summarized in Table 8.1 on the next page.

Communicating through Body Movements

She's one of the most memorable movie villains in years, and the most loyal of Lord Voldemort's "Death Eaters." Across the various *Harry Potter* films in which she has appeared, Bellatrix Lestrange (played by Helena Bonham Carter) is almost always a flurry of motion. Her facial expression is soft and mocking

Table 8.1 **The Eight Codes of Nonverbal Communication**

Code	Description
Kinesics	Visible body movements, including facial expressions, eye contact, gestures, and body postures
Vocalics	Vocal characteristics such as loudness, pitch, speech rate, and tone
Haptics	Duration, placement, and strength of touch
Proxemics	Use of physical distance
Chronemics	Organization and use of time
Physical appearance	Appearance of hair, clothing, body type, and other physical features
Artifacts	Personal possessions displayed to others
Environment	Structure of physical surroundings

In the *Harry Potter* movies, Bellatrix Lestrange's body movements—from her vicious facial expressions to her vivid, unpredictable gestures—combine to make her one of the series' most unforgettable villains. What experiences have you had with people who use body movements to communicate traits such as strength, power, or even kindness?

one moment, hard and vicious the next. Her eyes are constantly watchful, and she stares intensely with hostility at any who oppose her. Her gestures are large and vivid, even as her body shifts quickly from one posture to the next, rarely remaining still. All of these movements combine to accentuate the anger, loathsomeness, and evil associated with her character.

As depicted in the movies, Lestrange exemplifies the power of **kinesics** (from the Greek *kinesis*, meaning "movement")—visible body movements. Kinesics is the richest nonverbal code in terms of its power to communicate meaning, and it includes most of the behaviors we associate with nonverbal communication: facial expression, eye contact, gestures, and body postures.

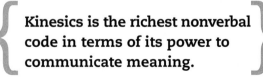

Kinesics is the richest nonverbal code in terms of its power to communicate meaning.

Facial Expression

"A person's character is clearly written on the face." As this traditional Chinese saying suggests, the face plays a pivotal role in shaping our perception of others. In fact, some scholars argue that facial cues rank first among all forms of communication in their influence on our interpersonal impressions (Knapp & Hall, 2002). We use facial expression to communicate an endless stream of emotions, and we make judgments about what others are feeling by assessing their facial expressions. Our use of emoticons (such as ☺) to communicate attitudes and emotions online testifies to our reliance on this type of kinesics, and the primacy of the face even influences our labeling of interpersonal encounters ("face-to-face") and Web sites devoted to social networking ("Facebook").

Eye Contact

Eye contact serves many purposes during interpersonal communication. We use our eyes to express emotions, signal when it's someone else's turn to talk, and show others that we're listening to them. We also demonstrate our interest in a conversation by increasing our eye contact, or signal relationship intimacy by locking eyes with a close friend or romantic partner.

Eye contact can convey hostility as well. One of the most aggressive forms of nonverbal expression is *prolonged staring*—fixed and unwavering eye contact of several seconds' duration (typically accompanied by a hostile facial expression). Although in the real world women seldom stare, men use this behavior to threaten others, invite aggression ("staring someone down" to provoke a fight), and assert their status (Burgoon, Buller, & Woodall, 1996).

Gestures

Imagine that you're driving to an appointment and someone is riding right on your bumper. Scowling at the offender in your rearview mirror, you're tempted to raise your middle finger and show it to the other driver, but you restrain yourself. The raised finger is an example of a *gesture*, a hand motion used to communicate messages (Streek, 1993). "Flipping" someone "the bird" falls into a category of gestures known as **emblems**, which represent specific verbal meanings (Ekman, 1976). With emblems, the gesture and its verbal meaning are interchangeable. You can say the words or use the gesture, and you'll send the same message.

Unlike emblems, **illustrators** accent or illustrate verbal messages. You tell your spouse about a rough road you recently biked, and as you describe the bumpy road you bounce your hand up and down to illustrate the ride.

Regulators control the exchange of conversational turns during interpersonal encounters (Rosenfeld, 1987). Listeners use regulators to tell speakers to keep talking, repeat something, hurry up, or let another person talk (Ekman & Friesen, 1969). Speakers use them to tell listeners to pay attention or to wait longer for their turn. Common examples include pointing a finger while trying to interrupt and holding a palm straight up to keep a person from interrupting. During online communication, abbreviations such as *BRB* ("be right back") and *JAS* ("just a second") serve as textual substitutes for gestural regulators.

Adaptors are touching gestures that serve a psychological or physical purpose (Ekman & Friesen, 1969). For example, you smooth your hair to make a better impression while meeting a potential new romantic partner.

Posture

The fourth kinesic is your bodily posture, which includes straightness of back (erect or slouched), body lean (forward, backward, or vertical), straightness of shoulders (firm and broad or slumped), and head position (tilted or straight up). Your posture communicates two primary messages to others: immediacy and power (Mehrabian, 1972). **Immediacy** is the degree to which you find someone interesting and attractive. Want to nonverbally communicate that you like someone? Lean forward, keep your back straight and your arms open, and hold your head up and facing toward the person when talking. Want to convey dislike? Lean back, close your arms, and look away.

(Left to right) Royalty-Free/Corbis; Robert Harding World Imagery/Getty Images

⬤ Our postures are determined by conditions and tools. In Western cultures, where many people work in offices, the chair greatly influences body posture. In agrarian and pastoral societies, where people spend most of their lives working outside, body postures are shaped accordingly. In Asia and Africa, for example, a common posture is the deep squat.

Power is the ability to influence or control other people or events (discussed in detail in Chapter 9). Imagine attending two job interviews in the same afternoon. The first interviewer sits upright, with a tense, rigid body posture. The second interviewer leans back in his chair, with his feet up on his desk and his hands behind his head. Which interviewer has more power? Most Americans would say the second. In the United States, high-status communicators typically use relaxed postures (Burgoon et al., 1996), but in Japan, the opposite is true. Japanese display power through erect posture and feet planted firmly on the floor.

Communicating through Voice

Grammy winner T-Pain has collaborated with an enviable who's who list of rap, hip-hop, and R&B stars from Ludacris to Kanye West. What makes T-Pain unique, and his songs so instantly recognizable, is his pioneering work with the pitch-correction program Auto-Tune. He was one of the first musicians to realize that Auto-Tune could be used not only to subtly correct singing errors, but to alter one's voice entirely. Running his vocals through the program, his normally full, rich voice becomes thin and reedy sounding, jumping in pitch precisely from note to note without error. The result is a sound that is at once musical yet robotic.

The popularity of T-Pain's vocal manipulations illustrates the impact that **vocalics**—vocal characteristics we use to communicate nonverbal messages—has upon our impressions. Indeed, vocalics rivals kinesics in its communicative power (Burgoon et al., 1996) because our voices communicate our social, ethnic, and individual identities to others. Consider a study that recorded people from diverse backgrounds answering a series of "small talk" questions such as "How are you?" (Harms, 1961). People who listened to these recordings were able to accurately judge participants' ethnicity, gender, and social class, often within only 10 to 15 seconds, based solely on their voices. Vocalics strongly shapes our perception of others when we first meet them. If we perceive a person's voice as calm and smooth (not nasal or shrill), we are more likely to view him or her as attractive, form a positive impression, and judge the person as extraverted, open, and conscientious (Zuckerman, Hodgins, & Miyake, 1990).

When we interact with others, we typically experience their voices as a totality—they "talk in certain ways" or "have a particular kind of voice." But people's voices are actually complex combinations of four characteristics: tone, pitch, loudness, and speech rate.

Tone

The most noticeable aspect of T-Pain's vocals is their unnatural, "computerized" tone. Tone is the most complex of human vocalic characteristics and involves a combination of richness and breathiness. You can control your vocal tone by allowing your voice to resonate deep in your chest and throat—achieving a full, rich tone that conveys an authoritative quality while giving a formal talk, for example. By contrast, letting your voice resonate through your sinus cavity creates a more whiny and nasal tone—often unpleasant to others. Your use of breath also affects tone. If you expel a great deal of air when speaking, you convey sexiness. If you constrict the airflow when speaking, you create a "thin" and "hard" tone that may communicate nervousness or anxiety.

◊ Rapper T-Pain regularly uses the pitch-correction program Auto-Tune to dramatically alter his voice, giving it an unnatural "computerized" tone. What impressions do you think he is trying to convey by changing his voice? Have you ever consciously modified or "corrected" your natural voice?

English-speakers use vocal tone to emphasize and alter the meanings of verbal messages. Regardless of the words you use, your tone can make your statements serious, silly, or even sarcastic, and you can shift tone extremely rapidly to convey different emphases. For example, when talking with your friends, you can suddenly switch from your normal tone to a much more deeply chest-resonant tone to mimic a pompous politician, then nearly instantly constrict your airflow and make your voice sound more like SpongeBob SquarePants. In online communication, we use italics to convey tone change ("I can't *believe* you did that").

Pitch

You're introduced to two new coworkers, Rashad and Paul. Both are tall and muscular. Rashad has a deep, low-pitched voice; Paul, an unusually high-pitched one. How do their voices shape your impressions of them? If you're like most people, you'll conclude that Rashad is strong and competent, while Paul is weak (Spender, 1990). Not coincidentally, people believe that women have higher-pitched voices than men and that women's voices are more "shrill" and "whining" (Spender, 1990). But although women across cultures do use higher pitch than men, most men are capable of using a higher pitch than they normally do but *choose* to intentionally limit their range to lower pitch levels to convey strength (Brend, 1975).

Self-Reflection

Think about someone you know whose voice you find funny, strange, or irritating. What is it about this person's voice that fosters your negative impression? Is it ethical to judge someone solely on his or her voice? Why or why not?

Loudness

Consider the following sentence: "Will John leave the room" (Searle, 1965). Say the sentence aloud, each time emphasizing a different word. Notice that emphasizing one word over another can alter the meaning from statement to question to command, depending on which word is emphasized ("WILL John leave the room" versus "Will JOHN leave the room").

Loudness affects meaning so powerfully that people mimic it online by USING CAPITAL LETTERS TO EMPHASIZE CERTAIN POINTS. Indeed, people who extensively cap are punished for being "too loud." For example, a member of a music Web site I routinely visit accidentally left his "cap lock" key on while posting, and all of his messages were capped. Several other members immediately pounced, scolding him, "Stop shouting!"

Speech Rate

The final vocal characteristic is the speed at which you speak. Talking at a moderate and steady rate is often considered a critical technique for effective speaking. Public-speaking educators urge students to "slow down," and people in conversations often reduce their speech rate if they believe that their listeners don't understand them. But MIT computer science researcher Jean Krause found that speech rate is not the primary determinant of intelligibility (Krause, 2001). Instead, it's pronunciation and articulation of words. People who speak quickly but enunciate clearly are just as competent communicators as those who speak moderately or slowly.

Communicating through Touch

Using touch to communicate nonverbally is known as **haptics**, from the ancient Greek word *haptein*. Touch is likely the first sense we develop in the womb, and receiving touch is a critical part of infant development (Knapp & Hall, 2002). Infants deprived of affectionate touch walk and talk later than others and suffer impaired emotional development in adulthood (Montagu, 1971).

Touch can vary based on its duration, the part of the body being touched, and the strength of contact, and these varieties influence how we interpret the physical contact (Floyd, 1999). Scholars distinguish between six types of touch. We use **functional-professional touch** to accomplish some type of task. Examples include touch between physicians and patients, between teachers and students, and between coaches and athletes. **Social-polite touch** derives from social norms and expectations. The most common form of social-polite touch is the handshake. Other examples include light hugging between friends or relatives, and the light cheek kiss. We rely on **friendship-warmth touch**—for example, gently grasping a friend's arm and giving it a squeeze—to express liking for another person. **Love-intimacy touch**—cupping a

> **Touch is likely the first sense we develop in the womb, and receiving touch is a critical part of infant development.**

romantic partner's face tenderly in your hands, giving him or her a big, lingering hug—lets you convey deep emotional feelings. **Sexual-arousal touch**, as the name implies, is intended to physically stimulate another person. Finally, **aggressive-hostile touch** involves forms of physical violence like grabbing, slapping, and hitting—behaviors designed to hurt and humiliate others.

Cultural upbringing has a strong impact on how people use and perceive touching. For example, many Hispanics use friendship-warmth touch more frequently than do Europeans and Euro-Americans. Researchers in one study monitored casual conversations occurring in outdoor cafés in two different locales: San Juan, Puerto Rico, and London, England. They then averaged the number of touches between conversational partners. The Puerto Ricans touched each other an average of 180 times per hour. The British average? Zero (Environmental Protection Agency, 2002).

Because people differ in the degree to which they feel comfortable giving and receiving touch, consider adapting your use of touch to others' preferences, employing more or less touch depending on your conversational partner's behavior responses to your touching. If you are talking with a "touchy" person, who repeatedly touches your arm gently while talking (a form of social-polite touch), you can probably presume that such a mild form of touch would be acceptable to reciprocate. But if a person offers you no touch at all, not even a greeting handshake, you would be wise to inhibit your touching.

Communicating through Personal Space

The fourth nonverbal communication code, **proxemics** (from the Latin *proximus*, meaning "near"), is communication through the use of physical distance. Edward T. Hall, one of the first scholars to study proxemics, identified four communication distances: intimate, personal, social, and public (Hall, 1966). **Intimate space** ranges from 0 to 18 inches. Sharing intimate space with someone counts among the defining nonverbal features of close relationships (see **Figure 8.1**). **Personal space** ranges between 18 inches and 4 feet and is the distance we occupy during encounters with friends. For most Americans and Canadians,

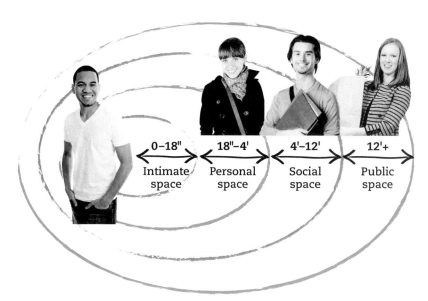

| 0–18″ | 18″–4′ | 4′–12′ | 12′+ |
| Intimate space | Personal space | Social space | Public space |

◆ Figure 8.1 Physical Distance in Communication

personal space is about your "wingspan"—that is, the distance from fingertip to fingertip when you extend your arms. **Social space** ranges from about 4 to 12 feet. Many people use it when communicating in the workplace or with acquaintances and strangers. In **public space**, the distance between persons ranges upward from 12 feet, including great distances; this span occurs most often during formal occasions such as public speeches or college lectures.

In addition to the distance we each claim for ourselves during interpersonal encounters, we also have certain physical areas or spaces in our lives that we consider our turf. **Territoriality** is the tendency to claim physical spaces as our own and to define certain locations as areas we don't want others to invade without permission (Chen & Starosta, 2005). Human beings react negatively to others who invade their perceived territory, and we respond positively to those who respect it (King, 2001). Imagine coming back to your dorm room and finding one of your roommate's friends asleep in your bed. How would you respond? If you're like most people, you would feel angry and upset. Even though your roommate's friend is not violating your personal space (distance from your body), he or she is inappropriately encroaching on physical space that you consider your territory.

Self-Reflection

Which locations in your physical spaces at home and work do you consider your most valued territories? How do you communicate this territoriality to others? What do you do when people trespass? Have your reactions to such trespasses caused negative personal or professional consequences?

What can you do to become more sensitive to differences in the use of personal space? Keep in mind that, as noted earlier in this chapter, North Americans'

notions of personal space tend to be larger than those in most other cultures, especially people from Latin America or the Middle East. When interacting with people from other cultures, adjust your use of space in accordance with your conversational partner's preferences. Realize, also, that if you're from a culture that values large personal space, others will feel most comfortable interacting at a closer distance than you're used to. If you insist on maintaining a large personal space bubble around yourself when interacting with people from other cultures, they may think you're aloof or distant or that you don't want to talk with them.

Communicating through Time

It's the middle of a busy workday. Looming over you is a 3 p.m. deadline for a report and a 3:30 appointment with the dentist. Suddenly your father calls. He wants to talk to you about plans for an upcoming surprise party for your mother. Should you disrupt your work schedule and talk or tell your father that another time would be more convenient?

Dilemmas such as this revolve around **chronemics**, the way you use time to communicate during interpersonal encounters. Edward Hall, who pioneered work on proxemics, also wrote extensively on chronemics (from the Greek word *khronos*, meaning "time"). As you learned in Chapter 5, Hall distinguished between two time orientations: *M-time* and *P-time* (Hall, 1997b). People who have an *M-time* (or monochronic) orientation value careful scheduling and time management. They view time as a precious resource: it can be saved, spent, wasted, lost, or made up, and it can even run out. So, if you have an M-time view, you likely would perceive your father's call as an interruption, and time taken during the workday to discuss a party as "misspent."

If you're an M-time person, "spending time" with someone, or "making time" in your schedule to share activities with him or her, sends the message that you consider that person and your relationship important (Hall, 1983). You may view time as a gift you give to others to show love or caring, or a tool with which you can punish ("I no longer have time for you").

In contrast to M-time people, people who have a *P-time* (or polychronic) orientation don't view time as a resource to be spent, saved, or guarded. And they rarely think of time as "wasted." If you're a P-time person, you might view your father's phone call as a welcome reprieve from the stress of work and an opportunity for an enjoyable and lengthy conversation.

Communicating through Physical Appearance

On the hit TLC show *Say Yes to the Dress*, Randy Fenoli and other sales associates at Kleinfeld Bridal in New York City help prospective brides find the ideal wedding dress. The show involves finding the dress that fits a bride's **ideal** image for how she should look. However, the **show** is not just about superficial allure. Instead, the choice of dress and accessories conveys a powerful communicative message to others about the bride's self-identity.

Although weddings are an extreme example in terms of the emphasis placed on how we look, our **physical appearance**—visible attributes such as hair, clothing, body type, and other physical features—profoundly influences all of our interpersonal encounters. In simple terms, how you look conveys as much about you as what you say. And beauty counts. Across cultures, people credit individuals they find physically attractive with higher levels of intelligence, persuasiveness, poise, sociability, warmth, power, and employment success than they credit to unattractive individuals (Hatfield & Sprecher, 1986).

This effect holds in online environments as well. For example, the physical attractiveness of friends who post their photos on your Facebook page has noteworthy effects on people's perceptions of *your* attractiveness (Walther, Van Der Heide, Kim, Westerman, & Tong, 2008). That is, if you have attractive friends' photos on your page, people will perceive

Photo by Amy Sussman/Getty Images for Discovery Communications

⬦ On *Say Yes to the Dress*, a bride's dress choice is not merely a fashion statement, but a statement about who she is as a person. Similarly, your daily physical appearance is a form of nonverbal communication that expresses how you want others to see you.

you as more physically and socially attractive; if you have unattractive friends, you'll seem less attractive to others.

Your clothing also has a profound impact on others' perceptions of you. More than 40 years of research suggests that clothing strongly influences people's judgments about profession, level of education, socioeconomic status, and even personality and personal values (Burgoon et al., 1996). The effect that clothing has on perception makes it essential that you consider the appropriateness of your dress, the context for which you are dressing, and the image of self you wish to nonverbally communicate. When I worked for a Seattle trucking company, I was expected to wear clothes that could withstand rough treatment. On my first day, I "dressed to impress" and was teased by coworkers and management for dressing as if I was an executive at a large corporation. But expectations like this can change in other situations. During job interviews, for example, dress as nicely as you can. Being even moderately formally dressed is one of the strongest predictors of whether an interviewer will perceive you as socially skilled and highly motivated (Gifford, Ng, & Wilkinson, 1985).

Communicating through Objects

Take a moment to examine the objects that you're wearing and that surround you: jewelry, watch, cell phone, computer, art or posters on the wall, and so forth. These **artifacts**—the things we possess that influence how we see ourselves and that we use to express our identity to others—constitute another code of nonverbal communication. As with our use of posture and of personal space, we use artifacts to communicate power and status. For example, by displaying expensive watches, cars, or living spaces, people "tell" others that they're wealthy and influential (Burgoon et al., 1996).

Communicating through the Environment

A final way in which we communicate nonverbally is through our **environment**, the physical features of our surroundings. As the photo of the Google office on the right illustrates, our environment envelops us, shapes our communication, and implies certain things about us, often without our realizing it.

Two types of environmental factors play a role in shaping interpersonal communication: fixed features and semifixed features (Hall, 1981). *Fixed features* are stable and unchanging environmental elements such as walls, ceilings, floors, and doors. Fixed features define the size of a particular environment, and size has an enormous emotional and communicative impact on people. For example, the size of structures communicates power, with bigger often being better. In corporations, it's often assumed that larger offices equal greater power for their occupants, and, historically, the square footage of homes has communicated the occupant's degree of wealth.

Semifixed features are impermanent and usually easy to change; they include furniture, lighting, and color. We associate bright lighting with environments that are very active and soft lighting with environments that are calmer and more intimate. Color also exerts a powerful effect on our mood and communication: we experience blues and greens as

Chris Gascoigne/VIEW/Livedinimages.com

◊ Examine how these Google employees have set up their shared office space. What do their choices in semifixed features like personal decorations, wall art, furniture, and lighting communicate about them?

relaxing, yellows and oranges as arousing and energizing, reds and blacks as sensuous, and grays and browns as depressing (Burgoon et al., 1996).

> **Self-Reflection**
>
> Look around the room you're in right now. How does this room make you feel? How do the size of the space, furniture, lighting, and color contribute to your impression? What kind of interpersonal communication would be most appropriate for this space—personal or professional? Why?

LearningCurve
bedfordstmartins.com/ipcandyou

Functions of Nonverbal Communication

It was 4th and 24 with 4 minutes to go in the 4th quarter and the Chicago Bears were down by 17 points to the New Orleans Saints.[3] As Bears' quarterback Jay Cutler dropped back to pass, Saints' defenders Roman Harper and Malcolm Jenkins converged from opposite sides and pounded him to the turf—turning the ball back to the Saints, and ensuring victory. Leaping up, the two defensive backs leaned back, looked skyward, let their arms dangle loosely, and began shuffling and flailing about. Harper and Jenkins were doing the "Bernie Dance," from the ISA song "Movin' Like Berney" and the film *Weekend at Bernie's*. In the movie (and its sequel), two hapless insurance agents try to convince people that their dead boss Bernie is actually alive, even to the point of making his corpse dance. Of

course, Harper and Jenkins weren't "moving like Bernie" just to honor a dance fad. Instead, they were using their nonverbal communication to rouse their hometown crowd in celebration and express their joy at having sacked Cutler and (in effect) ending the game.

Like Harper and Jenkins, we use nonverbal communication for many different purposes in our daily lives. Within interpersonal encounters, nonverbal communication serves five functions: it conveys meanings, expresses emotion, presents ourselves to others, helps manage interactions, and defines relationships (Argyle, 1969).

Conveying Meanings

Just as we use words to signify unique meanings, we often use nonverbal communication to directly convey meanings. Your boss flips you a thumbs-up gesture following a presentation, and you know she means "Good job!" A friend makes a two-finger "V" at a campus rally, and you recognize it as an emblem for peace.

At other times we use nonverbal communication more indirectly, as a means for accenting or augmenting verbal communication meanings (Malandro & Barker, 1983). We do this in five ways, the first of which is by *reiterating*. Nonverbal communication is used to reiterate or repeat verbal messages, as when you say "Up!" and then point upward. Second, we *contradict* our verbal messages with our nonverbal communication. For example, a friend may ask if you're angry, but you respond by scowling and angrily shouting "No, I'm not angry!" Third, we use nonverbal communication to *enhance* the meaning of verbal messages, such as when you tell an

> At times we use nonverbal communication more indirectly, as a means for accenting or augmenting verbal communication meanings.

---

[3]The information that follows is adapted from 1079ishot.com, "New Orleans Saints' Roman Harper & Malcolm Jenkins Move It Like Bernie," retrieved October 25, 2011.

© Andrew Boyd/The Times-Picayune

🜄 This photo was taken immediately after New Orleans Saints defenders Roman Harper and Malcolm Jenkins made a game-winning tackle during their 2011 season. Their eye-catching victory dance communicated their joy and excitement with no words at all.

learn to facially communicate anger and happiness to get what they want (Burgoon et al., 1996). Unintentional affect displays begin even earlier. Infants in the first few weeks of life instinctively and reflexively display facial expressions of distress, disgust, and interest. As adults, we communicate hundreds, if not thousands, of real and faked emotional states with our faces.

People also use vocalics to convey emotions. Consider how you communicate love through your voice. What changes do you make in pitch, tone, volume, and speech rate? How does your "loving" voice differ from your "angry" voice? Most people express emotions such as grief and love through lowered vocal pitch, and hostile emotions such as anger and contempt through loudness (Costanzo, Markel, & Costanzo, 1969). Pitch conveys emotion so powerfully that the source of the sound (human voice or other) is irrelevant, and words aren't necessary. Researcher Klaus Scherer (1974) mimicked voice patterns on a music synthesizer and had listeners judge the emotion conveyed. Participants strongly associated high pitch with emotions such as anger, fear, and surprise, and they linked low pitch with pleasantness, boredom, and sadness.

intimate "I love you" while smiling and offering a gentle touch to emphasize the point. Fourth, we sometimes use nonverbal communication to *replace* verbal expressions—such as when you shake your head instead of saying "no." Finally, we use nonverbal communication to *spotlight* certain parts of verbal messages, such as when you increase the loudness of just one word: "STOP hitting your brother with that light saber!"

Expressing Emotion

We communicate emotion nonverbally through **affect displays**—intentional or unintentional nonverbal behaviors that display actual or feigned emotions (Burgoon et al., 1996). In everyday interactions, affect displays are presented primarily through the face and voice. Intentional use of the face to communicate emotion begins during late infancy, when babies

Presenting Self

Think about your interactions with your manager at work. How do you let him or her know—without words—that you're a dedicated and hardworking employee? Chances are, you employ almost all the nonverbal codes discussed above, simultaneously. You convey attentiveness through focused eye contact and pleasant facial expression, and you communicate seriousness through moderate speech rate and pitch. You likely avoid crowding your boss and touching him or her. You strive to show up at meetings on time if you sense that your manager is M-time oriented. You also dress appropriately for the office and try to obey workplace norms regarding how you decorate your work space.

Now imagine that your manager confides to you a recent diagnosis of terminal illness. How would you use nonverbal communication to convey a different self—one who's compassionate and supportive? You'd likely adopt a facial expression conveying sadness and concern. You'd slow your speech rate and lower the pitch of your voice to convey empathy. You'd decrease your interpersonal distance to communicate support. And you might touch your boss lightly on the elbow or gently clasp his or her shoulder to signify caring.

As these examples suggest, nonverbal communication can help us present different aspects of our self to others. We all use nonverbal communication codes to create our identities during interpersonal encounters. An important part of being a competent nonverbal communicator is recognizing the need to shift our nonverbal communication quickly to present ourselves in different ways when the situation demands—for example, dedicated employee one moment, concerned fellow human being another.

Skills Practice

Professional Self-Presentation

Presenting yourself in a professional fashion in the workplace

1. Display a pleasant facial expression, make good eye contact, lean forward, and exhibit upright posture.
2. Use a moderately resonant and breathy vocal tone, medium pitch and volume, and moderate speech rate.
3. Adapt your use of proxemics to others' needs for personal space, and respect their territory.
4. Adjust your touching to match others' preferences.
5. Keep appointments or allow flexibility regarding punctuality.
6. Ensure that your physical appearance and artifacts are appropriate, asking your coworkers' and manager's opinions if you're uncertain.

Managing Interactions

Nonverbal communication also helps us to manage interpersonal interactions. For example, during conversations, we use regulators, eye contact, touch, smiling, head nods, and posture shifts to signal who gets to speak and for how long (Patterson, 1988). While chatting with a friend, you probably look at him or her anywhere from 30 to 50 percent of your talk time. Then, when you're approaching the end of your conversational turn, you invite your friend to talk by decreasing your pitch and loudness, stopping any gestures, and focusing your gaze on the other person. As your friend begins speaking, you now look at your partner almost 100 percent of his or her talk time, nodding your head to show you're listening (Goodwin, 1981).

During conversations, we also read our partners' nonverbal communication to check their level of interest in what we're saying—watching for signals like eye contact, smiles, and head nods. Yet we're usually unaware that we're doing this until people behave in unexpected ways. For example, if a partner *fails* to react to something we've said that we consider provocative or funny, we may shoot them a glance or frown to express our displeasure nonverbally.

Nonverbal communication also helps us regulate others' attention and behavior. For example, a sudden glance and stern facial expression from a parent or babysitter can stop a child from reaching for the forbidden cookie jar. In my sons' school, the principal gains students' attention by clapping loudly three times, a pattern that students then repeat back to him, falling silent afterward to listen for an important announcement.

Defining Relationships

You're sitting at a local diner, eating lunch and people-watching. Two couples are sitting in nearby booths. One couple sits with one partner very close to the other. They cuddle, touch, and occasionally kiss. When they're not touching, they're smiling and gazing at each other. The couple sitting at the

© Paula Lerner/Aurora

◊ Think about the functions nonverbal communication is playing in this photo. Can you tell what emotions are being expressed? What about the relationships and interactions between the women? What does this tell you about the influence of nonverbal communication in our daily experiences?

next booth over is behaving very differently. The man sits up tall and straight, his arms extended on both sides of the table. He glares at his partner, interrupts her, and doesn't look at her when she's talking. Her eyes are downcast, her hands are folded in her lap, and she speaks softly. What does the nonverbal communication of each of these couples tell you about the degree of intimacy in their relationship? The partners' relative dominance? A final function of nonverbal communication is to define the nature of our interpersonal relationships. In particular, we use our nonverbal communication to create intimacy and define

> We use nonverbal communication to create intimacy and define dominance or submissiveness in our relationships.

dominance or submissiveness in our relationships (Burgoon & Hoobler, 2002).

Intimacy

One crucial function nonverbal communication serves is to create **intimacy**, the feeling of closeness and "union" that exists between us and our partners (Mashek & Aron, 2004). We frequently communicate intimacy through touch (for example, placing a hand on a friends' arm while she speaks or snuggling with a romantic partner). But intimacy isn't defined solely through touch. Physical closeness, shared gaze, soft voices, relaxed postures, sharing of personal objects, and, of course, spending time together—each of these nonverbal behaviors highlights and enhances intimacy. Consider just a few specifics. Smiling and gazing are associated with intimacy (Floyd & Burgoon, 1999), something vividly illustrated in the Beaver family photo in our chapter opening. Individuals share more personal space with intimates and liked others than with strangers, and use proximity to convey affection (Floyd & Morman, 1999). Studies that have instructed people to communicate liking to others have found that the primary way people do so is through increasing gaze, smiling, and leaning forward (Palmer & Simmons, 1995). Conversely, one can communicate lack of intimacy and greater formality through distance, lack of eye contact, decreased vocal expressiveness, precise articulation, and tense postures (Burgoon & Hoobler, 2002).

In general, more intimate relationships—particularly romantic bonds—show higher levels of nonverbal involvement across all of the codes (more eye contact, more touch, more smiling, closer distance, and so forth). For romantic couples, the level of nonverbal involvement is a direct indicator of the relationship's health (Patterson, 1988). Think back to the highly engaged couple in the diner booth. Although you don't know who they are, what they're saying, or what culture they're from, you could reasonably conclude that they have a healthy relationship, based solely on their nonverbal behavior.

Self-Quiz

Test Your Nonverbal Dominance Knowledge

Knowing which behaviors people perceive as dominant is an important part of being a competent nonverbal communicator (Carney et al., 2005). Review the following list of behaviors, identify and rank the top five nonverbal cues that you think communicate dominance, and check your answers.

- (a)　Using a loud voice while you talk
- (b)　Exhibiting confident and self-assured facial expressions
- (c)　Initiating the shaking of an interaction partner's hand
- (d)　Having your arms crossed or folded on your chest during an encounter
- (e)　Displaying unresponsive facial expressions toward your conversational partner
- (f)　Using broad, large, and expansive hand gestures while you talk
- (g)　Showing facial disgust
- (h)　Paying attention to your conversational partner
- (i)　Manipulating objects during the conversation (such as playing with your pencil or fiddling with a piece of paper)
- (j)　Engaging in "invasive" behaviors with your conversational partner, such as standing too close, touching, and pointing

Note: Items in this *Self-Quiz* are derived from Table 1 of Carney et al. (2005).

Scoring: The most to least dominating nonverbal cues are: b, c, f, j, and g.

Dominance and Submissiveness

Recall the physically distant couple in the other diner booth. Rather than conveying intimacy, their nonverbal communication displays dominance and submissiveness. **Dominance** refers to the interpersonal behaviors we use to exert power and influence over others (Burgoon & Dunbar, 2000). Larger-than-normal use of space; access to other people's space, time, and possessions; one-sided use of touch (giving more, receiving less); indirect body orientation; direct gaze and staring; frowning and scowling; and silence—all of these codes signal the dominance of the person who employs them (Carney, Hall, & Smith LeBeau, 2005). And gender has little effect—these behaviors are perceived as dominant when displayed by either men or women (Carney et al., 2005).

In contrast, **submissiveness** is the willingness to allow others to exert power over us. We communicate submissiveness to others nonverbally by engaging in behaviors that are opposite to those that express dominance, such as taking up less space; letting others control our time, space, and possessions; smiling more; and permitting others to interrupt us.

LearningCurve
bedfordstmartins.com/ipcandyou

Postscript }

Reflect on the postures, dress, use of space, eye contact, and facial expressions depicted in the Beaver family photo. Then think about how nonverbal communication shapes your life. What judgments do you make about others, based on their scowls and smiles? Their postures? Their appearance and voice? Do you draw accurate conclusions about certain groups of people based on their nonverbal communication? How do others see you? As you communicate with others throughout a typical day, what do your facial expressions, posture, dress, use of space, and eye contact convey?

We began this chapter with a family of smiles. The smile is one of the simplest, most commonplace expressions. Yet like so many nonverbal expressions, the smile has the power to fundamentally shift interpersonal perceptions. In the case of the Beaver family, seeing the smiles that talking with a friend evoked 100 years ago helps erase more than a century of Native American stereotypes. But the power of the Beaver family's smiles goes beyond simply remedying a historical distortion. It highlights the power that even your simplest nonverbal communication has in shaping and shifting others' perceptions of you.

Chapter Review

KEY TERMS

CHAPTER ACTIVITIES

1. Journal about a time when unintentional nonverbal communication such as a sigh, yawn, or slouched posture led to miscommunication on the job, with a friend, in a class, or with a loved one. How did you discover the unintentional behavior was a problem? What did you do to repair the situation?

2. Work with a partner (a classmate, a friend, your romantic partner) to have a conversation on any topic for about two minutes. Then stop the conversation and proceed with no eye contact for two more minutes. Finally, complete one more round while maintaining *constant* eye contact. How did each round make you feel? Did you feel differently depending on who your partner was? Which partner/round was the most comfortable? The most uncomfortable?

3. ⊙ Watch the video on **vocalics**. Then find online videos or sound bites illustrating types of vocalics (monotone, breathy, nasal, friendly, hostile, etc.). For example, you might use Ben Stein as an example of monotone. Present your example(s) to your class or a small group and discuss the common perceptions associated with each.

4. Engage in a nonverbal behavioral violation outside of class. For example, you could break a personal space rule with a friend or violate elevator norms in a public space. Discuss your behavior, why it was a violation, and others' reactions to it in a short paper. Share the examples in class and discuss various informal rules for nonverbal expectations.

5. Create a slideshow by searching Google Images for pictures of various kinds of people. Look for stereotypes such as "the blonde," "the biker dude," "the businesswoman," "the nerd," and so on. Show the pictures in a small group (or share with the class) in order to spark a discussion about immediate perceptions of the individuals in the photos: What are their jobs? What do they enjoy doing? Consider how quickly perceptions are formed based on appearance alone.

6. Choose a personal belonging that is important to you (e.g., a favorite hat, iPad, wedding ring) and briefly write down why this artifact is important. If you're willing, display your item to the class and ask class members to indicate their perceptions of the items. How do others' perceptions match up to your own? Are you surprised by the results?

Look for **LearningCurve** throughout the chapter to help you review.
bedfordstmartins.com/ipcandyou.

9 } Managing Conflict and Power

When Amy Chua's *Battle Hymn of the Tiger Mother* hit bookstores, a firestorm of controversy erupted regarding her parenting.[1] Chua boasts of never letting daughters Sophia and Lulu watch TV or play computer games, drilling them in piano and violin for hours daily, and demanding that they never get a grade below an A. Although Chua intended *Tiger Mother* to be humorous and satirical, critics decried her behavior as abusive. Blogger Betty Ming Liu even declared, "Parents like Amy Chua are the reason Asian-Americans like me are in therapy." But Chua's book is about more than just parenting rules; it's a tale of power, conflict, and the negative outcomes of approaching disagreements destructively (Cullen, 2011).

Throughout her book, Chua describes her need to wield power over others. While on vacation in Greece, Chua demands that the entire family (including husband Jed and her parents) delay sightseeing of local ruins until after Lulu rehearses her violin. The marathon practice session that follows results in everyone missing their planned activities. "I wouldn't wish the misery that followed on anyone," Chua laments, not seeming to realize it was an outcome of her decision making (pp. 90–91).

Chua's approach to conflict involves demanding that others do what she wants, then verbally abusing them if they don't do so. When Lulu refuses to practice piano, Chua insults her for "being lazy, cowardly, self-indulgent, and pathetic!" When Jed intervenes—reminding her that Lulu has a different musical skill set than her prodigy sister Sophia—Chua sarcastically snipes, "Even losers are special in their own special way" (pp. 60–61).

---

[1] All content that follows is adapted from Chua (2011), Choi (2011), Cullen (2011), and Liu (2011).

◆ **Conflict is a normal part of all relationships.**
  Photo by Erin Patrice O'Brien

The conflicts escalate for years, culminating in a public blowup at a restaurant. When Lulu refuses to try caviar, Chua taunts her: "There is nothing more common and low than an American teenager who won't try things—You're boring, Lulu." Lulu explodes, "I HATE YOU! You don't love me. You make me feel bad about myself every second. You've wrecked my life. I can't stand to be around you. You're a terrible mother. You're selfish. You don't care about anyone but yourself!" Chua retaliates in kind, "You're a terrible daughter!" (pp. 204–206).

Although Chua attributes her behavior to her Chinese heritage, research suggests otherwise. Temple University psychologist Laurence Steinberg studied thousands of Latino, Euro-, African, and Asian American families and found that authoritarian parents occur in *all* ethnic groups. Chinese caregivers are *not* more likely than others to aggressively abuse power or manage conflict by insulting others (Choi, 2011). Steinberg concludes, "One can't talk about Chinese households as if there isn't variability there . . . that can be misleading" (as quoted in Choi, 2011, para. 13).

Importantly, managing conflict and power in Chua's fashion leads to decidedly negative outcomes. Such behaviors within family settings elevate anxiety, depression, and psychosomatic problems, and children whose parents bully them are less self-assured and socially poised as a result. Late in her book, Chua seems to realize this as she reflects on the destructive legacy of her communication choices: "I don't know how my daughters will look back on all this twenty years from now. Will they tell their own children, 'My mother was a controlling fanatic who even in India made us practice before we could see Bombay and New Delhi?' Or will they have softer memories?" (p. 91).

I t's easy to read Amy Chua's book, or watch videos of her appearance on *The Colbert Report*, and laugh at the extremity of her conflict style. Even she makes fun of the things she said and did while fighting with her daughters. But when we face a bullying parent, battle with a lover, or argue with a friend, the pain becomes personal. The words people most commonly associate with interpersonal conflict are *destruction*, *heartache*, and *hopelessness* (Wilmot & Hocker, 2010).

Yet conflicts don't have to be hopeless, because we're not helpless. Each of us has the ability to choose constructive approaches to managing conflicts that will help create positive outcomes for everyone involved. In this chapter, we explore interpersonal conflict and how best to manage it. You'll learn:

- The nature of conflict
- The role power plays in conflict
- Different approaches for handling interpersonal conflict
- Resolutions and long-term outcomes of conflict
- The challenges to resolving conflict in close relationships, and how to overcome them

> **Each of us has the ability to choose constructive approaches to managing conflicts that will help create positive outcomes for everyone involved.**

Conflict and Interpersonal Communication

We like to think of conflict as unusual, an unpleasant exception to the normal routine of our relationships. Each conflict seems freshly painful and unprecedented. "I can't believe it!" we text or post, "We had a *terrible* fight last night!" Friends immediately fire back messages echoing our shock: "OMG, really?!"

But conflict is a normal part of *all* relationships (Canary, 2003). Dealing with other human beings (and their unique goals, preferences, and opinions) means regularly having your wants and needs run up against theirs, triggering disputes (Malis & Roloff, 2006). On average, people report seven conflicts a week, mostly with relatives, friends, and lovers with whom they've argued before (Benoit & Benoit, 1990). Thus, the challenge you face is not how to avoid conflict, or how to live a conflict-free life, but instead how to constructively manage the conflicts that *will* arise in your interpersonal relationships.

What Is Conflict?

Almost any issue can spark conflict—money, sex, housework, politics—and almost anyone can get into a conflict: family members, friends, lovers, or coworkers. Despite such variations, all conflicts share similar attributes. **Conflict** is the process that occurs when people perceive that they have incompatible goals or that someone is interfering in their ability to achieve their objectives (Wilmot & Hocker, 2010). Four features characterize most conflicts: they begin with perception, they involve clashes in goals or behaviors, they unfold over time as a process, and they are dynamic.

Conflict Begins with Perception

Conflict occurs when people perceive incompatible goals or actions (Roloff & Soule, 2002). Because conflict begins with perception, perceptual errors (see Chapter 3) shape how conflicts unfold. As we'll discuss later in this chapter, during conflicts we blame others more than ourselves and perceive them as uncooperative and ourselves as helpful.

🔸 Conflict is fueled by the perception of opposition. As long as people perceive their goals to be incompatible, conflict will endure.

BEHROUZ MEHRI/AFP/Getty Images

These self-enhancing errors can lead us to manage conflict in ways that create unsatisfying outcomes.

Conflict Involves Clashes in Goals or Behaviors

At the heart of conflicts are clashes in goals or behaviors (Zacchilli, Hendrick, & Hendrick, 2009). Some conflicts revolve around incompatible goals, ranging from everyday leisure activity disputes ("I want to go out dancing!" vs. "I want to stay home!") to serious arguments regarding personal values ("I want our children to be raised Jewish!" vs. "I want them to be Catholic!"). Other disputes break out when one person's actions clash with another's, for example, when a friend texts you repeatedly while you're studying and you fire back a nasty message.

Conflict Is a Process

Although people often describe conflict as a series of unrelated events ("I sent her this carefully worded message, and for no reason, she blasted me in response!"), conflict is a process that unfolds over time. Its course is determined by the communication choices we make—everything we say and do during a conflict influences everything our partner says and does, and vice versa.

Moreover, most conflicts proceed through several stages, each involving decisions and actions that affect the conflict's direction and consequences. In its most basic form, the process of conflict involves people perceiving that a conflict exists, choosing an approach for how to handle it, and then dealing with the resolutions and outcomes that follow. Conflict is not a one-time-only event: how you handle a conflict with someone will have consequences for your future interactions and relationship with that person.

Conflict Is Dynamic

Because conflict typically unfolds over a series of exchanged messages, it is ever-changing and unpredictable. Research looking at the dynamic nature of conflict finds that in 66.4 percent of disputes, the focus shifts substantially as the conflict progresses (Keck & Samp, 2007). A fight over your father's snide remark regarding your job quickly becomes a battle about his chronic disapproval of you. When a conflict shifts topic, it can devolve into **kitchen-sinking** (from the expression, "throwing everything at them but the kitchen sink"), in which combatants hurl insults and accusations at each other that have little to do with the original disagreement. For example, a couple fighting over whether one of them was flirting with their server at dinner may say things like: "What about when you completely forgot our anniversary?!" and "Oh yeah?! Well, your family sucks!"

Since conflict often dynamically branches out into other troublesome topics, you can never fully anticipate the twists and turns that will occur. But remember: you have total control over what *you* say and do—and that can influence how someone responds. If you think a conflict is getting completely off track, choose your communication carefully to help bring it back on topic.

Conflict in Relationships

Most conflicts occur between people who know each other and are involved in close relationships, such as romantic partners, friends, family members, and coworkers (Benoit & Benoit, 1990). Unlike people who don't know each other well, people in close relationships experience prolonged contact and frequent interaction, which set the stage for disagreements over goals and behaviors.

In close relationships, conflicts typically arise from one of three issues (Peterson, 2002): *irritating partner behaviors* (e.g., a family member has an annoying personal habit), *disagreements regarding relationship rules* (e.g., you and your partner disagree about texting with ex-partners), and *personality clashes* (e.g., you have a sunny disposition but your roommate is a complainer).

Relationship partners often develop consistent patterns of communication for dealing with conflict that either promote or undermine their happiness. For example, happily married couples are more likely than unhappily married couples to avoid personal attacks during conflicts and instead focus their discussion on the differences at hand (Peterson, 2002). Such patterns are self-perpetuating: happy couples remain motivated to behave in ways guaranteed to keep them happy, and because they believe they can solve their problems, they are more likely to work together to resolve conflict (Caughlin & Vangelisti, 2000). In contrast, dissatisfied couples often choose to avoid important conflicts. Their failure to deal directly with their problems further fuels their unhappiness (Afifi, McManus, Steuber, & Coho, 2009).

> ### Self-Reflection
> Think of a relational partner with whom you have the same conflict over and over again. What effect does this conflict have on your relationship? In what ways do you contribute to continuing the conflict? How might you change your communication to end this repetitive cycle?

Managing conflicts in close relationships presents unique challenges. We feel connected to our intimate partners, and disputes threaten that sense of connection (Berscheid, 2002). This is why conflicts with loved ones are often intense and emotionally draining experiences. Conflicts also powerfully affect your future encounters and relationships. For example, if you and a sibling fight via text messages, this conflict will shape not only how the two of you communicate when you are next face-to-face, but how you'll feel about your relationship moving forward. As scholar Donald Peterson (2002) notes, "Every conflict and every resolution, as well as every failure at resolution, becomes a part of your overall relationship history" (p. 363).

LearningCurve
bedfordstmartins.com/ipcandyou

Power and Conflict

In Suzanne Collins's futuristic novel *The Hunger Games* (2008), North America has become Panem, consisting of a wealthy Capitol city surrounded by twelve outlying districts.[2] Following suppression of a mass rebellion by the districts, the Capitol creates the annual "Hunger Games." Children from each district are selected and pitted against each other in a fight to the death that is televised live. Child participants are chosen lottery-style, and for district residents there is no choice: to not participate in the lottery means death for all. As Katniss Everdeen, the story's central character, describes it:

> Taking kids from our districts, forcing them to kill one another while we watch—this is the Capitol's way of reminding us how totally we are at their mercy. Whatever words they use, the real message is clear: "look how we take your children and sacrifice them and there's nothing you can do. If you lift a finger, we will destroy every last one of you." (p. 18)

The dominant theme of *The Hunger Games* is **power**: the ability to influence or control people and events (Donohue & Kolt, 1992). Understanding power is critical for constructively managing conflict because people in conflict often wield whatever power they have to overcome the opposition and achieve their goals. In conflicts where one party has more power than the other—like the Capitol has over the districts— the more powerful tend to get what they want.

[2]All material that follows is adapted from Collins (2008).

© Lionsgate Photographer: Murray Close/Photofest

In *The Hunger Games*, Effie Trinket wields the Capitol's power by escorting children to the Hunger Games, a televised competition in which youth are forced to fight to the death. Main character Katniss Everdeen exercises her own power in volunteering to take her younger sister's place in the Games.

Power's Defining Characteristics

Most of us won't ever experience power wielded as brutally as in *The Hunger Games*. But power does permeate our everyday lives and is an integral part of interpersonal communication and relationships. Power determines how partners relate to one another, who controls relationship decisions, and whose goals will prevail during conflicts (Dunbar, 2004). Let's consider power's defining characteristics, as suggested by scholars William Wilmot and Joyce Hocker (2010).

Power Is Always Present
Whether you're talking on the phone with a parent, texting your best friend, or spending time with your lover, power is present in all your interpersonal encounters. Power may be balanced (e.g., friend to friend) or imbalanced (e.g., manager to employee). When power is balanced, **symmetrical relationships**

result. When power is imbalanced, **complementary relationships** are the outcome.

Although power is always present, we're typically not aware of it until people violate our expectations for power balance in the relationship, such as giving orders or "talking down" to us. For example, your supervisor grabs inventory you were stocking and says, "No—do it *this* way!" even though you were doing it properly. According to **Dyadic Power Theory** (Dunbar, 2004), people with only moderate power are most likely to use controlling communication. Because their power is limited, they can't always be sure they're going to get their way. Hence, they feel more of a need to wield power in noticeable ways (Dunbar, 2004). In contrast, people with high power feel little need to display it; they *know* that their words will be listened to and their wishes granted. This means that you're most likely to run into controlling communication and power-based bullying when dealing with people who have moderate amounts of power over you, such as mid-level managers, team captains, and class-project group leaders, as opposed to people with high power (in such contexts) like vice presidents, coaches, or faculty advisors.

Power Can Be Used Ethically or Unethically

Power itself isn't good or bad—it's the way people use it that matters. Many happy marriages, family relationships, and long-term friendships are complementary. One person controls more resources and has more decision-making influence than the other. Yet the person in charge uses his or her power only to benefit both people and the relationship. In other relationships, the powerful partner wields his or her power unethically or recklessly. For example, a boss threatens to fire her employee unless he sleeps with her.

> **Although power is always present, we're typically not aware of it until people violate our expectations for power balance in the relationship.**

Power Is Granted

Power doesn't reside within people. Instead, it is granted by individuals or groups who allow another person or group to exert influence over them. For example, a friend of mine invited his parents to stay with him and his wife for the weekend. His parents had planned on leaving Monday, but come Monday morning, they announced that they would stay through the end of the week. My friend accepted their decision, even though he could have insisted that they leave at the originally agreed-upon time. In doing so, he granted his parents the power to decide their departure date without his input.

Power Influences Conflicts

If you strip away the particulars of what's said and done during most conflicts, you'll find power struggles underneath. Who has more influence? Who controls the resources, decisions, and feelings involved? People struggle to see whose goals will prevail, and they wield whatever power they have to pursue their own goals. But power struggles rarely lead to mutually beneficial solutions. As we'll see, the more constructive approach is to set aside your power and work collaboratively to resolve the conflict.

Self-Reflection

Think of a complementary personal relationship of yours, in which you have more power than the other person. How does the imbalance affect how you communicate during conflicts? Is it ethical for you to wield power over the other person during a conflict to get what you want? Why or why not?

Power Currencies

Given that power is not innate but something that some people grant to others, how do you get power? To acquire power, you must possess or control some form of **power currency**, a resource that other people value (Wilmot & Hocker, 2010). Possessing or controlling a valued

(Left to right) Britt Erlanson/Getty Images; Blend Images/Punchstock/Getty Images; Britt Erlanson/Getty Images; Rick Diamond/Getty Images; Lou Bopp/StockShop/Aurora

Power expresses itself in the form of different power currencies. As shown here, these include resource currency, expertise currency, social network currency, personal currency, and intimacy currency.

resource gives you influence over individuals who value that resource. Likewise, if individuals have resources you view as valuable, you will grant power to them.

Five power currencies are common in interpersonal relationships. **Resource currency** includes material things such as money, property, and food. If you possess material things that someone else needs or wants, you have resource power over them. Parents have nearly total resource power over young children because they control all the money, food, shelter, clothing, and other items their children need and want.

Expertise currency comprises special skills or knowledge. The more highly specialized and unique the skill or knowledge you have, the more expertise power you possess. A Stuttgart-trained Porsche mechanic commands a substantially higher wage and choicer selection of clients than a minimally trained Quick Lube oil change attendant.

A person who is linked with a network of friends, family, and acquaintances with substantial influence has **social network currency**. Others may value his or her ability to introduce them to people who can land them jobs, "talk them up" to potential romantic partners, or get them invitations to exclusive parties.

Personal characteristics—beauty, intelligence, charisma, communication skill, sense of humor—that people consider desirable constitute **personal currency**. Even if you lack resource, expertise, and social network currency, you can still achieve a certain degree of influence and stature by being beautiful, athletic, funny, or smart.

Finally, you acquire **intimacy currency** when you share a close bond with someone that no one else shares. If you have a unique intimate bond with someone—a lover, friend, or family member—you possess intimacy power over him or her, and he or she may do you a favor "only because you are my best friend."

Power derives from the perception of power currencies, but views of power differ substantially across cultures. People are granted power not only according to which power currencies they possess, but also according to the degree to which those power currencies are valued in a given culture. In Asian and Latino cultures, high value is placed on resource currency; consequently, people without wealth, property, or other such material resources are likely to grant power to those who possess them (Gudykunst & Kim, 2003). In contrast, in northern European countries, Canada, and the United States, people with wealth may be admired or even envied, but they are not granted unusual power. If your rich neighbor builds a huge mansion, you might be impressed. But if her new fence crosses onto your property, you'll confront her about it ("Sorry to bother you, but your new fence is one foot over the property line"). Members of other cultures would be less likely to say anything, given her wealth and corresponding power.

LearningCurve
bedfordstmartins.com/ipcandyou

Handling Conflict

You're sprinting through the airport with your carry-on bag, desperately hoping to make your connecting flight. You see your gate in the distance, but the attendant is beginning to close the security door. You shout for him to wait, but he closes the door anyway. "I'm sorry," he says, "federal regulations require that we close the door 15 minutes prior to departure." Looking at your watch, you see that there still are 20 minutes left before the flight time. What would you do? Give up and walk away? Demand that he open the door? Flip out and yell at him?

In situations where others are interrupting your goals or actions, your most important decision is how to handle the conflict (Sillars & Wilmot, 1994). *Your choice about what you'll say and do will shape everything that follows—whether the situation will go unresolved, escalate, or be resolved.* This choice also influences whether your relationship with the other person (if one exists) will be damaged or grow stronger.

In this section, we examine the approaches people use for handling conflict. In addition, we look at the impact that gender, culture, and technology have upon selection of these approaches.

Approaches to Handling Conflict

People generally handle conflict in one of five ways: avoidance, accommodation, competition, reactivity, or collaboration (Lulofs & Cahn, 2000; Zacchilli et al., 2009).

Avoidance

One way to handle conflict is **avoidance**: ignoring the conflict, pretending it isn't really happening, or communicating indirectly about the situation. One common form of avoidance is **skirting**, in which a person

{ **Your choice about how to handle a conflict shapes everything that follows—whether the situation will go unresolved, escalate, or be resolved.** }

avoids a conflict by changing the topic or joking about it. You think your lover is having an affair and raise the issue, but he or she just laughs and says (in a Southern accent), "Don't you know we'll always be together, like Noah and Allie from *The Notebook?*" Another form of avoidance is **sniping**—communicating in a negative fashion and then abandoning the encounter by physically leaving the scene or refusing to interact further. You're fighting with your brother through Skype, when he pops off a nasty comment ("I see you're still a spoiled brat!") and signs off before you have a chance to reply.

> **Self-Reflection**
>
> Recall a conflict in which you chose avoidance. Why did you make this choice? What consequences ensued? Were there any positive outcomes? If you could relive the encounter, what, if anything, would you say and do differently to obtain more positive results?

Avoidance is the most frequently used approach to handling conflict (Sillars, 1980). People opt for avoidance because it seems easier, less emotionally draining, and lower risk than direct confrontation (Afifi & Olson, 2005). But avoidance poses substantial risks (Afifi et al., 2009). One of the biggest is **cumulative annoyance**, in which repressed irritation grows as the mental list of grievances we have against our partners builds (Peterson, 2002). Eventually, cumulative annoyance overwhelms our capacity to suppress it and we suddenly explode in anger. For example, you constantly remind your teenage son about his homework, chores, personal hygiene, and room cleanliness. This bothers you immensely because you feel these matters are his responsibility, but you swallow your anger because you don't want to make a fuss or be seen by him as "nagging." One evening, after reminding him twice to hang up his expensive new leather jacket, you walk into his bedroom to find the coat crumpled in a ball on the floor. You go on a tirade, listing all of the things he has done to upset you in the past month.

A second risk posed by avoidance is **pseudo-conflict**, the perception that a conflict exists when in fact it doesn't. For example, you mistakenly think your romantic partner is about to break up with you because you see tagged photos of him or her arm in arm with someone else on Facebook. So you decide to preemptively end your relationship even though your partner actually has no desire to leave you (the photos were of your partner and a cousin).

Despite the risks, avoidance can be a wise choice for managing conflict in situations where emotions run high (Berscheid, 2002). If everyone involved is angry, and yet you choose to continue the interaction, you run the risk of saying things that will damage your relationship. It may be better to avoid through leaving, hanging up, or not responding to texts or messages until tempers have cooled.

Accommodation

Through **accommodation**, one person abandons his or her own goals and acquiesces to the desires of the other person. For example, your supervisor at work asks you to stay an extra hour tonight because a coworker is showing up late. Although you had plans for the evening, you cancel them and act as if it's not a problem.

If you're like most people, you probably accommodate people who have more power than you. Why? If you don't, they might use their power to control or punish you. This suggests an important lesson regarding the relationship between power and conflict: people who are more powerful than you probably won't accommodate your goals during conflicts.

Another factor that influences people's decision to accommodate is love. Accommodation reflects a high concern for others and a low concern for self; you want to please those you love (Frisby & Westerman, 2010). Hence, accommodation is likely to occur in healthy, satisfied, close relationships where selflessness is characteristic (Hendrick & Hendrick, 1992). For example, your romantic partner is accepted into a summer study-abroad program in Europe.

Even though you had planned on spending the summer together, you encourage him or her to accept the offer.

Competition

An open and clear discussion of the goal clash that exists, coupled with the pursuit of one's own goals without regard for others' goals is known as **competition** (Sillars, 1980).

The choice to use competition is motivated in part by negative thoughts and beliefs, including a desire to control, a willingness to hurt others in order to gain, and a lack of respect for others (Bevan, Finan, & Kaminsky, 2008; Zacchilli et al., 2009). Consequently, you'll be less likely to opt for competition when you are in a conflict with someone whose needs you are interested in and whom you admire. Conversely, if people routinely approach conflict by making demands to the exclusion of your desires, they likely do not respect you (Hendrick & Hendrick, 2006).

At a minimum, competitive approaches can trigger *defensive communication* (described in Chapter 7)—someone refusing to consider your goals or dismissing them as unimportant, acting superior to you, or

AP Photo/*The News Tribune*/Russ Carmack

🔹 The competition for limited-supply products and deals is a notorious part of Black Friday shopping. Have you experienced or heard about how conflicts are handled in these potentially tense situations?

Self-Quiz }

How Do You Approach Conflict?

Read through the statements, placing a check mark next to each statement with which you agree.

During conflicts, I typically . . .

Avoidance

☐ keep my feelings about the disagreement to myself.

☐ avoid open discussion of the dispute.

☐ stay away from the topic of disagreement.

☐ avoid any type of unpleasant exchange.

Accommodation

☐ accommodate the other person's wishes.

☐ give in to the other person's desires.

☐ go along with the other person's suggestions.

☐ pretend to agree just to satisfy the other person's expectations.

Competition

☐ try to convince the other person that I'm right.

☐ take control so that the decision goes in my favor.

☐ pursue my side of the issue.

☐ use my power to win.

Reactivity

☐ explode violently with anger.

☐ say things that I know will hurt the other person.

☐ scream or yell loudly and throw things.

☐ accuse the other person of wrongdoing.

Collaboration

☐ investigate the issue of dispute to find a solution acceptable to both parties.

☐ try to work with the other person to find solutions that satisfy both our expectations.

☐ exchange information with the other person so we can solve the problem together.

☐ bring all of our concerns out in the open so the issue can be resolved.

Note: Adapted from Rahim and Mager (1995); Zacchilli, Hendrick, & Hendrick (2009).

Scoring: The category with the most check marks indicates how you primarily manage conflict. If you score equally high on two or more different approaches, you use more than one approach.

attempting to squelch your disagreement by wielding power over you (Waldron, Turner, Alexander, & Barton, 1993). But the primary risk of choosing a competitive approach is **escalation**, a dramatic rise in emotional intensity and increasingly negative and aggressive communication. If people in conflict both choose competition, and neither is willing to back down, escalation is guaranteed. Even initially trivial conflicts can quickly explode into intense exchanges.

Reactivity

A fourth way people handle conflict is by not pursuing any conflict-related goals at all; instead, they communicate in an emotionally explosive and negative fashion. This is known as **reactivity** and is characterized by accusations of mistrust, yelling, crying, and becoming verbally or physically abusive. Reactivity is decidedly nonstrategic. Instead, people simply "flip out." For example, one of my college dating partners was intensely reactive. When I noted that we weren't getting along, and suggested taking a break, she screamed, "I *knew* it! You've been cheating on me!" and hurled a flower vase at my head. Thankfully I ducked out of the way, but it took the campus police to calm her down. Her behavior had nothing to do with "managing our conflict." She simply *reacted*.

Similar to competition, reactivity is strongly related to a lack of respect (Bevan et al., 2008; Zacchilli et al., 2009). People prone to reactivity have little interest in others as individuals and do not recognize others' desires as relevant (Zacchilli et al., 2009).

> ### Self-Reflection
>
> Call to mind someone you know who consistently approaches conflict with reactivity. How has this shaped your willingness to broach issues of disagreement? Impacted your feelings? Given the relationship between reactivity and respect, is it possible to sustain a healthy, close relationship with a reactive person? Why or why not?

Collaboration

The most constructive approach to managing conflict is **collaboration**: treating conflict as a mutual problem-solving challenge. Often the result of using a collaborative approach is *compromise*, where everyone involved modifies their individual goals to come up with a solution to the conflict. (We'll discuss compromise more on page 191.) You're most likely to use collaboration when you respect the other person and are concerned about his or her desires as well as your own (Keck & Samp, 2007; Zacchilli et al., 2009). People who regularly use collaboration feel more trust, commitment, and overall satisfaction with their relationships than those who don't (Smith, Heaven, & Ciarrochi, 2008). Whenever possible, opt for collaboration.

To use a collaborative approach, try these suggestions from Wilmot and Hocker (2010). First, *attack problems, not people.* Talk about the conflict as something separate from the people involved, saying, for instance, "This issue has really come between us." This frames the conflict as the source of trouble and unites the people trying to handle it. At the same time, avoid personal attacks while being courteous and respectful, regardless of how angry you may be. This is perhaps the hardest part of collaboration because you likely *will* be angry during conflicts (Berscheid, 2002). Just don't let your anger cause you to say and do things you shouldn't. If someone attacks you and not the problem, don't get sucked into trading insults. Simply say, "I can see you're very upset; let's talk about this when we've both had a chance to cool off," and end the encounter before things escalate further.

Second, *focus on common interests and long-term goals.* Keep the emphasis on the desires you share in common, not the issue that's driving you apart. Use "we" language (see Chapter 8) to bolster this impression: "I know we both want what's best for the company." Arguing over positions ("I want this!" versus "I want that!") endangers relationships because the conflict quickly becomes a destructive contest of wills.

Third, *create options before arriving at decisions.* Be willing to negotiate a solution, rather than insist on one. Start by asking questions that will elicit options: "How do you think we can best resolve this?" Then propose ideas of your own. Be flexible. Most collaborative solutions involve some form of compromise, so be willing to adapt your original desires, even if it means not getting everything you want. Then combine the best parts of the various suggestions to come up with an agreeable solution. Don't get bogged down searching for a "perfect" solution—it may not exist.

Finally, *critically evaluate your solution.* Ask for an assessment: "Is this equally fair for both of us?" The critical issue is livability: Can everyone live with the resolution in the long run? Or, is it so unfair or short

Table 9.1 **Competitive versus Collaborative Conflict Approaches**

Situation	Competitive Approach	Collaborative Approach
Roommate hasn't been doing his or her share of the housework.	"I'm sick and tired of you never doing anything around here! From now on, you are doing all the chores!"	"We've both been really busy, but I'm concerned that things are not getting done. Let's make a list of all the chores and figure out how to fairly divide them up."
Coworker is draining large blocks of your work time by socializing with you.	"It's obvious that you don't care about your job or whether you get fired. But I need this job, so stop bugging me all the time and let me get my work done!"	"I enjoy spending time with you, but I'm finding I don't have enough time left to get my work done. Let's figure out how we can better balance hanging out and working."
Romantic partner wants you to abandon a beloved pastime because it seems too dangerous.	"I've been racing dirt bikes long before I met you, and there's no way I'm giving them up. If you really loved me, you'd accept that instead of pestering me to quit!"	"Sorry my racing worries you; I know the reason you're concerned is because you care about me. Let's talk about what we can both do so I don't worry you so much."

of original desires that resentments are likely to emerge? If anyone can answer "yes" to the latter question, go back to creating options (step 3) until you find a solution that is satisfactory to everyone.

Gender and Handling Conflict

Traditional gender socialization creates challenges for men and women as they seek to constructively resolve conflicts. Women are encouraged to avoid and suppress conflict and to sacrifice their own goals to accommodate others (Wood, 1998). Consequently, many women have little experience in constructively pursuing their goals during a dispute. Men, in contrast, learn to adopt competitive or even violent approaches to interpersonal clashes, as such approaches suggest strength and manliness (Wood, 1998). At the same time, they're taught not to harm women. Thus, during a contentious exchange with a woman, men face a dilemma: compete or avoid? Many men handle the dilemma by downplaying conflicts or simply leaving the scene instead of seeking constructive resolution.

Given that gender can sometimes interfere with constructive conflict management, reconsider how you approach conflict with men and women. When experiencing conflicts with women, encourage the open expression of goals to allow for a collaborative solution. Above all, avoid assuming that no conflict exists just because the other person hasn't voiced any concerns. When managing conflicts with men, be aware of the male emphasis on competitive approaches. Stress collaboration, and as you communicate, steadfastly avoid forms of communication such as personal criticism, insults, or threats that may escalate the conflict.

Culture and Handling Conflict

The strongest cultural factor that influences your conflict approach is whether you belong to an individualistic or a collectivistic culture (Ting-Toomey, 1997). People raised in collectivistic cultures often view direct messages regarding conflict as personal attacks (Nishiyama, 1971) and consequently are more

(Left to right) Photo by Craig Blankenhorn/CBS via Getty Images; ABC/Photofest; NBC/Photofest; Photofest

Popular television shows depict a variety of conflict management styles among married couples. How do these depictions match or contradict your own experiences?

likely to manage conflict through avoidance or accommodation. People from individualistic cultures feel comfortable agreeing to disagree and don't necessarily see such clashes as personal affronts (Ting-Toomey, 1985). They are more likely to compete, react, or collaborate.

Given these differences, how might you manage conflict competently across cultures? If you're an individualist embroiled in a dispute with someone from a collectivistic culture, consider the following practices (Gudykunst & Kim, 2003):

- Recognize that collectivists may prefer to have a third person mediate the conflict (Kozan & Ergin, 1998). Mediators allow those in conflict to manage their disagreement without direct confrontation, thereby helping to maintain harmony in the relationship—which is especially important to collectivists.

- Use more indirect verbal messages. For example, sprinkle your comments with "maybe" and "possibly," and avoid blunt responses such as "no."

- Let go of the situation if the other person does not recognize that the conflict exists or does not want to deal with it.

If you're a collectivist in contention with someone from an individualistic culture, the following guidelines may help:

- Recognize that individualists often separate conflicts from people. Just because you're in conflict doesn't mean that the situation is personal.

- Use an assertive style and be direct. For example, use "I" messages and candidly state your opinions and feelings.

- Manage conflicts when they arise, even if you'd much rather avoid them.

Technology and Handling Conflict

Given how much of our daily communication occurs via technology, it's no surprise that conflicts occur through text- or instant-messaging, e-mail, and Web posts. Nearly two-thirds of college students (61.2 percent) report using mediated channels to engage in conflicts, the most popular form being text-messaging (Frisby & Westerman, 2010). When asked why they choose mediated channels rather than face-to-face contact, respondents report "geographical distance" as the most common reason.

Without the means for immediately seeing someone, texting becomes a tempting alternative for handling conflict.

Unfortunately, such media are not well suited for resolving conflicts. The inability to see nonverbal reactions to messages makes people less aware of the consequences of their communication choices (Joinson, 2001). As a result, people are more likely to prioritize their own goals, minimize a partner's goals, and use hostile personal attacks in pursuit of their goals online than face-to-face (Shedletsky & Aitken, 2004).

Thus, the first and most important step in managing conflict constructively is to *take the encounter offline*. Doing so can dramatically reduce the likelihood of attributional errors and substantially boost empathy. If meeting face-to-face isn't an option at the time, you can try to stall the encounter by saying, "I think this is best handled in person. When can we get together and talk?" If you can't (or don't want to) meet, then switch to a phone call. That way, you'll at least have vocal cues to gauge a partner's reaction and enhance your empathy.

If, however, you're in a situation in which you must deal with the conflict online, try these suggestions (Munro, 2002):

1. *Wait and reread.* When you receive a message that triggers a conflict, don't respond right away. Instead, wait for a while, engage in other activities, and then reread it. This helps you to avoid communicating when your anger is at its peak. It also provides the opportunity for reassessment: often, in rereading a message, you'll find that your initial interpretation was mistaken.
2. *Assume the best and watch out for the worst.* When reviewing the trigger message, presume that the sender meant well but didn't express him- or herself competently. Keep in mind all you know about the challenges of online communication: anonymity and online disinhibition, empathy deficits, and inappropriate expression. At the same time, realize that some people enjoy conflict. Firing back a nasty message may be exactly what they want.

3. *Seek outside counsel.* Before responding to online conflict messages, discuss the situation offline (ideally, face-to-face) with someone who knows you well, and whose opinion you trust and respect. Having an additional viewpoint will help you perspective-take and make wise communication decisions.
4. *Weigh your options carefully.* Choose cautiously between engaging or avoiding the conflict. Consider the consequences associated with each option, and which is most likely to net you the long-term outcomes you desire. Ask yourself: will responding at this time help to resolve the conflict, or escalate things further?
5. *Communicate competently.* When crafting your response, draw upon all you know about competent interpersonal communication. Use "I" language, incorporate appropriate emoticons, express empathy and perspective-take, encourage the sharing of relevant thoughts and feelings, and make clear your willingness to negotiate mutually agreeable solutions. Perhaps most important, start and end your message with positive statements that support rather than attack the other person's viewpoints.

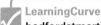

LearningCurve
bedfordstmartins.com/ipcandyou

Conflict Endings

Think about the most recent serious conflict you experienced, and consider the way it ended. Did one of you "win" and the other "lose"? Were you both left dissatisfied, or were you each pleased with the resolution? More important, were you able to resolve the underlying issue that triggered the disagreement in the first place, or did you merely create a short-term fix?

Given their emotional intensity and the fact that they typically occur in relationships, conflicts conclude more gradually than many people would like. You may arrive at a short-term resolution leading to the immediate end of the conflict. But afterward, you'll experience long-term outcomes as you remember, ponder, and possibly regret the incident. These outcomes will influence your relationship health and happiness long into the future.

Short-Term Conflict Resolutions

The approach you and your partner choose to handle the conflict usually results in one of five short-term conflict resolutions (Peterson, 2002). First, some conflicts end through **separation**, the sudden withdrawal of one person from the encounter. This resolution is characteristic of approaching conflict through avoidance. For example, you may be having a disagreement with your mother, when she suddenly hangs up on you. Separation ends the immediate encounter, but it does nothing to solve the underlying issue that triggered the dispute in the first place.

However, separation isn't always negative. In some cases, short-term separation may help bring about long-term resolution. For example, if you and your partner have both used competitive or reactive approaches, your conflict may have escalated so much that any further contact may result in irreparable relationship damage. In such cases, temporary separation may help you both to cool off. Then, you can come back together later and consider how to collaborate.

Second, **domination** occurs when one person gets his or her way by influencing the other to engage in accommodation and abandon goals. Conflicts that end with domination are often called *win-lose solutions*. The strongest predictor of domination is the power balance in the relationship. When one person has substantial power over the other, that person will likely prevail.

In some cases, domination may be acceptable. For example, when one person doesn't feel strongly about achieving his or her goals, being dominated may have few costs. However, domination is destructive when it becomes a chronic pattern and one individual always sacrifices his or her goals to keep the peace. Over time, the consistent abandonment of goals can spawn resentment and hostility. While the accommodating "losers" are silently suffering, the dominating "victors" may think everything is fine because they are used to achieving their goals.

Third, during **compromise**, both parties change their goals to make them compatible. Often, both people abandon part of their original desires, and neither feels completely happy about it. Compromise typically results from people using a collaborative approach and is most

Stuart Franklin/Magnum Photos

◦ Conflict resolutions depend on the balance of power in a relationship. For example, many parents resolve conflict with their children through domination.

effective in situations where both people treat each other with respect, have relatively equal power, and don't consider their clashing goals especially important (Zacchilli et al., 2009). In cases where the two parties do consider their goals important, however, compromise can foster mutual resentment and regret (Peterson, 2002). Say that you and your spouse want to spend a weekend away. You planned this getaway for months, but your spouse now wants to attend a two-day workshop that same weekend. A compromise might involve you cutting the trip short by a night, and your spouse missing a day of his or her workshop, leaving both of you with substantially less than you originally desired.

Fourth, through **integrative agreements**, the two sides preserve and attain their goals by developing a creative solution to their problem. This creates a *win-win solution* in which both people, using a collaborative approach, benefit from the outcome. To achieve integrative agreements, the parties must remain committed to their individual goals but be flexible in how they achieve them (Pruitt & Carnevale, 1993). An integrative agreement for the example given above might involve rescheduling the weekend away so that you and your spouse could enjoy both the vacation and the workshop.

Finally, in cases of especially intense conflict, **structural improvements** may result. This is when people agree to change the basic rules or understandings that govern their relationship to prevent further conflict. In such cases, the conflict itself becomes a vehicle for reshaping the relationship in positive ways—rebalancing power or redefining expectations about roles in the relationship. Structural improvements are only likely to occur when the

Digital Vision/Getty Images

◦ We may try to end a conflict through a "peace offering"—a gift or favor to smooth things over. However, it is important to ensure that the parties involved have all reached a resolution so no lingering conflict may remain.

people involved control their negative emotions and handle the conflict collaboratively.

Long-Term Conflict Outcomes

After short-term conflict resolutions, you may begin to ponder the long-term outcomes. In particular, you might consider whether the conflict was truly resolved, and how the dispute impacts your relationship. Research examining long-term conflict outcomes and relationship satisfaction has found that certain approaches for dealing with conflict—in particular, avoidant, reactive, and collaborative approaches—strongly predict relationship quality (Smith et al., 2008; Zacchilli et al., 2009).

The most commonly used conflict approach is avoidance. But because avoidance doesn't address the goal clash or actions that sparked the conflict, tensions will likely continue. People who use avoidance have lower relationship satisfaction and endure longer and more frequent conflicts than people who don't avoid (Smith et al., 2008). Consequently, try not to use avoidance unless you're certain the issue is unimportant. Of course, sometimes an issue that seems unimportant at the time ends up mattering to you over the long run. When in doubt, communicate directly about the issue.

Far more poisonous to relationship health, however, is reactivity. Individuals who handle conflict by (in effect) throwing tantrums end up substantially less happy in their relationships (Zacchilli et al., 2009). If you or your partner habitually uses reactivity, seriously consider more constructive ways to approach conflict. If you do not, your relationship is likely doomed to dissatisfaction.

In sharp contrast to the negative outcomes of avoidance and reactivity, collaborative approaches generally generate positive long-term outcomes (Smith et al., 2008). People using collaboration tend to resolve their conflicts, report higher satisfaction in their relationships, and experience shorter and fewer disputes. The lesson from this is to always treat others with kindness and respect, and strive to deal with conflict by openly discussing it in a way that emphasizes mutual interests and saves your partner's face.

If collaborating yields positive long-term outcomes and avoiding and reacting yield negative ones,

what about accommodating and competing? This is difficult to predict. Sometimes, you'll compete and get what you want, the conflict will be resolved, and you'll be satisfied. Or, you'll compete, the conflict will escalate wildly out of control, and you'll end up incredibly unsatisfied. Other times, you'll accommodate, the conflict will be resolved, and you'll be content. Or, you'll accommodate, and the other person will exploit you further, causing you deep discontent. Accommodation and competition are riskier because you can't count on either as a constructive way to manage conflict for the long term (Peterson, 2002).

LearningCurve
bedfordstmartins.com/ipcandyou

Challenges to Handling Conflict

You and your mother suffer a disagreement that threatens to tear your family apart. So you text her and schedule a lunch date. Sitting down face-to-face, you both express love and admiration for each other, and you agree that the conflict should be resolved in a mutually satisfying fashion. You then collaboratively brainstorm ideas, and "Voila!"—the perfect solution is discovered! You smile, hug, and part ways, each feeling satisfied with the relationship and contented with the resolution.

Yeah, right. If only resolving conflict could be so easy! Unfortunately, conflict in close relationships is rarely (if ever) as streamlined and stress-free as cooperative partners joining forces to reconcile surmountable differences. Instead, close relationship conflict is typically fraught with challenges. Let's take a look at some of the most potent: self-enhancing thoughts, destructive messages, serial arguments, physical violence, and unsolvable disputes.

Self-Enhancing Thoughts

Arguably the biggest challenge we face in constructively managing conflict is our own minds. During conflicts, we think in radically self-enhancing ways. In a detailed study of conflict thought patterns, scholar Alan Sillars and his colleagues found that, during disputes, individuals selectively remember information that supports

> **You can improve your conflict-management skills by routinely practicing critical self-reflection during disputes.**

themselves and contradicts their partners, view their own communication more positively than their partners', and blame partners for failure to resolve the conflict (Sillars, Roberts, Leonard, & Dun, 2000).

Sillars and his colleagues also found little evidence of complex thought. While conflicts are unfolding, people typically do *not* consider long-term outcomes ("How is this going to impact our relationship?") and do *not* perspective-take ("How is she feeling?"). Instead, their thoughts are locked into simple, unqualified, and negative views: "He's lying!" or "She's blaming me!" (Sillars et al., 2000, p. 491). In only 2 percent of cases did respondents attribute cooperativeness to their partners and uncooperativeness to themselves. This means that in 98 percent of fights, you'll likely think, "I'm trying to be helpful, and my partner is being unreasonable!" However, your partner will be thinking the exact same things about you.

Self-enhancing thoughts dominate conflict encounters, stifling the likelihood of collaboration. Consequently, *the most important thing you can do to improve your conflict-management skills is to routinely practice critical self-reflection during disputes.* You can work toward this goal by regularly going through this mental checklist:

- Is my partner *really* being uncooperative, or am *I* making a faulty attribution?
- Is my partner *really* solely to blame, or have *I* also done something to cause the conflict?
- Is the conflict *really* due to ongoing differences between us, or is it *actually* due to temporary factors such as stress or fatigue?

Destructive Messages

Think back to the chapter opener when Amy Chua had a fight with Lulu in a restaurant. They both were so irate that they said horrible and unforgivable things to one another. When conflicts escalate and anger peaks, our minds are filled with negative thoughts of all the grievances and resentments we feel toward others (Sillars et al., 2000). These thoughts often leap out of our mouths, in the form of messages that permanently damage our relationships (McCornack & Husband, 1986).

Sudden-death statements occur when people get so angry that they suddenly declare the end of the relationship, even though that wasn't a possibility before the conflict. When my wife Kelly and I had been married for two years, we had a major argument while visiting her parents. A small dispute over family differences quickly escalated into a full-blown conflict. After flinging a number of kitchen-sink messages at each other, we both shouted, "Why are we even together?! We're so different!" Fortunately, this sudden-death statement caused us to calm down. But many couples who blurt out such things during escalation follow through on them.

Perhaps the most destructive messages are **dirty secrets**: statements that are honest in content but have been kept hidden to protect a partner's feelings. Dirty secrets can include acts of infidelity ("I cheated, and it was great!"), intense criticism of a partner's appearance ("You know how I've always said I like your nose? Well, I hate it!"), and even a lack of feelings ("I haven't been in love with you for years!"). Dirty secrets are designed to hurt, and because the content is true, they can irreparably damage the recipient and the relationship.

Needless to say, destructive messages can destroy relationships. Couples who exchange critical and contemptuous messages during the first seven years of marriage are substantially more likely to divorce than couples who refrain from such negativity (Gottman & Levenson, 2000). Thus, no matter your level of anger, or the caustic thoughts that fill your

Self-Reflection
Recall a conflict in which you and the other person exchanged destructive messages such as sudden-death statements or dirty secrets. What led to them being said? What impact did these messages have on the conflict? How did they affect your relationship?

head, it's essential to always communicate toward your partner in a civil, respectful fashion.

Serial Arguments

Another conflict challenge is **serial arguments**: a series of unresolved disputes, all having to do with the same issue (Bevan, Finan, & Kaminsky, 2008). Serial arguments typically stem from deep disagreements, such as differing relationship expectations or clashes in values and beliefs. By definition, serial arguments occur over time and consist of cycles in which things "heat up" and then lapse back into a temporary state of truce (Malis & Roloff, 2006). During these "quiet" periods, individuals are likely to think about the conflict, attempt to repair the relationship, and cope with the stress resulting from the most recent fight (Malis & Roloff, 2006).

Serial arguments are most likely to occur in romantic and family involvements, where the frequency of interaction provides ample opportunity for repetitive disagreements (Bevan et al., 2008). They are also strongly predictive of relationship failure: couples who suffer serial arguments experience higher stress levels and are more likely to have their relationships end than those who don't (Malis & Roloff, 2006).

Although many serial arguments involve heated verbal battles, others take the form of **demand-withdraw patterns**, in which one partner in a relationship demands that his or her goals be met, and the other partner responds by withdrawing from the encounter (Caughlin, 2002). Demand-withdraw patterns typically are triggered when a person is bothered by a repeated source of irritation, but doesn't confront the issue until his or her anger can no longer be suppressed. At that point, the person explodes in a demanding fashion (Malis & Roloff, 2006).

If you find yourself in a close relationship in which a demand-withdraw pattern has emerged, discuss this situation with your partner. Using a collaborative approach, critically examine the forces that trigger the pattern, and work to generate solutions that will enable you to avoid the pattern in the future.

Physical Violence

The most destructive conflict challenge is physical violence, a strategy to which people may resort if they cannot think of a better way to deal with conflict or if they believe no other options are available (Klein, 1998). In the National Violence Against Women Survey (Tjaden & Thoennes, 2000), 52 percent of women and 66 percent of men reported that at some time in their lives they had been physically assaulted during conflicts. Both men and women use violence as a strategy for dealing with conflicts. However, women are substantially more likely to be injured or killed, owing to their lesser physical size and strength (Archer, 2000; O'Leary & Vivian, 1990). Physical violence doesn't restrict itself to heterosexual relationships; nearly 50 percent of lesbian and 30 to 40 percent of gay respondents have been victims of violence during interpersonal conflicts at some time in their lives (Peplau & Spalding, 2000).

One outcome of physical violence in close relationships is the **chilling effect**, whereby individuals stop discussing relationship issues out of fear of their partners' negative reactions (Solomon & Samp, 1998). In these relationships, individuals who are "chilled" constrain their communication and actions to a very narrow margin, avoiding all topics and behaviors they believe may provoke a partner (Afifi et al., 2009). The result is an overarching relationship climate of fear, suppression, anxiety, and unhappiness.

If you find yourself in a relationship in which your partner behaves violently toward you, seek help from family members, friends, and, if necessary, law

In the movie *Blue Valentine*, main characters Dean and Cindy struggle with serial arguments and are unable to resolve the conflicts that ultimately destroy their marriage.

Davi Russo/© The Weinstein Company/Courtesy Everett Collection

© Peter Coombs/Alamy

Conflicts do not need to destroy your closest interpersonal relationships. When navigating a challenging conflict with a loved one, remember that renewed intimacy and happiness may be just around the corner.

enforcement officials. Realize that your best option might be to end the relationship and avoid all contact with the person. We discuss tactics for dealing with relational violence in more detail in Chapter 10.

If you find that you are inclined to violence in relationships, revisit the anger management techniques described in Chapter 4 as well as the suggestions for constructively handling conflict described previously. Most aggression during conflicts stems from people's perception that they have no other options. Although situations may exist where there truly are no other options—for example, self-defense during a violent assault or robbery—within most encounters more constructive alternatives are available. If you are unable to control your impulses toward violence, seek professional counseling.

Unsolvable Disputes

Part of effectively managing conflict is accepting that some conflicts are unsolvable, or impossible to resolve. Sometimes, no amount of collaboration can solve fundamental differences. How can you recognize such disputes? Clues include: you and the other person aren't willing to change your negative opinions of one another; your goals are irreconcilable and strongly held; and at least one partner is uncooperative, chronically defensive, or violent. In these cases, the only options are to avoid the conflict, hope that your attitudes or goals will change over time, or abandon the relationship.

LearningCurve
bedfordstmartins.com/ipcandyou

Postscript }

This chapter began with a woman determined to dominate her children. Amy Chua made headlines and best-seller lists when she boasted of her dictatorial parenting style. Her book *Battle Hymn of the Tiger Mother* describes her dysfunctional approaches to managing conflict and power in painful detail, including taunts, tantrums, insults, and accusations.

What messages did you learn growing up about how conflict and power should best be managed? Did the way in which your parents or caregivers dealt with conflicts leave you feeling better about yourself and your relationship with them? Or did it leave a wake of interpersonal destruction and heartache behind?

Satirical or not, Chua's book provides a powerful lesson for us all regarding the relationship between choices, communication, and outcomes. When you consistently choose to manage disputes in unyielding, aggressive ways, the relationship outcomes will be as unsatisfying and unpleasant as the conflict itself.

Chapter Review

}

KEY TERMS

conflict, 179
kitchen-sinking, 180
⊙ power, 181
   symmetrical relationships, 181
   complementary relationships, 182
   Dyadic Power Theory, 182
   power currency, 182
⊙ resource currency, 183
⊙ expertise currency, 183
⊙ social network currency, 183
⊙ personal currency, 183

⊙ intimacy currency, 183
⊙ avoidance, 184
   skirting, 184
⊙ sniping, 184
   cumulative annoyance, 184
   pseudo-conflict, 185
⊙ accommodation, 185
⊙ competition, 185
   escalation, 186
   reactivity, 187
⊙ collaboration, 187

separation, 191
domination, 191
⊙ compromise, 191
   integrative agreements, 192
   structural improvements, 192
   sudden-death
     statements, 194
   dirty secrets, 194
   serial arguments, 195
   demand-withdraw patterns, 195
   chilling effect, 195

CHAPTER ACTIVITIES

1. Conflict is often the basis for the plots of TV comedies such as *How I Met Your Mother, New Girl, The Mindy Project, Friends,* and so on. Using a specific conflict from such a show (or Web series), analyze what occurred in a brief essay. Describe the scenario and provide examples of specific conflict strategies the characters used. What was constructive or destructive in the conflict? What was played "for laughs" and how did that impact the conflict? How could the characters have handled the situation better?

2. ⊙ Watch the video on **sniping** and write a short improvement paper analyzing the communication between the two roommates: How could the roommates in the video improve their communication? Have you experienced similar interactions? If so, how did you handle the conversation? What strategies could help repair the relationship?

3. Journal about a recent conflict with a romantic partner, coworker, family member, or friend. Describe the scenario, how each person handled the conflict, influences on the conflict, and the conflict ending, using concepts and theories from the chapter. Consider how you could have handled the situation differently and what lessons you learned for the next time you enter a conflict.

4. With a partner, discuss a time when you both avoided a conflict. Why did you choose this approach? What form of avoidance did you use? What were the results? Can avoiding conflict sometimes be a good strategy? How do the concepts of suppressing and venting emotions (from Chapter 4) affect avoidance as a way to handle conflict?

5. Consider this analogy: a small amount of salt is needed to balance the sugar level in cookies. Similarly, we don't want too much "salt" in relationships, but it can be useful to balance the sweet. Why would this be? What role does conflict play in relationships? When can conflict improve relationships?

6. Films and TV shows often feature sudden-death breakups such as in the film *The Break-Up,* when Jennifer Aniston's character breaks up with her boyfriend during a fight; or when Elaine's boyfriend, "The Bad Breaker-Upper" tells her she has a "big head" on *Seinfeld;* or when Rachel breaks up with Ross on *Friends* with "Let's take a break." Discuss the implications of sudden-death statements. Can relationships be repaired after such statements? How do you deal with the regret?

☑ Look for **LearningCurve** throughout the chapter to help you review.
bedfordstmartins.com/ipcandyou.

10 } Relationships with Romantic Partners

The temperature was –70°.[1] Although he was only a few miles from his supply depot—and salvation in the form of food and gear—the weather was impassable. Suffering from frostbite and malnutrition, Antarctic explorer Sir Robert Falcon Scott knew two things for certain: he would soon die, and a recovery team would eventually find his body. So he penned a letter to his wife, Kathleen. "To my widow," he began. What followed is one of the most moving testimonials to romantic love ever written.

Scott had led a British team trying to be the first to reach the South Pole. Arriving at their goal on January 17, 1912, they were stunned to find a tent erected on the site. Inside was a note left by Norwegian explorer Roald Amundsen: he had beaten Scott's team by a month. Defeated, Scott and his comrades began the 800-mile return trip, beset by snow blindness, hunger, and exhaustion. The weather worsened, and one by one his team members perished.

Huddled inside his shelter, Scott crafted a note to Kathleen that was at once passionate, practical, upbeat, and astonishingly selfless. Longing and sentiment poured from his pen: "You know I have loved you, you know my thoughts must have constantly dwelt on you . . . the worst aspect of this situation is the thought that I shall not see you again. . . . Oh what a price to pay—to forfeit the sight of your dear dear face!" He grieved the lost chance to see his son mature, ". . . what dreams I have had of his future." But he praised Kathleen's practicality and entreated her "to take the whole thing very sensibly as I am sure you will. . . . Make the boy interested in natural history, if you can, it is better than games."

_____

[1] All information and quotes that follow are adapted from the Scott Polar Institute. Retrieved from http://www.cam.ac.uk /news/caption=scott's=final=letters=home=go=on=display.

◆ **Romantic love may not be essential to life, but it may be essential to joy.**

Though suffering from frostbite, he remained relentlessly upbeat. "There is a painless end, so don't worry—How much better it has been than lounging in comfort at home." In the most striking passage of all, Scott granted Kathleen romantic liberty: "Cherish no sentimental rubbish about remarriage—when the right man comes to help you in life you ought to be your happy self again. I hope I shall be a good memory."

Eight months later a recovery team reached Scott's encampment. Searching the remnants of his tent, they found Scott's personal journal and his letter to Kathleen. In the years that followed, Scott would be honored across Britain as a tragic hero. Scott's letters and journal were even donated for display at the University of Cambridge in January 2007. But in the dim light of his tent in March 1912, with storms raging and death approaching, Sir Robert Falcon Scott was just another human being trying to capture in writing the multifaceted complexity of romantic love. To read his words is to be reminded that *love is not singular, but plural*: it is many things at once, including passion, practicality, commitment, respect, sentiment, and selflessness.

T hroughout time and across cultures, people have fallen in love. When each of us discovers love for ourselves, we honor that legacy, sharing in an experience that is both uniquely and universally human. We also find that romantic love contains multiple elements, some of which seem contradictory. Our affairs may be all about passion, but they also bring with them the rewards (and costs) of companionship. Our love for others may be selfless and giving, yet we're driven to build and sustain only those relationships that benefit us the most, and end those that don't. Although romance may be sentimental and otherworldly, the maintenance of love is decidedly practical. Romantic relationships are hard work, entailing constant upkeep to survive the innumerable and unforeseen challenges that threaten them.

In this chapter, the first of three on relationships, you'll learn:

- The defining characteristics of romantic love and relationships
- What drives your attraction to some people and not others
- How communication changes as your romantic relationships come together . . . and fall apart
- How to communicate in ways that keep your love alive
- Ways to deal effectively with the challenges to romantic relationships

Defining Romantic Relationships

Romantic love may not be essential to life, but it may be essential to joy. Life without love would be for many people like a black-and-white movie—full of events and activities but without the color that gives vibrancy and provides a sense of celebration. Beyond the theories, beyond the research, romantic love is one of life's compensations for drudgery, illness, and, perhaps in some small way, for mortality.[2]

—love researchers Clyde and Susan Hendrick

[2]The quote is excerpted from Hendrick & Hendrick (1992, p. 117).

{ **Liking and loving are separate emotional states, with different causes and outcomes.** }

We often think of romantic relationships as exciting and filled with promise—a joyful fusion of closeness, communication, and sexual connection. When researchers Pamela Regan, Elizabeth Kocan, and Teresa Whitlock (1998) asked several hundred people to list the things they associated most with "being in love," the most frequent responses were trust, honesty, happiness, bondedness, companionship, communication, caring, intimacy, shared laughter, and sexual desire. But apart from such associations, what exactly *is* romantic love? How does it differ from liking? How does interpersonal communication shape love relationships? The answers to these questions can help you build more satisfying romantic partnerships.

Liking and Loving

Most scholars agree that liking and loving are separate emotional states, with different causes and outcomes (Berscheid & Regan, 2005). **Liking** is a feeling of affection and respect that we typically have for our friends (Rubin, 1973). *Affection* is a sense of warmth and fondness toward another person, while *respect* is admiration for another person apart from how he or she treats you and communicates with you. **Loving**, in contrast, is a vastly deeper and more intense emotional experience and consists of three components: intimacy, caring, and attachment (Rubin, 1973).

- *Intimacy* is a feeling of closeness and "union" between you and your partner (Mashek & Aron, 2004).
- *Caring* is the concern you have for your partner's welfare and the desire to keep him or her happy.
- *Attachment* is a longing to be in your partner's presence as much as possible.

The ideal combination for long-term success in romantic relationships occurs when partners both like and love each other.

Different Types of Romantic Love

Though most people recognize that loving differs from liking, many also believe that to be *in* love, one must feel constant and consuming sexual attraction toward a partner. In fact, many different types of romantic love exist, covering a broad range of emotions and relationship forms. At one end of the spectrum is **passionate love**, a state of intense emotional and physical longing for union with another (Hendrick & Hendrick, 1992). For example, think of how the media depict couples who are passionately in love: Jacob and Anna in the film *Like Crazy*, Olivia Pope and Fitzgerald Grant on TV's *Scandal*, or even real-life couples like Beyoncé and Jay-Z. Their constant need for close contact (whether physical or communicative), expression of relationship happiness through social media posts or during conversations, and overall sense of delight permeates their entire lives.

If you've been passionately in love before, these feelings likely are familiar. Studies of passionate love support the universality of these sentiments and suggest that five things are true about the experience and expression of passion. First, people in the throes of passionate love often view their loved ones and relationships in an excessively idealistic light; talking about how "perfect" they are for each other and how their relationship is the "best ever."

Second, people from all cultures feel passionate love. Studies comparing members of individualistic versus collectivistic cultures have found no differences in the amount of passionate love experienced (Hatfield & Rapson, 1987). Although certain ethnicities, especially Latinos, often are stereotyped as more "passionate," studies comparing Latino and non-Latino experiences of romantic love suggest no differences in intensity (Cerpas, 2002).

Third, no gender or age differences exist in people's experience of passionate love. Men and women report experiencing this type of love with equal frequency and intensity, and studies that exclude reference to sexual feelings have found that children as young as age 4 report passionate love toward others (Hatfield & Rapson, 1987).

Fourth, for adults, passionate love is integrally linked with sexuality and sexual desire (Berscheid & Regan, 2005). In one study, undergraduates were asked whether they thought there was a difference between "being in love" and "loving" another person (Ridge & Berscheid, 1989). Eighty-seven percent of respondents said that there was a difference and that sexual attraction was the critical distinguishing feature of being in love.

Finally, passionate love is *negatively* related to relationship duration. Like it or not, the longer you're with a romantic partner, the less intense your passionate love will feel (Berscheid, 2002).

Although the "fire" of passionate love dominates media depictions of romance, not all people view being in love this way. At the other end of the romantic spectrum is **companionate love**: an intense form of liking defined by emotional investment and deeply intertwined lives (Berscheid & Walster, 1978). Many long-term romantic relationships evolve into companionate love. As Clyde and Susan Hendrick (1992) explain, "Sexual attraction, intense communication, and emotional turbulence early in a relationship give way to quiet intimacy, predictability, and shared attitudes, values, and life experiences later in the relationship" (p. 48).

Philip Jones Griffiths/Magnum Photos

◔ People who are passionately in love experience an intense longing to be physically near one another. What other traits or experiences do you associate with passionate love?

Between the poles of passionate and companionate love lies a range of other types of romantic love. Sociologist John Alan Lee (1973) suggested six different forms that range from friendly to obsessive and gave them each a traditional Greek name: *storge, agape, mania, pragma, ludus,* and *eros* (see Table 10.1 for an explanation of each). As Lee noted, there is no "right" type of romantic love—different forms appeal to different people.

> **Self-Reflection**
>
> Is passion the critical defining feature of being in love? Or can you fall in love without ever feeling passion? Given that passion typically fades, is romantic love always doomed to fail, or can you still be in love after passion leaves?

Key Elements of Romantic Relationships

If loving differs from liking, and people experience different types of love, what exactly does it mean to have a romantic relationship? A **romantic relationship** is a chosen interpersonal involvement forged through communication in which the participants perceive the bond as romantic. Six elements of romantic relationships underlie this definition: perception, diversity, choice, commitment, tensions, and communication.

Perception

A romantic relationship exists whenever the two partners perceive that it does. As perceptions change, so too does the relationship. For example, a couple may consider their relationship "casual dating" but still define it as "romantic" (rather than friendly). Or, a long-term couple may feel more companionate than passionate but still consider themselves "in love." If two partners' perceptions of their relationship differ—for example, one person feels romantic and the other does not—they do not have a romantic relationship (Miller & Steinberg, 1975).

Table 10.1 **Romantic Love Types**

Type	Description	Attributes of Love
Storge	Friendly lovers	Stable, predictable, and rooted in friendship
Agape	Forgiving lovers	Patient, selfless, giving, and unconditional
Mania	Obsessive lovers	Intense, tumultuous, extreme, and all consuming
Pragma	Practical lovers	Logical, rational, and founded in common sense
Ludus	Game-playing lovers	Uncommitted, fun, and played like a game
Eros	Romantic lovers	Sentimental, romantic, idealistic, and committed

Diversity

Romantic relationships exhibit remarkable diversity in the ages and genders of the partners, as well as in their ethnic and religious backgrounds and sexual orientations. Yet despite this diversity, most relationships function in a similar manner. For example, whether a romantic relationship is between lesbian, gay, or straight partners, the individuals involved place the same degree of importance on their relationship, devote similar amounts of time and energy to maintaining their bond, and demonstrate similar openness in their communication (Haas & Stafford, 2005). The exact same factors that determine marital success between men and women (such as honesty, loyalty, commitment, and dedication to maintenance) also predict stability and satisfaction within same-sex couples (Kurdek, 2005). As relationship scholar Sharon Brehm sums up, gay and lesbian couples "fall in love in the same way, feel the same passions, experience the same doubts, and feel the same commitments as straights" (Brehm, Miller, Perlman, & Campbell, 2002, p. 27).

Choice

We enter into romantic relationships through choice, selecting not only with whom we initiate involvements but also whether and how we maintain these bonds. Thus, contrary to widespread belief, love doesn't "strike us out of the blue" or "sweep us away." Choice plays a role even in arranged marriages: the spouses' families

and social networks select an appropriate partner, and in many cases the betrothed retain at least some control over whether the choice is acceptable (Hendrick & Hendrick, 1992).

Erich Lessing/Art Resource, NY

◊ Depictions of romantic love are often found in art, movies, literature, poetry, music, and other media, but they rarely detail the everyday interpersonal communication that makes successful relationships work.

Commitment

Romantic relationships often involve **commitment**: a strong psychological attachment to a partner and an intention to continue the relationship long into the future (Arriaga & Agnew, 2001). When you forge a commitment with a partner, positive outcomes often result. Commitment leads couples to work harder on maintaining their relationships, resulting in greater satisfaction (Rusbult, Arriaga, & Agnew, 2001). Commitment also reduces the likelihood that partners will cheat sexually when separated by geographic distance (Le, Korn, Crockett, & Loving, 2010).

Although men are stereotyped in the media as "commitment-phobic," this stereotype is false. *Both* men and women view commitment as an important part of romantic relationships (Miller, Perlman, & Brehm, 2007). Studies even suggest that men often place a higher value on commitment than do women. For example, when asked which they would choose, if forced to decide between a committed romance or an important job opportunity, more men than women chose the relationship (Mosher & Danoff-Burg, 2007). Men have also reported more of a desire for marriage than have women, and described "desire for a committed relationship" as more of a motivation for dating (Rubin, Peplau, & Hill, 1981).

Tensions

When we're involved in intimate relationships, we often experience competing impulses, or tensions, between our selves and our feelings toward others, known as **relational dialectics** (Baxter, 1990). Relational dialectics take three common forms. The first is *openness versus protection*. As relationships become more intimate, we naturally exchange more personal information with our partners. Most of us enjoy the feeling of unity and mutual insight created through such sharing. But while we want to be open with our partners, we also want to keep certain aspects of our selves—such as our most private thoughts and feelings—protected. Too much openness provokes an uncomfortable sense that we've lost our privacy and must share *everything* with our lovers.

The second dialectic is *autonomy versus connection*. We elect to form romantic relationships largely out of a desire to bond with other human beings. Yet if we come to feel so connected to our partners that our individual identity seems to dissolve, we may choose to pull back and reclaim some of our autonomy.

The final dialectic is the clash between our need for stability and our need for excitement and change—known as *novelty versus predictability*. We all like the security that comes with knowing how our partners will behave, how we'll behave, and how our relationships will unfold. Romances are more successful when the partners behave in predictable ways that reduce uncertainty (Berger & Bradac, 1982). However, predictability often spawns boredom. As we get to know our partners, the novelty and excitement of the relationship wears off, and things seem increasingly monotonous. Reconciling the desire for predictability with the need for novelty is one of the most profound emotional challenges facing partners in romantic relationships.

Communication

Romantic involvements, like all interpersonal relationships, are forged through interpersonal communication. By interacting with others online, over the phone, and face-to-face, we build a variety of relationships—some of which blossom into romantic love. And once love is born, we use interpersonal communication to foster and maintain it.

LearningCurve
bedfordstmartins.com/ipcandyou

Romantic Attraction

On the hit TV show *Glee*, Artie excitedly wheels his chair to the sign-up sheet for the new school song-and-dance club.[3] When he struggles to reach the list,

---

[3]All information that follows is from www.fox.com/glee.

Tina intervenes and helps him. An instant attraction is sparked. As they spend time together, they quickly learn that they share much more in common than music. Both are intensely intellectual and somewhat "offbeat" in their views. Both struggle with disabilities— Artie is paralyzed from the waist down, and Tina wrestles with a speech impediment. The degree to which they rise above their respective limitations spawns a strong foundation of shared respect. Their mutual attraction deepens and eventually culminates in a kiss—Artie's first. But when Tina reveals that she was faking her disability, Artie is shattered, and he angrily breaks off their relationship.

Every day, you meet and interact with new people while in class, standing in line at the local coffee shop, or participating in clubs like the one depicted on *Glee*. Yet few of these individuals make a lasting impression on you, and even fewer strike a chord of romantic attraction. What draws you to those special few? Many of the same factors that drew Artie and Tina together: proximity, physical attractiveness, similarity, reciprocal liking, and resources (Aron et al., 2008). These factors influence attraction for both men and women, in both same- and opposite-sex romances (Felmlee, Orzechowicz, & Fortes, 2010; Hyde, 2005).

Proximity

The simple fact of physical proximity—being in one another's presence frequently—exerts far more impact on romantic attraction than many people think. In general, you'll feel more attracted to those with whom you have frequent contact and less attracted to those with whom you interact rarely, a phenomenon known as the **mere exposure effect** (Bornstein, 1989).

Proximity's pronounced effect on attraction is one reason that mixed-race romantic relationships are much rarer than same-race pairings in the United States. Despite this nation's enormous ethnic diversity, most Americans cluster into ethnically homogeneous groups, communities, and neighborhoods. This clustering reduces the likelihood that individuals will meet, regularly interact with, and eventually become attracted to those outside their own cultural

Carin Baer © FOX/Courtesy Everett Collection

🔵 On *Glee*, Artie and Tina's instant attraction is disrupted when it is revealed that Tina isn't as similar to Artie as it first seemed. Have you ever misled a romantic interest into thinking you shared a common concern or value? If so, did you eventually confess? What was the outcome?

group (Gaines, Chalfin, Kim, & Taing, 1998). Those who do form interethnic romances typically have living arrangements, work situations, or educational interests that place them in close proximity with diverse others, fostering attraction (Gaines et al., 1998).

Self-Reflection

How much daily contact do you have with people of other ethnicities, based on where you live, work, and go to school? Do you date outside your own ethnic group? How has the frequency with which you've had contact with diverse others shaped your dating decisions?

Physical Attractiveness

It's no secret that many people feel drawn to those they perceive as physically attractive. In part this is because we view beautiful people as competent communicators, intelligent, and well-adjusted, a phenomenon known as the **beautiful-is-good effect** (Eagly, Ashmore, Makhijani, & Longo, 1991). But although most of us find physical beauty attractive, we tend to form long-term romantic relationships with people we judge as similar to ourselves in physical attractiveness. This is known as **matching** (Feingold, 1988). Research documents that people don't want to be paired with those they think are substantially "below" or "above" themselves in looks (White, 1980).

Similarity

No doubt you've heard the contradictory clichés regarding similarity and attraction: "Opposites attract" versus "Birds of a feather flock together." Which is correct? Scientific evidence suggests that we are attracted to those we perceive as similar to ourselves (Miller et al., 2007). This is known as the **birds-of-a-feather effect**. One explanation for this phenomenon is that people we view as similar to us are less likely to provoke uncertainty. In first encounters, they seem easier to predict and explain than people we perceive as dissimilar (Berger & Calabrese, 1975). Thus, we feel more comfortable with them.

Similarity means more than physical attractiveness; it means sharing parallel personalities, values, and likes and dislikes (Markey & Markey, 2007). Having fundamentally different personalities or widely disparate values erodes attraction between partners in the long run. At the same time, differences in mere tastes and preferences have no long-term negative impact on relationship health, as long as you and your partner are similar in other, more important ways. For example, I like heavier music (Motörhead, Mastodon, Pantera), and my wife hates it. But we have very similar personalities and values, so our attraction and our relationship endure.

Because differences in tastes and preferences don't predict relationship success, you shouldn't dismiss potential romantic partners because of their minor likes and dislikes. Instead, first see whether you share similarities in personality and values.

Reciprocal Liking

A fourth determinant of romantic attraction is one of the most obvious and often overlooked: whether the person we're attracted to makes it clear, through communication and other actions, that the attraction is mutual, known as **reciprocal liking** (Aron et al., 2008). Reciprocal liking is a potent predictor of attraction; we tend to be attracted to people who are attracted to us. Studies examining people's narrative descriptions of "falling in love" have found that reciprocal liking is *the* most commonly mentioned factor leading to love (Riela, Rodriguez, Aron, Xu, & Acevedo, 2010).

Resources

A final spark that kindles romantic attraction is the unique resources that another person offers. Resources include qualities such as sense of humor,

(Left to right) © Rhoda Sidney/The Image Works; sarune zurba/Getty Images; © ableimages/Alamy; © Arnold Gold/*New Haven Register*/The Image Works

💧 Although people lust after gorgeous others, most of us end up in long-term relationships with those we perceive to be our equals in physical attractiveness.

intelligence, kindness, supportiveness, and whether the person seems fun, and these attributes are viewed as valuable by both straight persons and gays and lesbians (Felmlee et al., 2010). But what leads *you* to view a person's resources as desirable?

Social exchange theory proposes that you'll feel drawn to those you see as offering substantial benefits (things you like and want) with few associated costs (things demanded of you in return). Two factors drive whether you find someone initially attractive: whether you perceive them as offering the kind of rewards you think you deserve in a romantic relationship (affection, emotional support, money, sex, etc.), and whether you think that the rewards they can offer you are superior to those you can get elsewhere (Kelley & Thibaut, 1978). In simple terms, you're attracted to people who can give you what you want, and who offer better rewards than others.

Once you've experienced attraction because of perceived rewards, the balance of benefits and costs exchanged by you and the other person, known as **equity**, determines whether a relationship will take root (Stafford, 2003). Romantic partners are happiest when the balance of giving and getting in their relationship is equal for both, and they're least happy when inequity exists (Hatfield, Traupmann, Sprecher, Utne, & Hay, 1985).

What is *inequity?* People in relationships have a strong sense of proportional justice: the balance between benefits gained from the relationship versus contributions made to the relationship (Hatfield, 1983). Inequity occurs when the benefits or contributions provided by one person are greater than those provided by the other. People who get more rewards from their relationships for fewer costs than their partners are *overbenefited*; those who get fewer rewards from their relationships for more costs than their partners are *underbenefited*. Overbenefited individuals experience negative emotions such as guilt, while underbenefited partners experience emotions such as sadness and anger (Sprecher, 2001).

Equity strongly determines the short- and long-term success of romantic relationships. One study found that only 23 percent of equitable romances broke up during a several-month period, whereas

◊ Approximately 50 percent of students surveyed think interracial dating is acceptable, but this masks substantial race and gender differences. While 81 percent of European American and 75 percent of African American men express willingness to date outside their ethnicity, the majority of European American and African American women report negative attitudes toward interracial dating.

54 percent of inequitable romantic relationships broke up (Sprecher, 2001).

Technology and Romantic Attraction

Today, the enormous range of communication technologies available has refined and enhanced the attraction process. You can establish virtual proximity to attractive others by befriending them on social networking sites (Instagram, Twitter) and then exchanging daily (or even hourly) updates and posts. You can assess a prospective partner's similarity to you and the rewards he or she could offer you by interacting with the person through text-messaging or simply by checking their personal Web pages and online profiles. You can assess physical attractiveness by viewing online photo albums and video clips. On dating sites such as Match.com, OkCupid, or even the "Personals" pages of Craigslist, you can enter a

Courtesy of howaboutwe.com

💧 A challenge of online dating is transferring the romance from online to offline. Newer online dating services like HowAboutWe focus on just that by encouraging users to plan specific activities with one another. What challenges, if any, have you faced in this transition?

set of search parameters—desired age, profession, appearance, interests, sexual orientation—and immediately see a broad range of potential partners.

But despite the conveniences they offer, these technologies also evoke tensions. For one thing, you have to decide how honest to be in your online self-presentations (Ellison, Heino, & Gibbs, 2006). Because so many people now use online communication to gauge each other, you may feel great pressure to present yourself as highly attractive—even if that means providing a distorted self-description. In a survey of more than 5,000 online dating service users, misrepresentation of self was commonplace (Hall, Park, Song, & Cody, 2010). Men were more likely than women to exaggerate their education level and income, and women were more likely to lie about their weight. And both men and women over 50 routinely distorted their ages to appear younger. Correspondingly, people view

others' online dating profiles skeptically. Users liken profiles to "résumés"; that is, they are vehicles for marketing one's "best self," rather than accurate glimpses into one's authentic identity (Heino, Ellison, & Gibbs, 2010). As one online dating service user describes, "Everyone is so wonderful over the Internet. What the Internet doesn't tell you is that, 'I'm defensive, I talk about my problems all the time, I can't manage my money' " (Heino et al., 2010, p. 435).

If your goal is to forge an offline romantic relationship, distorting your online self-description is ultimately self-defeating (Ellison et al., 2006). When you mislead someone online about your appearance or other personal attributes and then take your romance offline, your partner *will* discover the truth. Such unpleasant revelations are commonplace: one study found that 86 percent of people using online dating sites report having met others whom they felt had misrepresented their physical attractiveness (Gibbs, Ellison, & Heino, 2006). When people feel misled, the outcome is often a damaged impression, negative emotions (such as resentment or anger), and an injured or even ruined relationship (McCornack & Levine, 1990). The most ethical and practical thing you can do in your online self-descriptions is to accentuate your attractive attributes without resorting to distortion or dishonesty.

LearningCurve
bedfordstmartins.com/ipcandyou

Relationship Development and Deterioration

Romantic relationships come together and apart in as many different ways and at as many different speeds as there are partners who fall for each other (Surra & Hughes, 1997). Many relationships are of the "casual dating" variety—they flare quickly, sputter, and then fade. Others endure and evolve with deepening levels of commitment. But all romantic relationships undergo stages marked by distinctive patterns in partners' communication, thoughts, and feelings. Communication scholar Mark Knapp (1984)

| Initiating | Experimenting | Intensifying | Integrating | Bonding |

◐ Figure 10.1 Stages of Coming Together

modeled these patterns as ten stages: five of "coming together" and five of "coming apart."

Coming Together

Knapp's stages of coming together illustrate one possible flow of relationship development (see **Figure 10.1**). As you read through the stages, keep in mind that these suggest turning points in relationships and are not fixed rules for how involvements should or do progress. Your relationships may go through some, none, or all of these stages. They may skip stages, jump back or forward in order, or follow a completely different and unique trajectory.

Initiating

During the **initiating** stage, you size up a person you've just met or noticed. You draw on all available visual information (physical attractiveness, body type, age, ethnicity, gender, clothing, posture) to determine whether you find him or her attractive. Your primary concern at this stage is to portray yourself in a positive light. You also ponder and present a greeting you deem appropriate. This greeting might be in person or through an online site.

Experimenting

Once you've initiated an encounter with someone, you enter the **experimenting** stage, during which you exchange demographic information (names, majors, hometowns). You also engage in *small talk*—disclosing facts you and the other person consider relatively unimportant but that enable you to introduce yourselves in a safe and controlled fashion. As you share these details, you look for points of commonality on which you can base further interaction. This is the "casual dating" phase of romance, and most involvements never progress beyond this stage. We go through life experimenting with many people but forming deeper connections with very few.

Intensifying

Occasionally, you'll progress beyond casual dating and find yourself experiencing strong feelings of attraction toward another person. When this happens, your verbal and nonverbal communication becomes increasingly intimate. During this **intensifying** stage, you and your partner begin to reveal previously withheld information, such as secrets about your past or important life dreams and goals. You may begin using informal forms of address or terms of endearment ("honey" versus "Joe") and saying "we" more frequently. One particularly strong sign that your relationship is intensifying is the direct expression of commitment. You might do this verbally ("I think I'm falling for you") or online by marking your profile as "in a relationship" rather than "single." You may also spend more time in each other's personal spaces, as well as begin physical expressions of affection, such as hand-holding, cuddling, or sexual activity.

Integrating

During the **integrating** stage, your and your partner's personalities seem to become one. This integration is

"Conversation? I thought we were just meeting for coffee."

reinforced through sexual activity and the exchange of belongings (items of clothing, music, photos, etc.). When you've integrated with a romantic partner, you cultivate attitudes, activities, and interests that join you together as a couple —"*our* favorite movie" or "*our* song." Friends, colleagues, and family members begin to treat you as a couple —for example, always inviting the two of you to parties or dinners. Not surprisingly, many people begin to struggle with the dialectical tension of *connectedness versus autonomy* at this stage. As a student of mine once told his partner when describing this stage, "I'm not me anymore, I'm *us*."

Bonding

The ultimate stage of coming together is **bonding**, a public ritual that announces to the world that you and your partner have made a commitment to one another. Bonding is something you'll share with very few people—perhaps only one—during your lifetime. The most obvious example of bonding is marriage.

Bonding institutionalizes your relationship. Before this stage, the ground rules for your relationship and your communication within it remain a private matter, to be negotiated between you and your partner. In the bonding stage, you import into your relationship a set of laws and customs determined by governmental authorities and perhaps religious institutions. Although these laws and customs help to solidify your relationship, they can also make your relationship feel more rigid and structured.

Coming Apart

Like coming together, coming apart unfolds over stages marked by changes in thoughts, feelings, and

(Left to right) Norm Betts/Bloomberg/Getty Images; Digital Vision/Punchstock/Getty Images

There are many ways for couples to bond, but the key is that both partners agree and make a deep commitment to each other.

Differentiating	Circumscribing	Stagnating	Avoiding	Terminating

◑ Figure 10.2 **Stages of Coming Apart**

communication (see Figure 10.2). But unlike coming together, these stages often entail emotional turmoil that makes them difficult to negotiate skillfully. Learning how to communicate supportively while a romantic relationship is dissolving is a challenging but important part of being a skilled interpersonal communicator.

Differentiating

In all romantic relationships, partners share differences as well as similarities. But during the first stage of coming apart, **differentiating**, the beliefs, attitudes, and values that distinguish you from your partner come to dominate your thoughts and communication ("I can't *believe* you think that!").

Most healthy romances experience occasional periods of differentiating. These moments can involve unpleasant clashes and bickering over contrasting viewpoints, tastes, or goals. But you can move your relationship through this difficulty—and thus halt the coming-apart process—by openly discussing your points of difference and working together to resolve them. To do this, review the constructive conflict skills discussed in Chapter 9.

Skills Practice
Differentiating
Overcoming the challenge of differentiating

1. Identify when you and your romantic partner are differentiating.
2. Check your perception of the relationship, especially how you've punctuated encounters and the attributions you've made.
3. Call to mind the similarities that originally brought you and your partner together.
4. Discuss your concerns with your partner, emphasizing these similarities and your desire to continue the relationship.
5. Mutually explore solutions to the differences that have been troubling you.

Circumscribing

If one or both of you respond to problematic differences by ignoring them and spending less time talking, you enter the **circumscribing** stage. You actively begin to restrict the quantity and quality of information you

exchange with your partner. Instead of sharing information, you create "safe zones" in which you discuss only topics that won't provoke conflict. For example, saying, "Let's not talk about that anymore."

Stagnating

When circumscribing becomes so severe that almost no safe conversational topics remain, communication slows to a standstill, and your relationship enters the **stagnating** stage. You both presume that communicating is pointless because it will only lead to further problems. People in stagnant relationships often experience a sense of resignation; they feel "stuck" or "trapped." However, they can remain in the relationship for months or even years. Why? Some believe that it's better to leave things as they are rather than expend the effort necessary to break up or rebuild the relationship. Others simply don't know how to repair the damage and revive their earlier bond.

Avoiding

During the **avoiding** stage, one or both of you decide that you no longer can be around each other, and you begin distancing yourself physically. Some people communicate avoidance directly to their partner ("I don't want to see you anymore"). Others do so indirectly—for example, by going out when the partner's at home, screening cell-phone calls, ignoring texts, and changing their Facebook status from "in a relationship" to "single."

Terminating

In ending a relationship, some people want to come together for a final encounter that gives a sense of closure and resolution. During the **terminating** stage, couples might discuss the past, present, and future of the relationship. They often exchange summary statements about the past—comments on "how our relationship was" that are either accusations ("No one has ever treated me so badly!") or laments ("I'll never be able to find someone as perfect as you"). Verbal and nonverbal behaviors indicating a lack of intimacy are readily apparent—including physical distance between the two individuals and reluctance to make eye contact. The partners may also discuss the future status of their relationship. Some couples may agree to end all contact going forward. Others may choose to remain friends.

◊ Gender stereotypes dominate our thinking about men and women in romantic relationships, but research discredits many of these damaging presumptions. For example, although in Western cultures women are depicted as sentimental and men as rational, women actually are more likely than men to base their romantic relationship decisions on practical considerations.

Many people find terminating a relationship painful or awkward. It's hard to tell someone that you no longer want to be involved, and it is equally painful to hear it. Draw on your interpersonal communication skills to best negotiate your way through this dreaded moment. In particular, express empathy—offering empathic concern and perspective-taking (see Chapter 3). Realize that romantic breakups are a kind of death, and that it's normal to experience grief, even when breaking up is the right thing to do. Consequently, offer supportive communication ("I know this is going to be painful for both of us") and use grief management tactics (see Chapter 4). While termination conversations are never easy, your communication skills can help you minimize the pain and damage, enabling you and your former partner to move on.

💧 In *Eternal Sunshine of the Spotless Mind*, Joel and Clementine decide to take another shot at their relationship despite the risks.

Maintaining Romantic Relationships

In the movie *Eternal Sunshine of the Spotless Mind*, Joel (Jim Carrey) and Clementine (Kate Winslet) are lovers struggling to maintain a bittersweet romance (Bregman, Golin, Gondry, & Kaufman, 2004). Clementine, an outgoing, self-described "high-maintenance girl," is the opposite of quiet, bookish Joel, who communicates more with his private journal than with her. Following a fight, Clementine impetuously visits a clinic that specializes in memory erasure and has Joel expunged from her mind. Despondent, Joel follows suit. But the two meet again and find themselves attracted. Eventually discovering the truth—that they aren't strangers at all but longtime lovers—they face a momentous decision. Do they invest the time and energy necessary to maintain their romance a second time, knowing that they failed so terribly before that they chose to destroy their memories? Or do they end it before their history of relational disaster can repeat itself? They ultimately decide to defy their past failure and stay together.

Romantic relationships aren't always about happiness and celebration. No matter how much you love your partner, you will still experience unpleasant moments such as feeling irked, bored, or trapped. In fact, on any given day, 44 percent of us are likely to be seriously annoyed by a close relationship partner (Kowalski, Walker, Wilkinson, Queen, & Sharpe, 2003).

Though such experiences are normal, many people find them disturbing and wonder whether they should end the relationship. But Clementine's and Joel's choice in the conclusion of *Eternal Sunshine*—to accept the inevitable negatives as natural and move forward regardless—offers a message of hope. Wiping our mental slates clean and leaving our partners behind is not the only solution to romantic relationship challenges. Instead, we can choose to harness our interpersonal communication skills and invest the effort necessary to maintain satisfying, healthy romantic relationships.

Maintenance Strategies

Many people believe that love just happens—that once it strikes, it endures. But that isn't the case. Romantic love requires maintenance to keep it from deteriorating (Stafford, 2003). **Relational maintenance** refers to using communication and supportive behaviors to sustain a desired relationship status and level of satisfaction (Stafford, Dainton, & Haas, 2000). Communication scholar Laura Stafford has observed several strategies that satisfied couples—no matter their ethnicity or sexual orientation—routinely use to maintain their romances (Stafford, 2010). Three of these are positivity, assurances, and self-disclosure.

(Left to right) Ian Berry/Magnum Photos; © Russell Underwood/CORBIS; © Annebicque Bernard/Corbis Sygma

🔴 Constant, daily maintenance is needed to keep romantic relationships alive and healthy.

Positivity

Positivity includes communicating in a cheerful and optimistic fashion, doing unsolicited favors, and giving unexpected gifts. Partners involved in romantic relationships cite positivity as *the* most important maintenance tactic for ensuring happiness (Dainton & Stafford, 1993). This holds true for men and women in straight relationships (Stafford, 2010), and for same-sex partners in gay and lesbian romances (Haas & Stafford, 2005). You use positivity when:[4]

- You try to make each interaction with your partner enjoyable.
- You try to build your partner up by giving him or her compliments.
- You try to be fun, upbeat, and romantic with your partner.

You undermine positivity when:

- You constantly look for and complain about problems in your relationship without offering solutions.
- You whine, pout, and sulk when you don't get your way.
- You criticize favors and gifts from your partner.

Assurances

An additional maintenance tactic is assurances: messages that emphasize how much a partner means to you, how important the relationship is, and that describe a secure future together. Assurances may be expressed directly, such as saying, "I love you" or "I can't see myself ever being with anyone but you." You may also communicate assurances more indirectly, by emphasizing the value you place on your time together—for example, sending a text message saying, "I can't wait to see you again" (Rabby, 1997). You use assurances when:

- You regularly tell your partner how devoted you are to your relationship.
- You talk about future plans and events to be shared together (e.g., anniversaries, vacations, marriage, children).
- You do and say things to demonstrate the depth of your feelings for your partner.

You undermine assurances when:

- You flirt with others and talk about how attractive they are in front of your partner.
- You tell your partner not to count on anything long term.
- You systematically avoid pledging love or fidelity to your partner.

---

[4]All bulleted items that follow are adapted from the revised relationship maintenance behavior scale of Stafford (2010).

{ **An essential part of maintaining intimacy is creating a climate of security and trust within your relationship.** }

Self-Disclosure

An essential part of maintaining intimacy is creating a climate of security and trust within your relationship. This allows both partners to feel that they can disclose fears and feelings without repercussions. To foster self-disclosure, each person must behave in ways that are predictable, trustworthy, and ethical. Over time, consistency in behavior evokes mutual respect and the perception that self-disclosure will be welcomed. You use self-disclosure when:

- You tell your partner about your fears and vulnerabilities.
- You share your feelings and emotions with your partner.
- You encourage your partner to disclose his or her thoughts and feelings, and offer empathy in return.

You undermine self-disclosure when:

- You disparage your partner's perspective.
- You routinely keep important information hidden from your partner.
- You betray your partner by sharing confidential information about him or her with others.

Maintaining Romance across Distance

A common challenge to maintaining romantic relationships is geographic separation. At any one time, nearly half of college students are involved in romances separated by geography, and 75 percent will experience a long-distance dating relationship while in school (Aylor, 2003).

People often think that long-distance relationships are doomed to fail. However, long-distance romantic relationships have actually been found to be *more* satisfying and stable than those that are geographically close (Stafford, 2010). On measures of love, positivity, agreement, and overall communication quality,

geographically distant couples score *higher* than local partners (Stafford & Merolla, 2007). Why? Stafford (2010) offers several reasons. Couples separated by distance often constrain their communication to only that which is positive, steadfastly shying away from troublesome topics that provoke conflict. Geographically distant couples also idealize their partners more. When you're not around your partner every day, it's easy to cherish misconceptions about his or her "perfection." And visits between partners are typically occasional, brief in duration, and passionate. This amplifies the feeling that all their time together is intense and positive—an unsustainable illusion when people see each other regularly (Sahlstein, 2004).

The most difficult maintenance challenge long-distance couples face is not the separation but their eventual reunion. Almost all couples separated by distance express a desire to be near each other again, and they anticipate that being together will result in dramatic relationship improvements (Stafford, Merolla, & Castle, 2006). But the reality is more complicated. Couples who are reunited following separation are twice as likely to break up, compared with those who remain long-distance (Stafford & Merolla, 2007). Rather than being "all bliss, all the time," living locally presents a blend of rewards and costs (Stafford et al., 2006). On the plus side, couples get to spend more time together, savoring each other's company and sharing in the "little" things they missed when apart. On the minus side, partners' cherished illusions about each other are shattered. Reunited couples report realizing for the first time their lovers' negative characteristics, such as laziness, sloppiness, immaturity, or failure to invest effort in the relationship. They also report increased conflict, as formerly "taboo" topics become regularly discussed and fought over.

Despite the challenges, you can have a happy and enduring long-distance romance. Here are some suggestions to help maintain such relationships:

1. While separated, use technology to regularly communicate with your partner. Using text message, e-mail, instant messaging, Facebook, Skype, and even shared dropboxes can have a significant

In the movie *Like Crazy*, college students Jacob and Anna fall in love during their senior year. When immigration laws force Anna to return to her native England, they begin a long-distance relationship. Despite texting, e-mails, and phone calls, the relationship becomes strained. If you have ever been in a long-distance relationship, how did you use communication to ease the distance?

impact on improving relationship health (Dainton & Aylor, 2002).

2. When communicating with your distant partner, follow the maintenance tactics discussed in the previous section. Focus on positivity and assurances—keeping your interactions upbeat and filled with discussions of shared future plans and dreams.

3. When you permanently reunite, expect a significant period of adjustment, one that is marked by tension (as you rebalance autonomy versus connection), disappointment (as idealistic illusions of your partner are replaced by the reality), and conflict (as you begin talking about topics you shelved during the separation). Avoid expecting everything to be perfect, and use the strategies from our discussion of conflict (Chapter 9) to manage difficult dilemmas when they arise.

Deciding Whether to Maintain

Of course, not all romantic involvements are worth the effort to maintain. In some cases, it may be healthier to end the involvement rather than try to foster its survival. The decision of whether to maintain or dissolve a struggling romance is one of the most challenging interpersonal decisions we face.

As one way to work through this decision, familiarize yourself with the characteristics of couples whose relationships survive. Three factors—each of which we've discussed—can help predict survival of a romantic relationship. First is *the degree to which the partners consider themselves "in love."* Partners are more likely to stay together if they think of themselves as in love, are considering marriage or a lifelong commitment, rate their relationship as high in closeness, or date each other exclusively (Hill et al., 1976). Second is *equity*. Romantic relationships are happiest and most stable when the balance of giving and getting is equal for both partners (Hatfield et al., 1985). Third is *similarity*. Highly similar partners are more likely to stay together than partners who are dissimilar (Hill et al., 1976). To determine how well your relationship meets these criteria, ask yourself the following questions:

1. Are you still in love with your partner?

2. Is your relationship equitable?

3. Do you and your partner share values and personality traits?

If you answer "yes" to these questions, your relationship may warrant investment in maintenance. But remember: *deciding whether to maintain a struggling relationship or to let it go is a choice only you can make.* Friends, family members, pop-culture relationship experts, and even textbooks can't tell you when to keep or when to leave a romantic involvement. That being said, romantic relationships are in many ways practical endeavors. Your decision to maintain or end a struggling romance should be based on a long-term forecast of your relationship. Stacking your relationship up against those three criteria can give you insight into whether your relationship has a solid foundation on which to invest further effort.

Workplace Romances

While the maintenance strategies we've discussed so far hold true no matter where you met your partner, romances that form at work have some additional considerations. First, know that the workplace is a natural venue for romantic attraction to unfold, as many of the elements that foster attraction are present: a wide variety of attractive and available partners, large amounts of time spent together, physical proximity, and similarity in interests and attitudes (Appelbaum, Marinescu, Klenin, & Bytautas, 2007). Over 80 percent of North American employees have experienced a romantic relationship at work (Schaefer & Tudor, 2001), and 10 million new workplace romances are forged each year (Pierce & Aguinis, 2009), usually among peers.

Second, despite historical discouragement, many workplaces have begun to shift their policies, as research supports that romantic involvement does not hurt worker productivity (Boyd, 2010). In fact, romantically involved workers are usually perceived by people in their organization as being friendly and approachable (Hovick, Meyers, & Timmerman, 2003), and having romances in the workplace is seen as creating a positive work climate (Riach & Wilson, 2007). Relationship outcomes are often positive too: married couples who work in the same location have a 50 percent *lower* divorce rate than those employed at different workplaces (Boyd, 2010).

Third, workplace romances face challenges. Involvement in a romance can create the perception among coworkers that the partners are more interested in each other than in their work, leading to rumors and gossip (Albrecht & Bach, 1997). As a consequence, you can't cultivate a workplace romance without expecting the relationship to become a focus of workplace gossip.

With all this in mind, how can you successfully maintain a workplace romance? Make sure to leave your love at home, so to speak, and communicate with your partner in a strictly professional fashion during work hours. When romantic partners maintain a professional demeanor toward each other and communicate with all their coworkers in a consistent and positive fashion, the romance is usually ignored or even encouraged (Buzzanell, 1990).

This is why it is especially important to use e-mail, texting, Skype, Twitter, and instant-messaging carefully. When used properly, these technologies enable romantic partners to communicate frequently and maintain professional decorum (Hovick et al., 2003). Such communication should never contain overly intimate or controversial messages. Even when using business accounts for personal reasons, it is wise to write messages that comply with official policies—no matter who the recipient is. Remember that social media accounts and electronic messages are not secure. Anyone with the motivation and know-how can gain access to the messages you and your partner exchange. Keep the content professional when at work or when using company-provided devices.

LearningCurve
bedfordstmartins.com/ipcandyou

Romantic Relationship Challenges

Think about the Robert Falcon Scott story that began this chapter. His letter to Kathleen reminds us of the high ideals that love can inspire: compassion, caring, generosity, selflessness. But romance has a dark side as well. As scholar Robin Kowalski pointedly puts it, "people in romantic relationships do a lot of mean and nasty things to one another" (Kowalski et al., 2003, p. 472). And when they do, the result is often unparalleled pain and despair. In this section, we explore some of the most troubling issues related to romance—betrayal, jealousy, and violence.

Betrayal

Betrayal is one of the most devastating experiences that can occur in a close involvement (Haden & Hojjat, 2006). **Romantic betrayal** is defined as an act that goes against expectations of a romantic relationship and, as a result, causes pain to a partner (Jones, Moore, Scratter, & Negel, 2001). Common examples include *sexual infidelity* (engaging in sexual activity with someone else), *emotional infidelity* (developing a strong romantic attachment to someone else), *deception* (intentional manipulation of information), and *disloyalty* (hurting your partner to benefit yourself). But any behavior that violates norms of loyalty and trustworthiness can be considered betrayal.

In romantic relationships, partners inevitably behave in ways that defy one another's expectations

In the wake of betrayal, we may feel that all the time and effort we invested in our partner and the relationship were a waste, and that intimacy, commitment, and trust have been permanently destroyed (Haden & Hojjat, 2006). Consequently, when you are betrayed by a lover, expect to feel *grief* over the loss of the relationship that was. (See Chapter 4 for more on grief management.)

Sexual Infidelity

The most destructive form of romantic betrayal is sexual infidelity. A partner who cheats on you has broken a fundamental sacrament—the spoken or unspoken pledge to remain faithful. Not surprisingly, many people react to infidelity with a strong urge to leave their partner. One study found that more than 20 percent of American women and men would consider divorce if a spouse passionately kissed someone else, more than 30 percent would consider divorce if their spouse had a romantic date with another person, and more than 60 percent would consider divorce if their spouse had a serious (sexual) affair (Shackelford & Buss, 1997). Whether or not a sexual dalliance is planned matters little: cheaters' original intentions have no impact on subsequent feelings of blame by their partners (Mongeau, Hale, & Alles, 1994).

Although both men and women view infidelity as treasonous, their perceptions diverge when they're asked to compare sexual with emotional cheating. Infidelity researcher David Buss presented study respondents with the following dilemma (Buss, Larsen, Westen, & Semmelroth, 1992). Imagine you discover that your partner has become interested in someone

💧 Most people discover lies indirectly through hearing about them from a third party or stumbling across damning evidence.

and cause disappointment. But betrayal is different. Betrayal is *intentional*. As a result, it typically evokes two intense, negative reactions in betrayed partners. The first is an overwhelming sense of relational devaluation—the realization that our partners do not love and respect us as much as we thought they did (Leary, 2001). This sense of devaluation, which is triggered most by sexual infidelity and deception, is difficult to overcome and often leads us to abandon our relationships. The second is a profound sense of loss.

Self-Reflection

Think about Buss's challenge. Which would you find more upsetting: discovering that your romantic partner had formed an emotional attachment outside the relationship or that he or she had been sexually unfaithful? If your partner did betray you in one of these ways, how would you respond?

Self-Quiz }

How Often Do You Betray Romantic Partners?
Read each statement and rate how often you have done the activity:
1 (never), 2 (once), 3 (a few times), 4 (several times), 5 (many times).
Get your score by adding up your answers.

Snubbing a romantic partner when you are with a group you want to impress

Gossiping about a romantic partner behind his or her back

Making a promise to a romantic partner with no intention of keeping it

Telling others information given to you in confidence by a romantic partner

Lying to a romantic partner

Failing to stand up for a romantic partner when he or she is being criticized or belittled by others

Note: Information in this Self-Quiz adapted for romantic relationships is from Jones and Burdette (1994).

Scoring: 6–14 = You're an infrequent betrayer; 15–23 = You're a moderate betrayer; 24–30 = You're a frequent betrayer.

else. What would distress you more: your partner forming a deep emotional attachment to that person, or your partner enjoying passionate sex with that person? Sixty percent of men said that sex would upset them more, but 83 percent of women said they'd find the emotional attachment more distressing. The same pattern of results was found in samples of men and women from Sweden, the Netherlands, Germany, Korea, and Japan (Buss et al., 1999; Buunk, Angleitner, Oubaid, & Buss, 1996; Wiederman & Kendall, 1999).

Deception

As defined in Chapter 7, deception involves misleading your partner by intentionally withholding information, presenting false information, or making your message unnecessarily irrelevant or ambiguous (McCornack, 1997). Despite media images depicting romantic partners catching each other in lies, most people discover lies indirectly through hearing about them from a third party or stumbling across damning evidence, such as a text message or e-mail (Park, Levine, McCornack, Morrison, & Ferrara, 2002). When partners discover a lie, the experience typically is emotionally intense and negative. One study looking

at the emotional and relational aftermath of lies found that 16 percent of people who recalled having discovered a lie reported breaking up because of it (McCornack & Levine, 1990). That decision was usually determined by the severity of the lie. If the lie was "important" (for example, lying about relationship feelings), people were more likely to end their involvement (McCornack & Levine, 1990).

Dealing with Betrayal

The truth about romantic betrayal is that no simple solution or skill set will remedy the sense of devaluation and loss that results. The strongest predictor of what happens afterward is the seriousness of the betrayal. If a betrayal permanently stains your perception of your partner, the relationship probably won't survive. If you believe you can eventually overcome the pain, then your relationship has a chance.

People struggling to cope with betrayal commonly adopt one of four general communication approaches (Rusbult, 1987). You can actively confront the betrayal, seeking to understand the conditions that led to it and jointly working with your partner to change those causes. You can quietly stand by your partner, choosing to forgive and forget and trusting that, in time, your love will heal the pain you feel. You can stand by your partner but simmer with pain and rage, venting your anger by constantly reminding the person of his or her transgression or withholding sex or other rewards. Or you can simply end the relationship, believing that the emotional costs associated with the betrayal are too substantial to surmount.

Regardless of which approach you take, the hard truth is that, after a betrayal, your relationship will never be the same, and it will never be "better" than it previously was in terms of trust, intimacy, and satisfaction. You certainly can rebuild a strong and enduring relationship, but it will always be scarred. As my therapist friend Joe says, "You will *never* get over it. You just learn to live with it."

Jealousy

A second problem for romantic relationships is **jealousy**—a protective reaction to a perceived threat

Josh Haner/The New York Times/Redux Pictures

◊ Jealousy can easily form if you see flirty wall posts or suggestive photos on your lover's social networking pages. If you feel threatened, it's important to communicate in a cooperative and constructive manner when discussing your feelings with your partner. What experiences have you had with jealousy of this kind?

> **The most effective way to deal with jealousy is *self-reliance*: allowing yourself to feel jealous but not letting whatever sparked your jealousy to interrupt you.**

to a valued relationship (Hansen, 1985). Most scholars agree that jealousy isn't a single emotion but rather a combination of negative emotions—primarily anger, fear, and sadness (Guerrero & Andersen, 1998).

Jealousy especially plagues users of social media. Such sites open the possibility for people other than your romantic partner to post provocative photos, write enticing posts on your wall, and send alluring messages—all of which can trigger your partner's jealousy. Imagine how you'd feel if you saw such communication on your partner's page. Studies of Facebook have found that jealousy is one of the most frequent problems reported by users (Morrison, Lee, Wiedmaier, & Dibble, 2008). Jealousy can intensify even further if site users engage in what communication scholar Kelly Morrison calls **wedging**. Through wedging, a person deliberately uses messages, photos, and posts to try and "wedge" him- or herself between partners in a romantic couple because he or she is interested in one of the partners (Morrison et al., 2008).

The most effective way to deal with jealousy is *self-reliance*: allowing yourself to feel jealous but not letting whatever sparked your jealousy to interrupt you. You should continue your current activities and give yourself time to cool off (Salovey & Rodin, 1988). Avoid communicating with your partner until you're able to do so in a cooperative and constructive fashion. When you *are* ready to talk, don't be afraid to candidly acknowledge your own jealousy, and discuss your perception of threat with your partner: "I saw that post from your old girlfriend, and I'm worried that she wants to get back together with you. Am I reading too much into this, or should I really feel threatened?"

Dating Violence

Scott and I became friends in grad school, when we both served as instructors with a campus karate club. Originally from Southern California, Scott was a kickboxing champion.[5] He was 6 foot 3, all muscle, and had a very long reach—something I learned the hard way when he caught me with an unexpected backfist on my nose while sparring!

Soon after our friendship began, Scott met Pam, and the two fell for each other hard and fast. But within a few weeks, Scott confessed to me several concerns: Pam was extremely jealous and constantly accused him of cheating. She called him names, swore at him, and ridiculed his sexual performance. She demanded that he no longer go out with his friends, and when he refused, she threatened to

leave him. Visiting him one afternoon, I was stunned to see the glass frame of his black-belt certificate shattered. "Yeah," he admitted, "Pam threw it at me the other night." When she learned that Scott was confiding in me, Pam told him a series of lies to alienate him from me: I had "stolen money from him," I had "hit on her," I was "gay and wanted him to myself" (never mind that the last two were contradictory). But Scott stayed with her until she put him in the hospital with a broken nose and third-degree burns across his face. She had demanded that he quit karate, and when he refused, she had hit him in the face with a heated clothes iron. When I asked why he didn't fight back, or at least defend himself (given his abundant skills), he looked at me in disbelief. "I can't hit *a girl*, man. I'm not that kind of guy!"

Dating violence affects millions of people, and as Scott's story shows, despite common beliefs, dating violence knows no demographic boundaries: men and women of all ages, sexual orientations, social classes, ethnicities, and religions experience violence in romantic relationships. According to the National Center for Victims of Crimes, 21 percent of college students report having experienced dating violence (National Center for Victims of Crimes, 2008). In addition to physical injuries (and in extreme cases, death), victims of dating violence are more likely than others to suffer from substance abuse, low self-esteem, suicidal thoughts, and eating disorders (Ackard & Neumark-Sztainer, 2002).

It's easy, if you haven't experienced a violent relationship, to think, "Well, the person should have seen it coming!" But this is false, for at least two reasons (Eisikovits & Buchbinder, 2000). First, violence doesn't happen all at once—it typically escalates slowly over time. Also, it often doesn't evolve into full-blown physical violence until relationships are firmly established—making victims all that much more vulnerable because of their love and commitment. Second, potential abusers often mask their jealousy, violent anger, and excessive need for control in the early stages of a relationship, making it difficult to discern any possible warning signs. In Scott's case, both of these reasons played a role in

[5]Although the facts of this story are true, the names and demographic information have been changed to protect the identities of the parties involved.

making him vulnerable. Pam seemed perfectly "normal" in the first few weeks of their relationship. She was funny, attractive, smart, and outgoing. By the time the first incidents occurred, he was already in love. Plus, the destructiveness of her behaviors escalated slowly—starting with minor jealous tantrums, and only evolving into violence after many months. As a consequence, Scott didn't perceive Pam's abusiveness as particularly "severe," until she put him in the hospital.

What should *you* do if you find yourself in a relationship with a violent partner? First and foremost, let go of the belief that you can "heal" your partner through love, or "save" him or her by providing emotional support. Relationship repair strategies will not prevent or cure dating violence. Your only option is to extricate yourself from the relationship.

As you move toward ending the involvement, keep in mind that the most dangerous time comes immediately after you end the relationship, when the abuser is most angry. So, make sure you cut all ties to the abuser, change your phone numbers, and have ready a *safety plan*: a road map of action for departing the relationship that provides you with the utmost protection. For information on how to develop such a plan, or for help in dealing with an abusive relationship, call the National Domestic Violence Hotline, 1-800-799-SAFE, or visit www.thehotline.org.

LearningCurve
bedfordstmartins.com/ipcandyou

Postscript }

We began this chapter with the dying words of a doomed explorer. As Sir Robert Falcon Scott huddled inside his tent, awaiting death, he penned a last letter to his "widow." Of all the possible things he could say during those final moments—the limitless selection of topics and words available to sum up his life—what did he choose to focus upon? *Love.*

When the impassable storms of your life rage around you, what shelter does love provide? If you had but a few hours to live, and were going to craft a final statement, what view of love would you elaborate?

Scott's letter reminds us that love is not one thing, but many. To experience romantic love means to feel passion, practicality, commitment, respect, sentiment, and selflessness—all at the same time. Although no two people ever experience love in exactly the same way, we do share this in common: romantic love may not be essential to life, but it may be essential to joy.

Chapter Review

Visit LaunchPad for *Interpersonal Communication and You* to watch brief, illustrative ⊙ videos of these terms and to access ☑ LearningCurve. **bedfordstmartins.com/ipcandyou**

KEY TERMS

liking, 201
loving, 201
passionate love, 201
companionate love, 202
romantic relationship, 202
commitment, 204
⊙ relational dialectics, 204
mere exposure effect, 205
beautiful-is-good effect, 206
matching, 206

birds-of-a-feather
 effect, 206
reciprocal liking, 206
social exchange theory, 207
equity, 207
initiating, 209
⊙ experimenting, 209
intensifying, 209
⊙ integrating, 209
⊙ bonding, 210

⊙ differentiating, 211
circumscribing, 211
⊙ stagnating, 212
avoiding, 212
terminating, 212
⊙ relational maintenance,
 213
romantic betrayal, 217
jealousy, 220
wedging, 220

CHAPTER ACTIVITIES

1. Write a short essay applying one of the relational tensions or dialectics that were discussed in the text to a past or current romantic relationship, or a relationship you have observed. Carefully define the tension, briefly describe the relationship, and provide thorough examples of the tension. Describe how you or the other couple dealt with the tension in the relationship.

2. Do "birds of a feather flock together" or do "opposites attract"? Take a stance on the question and prepare a rationale to share with the class. Do culture or gender influence different perspectives on similarity and attraction?

3. Choose a romantic relationship from literature, film, or television to analyze using Knapp's relational stages of coming together or coming apart. Write a brief description of the relationship in general. Then, in an analysis essay, carefully define each stage the couple experienced and provide examples. Discuss how the relationship both conformed to and defied Knapp's stages.

4. View the Web site iBreakUp.net, which claims to be the "premiere full-service relationship separation service." Would you use this site to terminate a romantic relationship? If so, under what circumstances? How would you feel if a partner ended a relationship in this manner? Is this type of technology useful, or more of a hindrance to romantic relationships?

5. ⊙ Watch the video on **relational maintenance** with a small group of classmates. Then, create a role play demonstrating one of the three strategies for relational maintenance. Be prepared to discuss different ways in which the relational maintenance strategy can be enacted in relationships and what could happen if couples lack maintenance.

6. While social media like Facebook can help create and maintain relationships, they can also lead to jealousy. Consider your experiences of jealousy due to online communication. What triggered the jealousy? How did you combat it? Is Facebook the cause of jealousy, or is it more about individual personality?

7. With a partner, research an organization developed to prevent violence (such as loveisrespect.org) or emotional abuse in romantic relationships. Make a five-minute presentation to your class explaining what the organization does and their suggestions for preventing physical and emotional abuse.

Look for **LearningCurve** throughout the chapter to help you review.
bedfordstmartins.com/ipcandyou

11 } Relationships with Family Members

She's one of the greatest water polo players ever.[1] She is an NCAA Women's Player of the Year, a 2012 Olympic gold medalist, a three-time World Champion, and a World Cup Champion. But when Brenda Villa is asked about her abilities and accomplishments, she is quick to credit her family, especially her mother. "I get my confidence and 'swagger' from my mom. She's one tough woman. She always supports me, but is unafraid to tell me when I'm not being humble."

Brenda grew up in Commerce, California—a working-class suburb of Los Angeles. At a young age, her mother enrolled her in swimming classes. Brenda excelled and gravitated to water polo after seeing her older brother, Edgar, compete. Although her parents had no experience with the sport, they encouraged Brenda's

interest. "They taught me that you should always be open to new things."

Growing up, four themes were foundational in the Villa family: *support, honesty, sacrifice,* and *love*. As Brenda describes, "Both my parents worked full-time. Yet they were at all my swim meets, water polo games, school activity nights, and assemblies. They knew that I was committed to both school and sports, and they supported me in every way so that I could achieve my goals." Her parents are also scrupulously honest with her, in good times and bad. "They know when I need a kick in the butt and when I need someone to listen. Recently I was feeling sorry for myself after missing a penalty shot at a tournament. My mother found out from my boyfriend, and the next thing you know I get a comforting text message from my dad and a phone call from my mom. She reminded me that it's my choice to continue to play and if I'm going to dwell on mistakes that I shouldn't play

[1]All information that follows is adapted from personal interviews with the author, July 2011, and published with permission.

Families have a primacy that no other relationships rival.
MCT/Newscom

anymore. She wants me to be the champion I am—no fear. Gotta love her!"

The Villa family is always willing to sacrifice for one another. For example, Brenda's training camps for the U.S. Team were in Chula Vista—a two-hour commute from Commerce. Her parents drove her, without debate or resentment. As Brenda describes, "I don't remember asking my parents to do this—they just did it. And I never realized how hard it was for them. My mother would accompany my dad because she was afraid he would fall asleep on the drive home. I didn't appreciate the depth of their sacrifice at the time, as a kid, but now that I'm older, I'm so thankful that they put me first." The willingness to sacrifice communicated a powerful message of love. "Their love is unconditional. It warms my heart to think that my mom would accompany my dad just to keep him awake. *That's love!*"

Though she's one of America's most talented and celebrated female athletes, Brenda Villa remains humble about her accolades. As the Women's Sports Foundation notes, "[Brenda] seems unaware of the splash she has made as role model and hero to Latina athletes. Maybe she's just too busy and too modest by nature" (Lewellen, 2008). But the truth is, Brenda doesn't think of herself as a role model—she thinks of her *parents* that way. "I look at their 30-plus years of marriage and how they still always put their kids first. I hope to be as selfless as them with my own children."

F amilies have a primacy that no other relationships rival. Family members are the first people we see, hear, touch, and interact with. As we grow from infancy to childhood, we learn from family the most basic of skills: how to walk, talk, and feed and clothe ourselves. As we develop further, our families teach us deeper lessons about life akin to those learned by Brenda Villa from her parents: the importance of support, honesty, sacrifice, and love. As our relationships broaden to include friendships and romances, we still use kinship as a metaphor to describe closeness: "How close are we? We're like *family!*" (Rubin, 1996). But family relationships are also compulsory. We don't *choose* our families—we are brought into them by birth, adopted into them by law, or integrated into them by remarriage. When problems arise in our family relationships, the stress is unrivaled. Day in and day out, family relationships provide us with our greatest joys and most bitter heartaches (Myers, 2002).

In this chapter, we look at the most influential and enduring of our close involvements: family relationships. You'll learn:

- The defining features of family
- The different ways in which families communicate
- Communication strategies to maintain healthy family relationships
- Challenges that families face, and how to manage them

Defining Family

When many of us think of family, iconic TV images come to mind, like Chris's family in *Everybody Hates Chris* or the Dunphys from *Modern Family*. These images are simple and comforting: families consist of happily married heterosexual couples raising their biological children, bonded by love, and united in facing any challenges that confront them (Braithwaite et al., 2010).

(Left to right) ©Tony Avelar/*Christian Science Monitor*/The Image Works; ©The Star-Ledger/Aristide Economopoulos/The Image Works

💧 Although every family possesses its own distinct identity, all families hold certain things in common. Whether bound together by marriage, blood, or commitment, each family has a profound, shared history made up of the small, everyday moments they spend together.

But families today are more diverse than such depictions suggest. Between 1970 and 2010, the percentage of households composed of married couples with biological children in the United States declined from 40 percent to just 20 percent (Tavernise, 2011). In Canada, this kind of family declined from 55 percent in 1981 to 34.6 percent in 2006 (HRSDC, 2006). Instead, couples are increasingly living together rather than getting married, making marriage less common than at any prior time in history (Cherlin, 2004). Rising divorce rates over the past half century have also decreased the average size of households, as families divide into smaller units and re-form into blended arrangements featuring stepparents and stepchildren. Adding to this complexity, individual families are constantly in flux, as children move out, then lose jobs and move back in with parents; grandparents join the household to help with daycare or receive care themselves; and spouses separate geographically to pursue job opportunities (Crosnoe & Cavanagh, 2010).

Defining Characteristics of Family

The enormous diversity in contemporary families requires a broad, inclusive definition. **Family** is a network of people who share their lives over long periods of time and are bound by marriage, blood, or commitment; who consider themselves as family; and who share a significant history and anticipated future of functioning in a family relationship (Galvin, Brommel, & Bylund, 2004). This definition highlights six characteristics that distinguish families from other social groups.

First, families possess a strong sense of family identity, created by how they communicate (Braithwaite et al., 2010). The way you talk with family members, the stories you exchange, and even the manner in which members of your family deal with conflict all contribute to a shared sense of what your family is like (Tovares, 2010).

Second, families use communication to define boundaries, both inside the family and to distinguish family members from outsiders (Afifi, 2003; Koerner & Fitzpatrick, 2006). As we'll discuss later, some families constrict information that flows out ("Don't talk about our family problems with others"). Some also restrict physical access to the family—for example, by dictating with whom family members can romantically bond ("No son of mine is going to marry a Protestant!"). Others set few such boundaries. For

(Left to right) David M. Grossman/The Image Works; Brand X Pictures/Getty Images; Erin Patrice O'Brien/Getty Images; Jose Luis Pelaez Inc./Getty Images

💧 No matter who is in them, families are some of the most central and formative interpersonal relationships that we have.

instance, a family may welcome friends as unofficial members, such as an "aunt" who isn't biologically related to your parents (Braithwaite et al., 2010). A family may even welcome others' children, such as the neighbors across the street, whom you think of as your "family away from home." If remarriage occurs and stepfamilies form, these boundaries are renegotiated (Golish, 2003).

Third, the emotional bonds underlying family relationships are intense and complex. Family members typically hold both warm *and* antagonistic feelings toward one another (Silverstein & Giarrusso, 2010). As author Lillian Rubin (1996) notes, family relationships have "an elemental quality that touches the deepest layers of our inner life and stirs our most primitive emotional responses" (p. 256). Consider the strength of feeling that arises in you when you get into an argument with a parent or sibling, or when you celebrate an important milestone (a graduation, a wedding, a new job) with family members.

Fourth, families share a history (Galvin et al., 2004). Such histories can stretch back for generations and feature family members from a broad array of cultures. These histories often set expectations regarding how family members should behave ("We Ngatas have always been an honest bunch, and we're not about to change that now"). Families also share a common future: they expect to maintain their bonds indefinitely. For better or worse, everything you say and do becomes a part of your family history,

shaping future interactions and determining whether your family relationships are healthy or destructive.

Fifth, family members may share genetic material (Crosnoe & Cavanagh, 2010). This can lead to shared physical characteristics as well as similar personalities, outlooks on life, mental abilities, and ways of relating to others. Such similarities may include shyness and aggressiveness, which some studies suggest are influenced by genes (Carducci & Zimbardo, 1995).

Finally, family members juggle multiple and sometimes competing roles (Silverstein & Giarrusso, 2010). Within your family, you're not just a daughter or son, but perhaps a sibling, a spouse, or an aunt or uncle as well. By the time you reach middle age, you simultaneously may be a parent, spouse, grandparent, daughter or son, *and* sibling—and each of these roles carries with it varying expectations and demands. This makes communicating competently within families challenging.

Types of Family

No "typical" family type exists. Instead, families come in many different forms (Braithwaite et al., 2010). But even these forms are not fixed: you may experience several different family structures as you progress through life. For example, 60 years ago, the **nuclear family**—a wife, husband, and their biological or adopted children—was the most common family type in North America. Today, it is in the minority. Instead, families may include children or not; have one, two, or several parents; be headed by heterosexual, lesbian, gay, bisexual, or transgendered people; include other relatives such as grandparents; include stepparents and stepsiblings; or any other combination you can imagine! While we discuss the family types below, consider how your family experiences align with or depart from these depictions. But, perhaps most important, keep this in mind: *what matters most is not the "type" of family you have, but whom you consider part of your family in terms of love, respect, and communication.*

When relatives such as aunts, uncles, parents, children, and grandparents live together in a common household, the result is an **extended family**. By the year 2050, 100 million people in the United States will be over the age of 65, and many of these individuals will be sharing a household with relatives. Numerous Italian American, African American, and Asian American families fall into this category.

Approximately half of marriages in the United States and Canada are remarriages for one or both partners (Coleman, Ganong, & Fine, 2000). This often creates a **stepfamily** in which at least one of the adults has a child or children from a previous relationship (Ganong & Coleman, 1994). Stepfamilies often are called "blended" or "remarried" families. More than 50 percent of children born throughout the twenty-first century will grow up in stepfamilies (Crosnoe & Cavanagh, 2010).

Some couples live together prior to or instead of marriage. These **cohabiting couples** consist of two unmarried, romantically involved adults living together in a household, with or without children. Cohabitation is steadily increasing in Western societies (Adams, 2004). This is partly due to an increase in cohabitation among middle-aged and older adults, many of whom were formerly married but now want the relational flexibility that cohabitation affords (Silverstein & Giarrusso, 2010).

In a **single-parent family**, only one adult resides in the household, possessing sole responsibility as caregiver for the children. As of 2011, 27 percent of children in the United States (U.S. Census Bureau,

2011) and about 16 percent of children in Canada (HRSDC, 2006) were growing up in single-parent households.

Family Stories

Characteristics and types define families from the outside looking in. But from the inside, one of the most powerful ways we define our collective family identity is to share stories (Tovares, 2010). **Family stories** are narrative accounts shared repeatedly within a family that retell historical events and are meant to bond the family together (Stone, 2004). For example, when I was growing up, family storytelling was a nightly ritual. Tales ranged from how my parents met at college to shared family experiences, like the great lengths I would go to avoid eating scrambled eggs. Even now, when we get together for visits, we relive and retell these stories and others like them, enjoying the sense of family history they provide.

Family stories help create and promote a unique family identity by teaching individuals about their role in the family and about the family's norms, values, and goals (Kellas, 2005). They also provide powerful images of family relationships. When people

> What matters most is not the "type" of family you have, but whom you consider part of your family in terms of love, respect, and communication.

tell family stories, they typically lace their narratives with opinions and emotions that make clear how they feel about other family members (Vangelisti, Crumley, & Baker, 1999). Importantly, it's not just the content of the stories that bonds families together; it's the activity of storytelling. Family members often collaborate in telling stories: adding details, disagreeing, correcting discrepancies, and confirming perspectives (Kellas, 2005).

However, family stories aren't always positive; some criticize family values, condemn specific family members' actions, or discourage dissent. These stories may also involve family histories of abandonment, abuse, or parental oppression—and corresponding lessons about how *not* to parent (Goodsell, Bates, & Behnke, 2010).

The breadth and depth of your family experiences provide a rich resource to share with family members. But not all shared experiences are ones your family members would like to relive. To ensure that family stories strengthen, rather than erode, family relationships, select experiences that cast the family and individual members in a positive light and that emphasize unity rather than discord. When sharing stories with younger family members, keep in mind that they will learn values from your story (Tovares, 2010). Ask yourself whether the story sends the message you intend about your family's values.

Stories that cast individual family members in a humorous light require special care. Although such stories may be perfectly appropriate to share, make sure that the "target" family member enjoys and agrees to the telling. Avoid sharing stories that breach personal confidences ("John never told any of you what *really* happened, but here it is!") or that make sport of family members in ways they don't enjoy. When in doubt, simply (but privately) ask the family member whether he or she wants you to share the story. If the answer is "no," keep silent.

LearningCurve
bedfordstmartins.com/ipcandyou

Communicating in Families

Few literary families rival the Weasleys from the *Harry Potter* series in terms of closeness and camaraderie.[2] Their intimacy is shown through their communication: the importance they place upon sharing conversation and the diversity of topics they discuss. Mr. Weasley even talks about a subject loathsome to most magical people: the study of Muggles (nonmagical folk). "Mr. Weasley liked Harry to sit next to him at the dinner table so that he could bombard him with questions about life with the Muggles, asking him to explain how things like plugs and the postal service worked" (1999, p. 42). Harry, who has never experienced such intimacy and openness in a family, is awed: "This is the best house I've ever been in!" His life at home with the Dursleys is the complete opposite. There is little interest in sharing conversation, and they are fiercely incurious about activities or people outside their own, narrow sphere of interests. Growing up, Harry learns, "Don't ask questions—that was the first rule for a quiet life with the Dursleys" (1997, p. 20). Another rule discouraged bringing up unusual topics: "If there was one thing the Dursleys hated even more than [Harry's] asking questions, it was his talking about anything acting in a way it shouldn't, no matter if it was in a dream or even a cartoon" (p. 26).

Like the fictional Weasleys and Dursleys, our own families' communication is guided by shared beliefs about how families should converse. These

---

[2]The content that follows is adapted from Rowling (1997) and Rowling (1999).

Self-Reflection

What are the most memorable family stories that were shared with you during your upbringing? What lessons did they teach you about your family and the values that you share? Did the stories function to bring you together as a family, or drive you apart?

(Left to right) ©Warner Brothers/Courtesy Everett Collection; Mary Evans/WARNER BROS/JK ROWLING/Ronald Grant/Everett Collection

In the *Harry Potter* series, the Weasleys are high on conversation orientation and low on conformity orientation, encouraging individual expression and appreciating one another's ideas, while the Dursleys are low on conversation orientation and high on conformity orientation, avoiding conversation with one another and valuing uniformity above all else. Where does your family fall on the conformity and conversation orientation spectrum?

beliefs, and the resulting communication, are known as *family communication patterns* (Koerner & Fitzpatrick, 2002) and evolve from two communication dimensions, which we'll discuss next.

Communication Dimensions

According to **Family Communication Patterns Theory** (Koerner & Fitzpatrick, 2006), two dimensions underlie the communication between family members. The first is **conversation orientation**: the degree to which family members are encouraged to participate in unrestrained interaction about a wide array of topics. Families with a high conversation orientation are like the Weasleys: they believe that open and frequent communication is essential to an enjoyable and rewarding family life. Consequently, they interact often, freely, and spontaneously without many limitations placed on time spent together and topics discussed.

In contrast, families with a low conversation orientation are like the Dursleys; they view interpersonal communication as something irrelevant and unnecessary for a satisfying, successful family life.

Such families interact only infrequently and limit their conversations to a few select topics—weather, daily activities, current events, and the like. Disclosure of intimate thoughts and feelings between family members is discouraged, as is debate of attitudes and perspectives.

The second dimension is **conformity orientation**, the degree to which families believe that communication should emphasize similarity in attitudes, beliefs, and values. Like the Dursleys, high conformity families use their interactions to highlight and enforce uniformity of thought. Such families are sometimes perceived as more "traditional" because children are expected to obey parents and other elders, who (in turn) are counted on to make family decisions. Members of these families tend to prioritize family relationships over outside connections such as friendships and romantic involvements. Moreover, they are expected to sacrifice their personal goals for the sake of the family.

Low conformity families like the Weasleys communicate in ways that emphasize diversity in attitudes, beliefs, and values, and that encourage members'

Self-Quiz

}

What Communication Pattern Does Your Family Have?

Place a check mark next to each statement with which you agree. Then check your score to determine your family communication pattern.

Conversation Orientation

☐ In my family, we often talk about our plans and hopes for the future.

☐ We frequently talk as a family about the things we have done during the day.

☐ My parents tend to be very open about their emotions.

☐ I really enjoy talking with my parents, even when we disagree.

☐ My parents and I often have long, relaxed conversations about nothing in particular.

☐ In our family, we often discuss our feelings together.

☐ I can tell my parents almost anything.

☐ My parents often ask my opinion when the family is talking about something important.

☐ My parents frequently say things like, "Every member of this family should have some say in decisions."

Conformity Orientation

☐ When anything really important is involved, my parents expect me to obey without question.

☐ In our home, my parents usually have the last word.

☐ My parents feel that it is important that they be the boss.

☐ My parents sometimes become irritated when my views differ from theirs.

☐ If my parents don't approve of a particular behavior, they don't want to know about it.

☐ When I am at home, I am expected to obey my parents' rules.

☐ My parents often say things like, "My ideas are right, and you shouldn't question them."

☐ My parents often say things like, "There are some things that just shouldn't be talked about."

☐ My parents often say things like, "You'll know better when you're older."

Note: This *Self-Quiz* is adapted from the Revised Family Communication Pattern Instrument (Ritchie & Fitzpatrick, 1990).

Scoring: For each orientation, a total number of check marks of 0–4 indicates "Low," and a total of 5–9 indicates "High." High conversation/high conformity suggests that your family is consensual; high conversation/low conformity, pluralistic; low conversation/high conformity, protective; and low conversation/low conformity, laissez-faire.

uniqueness, individuality, and independence. These families typically view outside relationships as equally important to those within the family, and they prioritize individual over family interests and goals. In low conformity families, children contribute to family decision making, and members view the family as a vehicle for individual growth rather than a collective

in which members must sacrifice their own interests for the good of the whole.

Family Communication Patterns

According to communication scholars Ascan Koerner and Mary Anne Fitzpatrick (2006), conversation and conformity dimensions give rise to four possible family communication patterns: consensual, pluralistic, protective, and laissez-faire.

Consensual Families

Families high in both conversation and conformity are **consensual families**. In such families, members are encouraged to openly share their views with one another as well as debate these beliefs. Consensual family communication is marked by high disclosure, attentive listening, and frequent expressions of caring, concern, and support toward one another (Rueter & Koerner, 2008). At the same time, consensual family members are expected to steadfastly share a single viewpoint. Parents in such households typically exert strong control over the attitudes, behaviors, and interactions of their children (Rueter & Koerner, 2008). For example, parents may encourage their children to share their thoughts and feelings about important issues ("What do you think we should do?") but then make clear that only one perspective (the parents') is acceptable. Because of their emphasis on conformity, consensual families perceive conflict as intensely threatening. Consequently, they address conflicts as they occur and seek to resolve them as constructively as possible to preserve family unity.

Pluralistic Families

Families high in conversation but low in conformity are **pluralistic families**. They communicate in open and unconstrained ways, discussing a broad range of topics and exploring them in depth. Pluralistic families enjoy debating the issues of the day and judge one another's arguments on their merit rather than whether they mesh with other members' attitudes. People in pluralistic families typically don't try to control other family members' beliefs or attitudes (Rueter & Koerner, 2008). Since parents don't feel compelled to wield power over their children, children's contributions to family discussions and decision making are treated as relevant and equally valid. For example, parents in a pluralistic family might ask for their children's opinions regarding a job opportunity ("Should Mom accept the offer from TelCo?") or a family vacation ("Where should we go this

Sitting down and sharing a meal often gives families the opportunity to catch up on daily events, discuss issues large and small, make decisions, and even deal with conflicts. When your family has a meal together, what do you talk about? How does this align with what you perceive as your family communication pattern?

year?"). Pluralistic families deal directly with conflict, seeking to resolve disputes in productive, mutually beneficial ways. They may, for instance, establish "official" times (such as mealtimes or family meetings) when members can vent their concerns and work collaboratively to settle them. For this reason, pluralistic family members report the highest rates of conflict resolution of any of the four family types.

Protective Families

Protective families are low on conversation and high on conformity. Communication in these families functions to maintain obedience and enforce family norms, and little value is placed on the exchange of ideas or the development of communication skills. Parent-child power differences are firmly enforced, and children are expected to quietly obey. Sayings such as "Children should be seen and not heard" reflect this mind-set. Parents invest little effort in creating opportunities for family discussion, and the result is low levels of disclosure amongst family members (Rueter & Koerner, 2008). Protective families avoid conflict because it threatens the conformity they value and because they often lack the skills necessary to manage conflicts constructively. Members may tell each other "You don't want to cause trouble."

Laissez-Faire Families

Families low in both conversation and conformity are **laissez-faire families**. Few emotional bonds exist between their members, resulting in low levels of caring, concern, and support expressed within the family (Rueter & Koerner, 2008). Their detachment shows itself in a lack of interaction and a decided disinterest in activities that might foster communication or maintenance of the family as a unit. Similar to parents in pluralistic families, laissez-faire parents believe that children should be independent thinkers and decision makers. But this belief derives from their disinterest in their children's thoughts and decisions. Such parents tend to leave it up to their children to form their own opinions regarding sexual behavior, drug and alcohol usage, and educational achievement. Because members of such families interact infrequently, they rarely get embroiled in conflict. If a disagreement does erupt, they avoid it or (if they feel strongly invested in the issues at stake) they compete to "win" the debate.

LearningCurve
bedfordstmartins.com/ipcandyou

Maintaining Family Relationships

When Arizona caseworker Heather Shew-Plummer met Steven and Roger Ham, she knew they would be ideal adoptive parents.[3] They were "patient, loving, fun and ceaseless advocates for kids." Shew-Plummer helped the Hams adopt a young Hispanic boy, Michael. But Michael worried about his four younger siblings, who were still in foster care. "These kids obviously loved one another," Steven says. "I knew they had to be together, and I was going to make

---

[3]All information that follows is adapted from Bland (2011).

> { **We create our families through how we communicate.** }

that happen." Eventually, the couple adopted all of Michael's siblings and worked to reassure the children about the family's stability by telling them, "This [family] is forever." Seeing their success, caseworkers began placing children of all ethnicities, ages, and abilities with the Hams. They now have twelve.

Critical to their family success is the positive atmosphere Steven and Roger create. "They are really supportive of anything I do," says their daughter Vanessa, and their constant encouragement traverses many varied activities: basketball, karate, ROTC, and cheerleading. The Hams also emphasize open, honest communication. Some of their kids are old enough to remember their troubled previous lives, and the Hams discuss their pasts forthrightly, helping the children to grieve and move forward. "Children should be able to come to you about anything," Steven says. But more than anything else, the Ham family focuses on love. "A loving home is a loving home," Roger says. "Our kids have two parents who love them; not all of their friends do."

The story of the Ham family reminds us of a simple truth: *we create our families through how we communicate.* Although you're only one member of your family, the interpersonal choices you make—and what you say and do as a result—ripple outward. To help boost your family's closeness and happiness, use your interpersonal communication skills to maintain your family relationships and work carefully to balance ongoing family tensions.

Maintenance Strategies for Families

Many people take their family relationships for granted. Instead of communicating in ways designed to maintain these relationships, people assume that "your family is always there for you" (Vogl-Bauer, 2003). As a consequence, we often treat family members less favorably than we treat individuals who have no biological or legal connection to us. But all family relationships need

© ABC/Photofest

🌢 On the sitcom *Modern Family*, Phil and Claire Dunphy encourage their family to make time for one another and to practice positive, respectful communication. By doing so, Phil and Claire uphold positive family maintenance strategies and cultivate a supportive environment for the family (even when that means getting Phil to do something he doesn't want to do).

constant maintenance to be sustained. Three strategies that help you foster your bonds are positivity, assurances, and self-disclosure (Vogl-Bauer, 2003).

Positivity

The most powerful maintenance tactic for families is *positivity* (Stafford, 2010). This means communicating with your family members in an upbeat and hopeful fashion. To implement positivity in your family encounters, do favors for other family members without being asked, and unexpectedly gift them in little ways that show you care. Invest energy into making each encounter with family members enjoyable. Avoid complaining about family problems that have no solutions; ridiculing family members; whining or sulking when you don't get your way; and demanding that caregivers, siblings, or other kin give you favored treatment.

Assurances

The second way you can bolster your family relationships is by offering regular *assurances* of how much

your family means to you. Let other family members know that you consider your relationship with each of them unique and valuable, and that you are committed to maintaining these bonds well into the future ("I will always be here for you," "I miss you," or "I can't wait to be home again so I can spend time with you"). Avoid devaluing family relationships in front of others ("They're *just* my family") and commenting on how other families are superior to yours ("I'd give anything to have other parents").

Self-Disclosure

Self-disclosure in family relationships means sharing your private thoughts and feelings with family members and allowing them to do the same without fear of betrayal. You do this by treating other family members in ways that are consistent, trustworthy, and ethical. Ways to practice self-disclosure include making time in your schedule to talk with parents, siblings, or children about how they are doing; encouraging them to share their feelings and concerns with you; and offering your perspectives in a cooperative, respectful way. It also means avoiding communication practices that undermine disclosure, such as betraying confidences, refusing to make time for family conversation, reacting defensively when family members share their feelings with you, disparaging family members' viewpoints, and hiding things from your family.

Technology and Family Maintenance

My parents live 2,000 miles away from me, in an isolated valley in southern Oregon. But we "talk" several times each week by e-mail—exchanging cartoons, photos, and articles of interest. My nephew John, a student at the University of Washington, regularly keeps in touch via the messaging application WhatsApp. And my son Colin, while doing his homework upstairs, routinely sends me music and movie clips—even as I sit in our living room below, working.

Although some lament that technology has replaced face-to-face interaction and reduced family intimacy, families typically use online and face-to-face communication in a complementary, rather than substitutive, fashion. Families who communicate frequently via e-mail, Facebook, and instant messaging *also* communicate frequently face-to-face or on the phone. They typically choose synchronous modes of communication (face-to-face, phone) for personal or urgent matters, and asynchronous modes (e-mail, text, Facebook) for less important issues (Tillema, Dijst, & Schwanen, 2010).

What's more, technology, especially the use of cell phones, allows families to connect, share, and coordinate their lives to a degree never before possible, resulting in boosted intimacy and satisfaction (Kennedy, Smith, Wells, & Wellman, 2008). Similarly, families whose members are geographically separated but who use online communication to stay in touch report higher satisfaction, stronger intimacy, more social support, and reduced awareness of the physical separation, compared to families who don't (McGlynn, 2007).

Despite being comparatively "old school," e-mail is the dominant electronic way families communicate. Interpersonal scholar Amy Janan Johnson and her colleagues found that more than half of college students reported interacting with family members via e-mail in the preceding week, and that the primary purpose of these e-mails was relationship maintenance (Johnson, Haigh, Becker, Craig, & Wigley, 2008). Students used e-mail to maintain *positivity* ("Have a great day!"), provide *assurances* ("I love you and miss you!"), and *self-disclose* ("I'm feeling a bit scared about my stats exam tomorrow").

Skills Practice

Technology and Family Maintenance

Ways to communicate positivity and assurances to family members

1. Send an e-mail to a family member with whom you've been out of touch, letting him or her know you care.
2. Offer congratulations via text or e-mail to a family member who has recently achieved an important goal.
3. Post a message on the Facebook page of a family member with whom you've had a disagreement, saying that you value his or her opinions and beliefs.
4. Send an e-card to a long-distance family member, sharing a message of affection.
5. Post a supportive response to a family member who has expressed concerns via Twitter or Facebook.

Dealing with Family Dialectics

Within all families, tension exists between competing impulses, known as *relational dialectics* (see Chapter 10). Two dialectics are especially pronounced in families: *autonomy versus connection* and *openness versus protection*. As we mature, each of us must balance our desire

for autonomy against the connection that we share with our families and the corresponding expectations and obligations regarding who we "should" be as family members. We also face frequent decisions regarding how openly we should communicate with other family members, as well as how much information about our families we should share with those outside the family unit. Balancing these tensions is challenging. However, you *can* strike a balance—by applying the techniques described below.

Balancing Autonomy and Connection

Even though you may feel intensely connected to your family, you probably also struggle to create your own separate identity. You may enjoy the feeling of intimacy that connectedness brings, while resenting how your family seems blind to your true abilities: "My family doesn't think I can make mature decisions because I'm the youngest."

The tension between autonomy and connection in families is especially difficult to manage during adolescence (Crosnoe & Cavanagh, 2010). As children move through their teen years, they begin to assert their independence from parents. Their peers eventually replace parents and other family members as having the most influence on their interpersonal decisions (Golish, 2000).

How can you best manage the tension between autonomy and connection in your family? Keep two additional relationship maintenance strategies in mind—sharing tasks and cultivating social networks. With these, you want to strike a balance between family relationships and outside relationships. First, for sharing tasks you want to balance your dependence on family members to help you carry out everyday chores with a reliance on yourself and people outside your family. Too much dependence on family members—especially for tasks you could accomplish on your own—can erode your self-reliance, self-confidence, and independence (Strauss, 2006).

Second, examine your social networks (including your family), and assess the degree to which family members constitute the closest people in your life. If you have few or even no close ties with anyone outside the family sphere, you may feel intensely dependent on your family and experience a corresponding loss of autonomy. Likewise, having no close ties to any family members can create a sense of independence so extreme that you feel little emotional bond with your family.

Self-Reflection

Who has more influence in shaping your relationship decisions: your family or your friends? Whom do you look to for emotional support in times of need? Has the degree to which you depend on your family versus your friends changed over time? If so, why?

Balancing Openness and Protection

Families also experience tension between openness and protection. In any close relationship—family bonds included—we want both to share personal

◊ In the movie *The Descendants*, the family dialectics for Matt King (George Clooney) shift dramatically when he becomes a single parent to daughters Alexandra and Scottie. In his new role, Matt faces family obligations and expectations previously unknown to him, while Alexandra and Scottie are disoriented by their mother's absence and the greater autonomy it affords them.

information and to protect ourselves from the possible negative consequences of such sharing (Afifi & Steuber, 2010). In families, the tension between these two needs is even more pronounced. For example, your family may be extremely close, and as a consequence almost anything that you tell one family member quickly becomes common knowledge. This creates a dilemma when you want to share something with only one family member. Do you disclose the information, knowing that within a week's time your entire family will also know it, or do you withhold it?

According to **Communication Privacy Management Theory** (Petronio, 2000), individuals create informational boundaries by carefully choosing the kind of private information they reveal and the people with whom they share it. These boundaries are constantly shifting, depending on the degree of risk associated with disclosing information. The more comfortable people feel disclosing, the more likely they are to reveal sensitive information. Inversely, people are less likely to share when they expect negative reactions to the disclosure (Afifi & Steuber, 2010).

Within families, these boundaries are defined by **family privacy rules**: the conditions governing what family members can talk about, how they can discuss such topics, and who should have access to family-relevant information (Petronio & Caughlin, 2006). In some families, members feel free to talk about any topic, at any time, and in any situation. In other families, discussion of more sensitive topics such as politics and religion may be permissible only in certain settings (for example, discussing politics over dinner but not during breakfast). Or, some topics may be permanently excluded from your family discussion altogether: personal sexual history, assault, or abuse; financial woes; or health problems. Breaking a family privacy rule by forcing discussion of a "forbidden" topic can cause intense emotional discomfort among other family members and may prompt the family to exclude the "rule breaker" from future family interactions. Keep this in mind before you force discussion of an issue that other family members consider off-limits.

Family privacy rules govern *how* family members talk about topics as well—including what's considered an acceptable opinion and how deeply family members can explore these opinions. It may be acceptable to talk at any time about the personal lives of family members, for instance, but only if your comments are positive.

Additionally, family privacy rules identify the people with whom family members can talk. If your family holds a particular religious or political viewpoint that is at odds with surrounding neighbors' views, you might be instructed to avoid these topics when conversing with neighborhood friends (e.g. "This stays within the family").

Although family privacy rules help guide members in balancing openness and protection, they can also amplify tension within families as people age. When children grow up, the parent-child relationship often shifts from being authority based to friendship based (Silverstein & Giarrusso, 2010). As this occurs, people may feel pressure to change long-standing privacy rules. For example, even if your family has never openly discussed severe illness, you may feel compelled to talk about this topic if your mother starts displaying early symptoms of Alzheimer's disease.

> ### Self-Reflection
> What topics, if any, are off-limits for discussion within your family? Why are these topics taboo? What would be the consequences of forcing a discussion on these issues? How does not being able to talk about these things with family members make you feel about your family?

How can you improve your family privacy rules and, in doing so, bring about a better balance of openness and protection? First, remember that all families have approved and taboo conversational topics, certain viewpoints they promote over others, and people whom they include or exclude from receiving information about the family. Effective family privacy rules aren't "one size fits all." Instead, they should strike the balance between openness and protection that best fits *your* family. Second, be respectful of the varying opinions and preferences individual family members have regarding openness and protection. Keep in mind that if your family communication pattern is low on conversation orientation and high on conformity orientation, any push for a change in privacy rules may strike others as a threat to the family.

Finally, if you believe that your family privacy rules should be altered to allow greater openness or increased protection, avoid abrupt, dramatic, and demanding calls for change—"We need to learn how to talk more openly about sex!" Such pronouncements will likely offend family members and put them on the defensive. Instead, identify a single family member who you think might share your views. Discuss your desire for change with him or her by using your interpersonal competence skills and cooperative language (Chapters 1 and 7). Ask this person's opinion on the possibility of modifying your family's privacy rules, and invite him or her to suggest ideas for implementing the change. If he or she agrees that change is needed, identify an additional family member who might also concur. Then initiate a three-way discussion. Changes in long-standing family privacy rules—especially for low conversation, high conformity families—are best accomplished slowly through interactions with one family member at a time.

LearningCurve
bedfordstmartins.com/ipcandyou

Family Relationship Challenges

We like to think of family relationships as simple, straightforward, and uniformly positive. Family consists of the most supportive people in our lives—individuals whom we like, love, and depend on. For many people this is true. But this isn't always the case; family relationships also face daunting challenges. To help you manage such difficulties, let's explore two common issues: stepfamily transitions and interparental conflict.

Stepfamily Transitions

Transitioning to a stepfamily is a common challenge, given that approximately half of the marriages in the United States and Canada involve a remarriage for one or both partners (Coleman, Ganong, & Fine, 2000). While most people enter into stepfamilies with the best intentions for a new start, not all stepfamily members experience the transition equally. Studies have found that children in stepfamilies have more frequent behavioral problems, more turbulent relationships, and lower self-esteem than children in first-marriage families (Golish, 2003).

The majority of stepfamilies confront very similar challenges, including negotiating new family privacy rules, discrepancies in conflict management styles, and building solidarity as a family unit (Golish, 2003). But the most frequent and perplexing challenge is **triangulation**: loyalty conflicts that arise when a coalition is formed, uniting one family member with another against a third person (Schrodt & Afifi, 2007). Two forms of triangulation are common within stepfamilies: children feeling caught between their custodial and noncustodial parents, and stepparents feeling caught between the children in their stepfamily (Golish, 2003). Family members caught in triangulation feel "torn" between different loyalties. As one daughter described her triangulation between her birth parents, "I would carry things from her, she'd say stuff about him, and he'd do the same and talk about her. It's kind of hard to get both sides of it. So I avoided them for a while . . . I just felt that I was caught in the middle" (Golish, 2003, p. 52).

Given such challenges, how can *you* help ease the transition to a stepfamily, should you experience it? Try these suggestions:

1. *Go slow, but start early.* Except for the couple getting married, the relationships between other stepfamily members are involuntary. Yet

(Left to right) © Bubbles Photolibrary/Alamy; Imageshop/Alamy

🔥 Whether you're getting used to a new sibling or a stepparent, stepfamily transitions can be a challenge and often involve conflict.

stepfamily members often feel pressure to immediately become intimate (Ganong, Coleman, Fine, & Martin, 1999). This can cause stress and anxiety, as no one enjoys feeling forced to be close to others. To avoid this, *go slow* in building ties with your stepparents, stepchildren, or stepsiblings. Take the time to get to know one another, forging relationships in the same way you would any other interpersonal involvements—by having fun and doing things together. If possible, *start early* in creating these bonds—ideally as soon as it becomes certain that a stepfamily will form.

2. *Practice daily maintenance.* Research on stepfamilies emphasizes the importance of displaying affection, attending important activities and events, engaging in everyday talk, and sharing humorous stories—the behaviors fundamental to all families (Afifi, 2003). Try to express your support for your new family members by doing at least some of these things every day.

3. *Create new family rituals.* A critical part of building a new family identity is creating *stepfamily rituals*: events or activities shared between stepfamily members that function to define the group as a family. This can be sharing a weekly dinner together or attending religious services together. Whatever form it takes, the most constructive stepfamily rituals are those that bring stepfamily members together as a family, but still recognize and value what was important from the previous families (Schrodt, 2006).

4. *Avoid triangulating family members.* You may feel it's strategic or even enjoyable to team up and triangulate against a stepparent or stepsibling. But such behavior damages your relationship with them and creates family stress (Schrodt & Afifi, 2007). If you're the one caught in the middle of triangulation, confront the perpetrators. Using your cooperative language and competent interpersonal communication skills, respectfully explain how their behavior is making you feel and the damage it is doing to the family. Remind them that stepfamilies are difficult enough to maintain without also having to deal with alliances, loyalty struggles, and power battles. Ask them to cease such behavior.

{ **Family members caught in triangulation feel "torn" between different loyalties.** }

5. *Be patient*. Whenever families experience a major transition, there is always a lengthy period of adjustment. In the case of remarriage, it typically takes anywhere from three to five *years* for a stepfamily to stabilize as a family unit (Hetherington, 1993). Consequently, be patient. Expect that new relationship bonds are going to take a long time to develop, that you will feel uncertain about your new family roles, and that disputes will arise over privacy rules and personal boundaries (Golish, 2003).

Self-Reflection

Does your family or stepfamily have rituals? Which rituals mean the most to you, and why? How does the regular practice of these rituals affect how you feel about your family or stepfamily?

Interparental Conflict

One of the most potent family challenges is **interparental conflict**: overt, hostile interactions between parents in a household. While such constant fighting is harmful to the parents' relationship, the impact upon children in the household is worse. Interparental conflict is associated with children's social problems, including lower levels of play with peers and lower friendship quality (Rodrigues & Kitzmann, 2007). Such children are also more likely to imitate their parents' destructive interaction styles and, consequently, are more at risk for aggressive and delinquent behaviors (Krishnakumar, Buehler, & Barber, 2003).

But the most devastating effects of interparental conflict are relational. Adolescents who perceive a high frequency of interparental conflict are more likely to report feelings of jealousy and fears of abandonment in their romantic relationships (Hayashi & Strickland, 1998). Interparental conflict also negatively impacts late teen and adult perceptions of interpersonal trust, love attitudes, sexual behaviors,

relationship beliefs, cohabitation, and attitudes toward marriage and divorce (Rodrigues & Kitzmann, 2007).

Why do children suffer so many profound and negative outcomes from fights between parents? One explanation is the **spillover hypothesis**: emotions, affect, and mood from the parental relationship "spill over" into the broader family, disrupting children's sense of emotional security (Krishnakumar et al., 2003). Children living in households torn by interparental conflict experience a chronic sense of instability—not knowing when the next battle will erupt and if or when their parents will break up. This gives them a deep-seated sense of emotional insecurity related to relationships (Rodrigues & Kitzmann, 2007), which manifests in their own intimate involvements, months and even years later.

Skills Practice

Managing Interparental Conflict
Helping parents better manage their conflicts

1. Following a significant conflict between parents or caregivers, reach out to each person individually, letting them know you're available to talk.
2. Encourage them to be mindful of how negative emotions and flawed attributions shape their conflict perceptions and decisions.
3. Remind them of the relational damage wrought by destructive messages.
4. Help them identify the causes of the conflict.
5. List goals and long-term interests they share in common.
6. Use these points of commonality to collaboratively create solutions that will prevent similar conflicts in the future.
7. Evaluate these solutions in terms of fairness for both of them.

What can you do to manage interparental conflict and its outcomes? If you're the child of parents who fight, encourage them individually to approach their conflicts more constructively. Share with them all you know about conflict from Chapter 9: competent approaches for managing conflict, the negative role of self-enhancing thoughts, the dangers of destructive messages, and the trap of serial arguments. If you feel that you are suffering negative outcomes from having grown up in a conflict-ridden household, seek therapy from a reputable counselor. And if you're a parent, realize this: everything you say and do within the family realm—including interactions you have with your spouse or partner—spills over into the emotions and feelings of your children.

LearningCurve
bedfordstmartins.com/ipcandyou

Postscript }

We began this chapter with a world champion and the family who encouraged her to excel. Throughout her life, Brenda Villa's parents have been a source of inspiration and motivation. Through their support, honesty, sacrifice, and love, they created the foundation upon which Brenda has built the most successful water polo career in U.S. history.

To whom do you turn to listen—or to provide you with a necessary kick in the butt—when you're feeling sorry for yourself? From whom did you get the confidence and swagger to face the competitions that life presents?

The story of Brenda Villa and her parents reminds us of a simple truth regarding the primacy of family. The successes, victories, and medals we achieve in our lives may be won through our own efforts, but they were made possible by the people who raised us.

Chapter Review

Visit LaunchPad for *Interpersonal Communication and You* to watch brief, illustrative ▶ videos of these terms and to access ✔ LearningCurve. **bedfordstmartins.com/ipcandyou**

KEY TERMS

family, 227
nuclear family, 228
extended family, 229
stepfamily, 229
cohabiting couples, 229
single-parent
    family, 229
family stories, 229

Family Communication
    Patterns Theory, 231
conversation orientation, 231
conformity orientation, 231
▶ consensual families, 233
▶ pluralistic families, 233
▶ protective families, 233
▶ laissez-faire families, 234

Communication Privacy
    Management Theory, 238
family privacy
    rules, 238
triangulation, 239
interparental conflict,
    241
spillover hypothesis, 241

CHAPTER ACTIVITIES

1. Working with a classmate, identify famous families from TV shows or movies that correspond to each family type, such as the Cosbys (nuclear), the Brady Bunch (stepfamily), and the Addams family (extended). Consider the communication styles of these families and how they handle conflict. How realistic do these media families seem? What are the major differences between media families and real-life ones?

2. Go to americanfamilystories.org and listen to a few examples of family stories on the site. Write a journal entry explaining what you heard and how the stories align to the types of stories described on pages 229–230. Then, write an essay about one of your own favorite family stories and include why the story is significant and how it affects family communication.

3. ▶ Watch the videos on **consensual families, protective families, pluralistic families**, and **laissez-faire families**. Identify which family communication pattern best represents your family. Using a real

example of behaviors and experiences, create your own video script demonstrating how the pattern works in your family.

4. With a small group of classmates, discuss the following questions: Do you add your family members as friends to your social networks? Why or why not? Do you monitor your communication with others due to this? Has being friends with family members on social networks caused conflict? How has technology changed the way you communicate with your family?

5. Write an essay applying the ideas of Communication Privacy Management Theory. Address these questions: What were the family privacy rules in your family of origin? How has privacy been beneficial or detrimental in your family? What changes did you experience in openness during different transitions in your childhood? Would you change or maintain the same privacy rules with your own children in your current or future families?

Look for LearningCurve throughout
the chapter to help you review.
bedfordstmartins.com/ipcandyou.

12 } Relationships with Friends

They met while working together at WJZ-TV in Baltimore. Oprah was the six o'clock news anchor and Gayle was a production assistant.[1] One night a snowstorm blew in, making the roads perilous. Oprah suggested that Gayle stay over at her place, rather than risk the drive home. Gayle accepted. As the two chatted in the warmth of Oprah's apartment, they learned of their radically different economic backgrounds. Gayle was from an upper-middle-class family; Oprah had grown up poor. "Gayle had a *pool* growing up!" exclaims Oprah. "She had a *maid*. My *mother* was a maid. You know what I'm saying?" But the more they talked, the more they realized their commonalities. "We became friends that first night because for the first time, I met somebody who I felt was like me," describes Gayle. "Oprah

and I had the same sensibilities. We liked the same kind of music. We both had been the only black girls in our schools. And we were the same age, we were both single, and we just immediately bonded. And we've been friends ever since."

The cornerstones of Gayle and Oprah's now-iconic friendship are communication, support, and trust. The two typically talk three or four times a day, regardless of how busy they are. But it isn't just the frequency of interaction that cements their bond; it's the degree of disclosure. "We talk about everything and anything," says Gayle. "I don't want to offend her, but I'm never afraid to be truthful with her."

Oprah and Gayle offer each other unconditional support. As Oprah describes, "We're talking about a relationship in which someone always loves you, always respects you, wants the best for you in every single situation of your life. Lifts you up. Supports you. Always!" The two

[1]The information that follows is adapted from Kogan (2006).

◆ **Our friends keep us grounded and provide us with support in times of crisis.**
Frazer Harrison/Getty Images for AFI

women trust each other to never betray their friendship. Oprah once hosted an episode of her TV show in which she interviewed women who had slept with their best friend's husbands. This type of betrayal is inconceivable to the two. "That is not possible in this relationship," says Oprah. Gayle added, "I know for sure: I will *never* sleep with [Oprah's boyfriend] Stedman!"

A common tabloid story about Oprah and Gayle is that they are actually lovers. This irks Oprah because, if she *was* a lesbian and Gayle *was* her lover, the two would be open and honest about it. At the same time, Oprah isn't surprised. "I understand why people think we're gay. There isn't a definition in our culture for this kind of bond between women. So I get why people have to label it—how can you be this close without it being sexual? How else can you explain this level of intimacy?"

Gayle and Oprah have been best friends for more than 30 years. But despite all the public scrutiny their friendship has undergone, and all the effort they've put in to maintain it, there's still an aspect of it that defies description. "There isn't a model for something like this," offers Oprah. "Something about this relationship feels otherworldly to me, like it was designed by a power and a hand greater than my own. Whatever this friendship is, it's been a very fun ride—and we've taken it together."

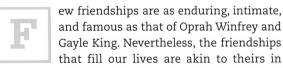

Few friendships are as enduring, intimate, and famous as that of Oprah Winfrey and Gayle King. Nevertheless, the friendships that fill our lives are akin to theirs in important ways. Like Oprah and Gayle, we are drawn to our friends through the realization of shared similarities. We count on our friends to provide support. We build our friendships by disclosing our thoughts, feelings, and vulnerabilities while trusting our friends to not betray us. At the same time, our friendships can be difficult to define. They lack the permanence of family bonds and the clear constraints and expectations of romantic involvements. This makes them more delicate and mysterious than other close relationships. Friendships often leave us pondering, like Oprah, "I know this is fun, but what exactly *is* this?"

In this chapter, we look at friendship. You'll learn:

- How friendships are unique and distinct
- Varied types of friendships you'll experience
- Ways you can communicate so that your friendships survive and thrive
- Challenges to friendships and how to overcome them

The Nature of Friendship

Like family and romantic bonds, friendship plays a crucial role in our lives. Friendship is an important source of emotional security and self-esteem (Rawlins, 1992). It also facilitates a sense of belonging when we're young, helps solidify our identity during adolescence, and provides satisfaction and social support when we're elderly (Miller, Hefner, & Scott, 2007). But what exactly is friendship?

Friendship Defined

Friendship is a voluntary interpersonal relationship characterized by intimacy and liking (McEwan, Babin Gallagher, & Farinelli, 2008). Whether it's casual or close, short- or long-term, friendship has several distinguishing characteristics.

Friendship Is Voluntary

We have greater liberty in choosing our friends than we do in choosing partners for any other relationship type (Sias et al., 2008). Whether a friendship forms is determined largely by the people involved, based on their mutual desire to create such a relationship. This is different from romantic and family involvements. Consider romantic relationships. You may face substantial familial or cultural constraints in your choice of romantic partners. You may be expected (or allowed) only to date people of a certain age, gender, ethnicity, religion, or income level. You may even have a spouse chosen *for* you in an arranged marriage. In your family, you're bound to others through birth, adoption, or the creation of a stepfamily. These ties are involuntary. As French poet Jacques Delille (1738–1813) put it, "Fate chooses your relations, you choose your friends."

Friendship Is Driven by Shared Interests

As shown by Oprah Winfrey and Gayle King, similarity is the primary force that draws us to our friends (Parks & Floyd, 1996). This is true across ages, genders, sexual orientations, and ethnicities. One practical implication of this is that when your interests and activities change, so do your friendships. If you change your political beliefs or suffer an injury that prevents you from playing a beloved sport, friendships related to those things may change as well. Some friendships will endure—the focus of the relationship shifting to new points of commonality—but others will fade away. One of the most common reasons for friendships ending is a change in shared interests and beliefs (Miller et al., 2007).

> { We have greater liberty in choosing our friends than we do in choosing partners for any other relationship type. }

Greg Gayne/CBS/Landov

💧 On *The Big Bang Theory*, close friends Leonard, Sheldon, Howard, and Rajesh regularly get together and indulge their mutual passion for physics, sci-fi movies, and intricate science experiments. Their shared interests are a point of commonality that began but also sustains their friendships over time. What first drew you to your closest friends?

Friendship Is Characterized by Self-Disclosure

We consider most people in our lives "acquaintances." Only a select few rise to the level of "friends." What distinguishes the two groups? *Self-disclosure.* Both men and women report that being able to freely and deeply disclose is *the* defining feature of friendship (Parks & Floyd, 1996). Self-disclosure between friends means sharing private thoughts and feelings, and believing (like Gayle and Oprah) that "we can tell each other anything." The relationship between friendship and self-disclosure is reciprocal as well. The more you consider someone a friend, the more you will disclose, and the more you disclose, the more you will consider that person a friend (Shelton, Trail, West, & Bergsieker, 2010).

Friendship Is Rooted in Liking

We feel affection and respect for our friends. In other words, we *like* them (Rubin, 1973). We enjoy their company and take pleasure in sharing time together (Hays, 1988). However, because friendships are rooted in liking—rather than love—we're not as emotionally attached to our friends as we are to other intimates, and we're not as emotionally demanding of them. Correspondingly, we're expected to be more loyal to and more willing to help romantic partners and family members than friends (Davis & Todd, 1985).

Friendship Is Volatile

Friendships are less stable, more likely to change, and easier to break off than family or romantic relationships (Johnson, Wittenberg, Villagran, Mazur, & Villagran, 2003). Why? Consider the differences in depth of commitment. We're bonded to friends by choice, rooted in shared interests. But we're bonded to families by social and legal commitment, and to lovers by deep emotional and sexual attachment. These loyalties mean we may choose or forgo professional opportunities to preserve romances or stay close to family. But most of us will choose to pursue our careers over staying geographically close to friends (Patterson, 2007).

Self-Reflection

Call to mind your three closest friends in middle school. Then do the same for high school. Now think about your three closest friends today. Are the lists the same? How have they changed? Why? What does this tell you about the volatility of friendships?

Friendship Functions

Friendships serve many different functions in our lives. Two of the most important are *companionship*—chances to do fun things together and receive emotional support—and *achieving practical goals*—friends help us deal with problems or everyday tasks (de Vries, 1996). These functions are not mutually exclusive, as many friendships facilitate both.

Communal Friendships

Friendships enable us to share life events and activities with others. Compared to family and work relationships, friendship interactions are the least task oriented and tend to revolve around leisure activities such as talking or eating (Argyle & Furnham, 1982). Scholar William Rawlins (1992) describes friendships that focus primarily on sharing time and activities together as **communal friendships**. Communal friends get together as often as possible and provide encouragement and emotional support to one another during times of need. Importantly, because emotional support is a central aspect of communal friendship, only when both friends fulfill the expectations of support for the relationship does the friendship endure (Burleson & Samter, 1994).

Agentic Friendships

Friends also help us achieve practical goals in both our personal and our professional lives. They help us study for exams, fix cars, move apartments, and complete professional projects. Friendships in which the parties focus primarily on helping each other achieve practical goals are known as **agentic friendships** (Rawlins, 1992). Agentic friends value sharing time together—but only if they're available and have no other priorities. They also aren't interested in the emotional

© Matthias Ritzmann/Corbis

◊ Although less intimate than communal friendships, people in agentic friendships can help each other with practical tasks and other goals like moving. Can you recall a time when an agentic friend helped you achieve a significant goal?

interdependence and intimate self-disclosure that characterize communal friendships. They're available when the need arises, but beyond that, they're uncomfortable with more personal demands or responsibilities. For example, an agentic friend from work may gladly help you write up a monthly sales report, but she may feel uncomfortable if you ask her for advice about your romantic problems.

© DreamWorks/Courtesy Everett Collection

◊ In the movie *I Love You, Man,* Peter Klaven (Paul Rudd) is happily engaged to Zooey (Rashida Jones) but feels pressure to make more male friends before getting married. When Peter meets Sydney Fife (Jason Segel) and they quickly become inseparable, their open displays of affection and eagerness to spend time together cause Zooey to worry she is no longer the primary source of intimacy in Peter's life.

> ### Self-Reflection
>
> Do you have more communal or agentic friends? How do you communicate differently with the two types of friends? Which type of friend do you depend on more, day to day? Why?

Friendship across the Life Span

The importance we attribute to our friendships changes throughout our lives. Up through the fourth grade, most children look to their family as their sole source of emotional support (Furman & Simon, 1998). When children suffer a disappointment at school, have frightening dreams, or just want to share the events of the day, they will turn to parents or siblings. But during adolescence, children slowly transfer their emotional attachment from their family to friends (Welch & Houser, 2010). For example, by the seventh grade, young people rely just as much on same-sex friends as they do on family for support. By tenth grade, same-sex friends are the principal providers of emotional support. This trend continues into early adulthood: for college students, friends are the primary relationship for fulfilling relational needs (McEwan et al., 2008).

By middle adulthood, many people form long-term romantic commitments and start families of their own. Consequently, their romantic partners and children become the primary providers of companionship, affection, and support. The importance of friendships begins to wane (Carbery & Buhrmester, 1998). This is especially the case for married men, who before marriage tend to spend most of their

time with male friends (Cohen, 1992). Late in life, however, the pattern shifts back once more, as spouses and siblings pass on and children form their own families. For the elderly, friendships are the most important relationships for providing social support and intimacy (Patterson, 2007).

Friendship, Culture, and Gender

People from different cultures have varied expectations regarding friendships. For example, most Westerners believe that friendships don't endure, that you'll naturally lose some friends and gain others over time (Berscheid & Regan, 2005). This belief contrasts sharply with attitudes in other cultures, in which people view friendships as deeply intimate and lasting. In one study, when asked to identify the closest relationship in their lives, Euro-Americans tended to select romantic partners, whereas Japanese tended to select friendships (Gudykunst & Nishida, 1993).

Across cultures, friendship interactions are also entangled with gender norms. In the United States and Canada, for instance, friendships between women are often stereotyped as communal, whereas men's friendships are thought to be agentic. But male and female same-sex friendships are more similar than they are different (Winstead, Derlaga, & Rose, 1997).[2] Men and women rate the importance of both communal and agentic friendships equally (Roy, Benenson, & Lilly, 2000), and studies of male friendships in North America have found that companionship is the primary need met by friendships (Wellman, 1992).

At the same time, Euro-American men, unlike women, learn to avoid direct expressions of affection and intimacy in their friendships with other males. Owing to traditional masculine gender roles, a general reluctance to openly show emotion, and homophobia (among other factors), many men avoid verbal and nonverbal intimacy, such as disclosing personal feelings, touching, and hugging, in their same-sex friendships (Bank & Hansford, 2000). But in many other cultures, both men and women look to same-sex friends as their primary source of intimacy. Traditional Javanese (Indonesian) culture holds that marriage should not be too intimate and that a person's closest relationship should be with his or her same-sex friends (Williams, 1992).

Friendship and Technology

As with other interpersonal relationships, communication technologies such as social networking sites, Twitter, smartphones, e-mail, and text-messaging have reshaped the way people create friendships. In the past, people forged friendships slowly. They took time to discover the values and interests of their neighbors, coworkers, and acquaintances, and only then built friendships with those who shared their values and interests. Now, however, you can form friendships quickly and with more people—some whom you may never actually meet in person—simply by friending them on Facebook or other online communities (Stafford, 2005). This provides a valuable resource to people suffering from chronic shyness. They can interact with others and garner social and emotional support, without suffering the anxiety that direct face-to-face contact may cause (Pennington, 2009).

Communication technologies make it possible for friends to stay constantly connected with one another. For better or worse, you now can keep your friends updated 24/7 on the latest news in your life through posts and messages. Interestingly, much like within families (see Chapter 11), technology does not replace in-person interaction. People who regularly use cell phones to call and text their friends are *more* likely to also seek face-to-face encounters (Wang & Andersen, 2007).

Despite all of this technology, people continue to recognize the superiority of offline relationships and communication. Studies comparing offline versus online friendships find that offline friendships have higher degrees of intimacy, understanding, interdependence, and commitment (Chan & Cheng, 2004). Additionally, people prefer face-to-face interactions with friends when discussing deeply personal or troubling topics (Pennington, 2009).

---

[2]As defined in Chapter 2, *gender* is the composite of social, psychological, and cultural attributes that characterize us as male or female (Canary, Emmers-Sommer, & Faulkner, 1997). *Sex* refers to the biological sex organs with which we're born. When communicating, people orient to gender, not sex (which they typically don't see!). But usage of the terms *sex* and *gender* by scholars often is inconsistent (Parks, 2007). For example, within the friendship literature, male-female friendships are referred to as opposite-*sex* and male-male and female-female friendships as same-*sex*, rather than opposite-gender and same-gender. Consequently, in this section, we use the terms *cross-sex* and *same-sex*.

Self-Reflection

Think of friends you only know and interact with online and compare them with the friends who populate your offline world. Which friends do you consider closer? When you're confronted with a challenging problem or personal crisis, which friends do you turn to for support? Why?

Nick David /Getty Images

 Communication technologies have reshaped the ways people create and maintain friendships. Even while socializing with friends face-to-face, it is now possible to stay connected to friends who aren't present. How do you maintain friendships using online communication?

LearningCurve
bedfordstmartins.com/ipcandyou

Types of Friendship

Like family and romantic bonds, friendships play a crucial role in our lives. They also constitute the most prevalent type of relationship we experience (Blieszner & Adams, 1992). Some friendships endure for decades, during which the friends involved become family. Others are formed for convenience, such as a friendship with a coworker that you meet with regularly via Skype. While you have a variety of different types of friends, three types stand out as unique, challenging, and significant: best friends, cross-category friends, and workplace friends.

Best Friends

Think of the people you consider *close friends*—those with whom you exchange deeply personal information and emotional support, share many interests

and activities, and around whom you feel comfortable and at ease (Parks & Floyd, 1996). How many come to mind? Chances are you can count them on one hand. A study surveying over one thousand individuals found that, on average, people have four close friends (Galupo, 2009).

But, what is the difference between a close friend and a *best friend*? Many things. First, best friends typically are same-sex rather than cross-sex (Galupo, 2009). Although we may have close cross-sex friendships, few of these relationships evolve to being a "best." Second, best friendship involves greater intimacy, more disclosure, and deeper commitment than close friendship (Weisz & Wood, 2005). People talk more frequently and more deeply with best friends about their relationships, emotions, life events, and goals (Pennington, 2009). This holds true for both women *and* men. Third, people count on their best friends to listen to their problems without judging, and to "have their back"—that is, provide unconditional support (Pennington, 2009). Fourth, best friendship is distinct in the degree to which shared activities commit the friends to each other in substantial ways. For example, best friends are more likely to join clubs together, participate on intramural sports teams, become roommates, and vacation together (Becker et al., 2009).

Finally, the most important factor that distinguishes best friends is unqualified provision of **identity support**: behaving in ways that convey understanding, acceptance, and support for a friend's valued social identities. **Valued social identities** are the aspects of your public self that you deem the most important in defining who you are—for example, musician, athlete, poet, dancer, teacher, mother, and so on. Whoever we are—and whoever we dream of being—our best friends understand us, accept us,

> **The most important factor that distinguishes best friends is unqualified provision of identity support.**

respect us, and support us, no matter what. Imagine that a good friend tells you that he is transgendered and henceforth will be living as a woman in accordance with his true gender. How would you respond? *Best* friends would distinguish themselves by supporting such identity shifts even if they found them surprising. Research following friendships across a four-year time span found that more than any other factor—including amount of communication and perceived closeness—participants who initially reported high levels of identity support from a new friend were more likely to describe that person as their *best* friend four years later (Weisz & Wood, 2005).

Self-Reflection

Call to mind your most valued social identities. Which friends provide the most acceptance, respect, and support of these identities? Which friends do you consider closest? What's the relationship between the two? What does this tell you about the importance of identity support in determining friendship intimacy?

Cross-Category Friendships

Given that friendships center on shared interests and identity support, it's no surprise that people tend to befriend those who are similar demographically (age, gender, economic status, etc.). As just one example, studies of straight, gay, lesbian, bisexual, and transgendered persons find that, regardless of sexual orientation or gender identity, people are more likely to have close friendships with others of the same ethnicity (Galupo, 2009). But people also regularly defy this norm, forging friendships that cross demographic lines, known as **cross-category friendships** (Galupo, 2009). Such friendships are a powerful way to break down ingrouper and outgrouper perceptions and purge people of negative stereotypes. The three most common cross-category friendships are cross-sex, cross-orientation, and interethnic.

Cross-Sex Friendships

One of the most radical shifts in interpersonal relationship patterns over the past few decades has been the increase in platonic (nonsexual) friendships between men and women in the United States and Canada. In the nineteenth century, friendships were almost exclusively same-sex, and throughout most of the twentieth century, cross-sex friendships remained a rarity (Halatsis & Christakis, 2009). As we move into the twenty-first century, however, this is changing.

Most cross-sex friendships are not motivated by sexual attraction (Messman, Canary, & Hause, 1994). Instead, men and women agree that through cross-sex friendships, they gain a greater understanding of how members of the other sex think, feel, and behave (Halatsis & Christakis, 2009). For men, forming friendships with women provides the possibility of greater intimacy and emotional depth than is typically available in male-male friendships (Monsour, 1997).

Despite changing attitudes toward cross-sex friendships, men and women face several challenges in building such relationships. For one thing, society tends to segregate the sexes from early childhood. In most schools, young boys and girls are put in separate gym classes, line up separately for class, and engage in competitions pitting "the boys against the girls" (Thorne, 1986). It's no surprise, then, that young children overwhelmingly prefer friends of the same sex (Reeder, 2003). As a consequence, most children enter their teens with only limited experience in building cross-sex friendships. Neither adolescence nor adulthood provides many opportunities for gaining this experience. Leisure-oriented activities such as competitive sports, community programs, and social organizations—including the Boy Scouts and Girl Scouts—typically are sex segregated (Swain, 1992).

Another challenge is that our society promotes only same-sex friendship and cross-sex coupling as the two most acceptable relationship options. So no matter how rigorously a pair of cross-sex friends insist that they're "just friends," their surrounding friends and family members will likely meet these claims with skepticism or even disapproval (Monsour, 1997). Family members who approve of the

(Left to right) David Alan Harvey/Magnum Photos; Wayne Miller/Magnum Photos; © Ann Cutting/Alamy; SassyStock/Fotosearch

🔵 In addition to the benefits of friendship such as companionship and shared interests, cross-category friends are often exposed to cultural experiences they may not have otherwise.

friendship often pester such couples to become romantically involved: "You and Jen have so much in common! Why not take things to the next level?" If families disapprove, they encourage termination of the relationship: "I don't want people thinking my daughter is hanging out casually with some guy. Why don't you hang out with other girls instead?" Romantic partners of people involved in cross-sex friendships often vehemently disapprove of such involvements (Hansen, 1985). Owing to constant disapproval from others and the pressure to justify the relationship, cross-sex friendships are far less stable than same-sex friendships (Berscheid & Regan, 2005).

Cross-Orientation Friendships

A second type of cross-category friendship is *cross-orientation*: friendships between lesbian, gay, bisexual, transgendered, or queer (LGBTQ) people and straight men or women. As within all friendships, cross-orientation friends are bonded by shared interests and activities, and provide each other with support and affection. But these friendships also provide unique rewards for the parties involved (Galupo, 2007). For straight men and women, forming a cross-orientation friendship can help correct negative stereotypes about persons of other sexual orientations and the LGBTQ community as a whole. For LGBTQ persons, having a straight friend can provide much-needed emotional and social support from outside of the LGBTQ community, helping to further insulate them from societal homophobia (Galupo, 2007).

Although cross-orientation friendships are commonplace on television and in the movies, they are less frequent in real life. Although LGBTQ persons often have as many cross-orientation friends as same-orientation, straight men and women overwhelmingly form friendships with other straight men and women (Galupo, 2009). The principal reason is homophobia, both personal and societal. By far the group that has the fewest cross-orientation friendships is straight men. In fact, the average number of cross-orientation friendships for straight men is *zero*: most straight men do not have a single lesbian, gay, bisexual, or transgendered friend (Galupo, 2009). This tendency may perpetuate homophobic sentiments because these men are never exposed to LGBTQ persons who might amend their negative attitudes. If biases are keeping you from developing friendships with diverse others, see the advice in Chapter 5 on overcoming prejudice as a way to start resetting your viewpoint.

Interethnic Friendships

The final type of cross-category friendship is *interethnic* friendship: a bond between people who share the same cultural background (for example, "American"), but who are of different ethnic groups ("African American," "Asian American," "Euro-American," and so forth). Similar to cross-orientation friendships,

Self-Quiz }

What Kind of Friend Are You?

Think about how you communicate with, relate to, and behave toward your friends. Then place a check mark next to the statements with which you agree and total the number you have marked. Check your score at the bottom.

▢ I strive to always maintain equal give-and-take in my friendships.

▢ I'm the kind of person my friends can talk with about anything and feel relaxed around.

▢ I think like my friends do and share a similar sense of humor with them.

▢ I don't hold my friends' mistakes against them.

▢ I can be trusted by my friends to keep a secret.

▢ I'm honest with my friends; I don't lie or hold things back.

▢ I can be serious with my friends, and I don't make fun of them when they want to talk about difficult issues.

▢ I'm considerate about my friends' feelings, and I don't do spiteful things.

▢ I can take care of myself, and I have my own ideals and beliefs apart from my friends'.

▢ I respect my friends' needs for privacy.

▢ I encourage my friends when they're up, and I cheer them up when they're down.

▢ I'm generous toward my friends and not self-centered.

▢ I'm fun to be around when I'm with my friends.

▢ I have an upbeat personality and stress the positive side of things when communicating with my friends.

▢ I always keep my promises to friends.

Note: This *Self-Quiz* is adapted from Maeda and Ritchie (2003).

Scoring: These statements represent the qualities people associate with close, trustworthy, and dependable friends. If you scored 11–15, you are an exceptionally trustworthy friend; 6–10, you are moderately trustworthy; 0–5, you exhibit low levels of trustworthiness.

interethnic friendships boost cultural awareness and commitment to diversity (Shelton, Richeson, & Bergsieker, 2009). In addition, interethnic friends apply these outcomes broadly. People who develop a close interethnic friendship become less prejudiced toward ethnicities and cultures of *all* types as a result (Shelton et al., 2009).

The most difficult barriers people face in forming interethnic friendships are attributional and perceptual errors. Too often we let our own biases and stereotypes stop us from having open, honest, and comfortable interactions with people from other ethnic groups. We become overly concerned with the "correct" way to act and end up behaving nervously. Such nervousness may lead to awkward, uncomfortable encounters and may cause us to avoid interethnic encounters in the future, dooming ourselves to friendship networks that lack diversity (Shelton, Trail, West, & Bergsieker, 2010).

How can you overcome these challenges and improve your ability to form interethnic friendships? Review the discussion in Chapter 3 of attributional errors and perception-checking. Look for points of commonality during interethnic encounters that might lead to the formation of a friendship—such as a shared interest in music, fashion, sports, movies, or video games. This effort is well worth it. Having friends from different ethnicities and cultures not only improves your world-mindedness but substantially increases the chances you will forge such friendships in the future (Sias et al., 2008). This is because you learn the enormous benefits that such relationships provide and decrease fear and uncertainty about "outgroupers."

Workplace Friendships

Considering the amount of time we spend at work, it is only natural that friendships develop among coworkers. Like all such relationships, these involvements are voluntary, based on liking and shared interests. But, the workplace environment impacts whom you befriend and how intimate the friendship gets.

Our most meaningful workplace friendships are those with **professional peers**, people holding positions of organizational status and power similar to our own. Peers are the most important source of personal and practical support for employees in any type of organization, whether it's a bank, a hospital, or a band (Rawlins, 1992). Although peer relationships strongly shape the quality of our work lives and are often intensely personal, not all peer relationships are the same (Fritz & Dillard, 1994). Instead, we categorize our peers by levels of intimacy.

- *Information peers* are equivalent-status coworkers with whom our communication is limited to work-related content. Information peer relationships typically are created through assignment rather than choice, and as a result, they lack trust and intimacy. Although these relationships are common, many people view information peers as less open and less communicatively skilled than collegial or special peers, discussed below (Myers, Knox, Pawlowski, & Ropog, 1999).

- *Collegial peers* are coworkers whom we consider friends. When we communicate with collegial peers, we talk about work and personal issues, and we feel moderate levels of trust and intimacy toward these individuals. Scholars sometimes describe these relationships as "blended" because they incorporate elements of both professional and personal relationships (Bridge & Baxter, 1992).

- *Special peers* are equivalent-status coworkers with whom we share very high levels of emotional support, career-related feedback, trust, self-disclosure, and friendship (Sias et al., 2002). The rarest type of peer relationship, special peers are those we consider our best friends in the workplace.

Professional peer relationships evolve from lesser to greater levels of intimacy over time. The first and most significant relationship transition is from information peer to collegial peer (Sias & Cahill, 1998). Workers who spend extended periods of time together, are placed in proximity with each other, or socialize together outside the workplace inevitably form stronger bonds with each other. However, sharing time and activities together is not enough to ensure that a coworker relationship will evolve from information to collegial peer. Like personal friendships, perceived similarity in interests, beliefs, and values is what decisively pushes a workplace relationship from acquaintanceship to friendship (Sias & Cahill, 1998).

The transition from collegial peer to special peer is different, however. Perceived similarity, shared time and tasks, and socializing are all important but are not sufficient to push coworker friendships to the level of best friend (Sias & Cahill, 1998). Instead, the evolution of a coworker friendship to a higher state of intimacy is usually spurred by negative events in partners' personal lives (serious illness, marital discord) or serious work-related problems that require an exceptional level of social support.

LearningCurve
bedfordstmartins.com/ipcandyou

Maintaining Friendships

In the movie *Zombieland*, four people known by the monikers of their former hometowns struggle to survive in a postapocalyptic world (Fleischer, Reesee, & Werrick, 2009). The central character, Columbus, is a self-described loner who never had close ties to friends or family. As he puts it, "I avoided people like they were zombies, even before they were zombies!" To deal with the challenge of constant flesh-eater attacks, he develops a set of rules, including Rule #1: *Cardio* (stay in shape to stay ahead of zombies); Rule #17: *Don't be a hero* (don't put yourself at risk to save others); and Rule #31: *Always check the backseat* (to avoid surprises). Eventually, he bands together with three other survivors—Tallahassee, Wichita, and Little Rock—and learns that they too have trust issues, regrets regarding their former lives, and fears about the future (above and beyond zombie attacks). As they travel across the country together, they learn to trust, support, defend, and depend upon each other. This leads to a friendship that eventually deepens to a family-like bond. Columbus even chooses to bend Rule #17 to save Wichita, by being a hero. As he

As Columbus, Wichita, Little Rock, and Tallahassee grow to trust, defend, and depend on one another in *Zombieland*, they realize that friendship is one of the key elements to surviving a zombie attack, and to being (and staying) human.

> { **Friendships don't endure on their own . . . they flourish only when you consistently communicate in ways that maintain them.** }

narrates in the final scene, "Those smart girls in the big black truck and that big guy in that snakeskin jacket—they were the closest to something I'd always wanted, but never really had—a family. I trusted them, and they trusted me. Even though life would never be simple or innocent again, we had hope—we had each other. And without other people, well, you might as well be a zombie!"

It's true. We *need* our friends. Most of us don't need them for survival, as we don't face daily zombie attacks. But our friends do provide a constant and important shield against the stresses, hardships, and threats of our everyday lives. We count on friends to be there when we need them and to provide support; in return we do the same. This is what bonds us together.

At the same time, friendships don't endure on their own. As with romantic and family involvements, friendships flourish only when you consistently communicate in ways that maintain them. Two ways that we keep friendships alive are by following friendship rules and by using maintenance strategies.

Following Friendship Rules

In *Zombieland*, Columbus follows a set of rules that allow him to survive. In the real world, one of the ways we can help our friendships succeed is by following **friendship rules**—general principles that prescribe appropriate communication and behavior within friendship relationships (Argyle & Henderson, 1984). In an extensive study of friendship maintenance, social psychologists Michael Argyle and Monica Henderson observed 10 friendship rules that people share across cultures. Both men and women endorse these rules, and adherence to them distinguishes happy from unhappy friendships (Schneider & Kenny, 2000). Not abiding by them may even cost you your friends: people around the globe describe failed friendships as ones that didn't follow these rules (Argyle & Henderson, 1984). The 10 rules for friendship are:

1. *Show support*. Within a friendship, you should provide emotional support and offer assistance in times of need, without having to be asked (Burleson & Samter, 1994). You also should accept and respect your friend's valued social identities. When he or she changes majors, tries out for team captain, or opts to be a stay-at-home mom or dad, support the decision—even if it's one you yourself wouldn't make.

2. *Seek support*. The flip side of the first rule is that when you're in a friendship you should not only deliver support but *seek* support and counsel when needed, disclosing your emotional burdens to your friends. Other than sharing time and activities, mutual self-disclosure serves as the glue that binds friendships together (Dainton, Zelley, & Langan, 2003).

3. *Respect privacy*. At the same time friends anticipate both support and disclosure, they also recognize that friendships have more restrictive boundaries for sharing personal information than do romantic or family relationships. Recognize this, and avoid pushing your friend to share information that he or she considers too personal. Also resist sharing information about yourself that's intensely private or irrelevant to your friendship.

4. *Keep confidences*. A critical feature of enduring friendships is trust. When friends share personal information with you, do not betray their confidence by sharing it with others.

5. *Defend your friends*. Part of successful friendships is the feeling that friends "have your back." Your friends count on you to stand up for them, so defend them online and off, in situations where they are being attacked either to their face or behind their back.

6. *Avoid public criticism*. Friends may disagree or even disapprove of each other's behavior on occasion. But airing your grievances publicly in ways that make your friends look bad will only hurt your friendships. Avoid questioning a friend's loyalty or commenting on a friend's weight in front of other people.

7. *Make your friends happy*. An essential ingredient to successful friendships is striving to make your friends feel good while you're in their company. You can do this by practicing positivity: communicating with them in a cheerful and optimistic fashion, doing unsolicited favors for them, and buying or making gifts for them.

8. *Manage jealousy*. Unlike long-term romantic relationships, friendships aren't exclusive. Your close friends likely will have other close friends, perhaps even friends who are more intimate than you. Accept that each of your friends has other good friends as well, and constructively manage any jealousy that arises in you.

9. *Share humor*. Successful friends spend a good deal of their time joking with and teasing each other in affectionate ways. Enjoying a similar sense of humor is an essential aspect of most long-term friendships.

10. *Maintain equity*. In enduring, mutually satisfying friendships, the two people give and get in roughly equitable proportions (Canary & Zelley, 2000). Help maintain this equity by conscientiously repaying debts, returning favors, and keeping the exchange of gifts and compliments balanced.

Self-Reflection

Consider the 10 universal rules that successful friends follow. Which of these rules do you abide by in your own friendships? Which do you neglect? How has neglecting some of these rules affected your friendships? What steps might you take to better follow rules you've previously neglected?

Maintenance Strategies for Friends

Most friendships are built on a foundation of shared activities and self-disclosure. To maintain your friendships, strive to keep this foundation solid by regularly doing things with your friends, and making time to talk.

Sharing Activities

Through *sharing activities*, friends structure their schedules to enjoy hobbies, interests, and leisure activities together. But even more important than the actual sharing of activities is the perception that each friend is willing to make time for the other. Scholar William Rawlins notes that even friends who don't spend much time together can still maintain a satisfying connection as long as each perceives the other as "being there" when needed (Rawlins, 1994).

Of course, most of us have several friends, but only finite amounts of time available to devote to

each one. Consequently, we are often put in positions where we have to choose between time and activities shared with one friend versus another. Unfortunately, given the significance that sharing time and activities together plays in defining friendships, your decisions regarding with whom you invest your time will often be perceived by friends as communicating depth of loyalty (Baxter et al., 1997). In cases where you choose one friend over another, the friend not chosen may view your decision as disloyal. To avert this, draw on your interpersonal communication skills. Express gratitude for the friend's offer, assure him or her that you very much value the relationship, and make concrete plans for getting together another time.

Self-Disclosure

A second strategy for friendship maintenance is self-disclosure. All friendships are created and maintained through the discussion of thoughts, feelings, and daily life events (Dainton et al., 2003). To foster disclosure with your friends, routinely make time just to talk—encouraging them to share their thoughts and feelings about various issues, whether online or face-to-face. Equally important, avoid betraying friends—that is, sharing with others personal information friends have disclosed to you.

But, as with romantic and family relationships, balance openness in self-disclosure with protection (Dainton et al., 2003). Over time, most friends learn that communication about certain issues, topics, or even people is best avoided to protect the relationship and preclude conflict. As a result, friends negotiate communicative boundaries that allow their time together and communication shared to remain positive. Such boundaries can be perfectly healthy as long as both friends agree on them and the issues being avoided aren't central to the survival of the friendship.

Nina Leen/Time & Life Pictures/Getty Images

⬦ Two important ways you can maintain your friendships are sharing activities and being open in your communication with friends.

LearningCurve
bedfordstmartins.com/ipcandyou

Friendship Challenges

Ashlee and Rachel were best friends throughout high school.[3] As Ashlee describes, "Rachel was brilliant, confident, blunt, and outgoing. She liked to mock people, but she could make me laugh like nobody else, and she loved the same things I did." After graduation, they were parted by distance: Rachel went to Stanford, while Ashlee attended the University of Washington. Although they regularly texted and e-mailed, they grew apart. The following summer they were reunited, this time as a foursome: Rachel was dating Mike (a friend from high school), and Ashlee was dating Ahmed, a Lebanese transfer student. The four hung out regularly, waterskiing, going to movies, and partying.

One day, after Mike bought a new iPhone, he offered his old one to Ashlee. Arriving home, Ashlee found that her SIM card wasn't compatible, so she started manually clearing Mike's information. When she got to his text in-box, she was stunned to see this message from Rachel: "Ashlee and Ahmed are the perfect couple: stupid sorority slut and steroided jock." As Ashlee describes, "My heart just stopped. I literally sat there, shaking. I thought it was a joke, until I scrolled down and found *hundreds* of similar messages." Text after text slammed Ashlee and mocked Ahmed's ethnicity. Later that night, crying hysterically, Ashlee summoned the courage to text Rachel: "I cleared out Mike's phone and found all your texts about me and Ahmed. You two are *horrible.* I want nothing to do with either of you." Rachel immediately texted back, "How dare you read our messages! Those were private! Whatever Ashlee—I'm sorry you're angry but Mike and I were just messing around. You're completely overreacting." In the aftermath, Ashlee returned Mike's iPhone, and refused all contact with Rachel. Back at school that fall, Ashlee received an e-mail with the subject line,

"please don't delete." The message read: "I don't even know where to begin. I know I messed up, but I can't lose you as a friend. We've been best friends forever, and I'd hate to lose you over something this dumb. I know I'm asking a lot of you to forgive me, but please think about it." Ashlee deleted the message.

To this point, we've talked about friendships as involvements that provide us with abundant and important rewards. Although this is true, friendships

Jose Luis Pelaez Inc/Getty Images

◊ Discovering that a friend has betrayed you is one of the most devastating friendship challenges you can face. After seeking any support you may need, ask yourself whether you can or even should attempt to restore the friendship, remembering that some betrayals might be harder to move past than others.

---

[3]All information in this example is true. The names and personal information of the people in question have been altered for confidentiality. This example is used with permission from "Ashlee."

also present us with a variety of intense interpersonal challenges. Three of the most common are friendship betrayal, geographic distance, and attraction.

Betrayal

Given the value friends place upon mutual support and defending each other, it's no surprise that betrayal is the most commonly reported reason for ending a friendship (Miller, Hefner, & Scott, 2007). Acts of friendship betrayal include breaking confidences, backstabbing (criticizing a friend behind his or her back), spreading rumors or gossip, and lying—all of which violate the friendship rules discussed earlier. When friends violate these rules, it's difficult for friendships to survive. Similar to romantic betrayal, friends who are betrayed experience an overwhelming sense of relationship devaluation and loss (Miller et al., 2007). And—as with the Ashlee and Rachel example—betrayal often leads people to realize things about their friends' characters that simply can't be tolerated.

How can you better manage friendship betrayal, when it occurs? If it's a close friendship, expect to experience grief as you suffer the loss of trust, intimacy, and the image of your friend you once held dear. Revisit the suggestions for grief management offered in Chapter 4, especially the value of *emotion-sharing*—that is, talking about your experience directly with people who have gone through the same thing. Importantly, avoid lashing out at the betrayer, or seeking revenge—both of which will simply make matters worse.

When you're able, ponder whether you can or should repair the friendship. Ask yourself the following questions to help guide your decision. First, how serious was the betrayal? Not all betrayals are of equal standing, so think carefully about whether this incident is something you can learn to live with, or not. Second, what was the context preceding and surrounding the betrayal? Did *you* do something to provoke the betrayal? Would you have done the same thing in the same situation—or *have* you done similar things in the past? Be careful about blaming others for behaviors that you caused, holding double standards,

and judging friends in ways you wouldn't wish to be judged yourself. Third, do the benefits of continuing the friendship outweigh the costs? Use the friendship rules as a guide: Does your friend follow most of these rules, most of the time? If so, he or she may actually be a desirable friend. Fourth, is this betrayal a one-time event, or part of a consistent pattern? Everyone falls from grace on occasion; what you want to avoid is a person who habitually abuses your trust. Last, and perhaps most important, does this betrayal reveal something about your friend's character that you simply can't live with? Be honest with yourself and realize that some friendships are best left broken following betrayal. In Ashlee's case, despite years of having Rachel as her best friend—and all the corresponding emotional, energy, and time investment—the betrayal revealed multiple aspects of Rachel's character that Ashlee simply couldn't tolerate, including sexism, racism, phoniness, and viciousness.

Skills Practice

Managing Friendship Betrayal

If you find yourself in a situation in which a friend betrays you:

1. Manage the intense anger and grief you experience.
2. Avoid seeking revenge or verbal retaliation.
3. Contact others who have experienced similar betrayals, and discuss your experience with them.
4. Evaluate the betrayal, including how serious it is, what caused it, whether it's a one-time event or part of a behavioral pattern, and whether you would have done something similar.
5. Assess the value of your friendship, compared against the damage of the betrayal.
6. End or repair the friendship, based on your analysis.

Geographic Separation

A contributing factor to Ashlee and Rachel's falling out was their geographic separation, which led them to grow apart. Separation is one of the most common and intense challenges friends face (Wang & Andersen, 2007). Upwards of 90 percent of people report having at least one long-distance friendship, and 80 percent report having a close friend who lives far away (Rohlfing, 1995). Physical separation prevents friends from adequately satisfying the needs that form the foundation of their relationship, such as sharing activities and intimate self-disclosure.

Although most friends begin long-distance separations with the intention of seeing each other regularly, they rarely visit solely for the sake of reuniting. Instead, they tend to see each other only when there's some other reason for them to be in the same area. This is because long-distance friends often don't have the money or time to travel only to visit a friend (Rohlfing, 1995). Instead, they visit when other commitments such as professional conferences, visits with relatives, or class reunions bring them together. Such contacts often leave friends feeling empty because their time together is so limited.

Which friendships tend to survive geographic distance, and which lapse? Friendships where the individuals have a particularly strong sense of liking and who "enjoy knowing each other" and "have great admiration for each other" are most likely to endure. Friends who overcome separation also accept change as a natural part of their relationship. If you get together with a good friend you haven't seen in a long while, you both likely will have changed in terms of profession, attitudes, and appearance. People who are comfortable with such changes, and offer identity support, tend to have relationships that survive. Friends who want their friends to "always stay the same," don't.

Moreover, friendships that survive separation involve friends who have a strong sense of shared history. In their conversations, they frequently celebrate the past as well as anticipate sharing events in the future. This sense of shared past, present, and future enables them to "pick up where they left off"

"Are you multitasking me?"

after being out of touch for a while. Successful long-distance friendships thus involve feeling a sense of relationship continuity and perceiving the relationship as solid and ongoing.

How can you communicate in ways that foster these qualities in your own long-distance friendships? Use technology (Skype, Facebook, phone, text, etc.) to regularly communicate with your friends. Focus your communication on activities and interests that you share. Doing this alleviates the feeling of loss that comes with the inability to actually spend time together (Rabby, 1997). So, for example, if a friend who now lives far away used to be your jogging buddy, send her regular updates on your marathon training and inquire about her local races.

Also, remind your long-distance friends that you still think of them with affection and hold them in high regard. Look for opportunities to appropriately express your feelings for your friend, such as: "I miss our Thursday movie nights! Have you seen any good films lately?" In addition, devote some of your communication to fondly recounting events and experiences you have shared in your past, as well as discussing plans for the future. Such exchanges bolster the sense of relational continuity critical to maintaining friendships.

Finally, when your long-distance friends go through dramatic life changes—as they inevitably will—communicate your continued support of their valued social identities. For instance, a close friend you haven't seen in a while may abandon previously shared religious beliefs, adopt new political viewpoints, or substantially alter his or her looks. In making these and other kinds of significant changes, your friend may look to you for identity support, as a friend. A good friend will express firm support and excitement regarding these decisions.

Skills Practice

Using Technology to Overcome Distance
Maintaining long-distance friendships through online communication

1. Think of a close friend who lives far away.
2. In your online interactions, focus your message content on common interests, making sure to ask about your friend's continued participation in these things.
3. Send text messages saying you're thinking of and missing her or him.
4. Craft e-mails that fondly recap past shared experiences.
5. Forward Web links with ideas for future activities you can share together.
6. When your friend discloses major life changes, provide support in the quickest fashion possible, whether by text, e-mail, phone call, or all three.

Attraction: Romance and FWB Relationships

A final challenge facing friends is attraction to one another beyond friendship: romantic, sexual, or both. Men typically report more of a desire for romantic involvement with their platonic cross-sex friends than

do women (Schneider & Kenny, 2000). However, one study found that 87 percent of college-age women and 93 percent of college-age men reported feeling sexually attracted to a friend at some point in their lives (Asada, Morrison, Hughes, & Fitzpatrick, 2003).

When attraction does blossom between friends, same-sex or cross-sex, pursuing a sexual or romantic relationship brings about challenges. Friends who feel attracted to one another typically report high uncertainty as a result: both regarding the nature of their relationship and whether or not their friend feels the same way (Weger & Emmett, 2009).

Friends cope with attraction by doing one of three things. Some simply repress the attraction, most commonly out of respect for their friendship (Messman, Canary & Hause, 2000). This usually occurs through *mental management*—doing things to actively manage how the friends think about each other so that the attraction is diminished (Halatsis & Christakis, 2009). These may include promises to not pursue the attraction, a strict avoidance of flirting, and the curtailing of activities (such as going out drinking) that might inadvertently lead to sexual interaction (Halatsis & Christakis, 2009). Alternatively, as we discuss below, some friends act on their attraction by either developing a full-fledged romantic involvement, or blending their friendship with sexual activity through a "friends-with-benefits" arrangement.

Romance between Friends

Many friends who develop an attraction opt to pursue a romantic relationship. The first and most powerful cue of such desire is a radical increase in the amount of time the friends spend flirting with each other (Weger & Emmett, 2009). Although people in Western cultures like to think of friendships and romantic relationships as strictly separate, many enduring and successful romances evolve from friendships. One of the strongest predictors of whether or not a friendship can successfully transition to romance is simply whether the friends already possess romantic beliefs that link friendship with love (Hendrick & Hendrick, 1992).

Although it's commonly believed that pursuing a romantic relationship will "kill the friendship" if or

> **One of the strongest predictors of whether or not a friendship can successfully transition to romance is simply whether the friends already possess romantic beliefs that link friendship with love.**

when the romance fizzles, the results actually are mixed. People who were friends prior to a romance are much more likely to be friends following a failed romance than those who were not friends first (Schneider & Kenny, 2000). However, postromance friendships tend to be less close than those with friends who have always been platonic. How can you successfully transition from friendship to romance, or back again? First, *expect difference*. Romantic relationships and friendships are fundamentally different in expectations, demands, commitment, and corresponding emotional intensity. Don't presume that your feelings, those of your partner, or the interplay between you two, will be the same. Second, *emphasize disclosure*. Relationship transitions tend to evoke high uncertainty, as partners worry about what the other thinks and feels, and wonder where the relationship is going. To reduce this uncertainty, share your feelings in an open and honest fashion, and encourage your partner to do the same. Finally, *offer assurances*. Let your partner know that whether you two are friends or lovers, you stand by him or her, and your relationship, regardless. This is especially important when transitioning back to friendship from romance, as your partner may believe that your relationship is now over.

Friends with Benefits

No jealousy. No flowers. No sleepovers. No cuddling. These and other rules are established by the characters Emma and Adam in the movie *No Strings Attached*, in an attempt to add sex to their friendship while avoiding romantic attachment. At first it works out great: Emma can focus on her medical career, and Adam can continue to date (and sleep with) other people. However, their deal sours as feelings arise

between them that clash with the rules they've established.

Like Emma and Adam in *No Strings Attached*, some friends deal with sexual attraction by forming a "friends-with-benefits" (FWB) relationship. In **FWB relationships**, the participants engage in sexual activity, but not with the purpose of transforming the relationship into a romantic attachment (Hughes, Morrison, & Asada, 2005). FWB relationships appear to be widespread. Studies suggest that around 50 percent of college students have had such a relationship (Mongeau, Ramirez, & Vorrell, 2003).

Those who form FWB relationships do so for two reasons: they welcome the lack of commitment (and all its attendant sacrifices), and they want to satisfy sexual needs (Asada et al., 2003). Both men and women cite these same reasons, contradicting stereotypes that women seek only emotional satisfaction in relationships while men want only sex.

Most partners in FWB relationships develop rules regarding emotional attachment, communication, and sex, akin to those depicted in *No Strings*

💧 Adam attempts to follow the rules of his FWB relationship by giving Emma a bouquet of carrots instead of flowers in *No Strings Attached*. However, like many FWB relationships, Adam and Emma eventually have to deal with the romantic impulses they feel toward each other.

Attached (Hughes et al., 2005). For example, they commonly strike an agreement to not fall in love. And they establish rules governing the frequency of phone calls, e-mails, and text messages as well as safe sex practices, frequency of sex, and sexual exclusivity. But despite these rules, the majority of FWB relationships fail eventually, costing the participants their original friendship as well as the sexual arrangement. Why? As with Emma and Adam, participants tend to develop romantic feelings despite their best efforts to avoid them, and many decide that the FWB relationship doesn't satisfy them enough emotionally (Hughes et al., 2005).

Self-Reflection

Have you had an FWB relationship? If so, what were the pros and cons? Did you and your friend establish rules for the relationship? If so, what were they? How well did you both follow those rules?

LearningCurve
bedfordstmartins.com/ipcandyou

Postscript }

We began this chapter with a snowstorm and two television employees trapped together. Huddled within the shelter of a warm apartment, Oprah Winfrey and Gail King learned that despite their different backgrounds, they shared the same sensibilities. The friendship that sparked would not only stand the test of time but would become world famous.

Which friends love you, respect you, and want the best for you? On whom can you count to lift you up and support you, in good times and bad?

Although the relationship between Oprah and Gayle may be iconic, it mirrors the friendships we experience in our own lives. Like us, they were drawn to each other through shared interests, viewpoints, and values. And like the bonds we forge with our friends, theirs remains cemented through trust, communication, and support.

Chapter Review }

KEY TERMS

friendship, 246
⊙ communal friendships, 248
⊙ agentic friendships, 248

identity support, 251
valued social identities, 251
cross-category friendships, 252

professional peers, 255
friendship rules, 256
FWB relationships, 263

CHAPTER ACTIVITIES

1. Consider this statement from scholar William Rawlins: "Friendships are permeated with ambiguities." What does it mean to you? If you consider the many types of friendship, how they are created, and all the different rules for each, is it even possible to fully define friendship? What characteristics of a friendship would you add to the ones listed in the chapter?

2. ⊙ Watch the videos on **communal friendships** and **agentic friendships**. Then write short journal entries describing two of your friendships, one of each type. What are the differences in the relationships? (Be as specific as possible.) Do friends ever change categories? Have the reasons for considering friends agentic or communal ever changed?

3. Researchers Blieszner and Adams (1992) study friendship by asking people "What does friendship mean to you?" They have discovered that social and individual characteristics, such as age or stage of life,

influence a person's view of friendship. Conduct your own version of this survey by asking several males and females, ranging in age and life experience, the same question. Then, write a short analysis about their responses: What did they say? How do male and female responses differ, or how are they similar? Do age or life experiences affect the responses?

4. Which one of Argyle and Henderson's (1984) 10 friendship rules is the most important in your life? Which rule is possibly the least important? Have you ever had a friendship end because one of these rules was broken? What kind of relationship repair is necessary after a rule is broken?

5. With a partner, discuss times you both faced a friendship challenge such as betrayal or geographic separation. How did you deal with the difficulty? Did the challenge end the friendship? What other friendship challenges have you faced? List some suggestions for handling these challenges and share them with the class.

GLOSSARY

accommodation: (p. 185) A way of handling conflict in which one person abandons his or her goals for the goals of another. For example, Louis gives in to Martel over where they should park their cars: "You can have the driveway. I'm tired of arguing about it."

action-oriented listeners: (p. 122) Those who prefer to receive brief, to-the-point, accurate information for decision making—for example, a supervisor who requires brief summaries from department heads and does not want to bat around details in long meetings.

actor-observer effect: (p. 55) The tendency to identify external forces as causes for our behaviors instead of internal factors. For instance, Leon says he snapped at a coworker because she was slow instead of blaming his own impatience.

adaptors: (p. 161) Touching gestures, often unconsciously made, that serve a physical or psychological purpose. For example, twirling hair while reading, jingling pocket change, and fingering jewelry may be gestures that provide comfort, signal anxiety, or are simply unconscious habits.

affect displays: (p. 170) Intentional or unintentional nonverbal behaviors that display actual or feigned emotions, such as a frown, a choked sob, or a smile intended to disguise fear.

agentic friendships: (p. 248) Voluntary relationships primarily focused on achieving specific practical goals, such as those among peers in a study group or colleagues at work.

aggressive-hostile touch: (p. 165) A touch designed to hurt and humiliate others, involving forms of physical violence like grabbing, slapping, and hitting.

aggressive listening: (p. 127) Listening in order to attack or collect information to use against the speaker, such as when a father encourages his son to describe his ambitions just to ridicule the son's goals. (Also known as *ambushing*.)

algebraic impressions: (p.65) Impressions of others that continually change as we add and subtract positive or negative information that we learn about them.

anger: (p. 85) The negative primary emotion that occurs when you are blocked or interrupted from attaining an important goal by what you see as the improper action of an external agent.

appropriateness: (p. 15) A measure of communication competence that indicates the degree to which your communication matches the situational, relational, and cultural expectations regarding how people should communicate.

artifacts: (p. 168) Things we possess that influence how we see ourselves and that we use to express our identity to others. Jewelry, for instance, can indicate economic means, marital status, religious affiliation, style preferences, and taste.

attending: (p. 114) The second stage of the listening process in which a listener devotes attention to received information. For example, you may *hear* a radio but *attend* only when a favorite song comes on.

attention focus: (p. 82) Preventing unwanted emotions by intentionally devoting your attention only to aspects of an event or encounter that you know will not provoke those emotions. For example, you disregard your uncle's snide comments while focusing all your interest on your aunt's conversation.

attributional complexity: (p. 107) The ability to acknowledge that other people's behaviors have complex causes.

attributions: (p. 54) Rationales we create to explain the comments or behaviors of others. For example, Ryan reasons that Jason's quietness in class means that Jason is shy.

avoidance: (p. 184) A way of handling conflict by ignoring it, pretending it isn't really happening, or communicating indirectly about the situation. For example, Martel hides behind the newspaper as Louis shouts, "Your car is blocking mine again. How many times do I have to ask you to park it to the side?" See also **skirting; sniping.**

avoiding: (p. 212) A relational stage in which one or both individuals in a couple try to distance themselves from each other physically. For example, Owen changes jobs to have an excuse to travel away from home frequently.

back-channel cues: (p. 118) Nonverbal or verbal responses that signal you've paid attention to and understood specific comments—for example, saying, "Okay, got it" after someone details extensive driving directions.

beautiful-is-good effect: (p. 206) A tendency for physical attractiveness to create the perception of competency and intelligence. For example, a witness is viewed favorably and seems credible because she is good-looking.

birds-of-a-feather effect: (p. 206) A tendency to be attracted to others if we perceive them to have similar levels of physical attractiveness, values, and interests.

blended emotions: (p. 78) Two or more primary emotions experienced at the same time. For instance, Melinda feels fear and anger when her daughter is not home after curfew.

bonding: (p. 210) A relational stage in which an official, public ritual unites two people by the laws or customs of their culture. For example, Ruth marries Owen in her hometown church.

catharsis: (p. 86) Within the field of interpersonal communication, the assumption that openly expressing emotions enables you to purge them.

channel: (p. 6) The sensory dimension (sound, sight, touch, scent, or taste) used to transmit information during communication. For example, you may apologize by showing someone a sad facial expression, lightly touching his shoulder, and saying, "I'm so sorry."

chilling effect: (p. 195) An outcome of physical violence in which individuals stop discussing relationship issues out of fear of their partners' negative reactions.

chronemics: (p. 166) A nonverbal code that represents the way you use time to communicate in interpersonal interactions.

chronic hostility: (p. 86) A persistent state of simmering or barely suppressed anger and constant negative thinking.

circumscribing: (p. 211) A relational stage in which partners avoid talking about topics that produce conflict. For instance, whenever Owen mentions he's interested in moving, Ruth becomes upset and changes the subject.

co-cultures: (p. 97) Groupings formed by members of a society who don't conform to the dominant culture but who are unified by any number of factors, including age, gender, social class, ethnicity, religion, mental and physical ability, sexual orientation, and other elements. For example, the LGBTQ community coexists with the dominant culture of the United States.

Co-Cultural Communication Theory: (p. 97) A theory suggesting that people who have more power within a given society determine the dominant culture of that society because they decide the prevailing views, values, and traditions.

cohabiting couple: (p. 229) Two unmarried adults who are involved romantically and live together with or without children.

collaboration: (p. 187) A way of handling conflict by treating it as a mutual problem-solving challenge. For example, housemates Jesus and Zhiang settle an argument about household chores by posting a schedule that lists responsibilities.

collectivistic cultures: (p. 100) Societies that emphasize group identity ("we" rather than "me"), interpersonal harmony, and the well-being of ingroups. Examples include Japan and Pakistan. See also **individualistic cultures.**

commitment: (p. 204) A strong psychological attachment to a partner and an intention to continue the relationship long into the future.

communal friendships: (p. 248) Voluntary relationships focused on sharing time and activities together.

communication: (p. 5) The process through which people use messages to generate meanings within and across contexts, cultures, channels, and media.

Communication Accommodation Theory: (p. 107) A theory stipulating that people are especially motivated to adapt their communication when they seek social approval, wish to establish relationships, and view others' language usage as appropriate.

communication apprehension: (p. 146) The fear or nervousness associated with communicating with others.

communication plans: (p. 146) Mental maps that describe exactly how communication encounters will unfold. For example, before calling to complain about her telephone bill, Marjorie mentally rehearses how she will explain her problem and what objections she might face.

Communication Privacy Management Theory: (p. 238) A theory suggesting that individuals create informational boundaries by choosing carefully the kind of private information they reveal and the people with whom they share it.

communication skills: (p. 15) Repeatable goal-directed behaviors and behavioral patterns that enable you to improve the quality of your interpersonal encounters and relationships. See also **appropriateness; interpersonal communication competence.**

companionate love: (p. 202) An intense form of liking defined by emotional investment and interdependent lives.

competition: (p. 185) A way of handling conflict in which the goal clash is discussed clearly and openly, and in which each person pursues his or her own goals without regard for the goals of others. For example, Teddy tells his coworker Elaine that he intends to secure the coveted promotion that Elaine is also pursuing.

complementary relationships: (p. 182) Relationships characterized by an unequal balance of power, such as a marriage in which one spouse is the decision maker.

compromise: (p. 191) The result that occurs when parties involved in a conflict change their goals to make them compatible. For example, Matt wants to watch a sci-fi movie and Jane wants to watch an animated film; they meet in the middle by finding an animated sci-fi feature to watch.

conflict: (p. 179) The process that occurs when people perceive that they have incompatible goals or that someone is interfering in their ability to achieve their objectives.

conformity orientation: (p. 231) The degree to which family members believe communication should emphasize similarity or diversity in attitudes, beliefs, and values.

connotative meaning: (p. 137) Understanding of a word's meaning based on the situation and the shared knowledge between communication partners (i.e., not the dictionary definition). For instance, calling someone *slender* suggests something more positive than the word *skinny* or *scrawny* does, though all three words mean "underweight." Contrast **denotative meaning.**

consensual families: (p. 233) Families characterized by high levels of conformity and conversation orientation. For example, Dan's parents encourage their son to be open but also expect him to maintain family unity through agreement or obedience.

constitutive rules: (p. 134) Guidelines that define word meaning according to a particular language's vocabulary. For instance, "pencil" is *Bleistift* in German and *matita* in Italian.

content-oriented listeners: (p. 123) Those who prefer to be intellectually challenged by messages—they prefer complex, detailed information. For example, a supervisor reviews the success of a fund-raising event by requesting data analyzing the effectiveness of her team's publicity campaign instead of asking to hear about team members' experiences.

contexts: (p. 5) Situations in which communication occurs. Context includes the physical locations, backgrounds, genders, ages, moods, and relationships of the communicators, as well as the time of day.

conversation orientation: (p. 231) The degree to which family members are encouraged to participate in unrestrained interaction about a wide array of topics.

Cooperative Principle: (p. 142) The idea that we should make our verbal messages as informative, honest, relevant, and clear as possible, given what the situation requires. For example, listening closely to your friend's problem with a coworker and then responding with support would demonstrate the Cooperative Principle; interrupting your friend to brag about your new laptop would not.

cooperative verbal communication: (p. 141) Producing messages that are easily understood, that you take ownership of by using "I" language, and that are inclusive of others (perhaps by using "we" language).

cross-category friendships: (p. 252) Voluntary relationships that cross demographic lines.

culture: (p. 95) An established, coherent set of beliefs, attitudes, values, and practices shared by a large group of people.

cumulative annoyance: (p. 184) A buildup of repressed irritations that grows as the mental list of grievances we have against someone grows. For example, office manager Jane becomes more and more annoyed every time she sees that custodian Marcus has failed to change a light bulb that burned out a week ago.

deactivation: (p. 82) Preventing unwanted emotions by systematically desensitizing yourself to emotional experience. For example, Josh insulates himself with numbness after his wife's death.

deception: (p. 149) Deliberately using uninformative, untruthful, irrelevant, or vague language for the purpose of misleading others.

defensive communication: (p. 147) Impolite messages delivered in response to suggestions, criticism, or perceived slights. For instance, when Stacy asks Lena to slow down her driving, Lena snaps back, "I'm not going that fast. If you don't like the way I drive, ride with someone else."

demand-withdraw pattern: (p. 195) A way of handling conflict in which one partner in a relationship demands that his or her goals be met, and the other partner responds by withdrawing from the encounter.

denotative meaning: (p. 137) The literal, or dictionary, definition of a word. Contrast **connotative meaning.**

dialects: (p. 134) Variations on language rules shared by large groups or particular regions; this may include differences in vocabulary, grammar, and pronunciation. For example, in various regions of the United States, carbonated beverages are called *soda, pop,* or *Coke.*

differentiating: (p. 211) A relational stage in which the beliefs, attitudes, and values that distinguish you from your partner come to dominate your thoughts and communication. For example, Ruth and Owen argue over whose family they are going to visit for Thanksgiving and how little time he has spent helping her fix up the house.

dirty secrets: (p. 194) Truthful but destructive messages used deliberately to hurt someone during a conflict. For example, Judith tells her sister, "That boy you like—Craig? I heard him tell Elaine you laugh like a horse."

dismissive attachment: (p. 33) An attachment style where individuals have low anxiety but high avoidance: they view close relationships as comparatively unimportant, instead prizing self-reliance.

display rules: (p. 102) Guidelines for when, where, and how to manage emotion appropriately.

dominance: (p. 173) The interpersonal behaviors we use to exert power or influence over others. Dominance may occur through nonverbal behavior, as in crowding threateningly into a person's intimate zone, or staring someone down, or keeping another person waiting.

domination: (p. 191) The result that occurs when one person gets his or her way in a conflict by influencing the other to engage in accommodation and abandon his or her goals. For example, when teenager Amed and his little brother Aziz disagree about who gets to ride in the front seat of the car with their father, Amed jumps into the front seat before Aziz can get there.

dyadic: (p. 10) Communication involving only two people.

Dyadic Power Theory: (p. 182) The idea that people with only moderate power are most likely to use controlling communication.

eavesdropping: (p. 126) Intentionally listening in on private conversations.

effectiveness: (p. 16) The ability to use communication to accomplish interpersonal goals.

embarrassment: (p. 36) A feeling of shame, humiliation, and sadness that comes when we lose face.

emblems: (p. 161) Gestures that symbolize a specific verbal meaning within a given culture, such as the "thumbs-up" or the "V for victory" sign.

emotion: (p. 75) An intense reaction to an event that involves interpreting the meaning of the event, becoming physiologically aroused, labeling the experience as emotional, attempting to manage your reaction, and communicating this reaction in the form of emotional displays and disclosures.

emotion-sharing: (p. 76) Disclosing your emotions to others.

emotional contagion: (p. 76) The rapid spreading of emotion from person to person, such as anger running through a mob.

emotional intelligence: (p. 81) The ability to accurately interpret your and others' emotions and use this information to manage emotions, communicate them competently, and solve relationship problems.

emotion management: (p. 81) Attempts to influence which emotions you have, when you have them, and how you experience and express them.

empathy: (p. 68) Understanding of another person's perspective and awareness of his or her feelings in an attempt to identify with him or her. For instance, Gill doesn't agree with Mike's protest against the new policies at work, but he can see why Mike was worried and angry.

encounter avoidance: (p. 82) Preventing unwanted emotions by keeping away from people, places, and activities likely to provoke them. For example, Jessica infuriates Roxanne, so Roxanne moves out of their shared apartment.

encounter structuring: (p. 82) Preventing unwanted emotions by intentionally avoiding discussion of difficult topics in encounters with others. For instance, Natalie and Julie avoid talking about living expenses because Natalie is jealous of Julie's income.

environment: (p. 168) The physical features of our surroundings.

equity: (p. 207) The balance of benefits and costs exchanged by you and a romantic interest that determines whether a romantic relationship will take root (after attraction is established).

escalation: (p. 186) A dramatic rise in emotional intensity and increasingly negative communication during conflict, such as teasing that inflates to a heated exchange of insults.

ethics: (p. 16) The set of moral principles that guide our behavior toward others. Ethical communication consistently displays respect, kindness, and compassion.

ethnocentrism: (p. 107) The belief that your own culture's beliefs, attitudes, values, and practices are superior to those of all other cultures.

experimenting: (p. 209) A relational stage in which two people become acquainted by sharing factual information about themselves and making light conversation or small talk. For instance, after Ruth is introduced to Owen, they talk about their jobs and where they went to school, and they discover they both like jazz.

expertise currency: (p. 183) Power that comes from possessing specialized skills or knowledge, such as knowing CPR. See also **intimacy currency, personal currency, power currency, resource currency, social network currency.**

extended family: (p. 229) A family type consisting of a group of people who are related to one another—such as aunts, uncles, cousins, or grandparents—and who live in the same household.

face: (p. 36) The self we allow others to see and know; the aspects of ourselves we choose to present publicly. For instance, you dress up and speak carefully for an important social occasion, though in private you're very casual.

family: (p. 228) A network of people who share their lives over long periods of time and are bound by marriage, blood, or commitment; who consider themselves as family; and who share a significant history and anticipated future of functioning in a family relationship.

Family Communication Patterns Theory: (p. 231) The idea that two dimensions—**conformity orientation** and **conversation orientation**—underlie the communication between family members.

family privacy rules: (p. 238) The conditions governing what family members can talk about, how they can discuss such topics, and who should have access to family-relevant information.

family stories: (p. 229) Narratives of family events retold to bond family members. For example, Katie's mother often recounts how Katie was born on the day of a crippling blizzard.

fearful attachment: (p. 33) An attachment style in which individuals are high in both attachment anxiety and avoidance: they fear rejection and thus shun relationships, preferring to avoid the pain they believe is an inevitable part of intimacy.

feedback: (p. 8) Verbal and nonverbal messages that receivers use to indicate their reaction to communication, such as a frown or saying, "I disagree." See also **interactive communication model.**

feelings: (p. 76) Short-term emotional reactions to events that generate only limited arousal, such as the fleeting nostalgia you experience hearing a familiar song.

feminine cultures: (p. 104) Societies that emphasize personal connections to others, relationship health, quality of life, and concern for the poor and elderly. Examples include Norway and Sweden. See also **masculine cultures.**

fields of experience: (p. 8) Beliefs, attitudes, values, and experiences that each communicator brings to an interaction.

friendship: (p. 246) A voluntary relationship characterized by intimacy and liking.

friendship rules: (p. 256) General principles for appropriate communication and behavior within friendships, such as keeping a confidence and showing support.

friendship-warmth touch: (p. 164) A touch used to express liking for another person, such as an arm placed across another's shoulders or a "high five" shared between teammates.

functional-professional touch: (p. 164) A touch used to accomplish a task, such as a physical therapist positioning a client's arm or a dancer gripping his partner's waist for a lift.

fundamental attribution error: (p. 54) The tendency to attribute someone's behavior solely to his or her personality rather than to outside forces.

FWB (friends with benefits) relationships: (p. 263) Friendships negotiated to include sexual activity but not intended to become romantic attachments.

gender: (pp. 20) The composite of social, psychological, and cultural traits associated with one sex or the other; unlike biological sex, with which we're born, gender is largely learned.

Gestalt: (p. 63) A general sense of a person that's either positive or negative. See also **halo effect; horn effect.**

grief: (p. 88) Intense sadness that follows a substantial loss, such as the death of a loved one.

halo effect: (p. 65) A tendency to interpret anything another person says or does in a favorable light because you have a positive Gestalt of that person.

haptics: (p. 164) A nonverbal code that represents messages conveyed through touch. See also **aggressive-hostile touch; friendship-warmth touch; functional-professional touch; love-intimacy touch; sexual-arousal touch; social-polite touch.**

hearing: (p. 114) The sensory process of taking in and interpreting sound.

high-context cultures: (p. 101) Societies in which people rely less on language than on widespread cultural knowledge to create meaning. Examples include China and Korea. See also **low-context cultures.**

honesty: (p. 143) Truthful communication, without exaggeration or omission of relevant information. Failing to tell someone something can be as dishonest as an outright lie.

horn effect: (p. 65) A tendency to interpret anything another person says or does in a negative light because you have a negative Gestalt of that person.

identity support: (p. 251) Behaving in ways that convey understanding, acceptance, and support for a friend's valued social identities.

I-It: (p. 10) A type of perception and communication that occurs when you treat others as though they are objects that are there for your use and exploitation—for example, when you dismiss someone by saying, "I don't have time for your stupid questions. Figure it out yourself."

"I" language: (p. 144) Communication that uses the pronoun *I* in sentence construction to emphasize ownership of your feelings, opinions, and beliefs—for example, "I'm frustrated because I think I'm doing more than you are on this project" instead of "You're really underperforming on this project." See also **"we" language; "you" language.**

illustrators: (p. 161) Gestures used to accent or illustrate a verbal message. For example, a fisherman holds his hands apart to show the size of his catch, or someone points emphatically at a door while saying, "Leave!"

immediacy: (p. 161) As expressed in your posture, the degree to which you find someone interesting and attractive.

impersonal communication: (p. 10) Messages that have negligible perceived impact on your thoughts, emotions, behaviors, or relationships, such as commenting about the television schedule or passing someone and saying, "How's it going?" without looking up.

implicit personality theories: (p. 62) Personal beliefs about different types of personalities and the ways in which traits cluster together. For instance, Bradley assumes that Will is a disorganized procrastinator because of Will's casual, friendly manner.

individualistic cultures: (p. 100) Societies in which people tend to value independence and personal achievement. Examples include Canada and the United States. See also **collectivistic cultures.**

ingroupers: (p. 57) People you consider fundamentally similar to yourself because of their interests, affiliations, or backgrounds. Contrast **outgroupers.**

initiating: (p. 209) A relational stage in which two people meet and form their first impressions of each other. For instance, Owen introduces himself in a message to Ruth after reading her profile on an online dating site, and she responds with her telephone number.

instrumental goals: (p. 14) Practical aims you want to achieve or tasks you want to accomplish through a particular interpersonal encounter.

integrating: (p. 209) A relational stage in which two people become a couple and begin to share an identity. For example, Ruth and Owen share an apartment together and spend time with each other's families.

integrative agreements: (p. 192) The result that occurs when parties involved in a conflict preserve and attain their goals by developing a creative solution to their problem. For example, because partners Hermes and Pierre can't decide what sort of live music they want to hear on a given evening, they opt to visit a comedy club instead.

intensifying: (p. 209) A relational stage characterized by deeper self-disclosures, stronger attraction, and intimate communication. For example, Owen and Ruth have been dating for more than a year and talk with excitement about a future together.

interaction: (p. 5) A series of messages exchanged between people, whether face-to-face or online.

interactive communication model: (p. 7) A depiction of communication messages that are exchanged back and forth between a sender and a receiver and are influenced by feedback and the fields of experience of both communicators.

intercultural communication competence: (p. 106) The ability to communicate appropriately, effectively, and ethically with people from diverse backgrounds.

interparental conflict: (p. 241) Overt, hostile interactions between parents in a household.

interpersonal communication: (p. 9) A dynamic form of communication between two (or more) people in which the messages exchanged significantly influence their thoughts, emotions, behaviors, and relationships.

interpersonal impressions: (p. 62) Mental pictures about who people are and how we feel about them. For instance, when Sarah and Georgia met, Georgia thought Sarah's boisterous laugh meant that Sarah was obnoxious.

interpersonal process model of intimacy: (p. 42) The idea that the closeness we feel toward others in our relationships is created through two things: self-disclosure and responsiveness of listeners to such disclosure.

interpretation: (p. 53) The stage of perception in which we assign meaning to the information we have selected. For instance, Randy thinks a man running down the sidewalk hurries because he is late, but Shondra infers that the man is chasing someone.

intimacy: (pp. 41) A feeling of closeness and "union" that exists between us and our relationship partners.

intimacy currency: (p. 183) Power that comes from sharing a close bond with someone that no one else shares. For example, your best friend will loan you books even though she usually dislikes loaning books to people. See also **expertise currency, personal currency, power currency, resource currency, social network currency.**

intimate space: (p. 165) The narrowest proxemic zone—0 to 18 inches of space—between communicators.

intrapersonal communication: (p. 10) Communication involving only one person, such as talking to yourself.

I-Thou: (p. 10) A way to perceive a relationship based on embracing fundamental similarities that connect you to others, striving to see things from others' points of view, and communicating in ways that emphasize honesty and kindness.

jealousy: (p. 220) A protective reaction when a valued relationship seems threatened. For instance, Tyler is jealous when his girlfriend, Mary, flirts with Scott.

Jefferson strategy: (p. 86) A strategy to manage your anger that involves counting slowly to 10 before responding to someone who says or does something that makes you angry. (The strategy was named after the third president of the United States.)

kinesics: (p. 160) A nonverbal code that represents messages communicated in visible body movements, such as facial expressions, posture, body movements, gestures, and eye contact.

kitchen-sinking: (p. 180) A response to a conflict in which combatants hurl insults and accusations at each other that have very little to do with the original disagreement. For example, although Mary and Pat are arguing about the budget, Mary adds, "I'm sick of the mess you left in the garage and these papers all over the family room."

laissez-faire families: (p. 234) Families characterized by low levels of conformity and conversation orientation. For example, Samantha's parents prefer limited communication and encourage their daughter to make her own choices and decisions.

liking: (p. 201) A feeling of affection and respect typical of friendship.

linear communication model: (p. 7) A depiction of communication messages that flow in one direction from a starting point to an end point.

linguistic determinism: (p. 138) The view that the language we use defines the boundaries of our thinking.

linguistic relativity: (p. 138) The theory that languages create variations in the ways cultures perceive and think about the world.

listening: (p. 113) The five-stage process of **receiving, attending** to, **understanding, responding** to, and **recalling** sounds and visual images during interpersonal encounters.

listening functions: (p. 120) The five general purposes that listening serves: to comprehend, to discern, to analyze, to appreciate, and to support.

listening style: (p. 122) An individual's habitual pattern of listening behaviors, which reflects one's attitudes, beliefs, and predispositions regarding the listening process. See also **action-oriented listeners; content-oriented listeners; people-oriented listeners; time-oriented listeners.**

long-term memory: (p. 117) The part of your mind devoted to permanent information storage.

looking-glass self: (p. 28) Sociologist Charles Horton Cooley's idea that we define our self-concepts through thinking about how others see us. For example, a young girl who believes others consider her poor in sports formulates an image of herself as uncoordinated, even though she is a good dancer.

love-intimacy touch: (p. 164) A touch indicating deep emotional feeling, such as two romantic partners holding hands or two close friends embracing.

loving: (p. 201) An intense emotional commitment based on intimacy, caring, and attachment.

low-context cultures: (p. 101) Societies in which people strive to be informative, clear, and direct in their communication. Examples include Germany and the United States. See also **high-context cultures.**

masculine cultures: (p. 103) Societies that prioritize personal ambition, competition, assertiveness, and material gain. Examples include Austria and Italy. See also **feminine cultures.**

mask: (p. 36) The public self designed to strategically veil your private self—for example, putting on a happy face when you are sad or pretending to be confident while inside you feel shy or anxious.

matching: (p. 206) A tendency to be attracted to others whom we perceive to be at our own level of attractiveness. For example, Michael dates Jennifer because she is pretty but not unapproachably gorgeous.

media: (p. 6) Tools used to exchange messages, including everything from newspapers, blackboards, and photographs to computers, smartphones, and television.

mental bracketing: (p. 116) Systematically putting aside thoughts that aren't relevant to the interaction at hand if your attention wanders when listening—for example, consciously dismissing your worries about an upcoming exam in order to focus on a customer's request at work.

mere exposure effect: (p. 205) A phenomenon in which you feel more attracted to those with whom you have frequent contact and less attracted to those with whom you interact rarely. For example, the more June sees of Tom, the more attracted to him she becomes.

message: (p. 5) The "package" of information transported during communication.

misunderstanding: (p. 143) Confusion resulting from the misperception of another's thoughts, feelings, or beliefs as expressed in the other individual's verbal communication.

mixed messages: (p. 156) Verbal and nonverbal behaviors that convey contradictory meanings, such as saying, "I'm so happy for you" in a sarcastic tone of voice.

mnemonics: (p. 119) Devices that aid memory. For example, the mnemonic *Roy G. Biv* is commonly used to recall the order of the seven colors in the rainbow.

monochronic time orientation: (p. 104) The view that time is a precious resource to be shared and/or withheld judiciously. See also **polychronic time orientation (P-time).**

moods: (p. 76) Low-intensity states of mind that are not caused by particular events and typically last longer than emotions. Examples include boredom, contentment, grouchiness, and serenity.

naming: (p. 138) Creating linguistic symbols to represent people, objects, places, and ideas.

narcissistic listening: (p. 127) A self-absorbed approach to listening in which the listener redirects the conversation to his or her own interests. For example, Neil acts bored while Jack describes a recent ski trip, interrupting Jack and switching the topic to his own recent car purchase.

negativity effect: (p. 64) A tendency to place emphasis on the negative information we learn about others.

noise: (p. 7) Environmental factors that impede a message on the way to its destination.

nonverbal communication: (p. 155) The intentional or unintentional transmission of meaning through an individual's nonspoken physical and behavioral cues.

nonverbal communication codes: (p. 159) Different ways to transmit information nonverbally, including **artifacts, chronemics, environment, haptics, kinesics, physical appearance, proxemics,** and **vocalics.**

nuclear family: (p. 228) A family type consisting of a father, a mother, and their biological or adopted children.

online communication: (p. 17) Interaction through communication technology such as social networking sites, e-mail, text- or instant-messaging, Skype, chatrooms, and even massively multiplayer online video games like *World of Warcraft.*

organization: (p. 52) The step of perception in which we mentally structure selected sensory data into a coherent pattern.

outgroupers: (p. 58) People you consider fundamentally different from you because of their interests, affiliations, or backgrounds. Contrast **ingroupers.**

paraphrasing: (p. 118) An active listening response involving summarizing or restating others' comments after they are finished speaking.

parental favoritism: (p. xx) When one or both parents allocate an unfair amount of valuable resources to one child over others.

passion: (p. 87) A blended emotion of joy and surprise coupled with other positive feelings like excitement, amazement, and sexual attraction.

passionate love: (p. 201) A state of intense emotional and physical longing for union with another.

people-oriented listeners: (p. 123) Those who view listening as an opportunity to establish commonalities between themselves and others. For example, Carl enjoys Elaine's descriptions of the triumphs and difficulties she's had learning to snowboard.

perception: (p. 51) The process of selecting, organizing, and interpreting information from our senses.

perception-checking: (p. 69) A five-step process to test your impressions of others and to avoid errors in judgment. It involves checking your punctuation, knowledge, attributions, perceptual influences, and impressions.

personal currency: (p. 183) Power that comes from personal characteristics that others admire, such as intelligence, physical beauty, charm, communication skill, or humor. See also **expertise currency, intimacy currency, power currency, resource currency, social network currency.**

personal idioms: (p. 134) Words and phrases that have unique meanings to a particular relationship, such as pet names or private phrases with special meaning. For example, Uncle Henry was known for his practical jokes; now, years after his death, family members still refer to a practical joke as "pulling a Henry."

personality: (p. 60) An individual's characteristic way of thinking, feeling, and acting based on the traits he or she possesses.

personal space: (p. 165) The proxemic zone that ranges from 18 inches to 4 feet of space between communicators. It is the spatial separation most often used in the United States for friendly conversation.

physical appearance: (p. 167) A nonverbal code that represents visual attributes such as body type, clothing, hair, and other physical features.

pluralistic families: (p. 233) Families characterized by low levels of conformity and high levels of conversation orientation. For example, Julie's parents encourage her to express herself freely, and when conflicts arise, they collaborate with her to resolve them.

polychronic time orientation: (p. 104) The view that time, as manifested in such things as deadlines and schedules, is less important than harmonious interaction with other people. See also **monochromic time orientation (M-time).**

positivity bias: (p. 64) A tendency for first impressions of others to be more positive than negative.

power: (pp. 162) The ability to influence or control events and people.

power currency: (p. 182) Control over a resource that other people value. See also **expertise currency, intimacy currency, personal currency, resource currency, social network currency.**

power-distance: (p. 102) The degree to which people in a particular culture view the unequal distribution of power as acceptable. In high-power-distance cultures, it is considered normal for those with greater power to receive greater deference and respect. In low-power-distance cultures, those who have more power seek to create parity with those who have less power via informality and openness.

prejudice: (p. 98) The destructive and unethical attitude that results from rigid beliefs about groups and their members.

preoccupied attachment: (p. 33) An attachment style in which individuals are high in anxiety and low in avoidance; they desire closeness, but are plagued with fear of rejection.

primary emotions: (p. 77) Six emotions that involve unique and consistent behavioral displays across cultures: anger, disgust, fear, joy, sadness, and surprise.

protective families: (p. 233) Families characterized by high levels of conformity and low levels of conversation orientation. For example, Brian's parents expect their son to be respectful, and they discourage family discussions.

provocateurs: (p. 127) Aggressive listeners who intentionally bait and attack others in online communication. For example, Timothy posts a meme about gun control on the Facebook page of a relative who belongs to the NRA solely for the purpose of starting an argument about the topic with the relative.

proxemics: (p. 165) A nonverbal code of communication representing physical distance. See also **intimate space; personal space; public space; social space.**

pseudo-conflict: (p. 185) A mistaken perception that a conflict exists when it doesn't. For example, Barbara thinks Anne is angry with her because Anne hasn't spoken to her all evening, but Anne is actually worried about a report from her physician.

pseudo-listening: (p. 126) Pretending to listen while preoccupied or bored.

public space: (p. 166) The widest proxemic zone, which ranges outward from 12 feet and is most appropriate for formal settings.

punctuation: (p. 52) A step during organization when you structure information you've selected into a chronological sequence that matches how you experienced the order of events. For example, Bobby claims his sister started the backseat argument, but she insists that he poked her first.

reactivity: (p. 187) A way of handling conflict by not pursuing conflict-related goals at all and communicating in an emotionally explosive and negative fashion instead.

reappraisal: (p. 82) Actively changing how you think about the meaning of emotion-eliciting situations so that their emotional impact is changed. For instance, though previously fearful of giving a speech, Luke reduces his anxiety by repeating positive affirmations and getting excited about the chance to share what he knows.

recalling: (p. 119) The fifth stage of the listening process in which a listener is able to remember information received.

receiver: (p. 7) The individual for whom a message is intended or to whom it is delivered.

receiving: (p. 114) The first stage of the listening process in which a listener takes in information by seeing and hearing.

reciprocal liking: (p. 206) When the person we're attracted to makes it clear, through communication and other actions, that the attraction is mutual.

regulative rules: (p. 134) Guidelines that govern how we use language when we verbally communicate—that is, spelling and grammar, as well as conversational usage. For example, we know how to respond correctly to a greeting, and we know that cursing in public is inappropriate.

regulators: (p. 161) Gestures used to control the exchange of conversational turns during interpersonal encounters—for example, averting eye contact to avoid someone or zipping up book bags as a class to signal to a professor that the lecture should end.

relational dialectics: (p. 204) Opposing tensions between ourselves and our feelings toward others that exist in interpersonal relationships, such as the tension between wishing to be completely honest with a partner yet not wanting to be hurtful.

relational maintenance: (p. 213) Efforts that partners make to keep their relationship in a desired condition. They may show devotion by making time to talk, spending time together, and offering help or support to each other.

relationship goals: (p. 14) Goals of building, maintaining, or terminating relationships with others through interpersonal communication.

resource currency: (p. 183) Power that comes from controlling material items others want or need, such as money, food, or property. See also **expertise currency, intimacy currency, personal currency, power currency, social network currency.**

responding: (p. 117) The fourth stage of the listening process in which a listener communicates, nonverbally or verbally, their attention and understanding—for example, by nodding or murmuring agreement.

romantic betrayal: (p. 217) An act that goes against expectations of a romantic relationship and, as a result, causes pain to a partner.

romantic relationship: (p. 202) An interpersonal involvement two people choose to enter that is perceived as romantic by both.

salience: (p. 51) The degree to which particular people or aspects of their communication attract our attention.

schemata: (p. 53) Mental structures that contain information defining the characteristics of various concepts (such as people, places, events), as well as how those characteristics are related to one another. We often use schemata when interpreting interpersonal communication. When Charlie describes his home as "retro," Amanda visualizes it before she even sees it.

secure attachment: (p. 33) An attachment style in which individuals are low in both anxiety and avoidance; they are comfortable with intimacy and seek close ties with others.

selection: (p. 51) The first step of perception during which we focus our attention on specific sensory data, such as sights, sounds, tastes, touches, or smells.

selective listening: (p. 125) Listening that captures only parts of a message (those that are the most interesting to the listener) and dismisses the rest.

self: (p. 27) The evolving composite of who one is, including **self-awareness, self-concept,** and **self-esteem.**

self-awareness: (p. 27) The ability to view yourself as a unique person distinct from your surrounding environment and reflect on your thoughts, feelings, and behaviors.

self-concept: (p. 27) Your overall idea of who you are based on the beliefs, attitudes, and values you have about yourself.

self-disclosure: (p.42) Revealing private information about yourself to others.

self-discrepancy theory: (p. 30) The idea that your self-esteem results from comparing two mental standards: your *ideal* self (the characteristics you want to possess based on your desires) and your *ought* self (the person others wish and expect you to be).

self-esteem: (p. 29) The overall value, positive or negative, you assign to yourself.

self-fulfilling prophecies: (p. 28) Predictions about future encounters that lead us to behave in ways that ensure the interaction unfolds as we predicted.

self-monitoring: (p. 16) The process of observing our own communication and the norms of the situation in order to make appropriate communication choices.

self-presentation goals: (p. 14) Presenting yourself in certain ways so that others perceive you as being a particular type of person.

self-serving bias: (p. 55) The tendency to attribute our success to internal, rather than external, factors. For example, Ruth attributes the success of a project to her leadership qualities rather than to the dedicated efforts of her team.

sender: (p. 7) The individual who generates, packages, and delivers a message.

separation: (p. 191) A sudden withdrawal of one person from a situation during a conflict. For example, you walk away from an argument to cool off, or you angrily retreat to your room.

serial arguments: (p. 195) A series of unresolved disputes, all having to do with the same issue. For example, husband and wife Brian and Marilyn quarrel repeatedly over whether Marilyn's mother is benevolent or manipulative.

sexual-arousal touch: (p. 165) A touch designed to physically stimulate another person.

sexual orientation: (p. 20) Enduring emotional, romantic, sexual, or affectionate attraction to others that exists along a continuum ranging from exclusive heterosexuality to exclusive homosexuality and that includes various forms of bisexuality.

short-term memory: (p. 117) The part of your mind that temporarily houses information while you seek to understand its meaning.

single-parent family: (p. 229) A household in which one adult has the sole responsibility to be the children's caregiver.

skirting: (p. 184) A means of avoiding conflict by changing the topic or joking about the conflict. For example, when Andrea's balding father, Jimmy, chides Andrea for dyeing her hair blue, Andrea teases, "You're just jealous that I still have hair."

sniping: (p. 184) A way of avoiding conflict by communicating in a negative fashion and then abandoning the encounter by physically leaving the scene or refusing to interact further. For example, when Shruti's brother says he wants to talk about her excessive drinking, she says, "When I want your opinion, I'll ask for it," before storming out of the room.

social comparison: (p. 27) Observing and assigning meaning to others' behaviors and then comparing their behavior to ours (when judging our own actions). For example, you might subtly check out how others are dressed at a party or how they scored on an exam to see if you compare favorably.

social exchange theory: (p. 207) The idea that you will be drawn to those you see as offering substantial benefits with few associated costs. For example, Meredith thinks Leonard is perfect for her because he is much more attentive and affectionate than her previous boyfriends and seems so easy to please.

social network currency: (p. 183) Power that comes from being linked with a network of friends, family, and acquaintances with substantial influence, such as being on a first-name basis with a famous athlete. See also **expertise currency, intimacy currency, personal currency, power currency, resource currency.**

social penetration theory: (p. 40) Altman and Taylor's model that you reveal information about yourself to others by peeling back or penetrating layers.

social-polite touch: (p. 164) A touch, such as a handshake, used to demonstrate social norms or culturally expected behaviors.

social space: (p. 166) The proxemic zone that ranges from 4 to 12 feet of space between communicators. It is the spatial separation most often used in the United States for conversations between acquaintances and strangers.

speech acts: (p. 139) The actions we perform with language, such as the question, "Is the antique clock in your window for sale?" and the reply, "Yes, let me get it out to show you."

spillover hypothesis: (p. 241) The idea that emotions, affect, and mood from the parental relationship "spill over" into the broader family, disrupting children's sense of emotional security.

stagnating: (p. 212) A relational stage in which communication comes to a standstill. For instance, day after day, Owen and Ruth speak only to ask if a bill has been paid or what is on television, without really listening to one another's answers.

stepfamily: (p. 229) A family type where at least one of the adults has a child or children from a previous relationship.

Stereotype Content Model: (p. 98)) The idea that prejudice centers on two judgments made about others: how warm and friendly they are, and how competent they are. These judgments create two possible kinds of prejudice: benevolent and hostile.

stereotyping: (p. 65) Categorizing people into social groups and then evaluating them based on information we have in our schemata related to each group.

structural improvements: (p. 192) When people agree to change the basic rules or understandings that govern their relationship to prevent further conflict.

submissiveness: (p. 173) The willingness to allow others to exert power over you, demonstrated by gestures such as a shrinking posture or lowered eye gaze.

sudden-death statements: (p. 194) Messages, communicated at the height of a conflict, that suddenly declare the end of a relationship, even if that wasn't an option before—for example, "It's over. I never want to see you again."

supportive communication: (p. 89) Sharing messages that express emotional support and that offer personal assistance, such as telling a person of your sympathy or listening to someone without judging.

suppression: (p. 81) Inhibiting thoughts, arousal, and outward behavioral displays of emotion. For example, Amanda stifles her anger, knowing that showing her anger would kill her chances of receiving a good tip.

symbols: (p. 133) Items used to represent other things, ideas, or events. For example, the letters of the alphabet are symbols for specific sounds in English.

symmetrical relationships: (p. 181) Relationships characterized by an equal balance of power, such as a business partnership in which the partners co-own their company.

terminating: (p. 212) A relational stage in which one or both partners end a relationship. For instance, Ruth asks Owen for a divorce once she realizes their marriage has deteriorated beyond salvation.

territoriality: (p. 166) The tendency to claim personal spaces as our own and define certain locations as areas we don't want others to invade without permission, such as spreading personal stuff to claim the entire library table.

time-oriented listeners: (p. 123) Those who prefer brief, concise messages to save time.

transactional communication model: (p. 8) A depiction of communication in which each participant equally influences the communication behavior of the other participants. For example, a salesperson who watches his customer's facial expression while describing a product is sending and receiving messages at the same time.

triangulation: (p. 239) Loyalty conflicts that arise when a coalition is formed, uniting one family member with another against a third family member.

uncertainty avoidance: (p. 101) The variance across cultures regarding the acceptance and tolerance of unpredictability. In high-uncertainty-avoidance cultures, control is valued, and in low-uncertainty-avoidance cultures, change, dissension, and diversity are welcomed.

Uncertainty Reduction Theory: (p. 56) A theory explaining that the primary compulsion during initial encounters is to reduce uncertainty about our conversational partners by gathering enough information about them so their communication becomes predictable and explainable.

understanding: (p. 117) The third stage of the listening process in which a listener interprets the meaning of another person's communication by comparing newly received information against past knowledge.

valued social identities: (p. 251) The aspects of your public self that you deem the most important in defining who you are—for example, musician, athlete, poet, dancer, teacher, mother, and so on.

venting: (p. 82) Allowing emotions to dominate your thoughts and explosively expressing them, such as by shrieking in happiness or storming into an office in a rage.

verbal aggression: (p. 148) The tendency to attack others' self-concepts—their appearance, behavior, or character—rather than their positions.

verbal communication: (p. 133) The exchange of spoken or written language with others during interactions.

vocalics: (p. 163) Vocal characteristics we use to communicate nonverbal messages, such as volume, pitch, rate, voice quality, vocalized sounds, and silence. For instance, a pause might signal discomfort or be used to heighten tension.

warranting value: (p. 38) The degree to which online information is supported by other people and outside evidence.

wedging: (p. 220) When a person deliberately uses online communication—messages, photos, and posts—to try to insert him- or herself between romantic partners because he or she is interested in one of the partners.

"we" language: (p. 144) Communication that uses the pronoun *we* to emphasize inclusion—for example, "We need to decide what color to paint the living room" instead of "I need you to tell me what color paint you want for the living room." See also **"I" language; "you" language.**

world-mindedness: (p. 106) The ability to demonstrate acceptance and respect toward other cultures' beliefs, values, and customs. This ability is developed by accepting others' cultural expressions as natural elements of their communication, by avoiding the temptation to judge others' cultural traits as "better" or "worse" than your own, and by treating people from all cultures with respect. See also **ethnocentrism.**

"you" language: (p. 144) Communication that states or implies the pronoun you to place the focus of attention on blaming others—such as "You haven't done your share of the work on this project." See also **"I" language; "we" language.**

REFERENCES

ABCnews.go.com. (2005, October 21). Do "helicopter moms" do more harm than good? Retrieved from http://abcnews.go.com/2020/Health/story?id=1237868&page=1

Ackard, D. M., & Neumark-Sztainer, D. (2002). Date violence and date rape among adolescents: Associations with disordered eating behaviors and psychological health. *Child Abuse and Neglect, 26,* 455–473.

Adams, B. N. (2004). Families and family study in international perspective. *Journal of Marriage and Family, 66,* 1076–1088.

Adamson, A., & Jenson, V. (Directors). (2001). *Shrek* [Motion picture]. United States: DreamWorks SKG.

Afifi, T. D. (2003). 'Feeling caught' in stepfamilies: Managing boundary turbulence through appropriate communication privacy rules. *Journal of Social and Personal Relationships, 20*(6), 729–755.

Afifi, T. D., McManus, T., Hutchinson, S., & Baker, B. (2007). Parental divorce disclosures, the factors that prompt them, and their impact on parents' and adolescents' well-being. *Communication Monographs, 74,* 78–103.

Afifi, T. D., McManus, T., Steuber, K., & Coho, A. (2009). Verbal avoidance and dissatisfaction in intimate conflict situations. *Human Communication Research, 35,* 357–383.

Afifi, T. D., & Olson, L. (2005). The chilling effect and the pressure to conceal secrets in families. *Communication Monographs, 72,* 192–216.

Afifi, T. D., & Steuber, K. (2010). The cycle of concealment model. *Journal of Social and Personal Relationships, 27*(8), 1019–1034.

Albrecht, T. L., & Bach, B. W. (1997). *Communication in complex organizations: A relational approach.* Fort Worth, TX: Harcourt Brace.

Allport, G. W. (1954). *The nature of prejudice.* Cambridge, MA: Addison-Wesley.

Altman, I., & Taylor, D. A. (1973). *Social penetration: The development of interpersonal relationships.* New York: Holt, Rinehart & Winston.

Andersen, P. A. (1997). Cues of culture: The basis of intercultural differences in nonverbal communication. In L. A. Samovar & R. E. Porter (Eds.), *Intercultural communication: A reader* (8th ed., pp. 244–255). Belmont, CA: Wadsworth.

Anderson, N. H. (1981). *Foundations of information integration theory.* Orlando, FL: Academic Press.

APA Online. (n.d.). *Just the facts about sexual orientation & youth: A primer for principals, educators, & school personnel.* Retrieved from http://www.apa.org/pi/lgbc/publications/justthefacts.html

Appelbaum, S. H., Marinescu, A., Klenin, J., & Bytautas, J. (2007). Fatal attractions: The mismanagement of workplace romance. *International Journal of Business Research, 7*(4), 31–43.

Arasaratnam, L. A. (2006). Further testing of a new model of intercultural communication competence. *Communication Research Reports, 23,* 93–99.

Archer, J. (2000). Sex differences in aggression between heterosexual partners: A meta-analytic review. *Psychological Bulletin, 126,* 651–680.

Argyle, M. (1969). *Social interaction.* New York: Atherton Press.

Argyle, M., & Furnham, A. (1982). The ecology of relationships: Choice of situations as a function of relationship. *British Journal of Social Psychology, 21,* 259–262.

Argyle, M., & Henderson, M. (1984). The rules of friendship. *Journal of Social and Personal Relationships, 1,* 211–237.

Argyle, M., & Lu, L. (1990). Happiness and social skills. *Personality and Individual Differences, 11,* 1255–1261.

Aron, A., Fisher, H., Strong, G., Acevedo, B., Riela, S., & Tsapelas, I. (2008). Falling in love. In S. Sprecher, A. Wenzel, & J. Harvey (Eds.), *Handbook of relationship initiation* (pp. 315–336). New York: Psychology Press.

Arriaga, X. B., & Agnew, C. R. (2001). Being committed: Affective, cognitive, and conative components of relationship commitment. *Personality and Social Psychology Bulletin, 27,* 1190–1203.

Asada, K. J. K., Morrison, K., Hughes, M., & Fitzpatrick, S. (2003, May). *Is that what friends are for? Understanding the motivations, barriers, and emotions associated with friends with benefits relationships.* Paper presented at the annual meeting of the International Communication Association, San Diego, CA.

Asch, S. E. (1946). Forming impressions of personality. *Journal of Abnormal and Social Psychology, 41,* 258–290.

Asian American Career Center. (n.d.). *Goldsea career success.* Retrieved from http://goldsea.com/Career/career.html

Aylor, B. A. (2003). Maintaining long-distance relationships. In D. J. Canary & M. Dainton (Eds.), *Maintaining relationships through communication: Relational, contextual, and cultural variations* (pp. 127–139). Mahwah, NJ: Erlbaum.

Balderrama, A. (2010, May 6). Are you paying attention to your online reputation? Employers are. *The Work Buzz.* Retrieved from http://www.theworkbuzz.com/featured/online-reputation

Bane, R. (2010, August 12). How splintered is your attention? [Blog post]. Retrieved from http://www.baneofyour resistance.com/2010/08/12/how-splintered-is-your-attention-take-the-quiz-and-find-out

Bank, B. J., & Hansford, S. L. (2000). Gender and friendship: Why are men's best same-sex friendships less intimate and supportive? *Personal Relationships, 7,* 63–78.

Baptiste, D. A., Jr. (1990). Therapeutic strategies with black-Hispanic families: Identity problems of a neglected minority. *Journal of Family Psychotherapy, 1,* 15–38.

Barker, L. L. (1971). *Listening behavior.* Englewood Cliffs, NJ: Prentice Hall.

Barker, L. L., & Watson, K. W. (2000). *Listen up.* New York: St. Martin's Press.

Barker, V. & Ota, H. (2011). Mixi diary versus Facebook photos: Social networking site use among Japanese and Caucasian American females. *Journal of Intercultural Communication Research, 40*(1), 39–63.

Barnes, S. B. (2001). *Online connections: Internet interpersonal relationships.* Cresskill, NJ: Hampton Press.

Barnett, O. W., Miller-Perrin, C. L., & Perrin, R. D. (1997). *Family violence across the life-span: An introduction.* Thousand Oaks, CA: Sage.

Barnlund, D. C. (1975). *Private and public self in Japan and the United States.* Tokyo: Simul Press.

Barry, D. (2011, May 15). A sports executive leaves the safety of his shadow life. *The New York Times.* Retrieved from http://www.nytimes.com/2011/05/16/sports/basketball/nba-executive-says-he-is-gay.html?pagewanted=all

Bartholomew, K., & Horowitz, L. M. (1991). Attachment styles among young adults: A test of a four-category model. *Journal of Personality and Social Psychology, 61*(2), 226–244.

Baxter, L. A. (1990). Dialectical contradictions in relationship development. *Journal of Social and Personal Relationships, 7,* 69–88.

Baxter, L. A., Mazanec, M., Nicholson, J., Pittman, G., Smith, K., & West, L. (1997). Everyday loyalties and betrayals in personal relationships. *Journal of Social and Personal Relationships, 14,* 655–678.

Baxter, L. A., Wilmot, W. W., Simmons, C. A., & Swartz, A. (1993). Ways of doing conflict: A folk taxonomy of conflict events in personal relationships. In P. J. Kalbfleisch (Ed.), *Interpersonal communication: Evolving interpersonal relationships* (pp. 89–108). Hillsdale, NJ: Erlbaum.

Beach, W. A. (2002). Between dad and son: Initiating, delivering, and assimilating bad cancer news. *Health Communication, 14,* 271–298.

Becker, J. A. H., Johnson, A. J., Craig, E. A., Gilchrist, E. S., Haigh, M. M., & Lane, L. T. (2009). Friendships are flexible, not fragile: Turning points in geographically-close and long-distance friendships. *Journal of Social and Personal Relationships, 26*(4), 347–369.

Beer, J. S., John, O. P., Scabini, D., & Knight, R. T. (2006). Orbitofrontal cortex and social behavior: Integrating self-monitoring and emotion-cognition interactions. *Journal of Cognitive Neuroscience, 18,* 871–879.

Bell, R. A., Buerkel-Rothfuss, N. L., & Gore, K. E. (1987). Did you bring the yarmulke for the Cabbage Patch Kid? The idiomatic communication of young lovers. *Human Communication Research, 14,* 47–67.

Bennett, S. H. (2003). *Radical pacifism: The War Resisters League and Gandhian nonviolence in America, 1915–1963.* Syracuse, NY: Syracuse University Press.

Benoit, P. J., & Benoit, W. E. (1990). To argue or not to argue. In R. Trapp & J. Schuetz (Eds.), *Perspectives on argumentation: Essays in honor of Wayne Brockriede* (pp. 55–72). Prospect Heights, IL: Waveland Press.

Berger, C. R., & Bradac, J. J. (1982). *Language and social knowledge: Uncertainty in interpersonal relations.* London: Edward Arnold.

Berger, C. R., & Calabrese, R. J. (1975). Some explorations in initial interaction and beyond: Toward a developmental theory of interpersonal communication. *Human Communication Research, 1,* 99–112.

Berkowitz, L., & Harmon-Jones, E. (2004). Toward an understanding of the determinants of anger. *Emotion, 4,* 107–130.

Berry, G. R. (2006). Can computer-mediated asynchronous communication improve team processes and decision-making? *Journal of Business Communication, 43*(4), 344–366.

Berscheid, E. (2002). Emotion. In H. H. Kelley et al. (Eds.), *Close relationships* (2nd ed., pp. 110–168). Clinton Corners, NY: Percheron Press.

Berscheid, E., & Peplau, L. A. (2002). The emerging science of relationships. In H. H. Kelley et al. (Eds.), *Close relationships* (2nd ed., pp. 1–19). Clinton Corners, NY: Percheron Press.

Berscheid, E., & Regan, P. (2005). *The psychology of interpersonal relationships.* Upper Saddle River, NJ: Pearson Education.

Berscheid, E., & Walster, E. (1978). *Interpersonal attraction* (2nd ed.). Reading, MA: Addison-Wesley.

Bevan, J. L., Finan, A., & Kaminsky, A. (2008). Modeling serial arguments in close relationships: The serial argument process model. *Human Communication Research, 34,* 600–624.

Bianconi, L. (2002). *Culture and identity: Issues of authenticity in another value system.* Paper presented at the XII Sietar-EU Conference, Vienna.

Bies, R. J., & Tripp, T. M. (1998). Two faces of the powerless: Coping with tyranny in organizations. In R. M. Kramer & M. A. Neale (Eds.), *Power and influence in organizations* (pp. 203–219). Thousand Oaks, CA: Sage.

Birdwhistell, R. L. (1970). *Kinesics and context: Essays on body motion communication.* Philadelphia: University of Pennsylvania Press.

Blakely, G. L., Blakely, E. H., & Moorman, R. H. (1995). The relationship between gender, personal experience, and perceptions of sexual harassment in the workplace. *Employee Responsibilities and Rights Journal, 8,* 263–274.

Bland, K. (2011). Phoenix gay dads adopt, raise 12 happy kids. *The Arizona Republic.* Retrieved from http://www.azcentral .com/news/azliving/articles/2011/05/02/20110502gay-dads-ham-family-12-adopted-kids.html?page=1

Blieszner, R., & Adams, R. G. (1992). *Adult friendship.* Newbury Park, CA: Sage.

Bochner, S., & Hesketh, B. (1994). Power distance, individualism/collectivism, and job related attitudes in a culturally diverse work group. *Journal of Cross-Cultural Psychology, 25,* 233–257.

Boddy, C. R. (2011). Corporate psychopaths, bullying and unfair supervision in the workplace. *Journal of Business Ethics, 100,* 367–379.

Bodenhausen, G. V., Macrae, C. N., & Sherman, J. W. (1999). On the dialectics of discrimination: Dual processes in social stereotyping. In S. Chaiken & Y. Trope (Eds.), *Dual process theories in social psychology* (pp. 271–290). New York: Guilford Press.

Bodhi, B., & Nanamoli, B. (1995). *The middle length discourse of the Buddha: A translation of the Majjhima Nikaya.* Somerville, MA: Wisdom Publications.

Bodie, G. D., & Worthington, D. L. (2010). Revisiting the listening styles profile (LSP-16): A confirmatory factor analytic approach to scale validation and reliability estimation. *The International Journal of Listening, 24,* 69–88.

Booth, A., & Hess, E. (1974). Cross-sex friendship. *Journal of Marriage and the Family, 36,* 38–46.

Bornstein, R. F. (1989). Exposure and affect: Overview and meta-analysis of research, 1968–1987. *Psychological Bulletin, 106,* 265–289.

Bowlby, J. (1969). *Attachment and loss: Vol. 1. Attachment.* New York: Basic Books.

Boyd, C. (2010). The debate over the prohibition of romance in the workplace. *Journal of Business Ethics, 97,* 325–338.

Braithwaite, D. O., Bach, B. W., Baxter, L. A., DiVerniero, R., Hammonds, J. R., Hosek, A. M., et al. (2010). Constructing family: A typology of voluntary kin. *Journal of Social and Personal Relationships, 27*(3), 388–407.

Brandes, S. (1987). Sex roles and anthropological research in rural Andalusia. *Women's Studies, 13,* 357–372.

Bregman, A., Golin, S. (Producers), Gondry, M. (Director), & Kaufman, C. (Writer). (2004). *Eternal sunshine of the spotless mind* [Motion picture]. United States: Focus Features.

Brehm, S. S., Miller, R. S., Perlman, D., & Campbell, S. M. (2002). *Intimate relationships* (3rd ed.). Boston: McGraw-Hill.

Brend, R. (1975). Male-female intonation patterns in American English. In B. Thorne & N. Henley (Eds.), *Language and sex: Difference and dominance* (pp. 84–87). Rowley, MA: Newbury House.

Brewer, M. B. (1993). Social identity, distinctiveness, and ingroup homogeneity. *Social Cognition, 11,* 150–164.

Brewer, M. B. (1999). The psychology of prejudice: Ingroup love or outgroup hate? *Journal of Social Issues, 55,* 429–444.

Brewer, M. B., & Campbell, D. T. (1976). *Ethnocentrism and intergroup attitudes: East African evidence.* Beverly Hills, CA: Sage.

Bridge, K., & Baxter, L. A. (1992). Blended relationships: Friends as work associates. *Western Journal of Communication, 56,* 200–225.

Brody, L. R., & Hall, J. A. (2000). Gender, emotion, and expression. In M. Lewis & J. M. Haviland (Eds.), *Handbook of emotions* (2nd ed., pp. 338–349). New York: Guilford Press.

Brontë, E. (1995). *Wuthering Heights.* Oxford: Oxford University Press. (Original work published 1848)

Brown, R. (1965). *Social psychology.* New York: Free Press.

Bruner, J., & Taguiri, R. (1954). The perception of people. In G. Lindzey (Ed.), *Handbook of social psychology* (Vol. 1, pp. 601–633). Cambridge, MA: Addison-Wesley.

Buber, M. (1965). *The knowledge of man: A philosophy of the interhuman.* New York: Harper & Row.

Bulfinch, T. (1985). *The golden age of myth and legend.* London: Bracken Books. (Original work published 1855)

Bunkers, S. S. (2010). The power and possibility in listening. *Nursing Science Quarterly, 23*(1), 22–27.

Burgoon, J. K., Buller, D. B., & Woodall, W. G. (1996). *Nonverbal communication: The unspoken dialogue* (2nd ed.). New York: McGraw-Hill.

Burgoon, J. K., & Dunbar, N. E. (2000). An interactionist perspective on dominance-submission: Interpersonal dominance as a dynamic, situationally contingent social skill. *Communication Monographs, 67,* 96–121.

Burgoon, J. K., & Hoobler, G. D. (2002). Nonverbal signals. In M. L. Knapp & J. A. Daly (Eds.), *Handbook of interpersonal communication* (3rd ed., pp. 240–299). Thousand Oaks, CA: Sage.

Burgoon, M. (1995). A kinder, gentler discipline: Feeling good about being mediocre. In B. R. Burleson (Ed.), *Communication yearbook 18* (pp. 464–479). Thousand Oaks, CA: Sage.

Buriel, R., & De Ment, T. (1997). Immigration and sociocultural change in Mexican, Chinese, and Vietnamese American families. In A. Booth, A. C. Crouter, & N. Landale (Eds.), *Immigration and the family: Research and policy on U.S. immigrants* (pp. 165–200). Mahwah, NJ: Erlbaum.

Burleson, B. R., & MacGeorge, E. L. (2002). Supportive communication. In M. L. Knapp & J. A. Daly (Eds.), *Handbook of interpersonal communication* (pp. 374–422). Thousand Oaks, CA: Sage.

Burleson, B. R., & Samter, W. (1994). A social skills approach to relationship maintenance: How individual differences in communication skills affect the achievement of relationship functions. In D. J. Canary & L. Stafford (Eds.), *Communication and relational maintenance* (pp. 61–90). New York: Academic Press.

Bushman, B. J., & Baumeister, R. F. (1998). Threatened egotism, narcissism, self-esteem, and direct and displaced aggression: Does self-love or self-hate lead to violence? *Journal of Personality and Social Psychology, 75,* 219–229.

Buss, D. M., Larsen, R. J., Westen, D., & Semmelroth, J. (1992). Sex differences in jealousy: Evolution, physiology, and psychology. *Psychological Science, 3,* 251–255.

Buss, D. M., Shackelford, T. K., Kirkpatrick, L. A., Choe, J. C., Lim, H. K., Hasegawa, M., et al. (1999). Jealousy and the nature of beliefs about infidelity: Tests of competing hypotheses about sex differences in the United States, Korea, and Japan. *Personal Relationships, 6,* 125–150.

Buunk, B. P., Angleitner, A., Oubaid, V., & Buss, D. M. (1996). Sex differences in jealousy in evolutionary and cultural perspective: Tests from the Netherlands, Germany, and the United States. *Psychological Science, 7,* 359–363.

Buzzanell, P. (1990, November). *Managing workplace romance.* Paper presented at the annual meeting of the Speech Communication Association, Chicago, IL.

Cacioppo, J. T., Klein, D. J., Berntson, G. G., & Hatfield, E. (1993). The psychophysiology of emotion. In M. Lewis & J. M. Haviland (Eds.), *Handbook of emotions* (pp. 119–142). New York: Guilford Press.

Campbell, R. G., & Babrow, A. S. (2004). The role of empathy in responses to persuasive risk communication: Overcoming resistance to HIV prevention messages. *Health Communication, 16,* 159–182.

Canary, D. J. (2003). Managing interpersonal conflict: A model of events related to strategic choices. In J. O. Greene & B. R. Burleson (Eds.), *Handbook of communication and social interaction skills.* Mahwah, NJ: Erlbaum.

Canary, D. J., Emmers-Sommer, T. M., & Faulkner, S. (1997). *Sex and gender differences in personal relationships.* New York: Guilford Press.

Canary, D. J., & Hause, K. S. (1993). Is there any reason to research sex differences in communication? *Communication Quarterly, 41,* 129–144.

Canary, D. J., & Zelley, E. (2000). Current research programs on relational maintenance behaviors. In M. E. Roloff (Ed.), *Communication yearbook 23* (pp. 305–339). Thousand Oaks, CA: Sage.

Carbery, J., & Buhrmester, D. (1998). Friendship and need fulfillment during three phases of young adulthood. *Journal of Social and Personal Relationships, 15,* 393–409.

Carducci, B. J., & Zimbardo, P. G. (1995, November/December). Are you shy? *Psychology Today, 28,* 34–41.

Carlson, J. G., & Hatfield, E. (1992). *Psychology of emotion.* Orlando, FL: Harcourt Brace.

Carney, D. R., Hall, J. A., & Smith LeBeau, L. S. (2005). Beliefs about the nonverbal expression of social power. *Journal of Nonverbal Behavior, 29,* 105–123.

Carr, N. (2010). *The shallows: What the Internet is doing to our brains.* New York: W. W. Norton & Co.

Castelli, L., Tomelleri, S., & Zogmaister, C. (2008). Implicit ingroup metafavoritism: Subtle preference for ingroup members displaying ingroup bias. *Personality and Social Psychology Bulletin, 34*(6), 807–818.

Caughlin, J. P. (2002). The demand/withdraw pattern of communication as a predictor of marital satisfaction over time: Unresolved issues and future directions. *Human Communication Research, 28,* 49–85.

Caughlin, J. P., & Huston, T. L. (2002). A contextual analysis of the association between demand/withdraw and marital satisfaction. *Personal Relationships, 9,* 95–119.

Caughlin, J. P., & Vangelisti, A. L. (2000). An individual difference explanation of why married couples engage in demand/withdraw patterns of conflict. *Journal of Social and Personal Relationships, 17,* 523–551.

Centers for Disease Control and Prevention. (2008). *Youth risk behavior surveillance—United States, 2007.* Retrieved from http://www.cdc.gov/mmwr/preview/mmwrhtml/ss5704a1.htm

Cerpas, N. (2002). Variation in the display and experience of love between college Latino and non-Latino heterosexual romantic couples. *Ronald E. McNair Scholarship research report*. University of California, Berkeley.

Chaffee, S. H., & Berger, C. R. (1987). What communication scientists do. In C. R. Berger & S. H. Chaffee (Eds.), *Handbook of communication science* (pp. 99–122). Newbury Park, CA: Sage.

Chan, D. K., & Cheng, G. H. (2004). A comparison of offline and online friendship qualities at different stages of relationship development. *Journal of Social and Personal Relationships, 21*(3), 305–320.

Chaplin, T. M., Cole, P. M., & Zahn-Waxler, C. (2005). Parental socialization of emotion expression: Gender differences and relations to child adjustment. *Emotion, 5*, 80–88.

Chen, G.-M., & Chung, J. (1997). The "Five Asian Dragons": Management behaviors and organization communication. In L. A. Samovar & R. E. Porter (Eds.), *Intercultural communication: A reader* (pp. 317–328). Belmont, CA: Wadsworth.

Chen, G.-M., & Starosta, W. J. (2005). *Foundation of intercultural communication*. Boston: Allyn and Bacon.

Cherlin, A. (2004). The deinstitutionalization of American marriage. *Journal of Marriage and Family, 66*, 848–861.

Chesebro, J. L. (1999). The relationship between listening styles and conversational sensitivity. *Communication Research Reports, 16*, 233–238.

Choi, C. Q. (2011, January 18). Does science support the punitive parenting of "tiger mothering"? *Scientific American*. Retrieved from http://www.scientificamerican.com/article.cfm?id=tiger-mother-punitive-parenting

Christofides, E., Muise, A., & Desmarais, S. (2009). Information disclosure and control on Facebook: Are they two sides of the same coin or two different processes? *CyberPsychology & Behavior, 12*(3), 341–345.

Chua, A. (2011). *Battle hymn of the tiger mother*. New York: Penguin Press.

Chung, J. H., Des Roches, C. M., Meunier, J., & Eavey, R. D. (2005). Evaluation of noise-induced hearing loss in young people using a web-based survey technique. *Pediatrics, 115*, 861–867.

Clair, R. P. (1993). The use of framing devices to sequester organizational narratives: Hegemony and harassment. *Communication Monographs, 60*, 113–136.

Clair, R. P. (1998). *Organizing silence*. Albany: State University of New York Press.

Clark, R. A., & Delia, J. (1979). Topoi and rhetorical competence. *Quarterly Journal of Speech, 65*, 187–206.

Cleveland, J. N., Stockdale, M., & Murphy, K. R. (2000). *Women and men in organizations: Sex and gender issues at work*. Mahwah, NJ: Erlbaum.

Cochran, C. C., Frazier, P. A., & Olson, A. M. (1997). Predictors of responses to unwanted sexual attention. *Psychology of Women Quarterly, 21*, 207–226.

Cohen, T. F. (1992). Men's families, men's friends: A structural analysis of constraints on men's social ties. In P. M. Nardi (Ed.), *Men's friendships: Vol. 2. Research on men and masculinities* (pp. 115–131). Newbury Park, CA: Sage.

Cole, M., & Cole, S. R. (1989). *The development of children*. New York: Freeman.

Coleman, M., Ganong, L., & Fine, M. (2000). Reinvestigating remarriage: Another decade in progress. *Journal of Marriage and the Family, 62*, 1288–1307.

Collins, N. L., & Feeney, B. C. (2004). An attachment theory perspective on closeness and intimacy. In D. J. Mashek & A. Aron (Eds.), *Handbook of closeness and intimacy* (pp. 163–187). Mahwah, NJ: Erlbaum.

Collins, S. (2008). *The hunger games*. New York: Scholastic Inc.

Conlin, J. (2011, October 2). The freedom to choose your pronoun. *The New York Times*. Retrieved from http://www.nytimes.com

Contractor, N. S., & Grant, S. (1996). The emergence of shared interpretations in organizations: A self-organizing systems perspective. In J. H. Watt & C. A. VanLear (Eds.), *Dynamic patterns in communication processes* (pp. 215–230). Thousand Oaks, CA: Sage.

Cooley, C. H. (1902). *Human nature and the social order*. New York: Scribner.

Corner, L. (2007, June 3). Mrs. Infidelity: Lust in translation author Pamela Druckerman. *The Independent*. Retrieved from http://www.belfasttelegraph.co.uk/lifestyle/mrs-infidelity-lust-in-translation-author-pamela-druckerman-13448101.html

Costanzo, F. S., Markel, N. N., & Costanzo, R. R. (1969). Voice quality profile and perceived emotion. *Journal of Counseling Psychology, 16*, 267–270.

Coupland, N., Giles, H., & Wiemann, J. M. (Eds.). (1991). *Miscommunication and problematic talk*. Newbury Park, CA: Sage.

Covarrubias, P. (2000). Of endearment and other terms of address: A Mexican perspective. In M. W. Lustig & J. Koestner (Eds.), *Among us: Essays on identity, belonging, and intercultural competence* (pp. 9–17). New York: Longman.

Crider, D. M., Willits, F. K., & Kanagy, C. L. (1991). Rurality and well-being during the middle years of life. *Social Indicators, 24*, 253–268.

Crosnoe, R., & Cavanagh, S. E. (2010). Families with children and adolescents: A review, critique, and future agenda. *Journal of Marriage and Family, 72*, 594–611.

Cross, S. E., & Madson, L. (1997). Models of the self: Self-construals and gender. *Psychological Bulletin, 122,* 5–37.

Cullen, J. (2011, April 18). *Battle hymn of the tiger mother:* A remarkably bad book [Book review]. *The Cutting Edge News.* Retrieved from http://www.thecuttingedgenews.com/index.php?article=51839

Cunningham, M. (1988). Does happiness mean friendliness? Induced mood and heterosexual self-disclosure. *Personality and Social Psychology Bulletin, 14,* 283–297.

Cupach, W. R., & Spitzberg, B. H. (1998). Obsessive relational intrusion and stalking. In B. H. Spitzberg & W. R. Cupach (Eds.), *The dark side of close relationships* (pp. 233–263). Hillsdale, NJ: Erlbaum.

Cupach, W. R., & Spitzberg, B. H. (2004). *The dark side of relational pursuit: From attraction to obsession to stalking.* Mahwah, NJ: Erlbaum.

Custudio, J. (2002). The divine Ms. C.H.O.: Margaret Cho on her new stand-up movie, Lea Delaria, Joan Rivers, and the meaning of gay pride. *The Montreal Mirror.* Retrieved from www.montrealmirror.com/ARCHIVES/2002/080102/divers7.html

Dainton, M., & Aylor, B. (2002). Patterns of communication channel use in the maintenance of long-distance relationships. *Communication Research Reports, 19,* 118–129.

Dainton, M., & Stafford, L. (1993). Routine maintenance behaviors: A comparison of relationship type, partner similarity and sex differences. *Journal of Social and Personal Relationships, 10,* 255–271.

Dainton, M., Zelley, E., & Langan, E. (2003). Maintaining friendships throughout the lifespan. In D. J. Canary & M. Dainton (Eds.), *Maintaining relationships through communication: Relational, contextual, and cultural variations* (pp. 79–102). Mahwah, NJ: Erlbaum.

Daly, J. (1975). *Listening and interpersonal evaluations.* Paper presented at the annual meeting of the Central States Speech Association, Kansas City, MO.

Daly, J. A., McCroskey, J. C., Ayres, J., Hopf, T., & Ayres, D. M. (Eds.). (2004). *Avoiding communication: Shyness, reticence, and communication apprehension* (3rd ed.). Cresskill, NJ: Hampton Press.

Daniels, D. (1986). Differential experiences of siblings in the same family as predictors of adolescent sibling personality differences. *Journal of Personality and Social Psychology, 51*(2), 339–346.

Dash, J. (2001). *The world at her fingertips: The story of Helen Keller.* New York: Scholastic Press.

Davey, M. (2004, December 6). 8 soldiers sue over Army's stop-loss policy. *The New York Times.* Retrieved from http://www.nytimes.com

Davis, K. E., & Todd, M. L. (1985). Assessing friendship: Prototypes, paradigm cases, and relationship description. In S. Duck & D. Perlman (Eds.), *Understanding personal relationships: An interdisciplinary approach* (pp. 17–38). London: Sage.

Deaf President Now. (n.d.). In *Wikipedia.* Retrieved from http://en.wikipedia.org/wiki/Deaf_President_Now

Deaf President Now Protest. (n.d.). Retrieved from http://www.gallaudet.edu/gallaudet_university/about_gallaudet/dpn_home.html

Dean, J. (2011). Smartphone user survey: A glimpse into the mobile lives of college students. *Digital New Test Kitchen.* Retrieved from http://testkitchen.colorado.edu/projects/reports/smartphone/smartphone-survey

DeAngelo, D. (2011). Reading body language and more. Retrieved from http://www.askmen.com/dating/dating_advice_150/197_dating_tips.html

Deardorff, D. K. (Ed.). (2009). *The Sage handbook of intercultural competence.* Thousand Oaks, CA: Sage.

Delgado-Gaitan, C. (1993). Parenting in two generations of Mexican American families. *International Journal of Behavioral Development, 16,* 409–427.

Delia, J. G. (1972). Dialects and the effects of stereotypes on interpersonal attraction and cognitive processes in impression formation. *Quarterly Journal of Speech, 58,* 285–297.

Devine, P. G. (1989). Stereotypes and prejudice: Their automatic and controlled components. *Journal of Personality and Social Psychology, 56,* 5–18.

de Vries, B. (1996). The understanding of friendship: An adult life course perspective. In C. Magai & S. McFadden (Eds.), *Handbook of emotion, aging, and the life course* (pp. 249–268). New York: Academic Press.

Dillard, J. (1987). Close relationships at work: Perceptions of the motives and performance of relational participants. *Journal of Social and Personal Relationships, 4,* 179–193.

Dindia, K., & Allen, M. (1992). Sex differences in self-disclosure: A meta-analysis. *Psychological Bulletin, 112,* 106–124.

Domingue, R., & Mollen, D. (2009). Attachment and conflict communication in adult romantic relationships. *Journal of Social and Personal Relationships, 26,* 678–696.

Donohue, W. A., & Kolt, R. (1992). *Managing interpersonal conflict.* Newbury Park, CA: Sage.

Dreyer, A. S., Dreyer, C. A., & Davis, J. E. (1987). Individuality and mutuality in the language of families of field-dependent and field-independent children. *Journal of Genetic Psychology, 148,* 105–117.

Druckerman, P. (2007). *Lust in translation.* New York: Penguin Press.

Duan, C., & Hill, C. E. (1996). The current state of empathy research. *Journal of Counseling Psychology, 43,* 261–274.

Dunbar, N. E. (2004). Dyadic power theory: Constructing a communication-based theory of relational power. *Journal of Family Communication, 4*(3/4), 235–248.

Duncan, S., Jr., & Fiske, D. W. (1977). *Face-to-face interaction: Research, methods, and theory.* New York: Wiley.

Dutton, L. B., & Winstead, B. A. (2006). Predicting unwanted pursuit: Attachment, relationship satisfaction, relationship alternatives, and break-up distress. *Journal of Social and Personal Relationships, 23*(4), 565–586.

Eagly, A. H., Ashmore, R. D., Makhijani, M. G., & Longo, L. C. (1991). What is beautiful is good, but . . . : A meta-analytic review of research on the physical attractiveness stereotype. *Psychological Bulletin, 110,* 109–128.

Ebbeson, E., Duncan, B., & Konecni, V. (1975). Effects of content of verbal aggression on future verbal aggression: A field experiment. *Journal of Experimental Social Psychology, 11,* 192–204.

Eisenberg, E. M., & Goodall, H. L., Jr. (2004). *Organizational communication: Balancing creativity and constraint* (4th ed.). Boston: Bedford/St. Martin's.

Eisikovits, Z., & Buchbinder, E. (2000). *Locked in a violent embrace.* Thousand Oaks, CA: Sage.

Ekman, P. (1972). Universals and cultural differences in facial expressions of emotion. In J. R. Cole (Ed.), *Nebraska Symposium on Motivation, Vol. 19* (pp. 207–283). Lincoln: University of Nebraska Press.

Ekman, P. (1976). Movements with precise meanings. *Journal of Communication, 26,* 14–26.

Ekman, P., & Friesen, W. V. (1969). The repertoire of nonverbal behavior: Categories, origins, usage, and coding. *Semiotica, 1,* 49–98.

Ekman, P., & Friesen, W. V. (1975). *Unmasking the face: A guide to recognizing emotions from facial clues.* Englewood Cliffs, NJ: Prentice-Hall.

Elci, M., & Alpkan, L. (2009). The impact of perceived organizational ethical climate on work satisfaction. *Journal of Business Ethics, 84,* 297–311.

Ellis, A., & Dryden, W. (1997). *The practice of rational emotive behavior therapy.* New York: Springer.

Ellison, N., Heino, R., & Gibbs, J. (2006). Managing impressions online: Self-presentation processes in the online dating environment. *Journal of Computer-Mediated Communication, 11*(2), article 2. Retrieved from http://jcmc.indiana.edu/vol11/issue2/ellison.html

Ellison, N. B., Steinfield, C., & Lampe, C. (2007). The benefits of Facebook "friends:" Social capital and college students' use of online social network sites. *Journal of Computer-Mediated Communication, 12*(4), article 1. Retrieved from http://jcmc.indiana.edu/vol12/issue4/ellison.html

Englehardt, E. E. (2001). Introduction to ethics in interpersonal communication. In E. E. Englehardt (Ed.), *Ethical issues in interpersonal communication: Friends, intimates, sexuality, marriage, and family* (pp. 1–27). Orlando, FL: Harcourt College.

Environmental Protection Agency. (2002, September). Cross-cultural communication. Retrieved from http://www.epa.gov/superfund/community/pdfs/12ccc.pdf

Escartín, J., Rodríguez-Carballeira, A., Zapf, D., Porrúa, C., & Martín-Peña, J. (2009). Perceived severity of various bullying behaviours at work and the relevance of exposure to bullying. *Work & Stress, 23*(3), 191–205.

Farace, R. V., Monge, P. R., & Russell, H. M. (1977). *Communicating and organizing.* Reading, MA: Addison-Wesley.

Feingold, A. (1988). Matching for attractiveness in romantic partners and same-sex friends: A meta-analysis and theoretical critique. *Psychological Bulletin, 104,* 226–235.

Felmlee, D., Orzechowicz, D., & Fortes, C. (2010). Fairy tales: Attraction and stereotypes in same-gender relationships. *Sex Roles, 62,* 226–240.

Felmlee, D. H. (2001). No couple is an island: A social network perspective on dyadic stability. *Social Forces, 79,* 1259–1287.

Fenigstein, A., Scheier, M. F., & Buss, A. H. (1975). Public and private self-consciousness: Assessment and theory. *Journal of Consulting and Clinical Psychology, 43,* 522–527.

Fiedler, K., Pampe, H., & Scherf, U. (1986). Mood and memory for tightly organized social information. *European Journal of Social Psychology, 16,* 149–165.

Field, A. (2005). Block that defense! Make sure your constructive criticism works. *Harvard Management Communication Letter, 2*(4), 3–5.

Field, A. E., Cheung, L., Wolf, A. M., Herzog, D. B., Gortmaker, S. L., & Colditz, G. A. (1999). Exposure to the mass media and weight concerns among girls. *Pediatrics, 103,* 36.

Fischer, A. H., Rodriguez Mosquera, P. M., van Vianen, A. E. M., & Manstead, A. S. R. (2004). Gender and culture differences in emotion. *Emotion, 4,* 87–94.

Fisher, B. A. (1983). Differential effects of sexual composition and interactional context on interaction patterns in dyads. *Human Communication Research, 9,* 225–238.

Fishman, P. M. (1983). Interaction: The work women do. In B. Thorne, C. Kramarae, & N. Henley (Eds.), *Language, gender, and society* (pp. 89–101). Cambridge, MA: Newbury House.

Fiske, S. T., & Taylor, S. E. (1991). *Social cognition* (2nd ed.). New York: McGraw-Hill.

Fitzgerald, L. F. (1993). Sexual harassment: A research analysis and agenda for the 1990s. *Journal of Vocational Behavior, 42,* 5–27.

Fleischer, R. (Director), Reese, R., & Wernick, P. (Writers). (2009). *Zombieland* [Motion picture]. United States: Sony Pictures.

Floyd, K. (1999). All touches are not created equal: Effects of form and duration on observers' interpretations of an embrace. *Journal of Nonverbal Behavior, 23,* 283–299.

Floyd, K., & Burgoon, J. K. (1999). Reacting to nonverbal expressions of liking: A test of interaction adaptation theory. *Communication Monographs, 66,* 219–239.

Floyd, K., & Morman, M. T. (1999). The measurement of affectionate communication. *Communication Quarterly, 46,* 144–162.

Floyd, K., & Morman, M. T. (2005). Fathers' and sons' reports of fathers' affectionate communication: Implications of a naïve theory of affection. *Journal of Social and Personal Relationships, 22*(1), 99–109.

Forgas, J. P., & Bower, G. H. (1987). Mood effects on person perception judgments. *Journal of Personality and Social Psychology, 53,* 53–60.

Forni, P. M. (2002). *Choosing civility: The twenty-five rules of considerate conduct.* New York: St. Martin's Griffin.

Foss, S. K., Foss, K. A., & Trapp, R. (1991). *Contemporary perspectives in rhetoric* (2nd ed.). Prospect Heights, IL: Waveland Press.

Fox, K. R. (1992). Physical education and development of self-esteem in children. In N. Armstrong (Ed.), *New directions in physical education: II. Towards a national curriculum* (pp. 33–54). Champaign, IL: Human Kinetics.

Fox, K. R. (1997). The physical self and processes in self-esteem development. In K. Fox (Ed.), *The physical self* (pp. 111–139). Champaign, IL: Human Kinetics.

Frederikse, M. E., Lu, A., Aylward, E., Barta, P., & Pearlson, G. (1999). Sex differences in the inferior parietal lobule. *Cerebral Cortex, 9,* 896–901.

Freides, D. (1974). Human information processing and sensory modality: Cross-modal functions, information complexity, memory, and deficit. *Psychological Bulletin, 81,* 284–310.

Frijda, N. H. (2005). Emotion experience. *Cognition and Emotion, 19,* 473–497.

Frisby, B. N., & Westerman, D. (2010). Rational actors: Channel selection and rational choices in romantic conflict episodes. *Journal of Social and Personal Relationships, 27,* 970–981.

Fritz, J. H., & Dillard, J. P. (1994, November). *The importance of peer relationships in organizational socialization.* Paper presented at the annual meeting of the Speech Communication Association, New Orleans, LA.

Fuendeling, J. M. (1998). Affect regulation as a stylistic process within adult attachment. *Journal of Social and Personal Relationships, 15,* 291–322.

Furger, R. (1996). I'm okay, you're online. *PC World, 14,* 310–312.

Furman, W., & Simon, V. A. (1998). Advice from youth: Some lessons from the study of adolescent relationships. *Journal of Social and Personal Relationships, 15,* 723–739.

Furr, R. M., & Funder, D. C. (1998). A multimodal analysis of personal negativity. *Journal of Personality and Social Psychology, 74,* 1580–1591.

Gaines, S. O., Jr., & Agnew, C. R. (2003). Relationship maintenance in intercultural couples: An interdependence analysis. In D. J. Canary & M. Dainton (Eds.), *Maintaining relationships through communication: Relational, contextual, and cultural variations* (pp. 231–253). Mahwah, NJ: Erlbaum.

Gaines, S. O., Jr., Chalfin, J., Kim, M., & Taing, P. (1998). Communicating prejudice in personal relationships. In M. L. Hecht (Ed.), *Communicating prejudice* (pp. 163–186). Thousand Oaks, CA: Sage.

Gaitonde, R. (2011). When it comes to telecommuting, companies save, but the U.S. lags. Retrieved from http://broadbandbreakfast.com/2011/06/when-it-comes-to-telecommuting-companies-save-but-the-u-s-lags/

Galupo, M. P. (2007). Friendship patterns of sexual minority individuals in adulthood. *Journal of Social and Personal Relationships, 24,* 139–151.

Galupo, M. P. (2009). Cross-category friendship patterns: Comparison of heterosexual and sexual minority adults. *Journal of Social and Personal Relationships, 26*(6–7), 811–831.

Galvin, K. M., Brommel, B. J., & Bylund, C. L. (2004). *Family communication: Cohesion and change* (6th ed.). New York: Pearson.

Ganong, L., Coleman, M., Fine, M., & Martin, P. (1999). Stepparents' affinity-seeking and affinity-maintaining strategies with stepchildren. *Journal of Family Issues, 20,* 299–327.

Ganong, L. H., & Coleman, M. (1994). *Remarried family relationships.* Thousand Oaks, CA: Sage.

Garcia, P., & Geisler, J. (1988). Sex and age/grade differences in adolescents' self-disclosure. *Perceptual and Motor Skills, 67,* 427–432.

Garrett, R. K., & Danziger, J. (2008). *Gratification and disaffection: Understanding personal Internet use during work.* Paper presented at the annual meeting of the International Communication Association, Montreal, Canada.

Gerdes, L. I. (1999). *Sexual harassment: Current controversies.* San Diego, CA: Greenhaven.

Gettings, J. (2005). Civil disobedience: Black medalists raise fists for civil rights movement. Retrieved from www.infoplease.com/spot/mm-mexicocity.html

Giannakakis, A. E., & Fritsche, I. (2011). Social identities, group norms, and threat: On the malleability of ingroup bias. *Personality and Social Psychology Bulletin, 37*(1), 82–93.

Gibbs, J. L., Ellison, N. B., & Heino, R. D. (2006). Self-presentation in online personals: The role of anticipated future interaction, self-disclosure, and perceived success in Internet dating. *Communication Research, 33,* 1–26.

Gibson, B., & Sachau, D. (2000). Sandbagging as a self-presentational style: Claiming to be less than you are. *Personality and Social Psychology Bulletin, 26,* 56–70.

Gifford, R., Ng, C. F., & Wilkinson, M. (1985). Nonverbal cues in the employment interview: Links between applicant qualities and interviewer judgments. *Journal of Applied Psychology, 70,* 729–736.

Giles, H., Coupland, N., & Coupland, J. (Eds.). (1991). *Contexts of accommodation: Developments in applied linguistics.* Cambridge, UK: Cambridge University Press.

Giles, H., & Street, R. L. (1994). Communicator characteristics and behavior. In M. L. Knapp & G. R. Miller (Eds.), *Handbook of interpersonal communication* (2nd ed., pp. 103–161). Beverly Hills, CA: Sage.

Gleason, L. B. (1989). *The development of language.* Columbus, OH: Merrill.

Glenn, D. (2010, February 28). Divided attention: In an age of classroom multitasking, scholars probe the nature of learning and memory. *The Chronicle of Higher Education.* Retrieved from http://chronicle.com/article/Scholars-Turn-Their-Attention/63746/

Glisson, C., & James, L. R. (2002). The cross-level effects of culture and climate in human service teams. *Journal of Organizational Behavior, 23,* 767–794.

Goffman, E. (1955). On facework: An analysis of ritual elements in social interaction. *Psychiatry, 18,* 319–345.

Goffman, E. (1959). *The presentation of self in everyday life.* Garden City, NY: Doubleday Anchor Books.

Goffman, E. (1979). Footing. *Semiotica, 25,* 124–147.

Goldstein, T. (2001). I'm not white: Anti-racist teacher education for white early childhood educators. *Contemporary Issues in Early Childhood, 2,* 3–13.

Goleman, D. (2006). *Social intelligence: The new science of human relationships.* New York: Bantam Dell.

Goleman, D. (2007a, February 20). Flame first, think later: New clues to e-mail misbehavior. *The New York Times.* Retrieved from http://www.nytimes.com

Goleman, D. (2007b, August 24). Free won't: The marshmallow test revisited [Blog post]. Retrieved from http://danielgoleman.info/2007/free-wont-the-marshmallow-test-revisited/

Golish, T. D. (2000). Changes in closeness between adult children and their parents: A turning point analysis. *Communication Reports, 13,* 79–97.

Golish, T. D. (2003). Stepfamily communication strengths: Understanding the ties that bind. *Human Communication Research, 29*(1), 41–80.

Goodsell, T. L., Bates, J. S., & Behnke, A. O. (2010). Fatherhood stories: Grandparents, grandchildren, and gender differences. *Journal of Social and Personal Relationships, 28*(1), 134–154.

Goodwin, C. (1981). *Conversational organization: Interaction between speakers and hearers.* New York: Academic Press.

Gosling, S. D., Gaddis, S., & Vazire, S. (2007, March). *Personality impressions based on Facebook profiles.* Paper presented at the International Conference on Weblogs and Social Media (ICWSM), Boulder, CO.

Gottman, J. M., & Levenson, R. W. (2000). The timing of divorce: Predicting when a couple will divorce over a 14-year period. *Journal of Marriage and Family, 62,* 737–745.

Grammer, K., & Thornhill, R. (1994). Human facial attractiveness and sexual selection: The role of averageness and symmetry. *Journal of Comparative Psychology, 108,* 233–242.

Grice, H. P. (1989). *Studies in the way of words.* Cambridge, MA: Harvard University Press.

Gross, J. J., & John, O. P. (2002). Wise emotion regulation. In L. Feldman Barrett & P. Salovey (Eds.), *The wisdom in feeling: Psychological processes in emotional intelligence* (pp. 297–319). New York: Guilford Press.

Gross, J. J., Richards, J. M., & John, O. P. (2006). Emotion regulation in everyday life. In D. K. Snyder, J. A. Simpson, & J. N. Hughes (Eds.), *Emotion regulation in couples and families: Pathways to dysfunction and health.* Washington, DC: American Psychological Association.

Gudykunst, W. B., & Kim, Y. Y. (2003). *Communicating with strangers: An approach to intercultural communication* (4th ed.). New York: McGraw-Hill.

Gudykunst, W. B., & Nishida, T. (1993). Closeness in interpersonal relationships in Japan and the United States. *Research in Social Psychology, 8,* 85–97.

Guerin, B. (1999). Children's intergroup attribution bias for liked and disliked peers. *Journal of Social Psychology, 139,* 583–589.

Guerrero, L. K., & Andersen, P. A. (1998). Jealousy experience and expression in romantic relationships. In P. A. Andersen & L. K. Guerrero (Eds.), *Handbook of communication and emotion* (pp. 155–188). San Diego, CA: Academic Press.

Gumperz, J. J., & Levinson, S. C. (Eds.). (1996). *Rethinking linguistic relativity.* New York: Cambridge University Press.

Haas, S. M., & Stafford, L. (1998). An initial examination of maintenance behaviors in gay and lesbian relationships. *Journal of Social and Personal Relationships, 15,* 846–855.

Haas, S. M., & Stafford, L. (2005). Maintenance behaviors in same-sex and marital relationships: A matched sample comparison. *Journal of Family Communication, 5,* 43–60.

Haden, S. C., & Hojjat, M. (2006). Aggressive responses to betrayal: Type of relationship, victim's sex, and nature of aggression. *Journal of Social and Personal Relationships, 23*(1), 101–116.

Halatsis, P., & Christakis, N. (2009). The challenge of sexual attraction within heterosexuals' cross-sex friendship. *Journal of Social and Personal Relationships, 26*(6–7), 919–937.

Hall, E. T. (1966). A system of the notation of proxemics behavior. *American Anthropologist, 65,* 1003–1026.

Hall, E. T. (1976). *Beyond culture.* Garden City, NY: Anchor.

Hall, E. T. (1981). *The silent language.* New York: Anchor/Doubleday.

Hall, E. T. (1983). *The dance of life: The other dimension of time.* New York: Doubleday.

Hall, E. T. (1997a). Context and meaning. In L. A. Samovar & R. E. Porter (Eds.), *Intercultural communication: A reader* (pp. 45–53). Belmont, CA: Wadsworth.

Hall, E. T. (1997b). Monochronic and polychronic time. In L. A. Samovar & R. E. Porter (Eds.), *Intercultural communication: A reader* (8th ed., pp. 277–284). Belmont, CA: Wadsworth.

Hall, E. T., & Hall, M. R. (1987). *Understanding cultural differences.* Yarmouth, ME: Intercultural Press.

Hall, J. A., Carter, J. D., & Horgan, T. G. (2000). Gender differences in nonverbal communication of emotion. In A. H. Fischer (Ed.), *Gender and emotion: Social psychological perspectives* (pp. 97–117). Cambridge, UK: Cambridge University Press.

Hall, J. A., Park, N., Song, H., & Cody, M. J. (2010). Strategic misrepresentation in online dating: The effects of gender, self-monitoring, and personality traits. *Journal of Social and Personal Relationships, 27*(1), 117–135.

Hammer, M. R., Bennett, M. J., & Wiseman, R. (2003). Measuring intercultural sensitivity: The intercultural development inventory. *International Journal of Intercultural Relations, 27,* 421–443.

Hansen, G. L. (1985). Dating jealousy among college students. *Sex Roles, 12,* 713–721.

Harms, L. S. (1961). Listener judgments of status cues in speech. *Quarterly Journal of Speech, 47,* 164–168.

Harrison, K. (2001). Ourselves, our bodies: Thin-ideal media, self-discrepancies, and eating disorder symptoms in adolescents. *Journal of Social and Clinical Psychology, 20,* 289–323.

Hastorf, A. H., & Cantril, H. (1954). They saw a game: A case study. *Journal of Abnormal and Social Psychology, 49,* 129–134.

Hatfield, E. (1983). Equity theory and research: An overview. In H. H. Blumberg, A. P. Hare, V. Kent, & M. Davies (Eds.), *Small groups and social interaction* (Vol. 2, pp. 401–412). Chichester, UK: Wiley.

Hatfield, E., & Rapson, R. L. (1987). Passionate love: New directions in research. In W. H. Jones & D. Perlman (Eds.), *Advances in personal relationships* (Vol. 1, pp. 109–139). London: Jessica Kingsley.

Hatfield, E. E., & Sprecher, S. (1986). *Mirror, mirror . . . the importance of looks in everyday life.* Albany: State University of New York Press.

Hatfield, E., Traupmann, J., & Sprecher, S. (1984). Older women's perceptions of their intimate relationships. *Journal of Social and Clinical Psychology, 2,* 108–124.

Hatfield, E., Traupmann, J., Sprecher, S., Utne, M., & Hay, M. (1985). Equity in close relationships. In W. Ickes (Ed.), *Compatible and incompatible relationships* (pp. 91–171). New York: Springer-Verlag.

Hauser, T. (2006). *Muhammad Ali: His life and times.* New York: Simon & Schuster.

Hausmann, R., Tyson, L. D., & Zahidi, S. (2010). *The global gender gap: Report 2010.* World Economic Forum Report, Geneva, Switzerland.

Hayashi, G. M., & Strickland, B. R. (1998). Long-term effects of parental divorce on love relationships: Divorce as attachment disruption. *Journal of Social and Personal Relationships, 15,* 23–38.

Hays, R. B. (1988). Friendship. In S. Duck (Ed.), *Handbook of personal relationships: Theory, research, and interventions* (pp. 391–408). Chichester, UK: Wiley.

Heider, F. (1958). *The psychology of interpersonal relations.* New York: Wiley.

Heino, R. D., Ellison, N. B., & Gibbs, J. L. (2010). Relationshopping: Investigating the market metaphor in online dating. *Journal of Social and Personal Relationships, 27*(4), 427–447.

Hendrick, C., & Hendrick, S. S. (1988). Lovers wear rose colored glasses. *Journal of Social and Personal Relationships, 5,* 161–183.

Hendrick, S. S., & Hendrick, C. (1992). *Romantic love.* Thousand Oaks, CA: Sage.

Hendrick, S. S., & Hendrick, C. (2006). Measuring respect in close relationships. *Journal of Social and Personal Relationships, 23,* 881–899.

Heritage, J. C., & Watson, D. R. (1979). Formulations as conversational objectives. In G. Pathas (Ed.), *Everyday language: Studies in ethnomethodology.* New York: Irvington.

Hertwig, R., Davis, J. N., & Sulloway, F. J. (2002). Parental investment: How an equity motive can produce inequality. *Psychological Bulletin, 128,* 728–745.

Herweddingplanner.com (2011, April 29). *Randy Fenoli 'Say Yes to the Dress' wedding gown tips with Chantal Patton of www.herweddingplanner.com*. Retrieved from http://www.youtube.com/watch?v=9T-R3LeFjLU

Heslin, R. (1974, May). *Steps toward a taxonomy of touching*. Paper presented at the annual meeting of the Midwestern Psychological Association, Chicago.

Hetherington, E. M. (1993). An overview of the Virginia longitudinal study of divorce and remarriage with a focus on early adolescence. *Journal of Family Psychology, 7*, 39–56.

Hickson, M., III, Grierson, R. D., & Linder, B. C. (1991). A communication perspective on sexual harassment: Affiliative nonverbal behaviors in asynchronous relationships. *Communication Quarterly, 39*, 111–118.

Higgins, E. T. (1987). Self-discrepancy: A theory relating self and affect. *Psychological Review, 94*, 319–340.

Hill, C. T., Rubin, Z., & Peplau, L. A. (1976). Breakups before marriage: The end of 103 affairs. *Journal of Social Issues, 32*, 147–168.

Hodgins, H. S., & Belch, C. (2000). Interparental violence and nonverbal abilities. *Journal of Nonverbal Behavior, 24*, 3–24.

Hodgson, L. K., & Wertheim, E. H. (2007). Does good emotion management aid forgiving? Multiple dimensions of empathy, emotion management and forgiveness of self and others. *Journal of Social and Personal Relationships, 24*(6), 931–949.

Hofstede, G. (1991). *Cultures and organizations*. London: McGraw-Hill.

Hofstede, G. (1998). I, we, they. In J. N. Martin, T. K. Nakayama, & L. A. Flores (Eds.), *Readings in cultural contexts* (pp. 345–357). Mountain View, CA: Mayfield.

Hofstede, G. (2001). *Culture's consequences* (2nd ed.). Thousand Oaks, CA: Sage.

Hofstede, G. (2009). National cultural dimensions. Retrieved from http://www.geert-hofstede.com/national-culture.html

Honeycutt, J. M. (1999). Typological differences in predicting marital happiness from oral history behaviors and imagined interactions. *Communication Monographs, 66*, 276–291.

Horne, C. F. (1917). *The sacred books and early literature of the East: Vol. II. Egypt*. New York: Parke, Austin, & Lipscomb.

Hovick, S. R. A., Meyers, R. A., & Timmerman, C. E. (2003). E-mail communication in workplace romantic relationships. *Communication Studies, 54*, 468–480.

Howard, P. E. N., Rainie, L., & Jones, S. (2001, November). Days and nights on the Internet: The impact of a diffusing technology. *American Behavioral Scientist, 45*, 383–405.

HRSDC (Human Resources and Skills Development Canada). (2006). Canadians in context—households and families. Retrieved from http://www4.hrsdc.gc.ca/.3ndic.1t.4r@-eng.jsp?iid=37

Hughes, M., Morrison, K., & Asada, K. J. K. (2005). What's love got to do with it? Exploring the impact of maintenance rules, love attitudes, and network support on friends with benefits relationships. *Western Journal of Speech Communication, 69*, 49–66.

Hurley, D. (2005, April 19). Divorce rate: It's not as high as you think. *The New York Times*, p. F7.

Hyde, J. S. (2005). The gender similarities hypothesis. *American Psychologist, 60*, 581–592.

Hyun, J. (2005). *Breaking the bamboo ceiling: Career strategies for Asians*. New York: HarperCollins.

Infante, D. A. (1995). Teaching students to understand and control verbal aggression. *Communication Education, 44*, 51–63.

Infante, D. A., Chandler, T. A., & Rudd, J. E. (1989). Test of an argumentative skill deficiency model of interspousal violence. *Communication Monographs, 56*, 163–177.

Infante, D. A., Myers, S. A., & Burkel, R. A. (1994). Argument and verbal aggression in constructive and destructive family and organizational disagreements. *Western Journal of Communication, 58*, 73–84.

Infante, D. A., & Wigley, C. J. (1986). Verbal aggressiveness: An interpersonal model and measure. *Communication Monographs, 53*, 61–69.

Institute of International Education (IIE). (2011, November 14). Open doors 2011: Report on international education exchange. Retrieved from http://www.iie.org/Research-and-Publications/~/media/Files/Corporate/Open-Doors/Open-Doors-2011-Briefing-Presentation.ashx

Jackson, D. C., Malmstadt, J. R., Larson, C. L., & Davidson, R. J. (2000). Suppression and enhancement of emotional responses to unpleasant pictures. *Psychophysiology, 37*, 515–522.

Jackson, M. (2008). *Distracted: The erosion of attention and the coming dark age*. Amherst, NY: Prometheus Books.

Jacobs, S. (1994). Language and interpersonal communication. In M. L. Knapp & G. R. Miller (Eds.), *Handbook of interpersonal communication* (2nd ed., pp. 199–228). Thousand Oaks, CA: Sage.

Jacobs, S., Dawson, E. J., & Brashers, D. (1996). Information manipulation theory: A replication and assessment. *Communication Monographs, 63*, 70–82.

Janusik, L. A. (2007). Building listening theory: The validation of the conversational listening span. *Communication Studies, 58*(2), 139–156.

John, O. P. (1990). The "Big Five" factor taxonomy: Dimensions of personality in the natural language and in questionnaires. In L. A. Pervin (Ed.), *Handbook of personality: Theory and research* (pp. 66–100). New York: Guilford Press.

John, O. P., Naumann, L., & Soto, C. J. (2008). Paradigm shift to the integrative Big Five trait taxonomy: Discovery, measurement, and conceptual issues. In O. P. John, R. W. Robins, & L. A. Pervin (Eds.), *Handbook of personality: Theory and research* (3rd ed., pp. 114–158). New York: Guilford.

John, O. P., & Gross, J. J. (2004). Healthy and unhealthy emotion regulation: Personality processes, individual differences, and lifespan development. *Journal of Personality, 72,* 1301–1334.

Johnson, A. J., Haigh, M. M., Becker, J. A. H., Craig, E. A., & Wigley, S. (2008). College students' use of relational management strategies in email in long-distance and geographically close relationships. *Journal of Computer-Mediated Communication, 13,* 381–404.

Johnson, A. J., Wittenberg, E., Villagran, M. M., Mazur, M., & Villagran, P. (2003). Relational progression as a dialectic: Examining turning points in communication among friends. *Communication Monographs, 70*(3), 230–249.

Johnson, H. (2004, April 1). Jimmy Jam: Three decades of hits; one seamless partnership. Retrieved from http://mixonline.com/mag/audio_jimmy_jam

Joinson, A. N. (2001, March/April). Self-disclosure in computer-mediated communication: The role of self-awareness and visual anonymity. *European Journal of Social Psychology, 31,* 177–192.

Jones, D. C., Vigfusdottir, T. H., & Lee, Y. (2004). Body image and the appearance culture among adolescent girls and boys: An examination of friends' conversations, peer criticism, appearance magazines, and the internalization of appearance ideals. *Journal of Adolescent Research, 19,* 323–339.

Jones, S. E., & LeBaron, C. D. (2002). Research on the relationship between verbal and nonverbal communication: Emerging integrations. *Journal of Communication, 52,* 499–521.

Jones, T. E. (1999). *If it's broken, you can fix it: Overcoming dysfunction in the workplace.* New York: AMACOM Books.

Jones, W., Moore, D., Scratter, A., & Negel, L. (2001). Interpersonal transgression and betrayals. In R. M. Kowalski (Ed.), *Behaving badly: Aversive behavior in interpersonal relationships* (pp. 233–256). Washington, DC: American Psychological Association.

Jones, W. H., & Burdette, M. P. (1994). Betrayal in relationships. In A. L. Weber & J. H. Harvey (Eds.), *Perspectives on close relationships* (pp. 243–262). Boston: Allyn and Bacon.

Jourard, S. M. (1964). *The transparent self.* New York: Van Nostrand Reinhold.

Kagawa, N., & McCornack, S. A. (2004, November). *Collectivistic Americans and individualistic Japanese: A cross-cultural comparison of parental understanding.* Paper presented at the annual meeting of the National Communication Association, Chicago.

Kaharit, K., Zachau, G., Eklof, M., Sandsjo, L., & Moller, C. (2003). Assessment of hearing and hearing disorders in rock/jazz musicians. *International Journal of Audiology, 42,* 279–288.

Kahneman, D. (1973). *Attention and effort.* Englewood Cliffs, NJ: Prentice Hall.

Kassing, J. W. (2008). Consider this: A comparison of factors contributing to employees' expressions of dissent. *Communication Quarterly, 56*(3), 342–355.

Katz, D., & Kahn, R. (1978). *The social psychology of organizations* (2nd ed.). New York: Wiley.

Katz, J. (1983). A theory of qualitative methodology. In R. M. Emerson (Ed.), *Contemporary field research: A collection of readings* (pp. 127–148). Prospect Heights, IL: Waveland Press.

Katz, J., & Farrow, S. (2000). Discrepant self-views and young women's sexual and emotional adjustment. *Sex Roles, 42,* 781–805.

Keashly, L., & Neuman, J. H. (2005). Bullying in the workplace: Its impact and management. *Employee Rights and Employment Policy Journal, 8,* 335–373.

Keashly, L., Trott, V., & MacLean, L. M. (1994). Abusive behavior in the workplace: A preliminary investigation. *Violence and Victims, 9,* 341–357.

Keck, K. L., & Samp, J. A. (2007). The dynamic nature of goals and message production as revealed in a sequential analysis of conflict interactions. *Human Communication Research, 33,* 27–47.

Keesing, R. M. (1974). Theories of culture. *Annual Review of Anthropology, 3,* 73–97.

Kellas, J. K. (2005). Family ties: Communicating identity through jointly told family stories. *Communication Monographs, 72*(4), 365–389.

Kellermann, K. (1989). The negativity effect in interaction: It's all in your point of view. *Human Communication Research, 16,* 147–183.

Kellermann, K. (1991). The conversation MOP: Progression through scenes in discourse. *Human Communication Research, 17,* 385–414.

Kelley, H. H., & Thibaut, J. W. (1978). *Interpersonal relations: A theory of interdependence.* New York: Wiley.

Kelly, A. E., & McKillop, K. J. (1996). Consequences of revealing personal secrets. *Psychological Bulletin, 120,* 450–465.

Kennedy, D. (2008). *Rock on.* Chapel Hill, NC: Algonquin Books.

Kennedy, T. L. M., Smith, A., Wells, A. T., & Wellman, B. (2008, October 19). Networked families: Parents and spouses are using the Internet and cell phones to create a "new connectedness" that builds on remote connections and shared Internet experiences. *Pew Internet & American Life Project.* Retrieved from http://www.pewinternet.org/

Kimpel, D. (2010). ASCAP Rhythm and Soul Heritage Award Jimmy Jam & Terry Lewis. Retrieved from http://www.ascap.com/eventsawards/awards/rsawards/2005/heritage.aspx

King, S. K. (2001). Territoriality. Retrieved from http://www.huna.org/html/territor.html

Klein, R. C. A. (1998). Conflict and violence in the family: Cross-disciplinary issues. In R. C. A. Klein (Ed.), *Multidisciplinary perspectives on family violence* (pp. 1–13). New York: Routledge.

Klopf, D. W. (2001). *Intercultural encounters: The fundamentals of intercultural communication* (5th ed.). Englewood, CO: Morton.

Kluger, J. (2011, October 3). Playing favorites. *Time.* Retrieved from http://www.time.com/time/magazine/article/0,9171,2094371,00.html

Knapp, M. (1984). *Interpersonal communication and human relationships.* Boston: Allyn & Bacon.

Knapp, M. L., & Hall, J. A. (2002). *Nonverbal communication in human interaction* (5th ed.). Belmont, CA: Wadsworth/Thomson Learning.

Knobloch, L. K. (2005). Evaluating a contextual model of responses to relational uncertainty increasing events: The role of intimacy, appraisals, and emotions. *Human Communication Research, 31*(1), 60–101.

Koerner, A. F., & Fitzpatrick, M. A. (2002). Toward a theory of family communication. *Communication Theory, 12,* 70–91.

Koerner, A. F., & Fitzpatrick, M. A. (2006). Family communication patterns theory: A social cognitive approach. In D. O. Braithwaite & L. A. Baxter (Eds.), *Engaging theories in family communication: Multiple perspectives* (pp. 50–65). Thousand Oaks, CA: Sage.

Koerner, S. S., Wallace, S., Lehman, S. J., & Raymond, M. (2002). Mother-to-daughter disclosure after divorce: A double-edged sword? *Journal of Child and Family Studies, 11,* 469–483.

Kogan, L. (2006, August). The O interview: Gayle and Oprah, uncensored. *O, the Oprah Magazine.* Retrieved from http://www.oprah.com/omagazine/Gayle-King-and-Oprah-Uncensored-The-O-Magazine-Interview/1

Kostiuk, L. M., & Fouts, G. T. (2002). Understanding of emotions and emotion regulation in adolescent females with conduct problems: A qualitative analysis. *The Qualitative Report, 7,* 1–10.

Kotzé, M., & Venter, I. (2011). Differences in emotional intelligence between effective and ineffective leaders in the public sector: An empirical study. *International Review of Administrative Sciences, 77*(2), 397–427.

Kowalski, R. M., Walker, S., Wilkinson, R., Queen, A., & Sharpe, B. (2003). Lying, cheating, complaining, and other aversive interpersonal behaviors: A narrative examination of the darker side of relationships. *Journal of Social and Personal Relationships, 20,* 471–490.

Kowner, R. (1996). Facial asymmetry and attractiveness judgments in developmental perspective. *Journal of Experimental Psychology: Human Perception and Performance, 22,* 662–675.

Kozan, M., & Ergin, C. (1998). Preference for third-party help in conflict management in the United States and Turkey. *Journal of Cross-Cultural Psychology, 29,* 525–539.

Kramarae, C. (1981). *Women and men speaking: Frameworks for analysis.* Rowley, MA: Newbury House.

Krause, J. (2001). *Properties of naturally produced clear speech at normal rates and implications for intelligibility enhancement.* Unpublished doctoral dissertation, Massachusetts Institute of Technology, Cambridge, MA.

Kreider, R. M. (2005). *Number, timing, and duration of marriages and divorces: 2001.* Washington, DC: U.S. Census Bureau.

Kreps, G. L. (1990). *Organizational communication.* New York: Longman.

Krishnakumar, A., Buehler, C., & Barber, B. K. (2003). Youth perceptions of interparental conflict, ineffective parenting, and youth problem behaviors in European-American and African-American families. *Journal of Social and Personal Relationships, 20*(2), 239–260.

Krusiewicz, E. S., & Wood, J. T. (2001). He was our child from the moment we walked in that room: Entrance stories of adoptive parents. *Journal of Social and Personal Relationships, 18*(6), 785–803.

Kubany, E. S., Richard, D. C., Bauer, G. B., & Muraoka, M. Y. (1992). Impact of assertive and accusatory communication of distress and anger: A verbal component analysis. *Aggressive Behavior, 18,* 337–347.

Kuhn, J. L. (2001). Toward an ecological humanistic psychology. *Journal of Humanistic Psychology, 41,* 9–24.

Kurdek, L. A. (2005). What do we know about gay and lesbian couples? *Current Directions in Psychological Science, 14,* 251–254.

Kurdek, L. A. (2008). Differences between partners from Black and White heterosexual dating couples in a path model of relational commitment. *Journal of Social and Personal Relationships, 25,* 51–70.

Kuttler, A. F., LaGreca, A. M., & Prinstein, M. J. (1999). Friendship qualities and social-emotional functioning of adolescents with close, cross-sex friends. *Journal of Research on Adolescence, 9,* 339–366.

LaFollette, H., & Graham, G. (1986). Honesty and intimacy. *Journal of Social and Personal Relationships, 3,* 3–18.

Langdridge, D., & Butt, T. (2004). The fundamental attribution error: A phenomenological critique. *British Journal of Social Psychology, 43,* 357–369.

Lareau, A. (2003). *Unequal childhoods: Class, race, and family life.* Berkeley: University of California Press.

Larsen, R. J., & Ketelaar, T. (1991). Personality and susceptibility to positive and negative emotional states. *Journal of Personality and Social Psychology, 61,* 132–140.

Larson, J. R. (1984). The performance feedback process: A preliminary model. *Organizational Behavior and Human Performance, 33,* 42–76.

Lasswell, H. D. (1948). The structure and function of communication in society. In L. Bryson (Ed.), *The communication of ideas* (pp. 32–51). New York: Harper & Row.

Lavy, S., Mikulincer, M., Shaver, P. R., & Gillath, O. (2009). Intrusiveness in romantic relationships: A cross-cultural perspective on imbalances between proximity and autonomy. *Journal of Social and Personal Relationships, 26*(6–7), 989–1008.

Le, B., Korn, M. S., Crockett, E. E., & Loving, T. J. (2010). Missing you maintains us: Missing a romantic partner, commitment, relationship maintenance, and physical infidelity. *Journal of Social and Personal Relationships, 28,* 653–667.

Leary, M. R. (2001). Toward a conceptualization of interpersonal rejection. In M. R. Leary (Ed.), *Interpersonal rejection* (pp. 3–20). New York: Oxford University Press.

Lee, J. A. (1973). *The colors of love: An exploration of the ways of loving.* Don Mills, Ontario: New Press.

Lehrer, J. (2009, May 18). Don't!: The secret of self-control. *The New Yorker.* Retrieved from http://www.newyorker.com/reporting/2009/05/18/090518fa_fact_lehrer

Leiner, D. (Director), Hurwitz, J. (Writer), Schlossberg, H. (Writer), Kahane, N. (Producer), & Shapiro, G. (Producer). (2004). *Harold and Kumar go to White Castle* [Motion picture]. United States: New Line Cinema.

Lemerise, E. A., & Dodge, K. A. (1993). The development of anger and hostile interactions. In M. Lewis and J. M. Haviland (Eds.), *Handbook of emotions* (pp. 537–546). New York: Guilford Press.

Lenard, D. M. (2006). Through the wall: A cross-cultural guide to doing business in China. *Asia Times Online.* Retrieved from www.atimes.com

Lenhart, A., Purcell, K., Smith, A., & Zickuhr, K. (2010). Social media & young adults. *Pew Internet & American Life Project.* Retrieved from http://www.pewinternet.org/Reports/2010/Social-Media-and-Young-Adults.aspx

Levine, T. R., McCornack, S. A., & Baldwin Avery, P. (1992). Sex differences in emotional reactions to discovered deception. *Communication Quarterly, 40,* 289–296.

Levinson, S. C. (1985). *Pragmatics.* Cambridge, UK: Cambridge University Press.

Lewellen, W. (2008, July 7). Brenda Villa: The American saint of water polo. *Women's Sports Foundation.* Retrieved from http://66.40.5.5/Content/Articles/Athletes/About-Athletes/B/Brenda-Villa-saint-of-Water-Polo.aspx

Lippa, R. A. (2002). *Gender, nature, and nurture.* Mahwah, NJ: Erlbaum.

Lippmann, W. (1922). *Public opinion.* New York: Harcourt Brace.

Liu, B. M. (2011, January 8). Parents like Amy Chua are the reason why Asian-Americans like me are in therapy [Blog post]. Retrieved from http://bettymingliu.com

Lopes, P. N., Salovey, P., Cote, S., & Beers, M. (2005). Emotion regulation abilities and the quality of social interaction. *Emotion, 5,* 113–118.

Luft, J. (1970). *Group processes: An introduction to group dynamics* (2nd ed.). Palo Alto, CA: National Press Books.

Lulofs, R. S., & Cahn, D. D. (2000). *Conflict: From theory to action* (2nd ed.). Needham Heights, MA: Allyn & Bacon.

Luscombe, B. (2010, November 18). Who needs marriage? A changing institution. *Time.* Retrieved from http://www.time.com/time/magazine/article/0,9171,2032116,00.html

Lustig, M. W., & Koester, J. (2006). *Intercultural competence: Interpersonal communication across cultures* (5th ed.). Boston: Allyn and Bacon.

Macrae, C. N., & Bodenhausen, G. V. (2001). Social cognition: Categorical person perception. *British Journal of Psychology, 92,* 239–255.

Maeda, E., & Ritchie, L. D. (2003). The concept of Shinyuu in Japan: A replication of and comparison to Cole and Bradac's study on U.S. friendship. *Journal of Social and Personal Relationships, 20,* 579–598.

Malandro, L. A., & Barker, L. L. (1983). *Nonverbal communication.* Reading, MA: Addison-Wesley.

Malcolm X. (1964). Personal letter. Retrieved from http://en.wikisource.org/wiki/Letter_from_Malcolm_X

Malis, R. S., & Roloff, M. E. (2006). Demand/withdraw patterns in serial arguments: Implications for well-being. *Human Communication Research, 32,* 198–216.

Manusov, V., & Hegde, R. (1993). Communicative outcomes of stereotype-based expectancies: An observational study of cross-cultural dyads. *Communication Quarterly, 41,* 338–354.

Markey, P. M., & Markey, C. N. (2007). Romantic ideals, romantic obtainment, and relationship experiences: The complementarity of interpersonal traits among romantic partners. *Journal of Social and Personal Relationships, 24*(4), 517–533.

Martin, J. N., & Nakayama, T. K. (1997). *Intercultural communication in contexts.* Mountain View, CA: Mayfield.

Martin, W., & LaVan, H. (2010). Workplace bullying: A review of litigated cases. *Employee Responsibilities and Rights Journal, 22*(3), 175–194.

Marzano, R. J., & Arredondo, D. E. (1996). *Tactics for thinking.* Aurora, CO: Mid Continent Regional Educational Laboratory.

Mashek, D. J., & Aron, A. (2004). *Handbook of closeness and intimacy.* Mahwah, NJ: Erlbaum.

Maslow, A. H. (1970). *Motivation and personality* (2nd ed.). New York: Harper & Row.

Massengill, J., & Nash, M. (2009). *Ethnocentrism, intercultural willingness to communicate, and international interaction amongst U.S. college students.* Paper presented at the annual meeting of the International Communication Association, Chicago, IL.

Matlin, M., & Stang, D. (1978). *The Pollyanna principle: Selectivity in language, memory, and thought.* Cambridge, MA: Schenkman.

Mauss, I. B., Levenson, R. W., McCarter, L., Wilhelm, F. H., & Gross, J. J. (2005). The tie that binds: Coherence among emotion experience, behavior, and physiology. *Emotion, 5,* 175–190.

Mayer, J. D., & Salovey, P. (1997). What is emotional intelligence? In P. Salovey & J. D. Sluyter (Eds.), *Emotional development and emotional intelligence* (pp. 3–31). New York: Basic Books.

Mayer, J. D., Salovey, P., & Caruso, D. R. (2004). Emotional intelligence: Theory, findings and implications. *Psychological Inquiry, 15*(3), 197–215.

McCornack, S. A. (1997). The generation of deceptive messages: Laying the groundwork for a viable theory of interpersonal deception. In J. O. Greene (Ed.), *Message production: Advances in communication theory* (pp. 91–126). Mahwah, NJ: Erlbaum.

McCornack, S. A. (2008). Information manipulation theory: Explaining how deception works. In L. A. Baxter & D. O. Braithwaite (Eds.), *Engaging theories in interpersonal communication: Multiple perspectives* (pp. 215–226). Thousand Oaks, CA: Sage.

McCornack, S. A., & Husband, R. (1986, May). *The evolution of a long-term organizational conflict: A design logic approach.* Paper presented at the annual meeting of the International Communication Association, Chicago, IL.

McCornack, S. A., & Levine, T. R. (1990). When lies are uncovered: Emotional and relational outcomes of discovered deception. *Communication Monographs, 57,* 119–138.

McCrae, R. R. (2001). Trait psychology and culture. *Journal of Personality, 69,* 819–846.

McCrae, R. R., & Costa, P. T., Jr. (2001). A five-factor theory of personality. In L. A. Pervin and O. P. John (Eds.), *Handbook of personality: Theory and research* (2nd ed., pp. 139–153). New York: Guilford Press.

McCroskey, J. C., & Richmond, V. P. (1987). Willingness to communicate. In J. C. McCroskey & J. A. Daly (Eds.), *Personality and interpersonal communication* (pp. 129–156). Beverly Hills, CA: Sage.

McEwan, B., Babin Gallagher, B., & Farinelli, L. (2008, November). *The end of a friendship: Friendship dissolution reasons and methods.* Paper presented at the annual meeting of the National Communication Association, San Diego, CA.

McGlynn, J. (2007, November). *More connections, less connection: An examination of computer-mediated communication as relationship maintenance.* Paper presented at the annual meeting of the National Communication Association, Chicago, IL.

McGuirk, R. (2011, September 14). Australian passport gender options: 'Transgender' will be included. *Associated Press.* Retrieved from http://www.huffingtonpost.com/2011/09/14/australia-passport-gender_n_963386.html

McIntosh, P. (1999). White privilege: Unpacking the invisible knapsack. In E. Lee, D. Menkart, & M. Okazawa-Rey (Eds.), *Beyond heroes and holidays: A practical guide to K–12 antiracist, multicultural education and staff development* (pp. 79–82). Washington, DC: Network of Educators on the Americas.

McLaughlin, M. L., & Cody, M. J. (1982). Awkward silences: Behavioral antecedents and consequences of the conversational lapse. *Human Communication Research, 8,* 299–316.

McNaughton, D., Hamlin, D., McCarthy, J., Head-Reeves, D., & Schreiner, M. (2007). Learning to listen: Teaching an active listening strategy to preservice education professionals. *Topics in Early Childhood Special Education, 27*(4), 223–231.

Mead, G. H. (1934). *Mind, self, and society.* Chicago: University of Chicago Press.

Mehrabian, A. (1972). *Nonverbal communication.* Chicago: Aldine.

Mercer, J. (1998, March 20). An unusual reunion at Gallaudet: 10 years after push for "Deaf President Now." *The Chronicle of Higher Education.* Retrieved from http://www.chronicle.com/article/An-Unusual-Reunion-at/99078/

Merriam-Webster dictionary online (2011). Definition of bear. Retrieved from http://www.merriam-webster.com/dictionary/bear

Messman, S. J., Canary, D. J., & Hause, K. S. (1994, February). *Motives, strategies, and equity in the maintenance of opposite-sex friendships.* Paper presented at the Western States Communication Association convention, San Jose, CA.

Messman, S. J., Canary, D. J., & Hause, K. S. (2000). Motives to remain platonic, equity, and the use of maintenance strategies in opposite-sex friendships. *Journal of Social and Personal Relationships, 17,* 67–94.

Metts, S., & Chronis, H. (1986, May). *Relational deception: An exploratory analysis.* Paper presented at the annual meeting of the International Communication Association, Chicago, IL.

Metts, S., & Planalp, S. (2002). Emotional communication. In M. L. Knapp & J. A. Daly (Eds.), *Handbook of interpersonal communication* (pp. 339–373). Thousand Oaks, CA: Sage.

Meyer, S. (2005). *Twilight.* New York: Little, Brown.

Michalos, A. C. (1991). *Global report on student well-being: Vol. 1. Life satisfaction and happiness.* New York: Springer-Verlag.

Michaud, S. G., & Aynesworth, H. (1989). *The only living witness: A true account of homicidal insanity.* New York: Signet.

Mickelson, K. D., Kessler, R. C., & Shaver, P. R. (1997). Adult attachment in a nationally representative sample. *Journal of Personality and Social Psychology, 73,* 1092–1106.

Mies, M. (1991). *Patriarchy and accumulation on a world scale: Women in the international division of labor.* London: Zed Books.

Miller, G. R., & Steinberg, M. (1975). *Between people: A new analysis of interpersonal communication.* Chicago: Science Research Associates.

Miller, H., & Arnold, J. (2001). Breaking away from grounded identity: Women academics on the Web. *CyberPsychology and Behavior, 4,* 95–108.

Miller, K. (1995). *Organizational communication: Approaches and processes.* Belmont, CA: Wadsworth.

Miller, L., Hefner, V., & Scott, A. (2007, May). *Turning points in dyadic friendship development and termination.* Paper presented at the annual meeting of the International Communication Association, San Francisco, CA.

Miller, R. S., Perlman, D., & Brehm, S. S. (2007). Love: Chapter 8. In R. S. Miller, D. Perlman, & S. S. Brehm (Eds.), *Intimate relationships* (pp. 244–275). New York: McGraw-Hill.

Millman, J. (1999, August 10). Brilliant careers: Fred Rogers. *Salon.com.* Retrieved from http://www.salon.com/1999/08/10/rogers_2/singleton/

Mister Rogers. (n.d.). *TVAcres.* Retrieved from http://www.tvacres.com/child_mrrogers.htm

Mitchell, M. (1936). *Gone with the wind.* New York: Macmillan.

Mohammed, R., & Hussein, A. (2008, August). *Communication climate and organizational performance.* Paper presented to the Eighth International Conference on Knowledge, Culture & Changes in Organizations, Cambridge University (UK).

Mongeau, P. A., Hale, J. L., & Alles, M. (1994). An experimental investigation of accounts and attributions following sexual infidelity. *Communication Monographs, 61,* 326–344.

Mongeau, P. A., Ramirez, A., & Vorrell, M. (2003, February). *Friends with benefits: Initial explorations of sexual, nonromantic relationships.* Paper presented at the annual meeting of the Western Communication Association, Salt Lake City, UT.

Monsour, M. (1997). Communication and cross-sex friendships across the life cycle: A review of the literature. In B. Burleson (Ed.), *Communication Yearbook 20* (pp. 375–414). Thousand Oaks, CA: Sage.

Montagu, M. F. A. (1971). *Touching: The human significance of the skin.* New York: Columbia University Press.

Morrison, K., Lee, C. M., Wiedmaier, B., & Dibble, J. L. (2008, November). *The influence of MySpace and Facebook events on interpersonal relationships.* Paper presented at the annual meeting of the National Communication Association, San Diego, CA.

Morrison, K., & McCornack, S. A. (2011). *Studying attitudes toward LGBT persons in mid-Michigan: Challenges and goals.* Technical report presented at the annual meeting of the Michigan Fairness Forum, Lansing, MI.

Mosher, C., & Danoff-Burg, S. (2007). College students' life priorities: The influence of gender and gender-linked personality traits. *Gender Issues, 24*(2). doi:10.1007/s12147-007-9002-z

Mulac, A., Bradac, J. J., & Mann, S. K. (1985). Male/female language differences and attributional consequences in children's television. *Human Communication Research, 11,* 481–506.

Mulac, A., Incontro, C. R., & James, M. R. (1985). Comparison of the gender-linked language effect and sex role stereotypes. *Journal of Personality and Social Psychology, 49,* 1098–1109.

Munro, K. (2002). Conflict in cyberspace: How to resolve conflict online. In J. Suler (Ed.), *The psychology of cyberspace.* Retrieved from http://www.usr.rider.edu/~suler/psycyber/conflict.html

Myers, D. G. (2002). *The pursuit of happiness: Discovering the pathway to fulfillment, well-being, and enduring personal joy.* New York: HarperCollins.

Myers, S. A., Knox, R. L., Pawlowski, D. R., & Ropog, B. L. (1999). Perceived communication openness and functional communication skills among organizational peers. *Communication Reports, 12,* 71–83.

National Communication Association (NCA). (1999). *NCA credo for ethical communication.* Retrieved from http://www.natcom.org

National Communication Association (NCA). (2002, October). *Communication research: Profile of a discipline.* Presentation made to the National Research Council. Retrieved from http://www.natcom.org/nca/Template2.asp?bid=1345

National Communication Association (NCA). (n.d.). *The field of communication.* Retrieved from http://www.natcom.org/Tertiary.aspx?id=236

Neuliep, J. W., & McCroskey, J. C. (1997). The development of a U.S. and generalized ethnocentrism scale. *Communication Research Reports, 14,* 385–398.

Nishiyama, K. (1971). Interpersonal persuasion in a vertical society. *Speech Monographs, 38,* 148–154.

Nofsinger, R. E. (1999). *Everyday conversation.* Prospect Heights, IL: Waveland Press.

Nutt, A. (2011). How to communicate in a global world. Woodridge Cross-Cultural Management Articles. Retrieved from http://cross-cultural-management.bestmanagementarticles.com/a-5711-how-to-communicate-in-a-global-world.aspx

Oetzel, J., Ting-Toomey, S., Matsumoto, T., Yokochi, Y., Pan, X., Takai, J., & Wilcox, R. (2001). Face and facework in conflict: A cross-cultural comparison of China, Germany, Japan, and the United States. *Communication Monographs, 68,* 235–258.

Ohbuchi, K., & Sato, K. (1994). Children's reactions to mitigating accounts: Apologies, excuses, and intentionality of harm. *Journal of Social Psychology, 134,* 5–17.

O'Keefe, B. J. (1988). The logic of message design. *Communication Monographs, 55,* 80–103.

O'Leary, K. D., & Vivian, D. (1990). Physical aggression in marriage. In F. D. Fincham & T. N. Bradbury (Eds.), *The psychology of marriage: Basic issues and applications* (pp. 323–348). New York: Guilford Press.

Ophir, E., Nass, C. I., & Wagner, A. D. (2012). Cognitive control in media multitaskers. *Proceedings of the National Academy of Sciences.* Retrieved from http://www.pnas.org/content/106/37/15583

Oravec, J. (2000). Internet and computer technology hazards: Perspectives for family counseling. *British Journal of Guidance and Counselling, 28,* 309–324.

Orbe, M. P. (1998). *Constructing co-cultural theory: An explication of culture, power, and communication.* Thousand Oaks, CA: Sage.

Palmer, M. T., & Simmons, K. B. (1995). Communicating intentions through nonverbal behaviors: Conscious and nonconscious encoding of liking. *Human Communication Research, 22,* 128–160.

Palmer Stadium. (n.d.). Retrieved from http://football.ballparks.com/NCAA/Ivy/Princeton/index.htm

Park, H. S., & Guan, X. (2006). The effects of national culture and face concerns on intention to apologize: A comparison of the USA and China. *Journal of Intercultural Communication Research, 35*(3), 183–204.

Park, H. S., Levine, T. R., McCornack, S. A., Morrison, K., & Ferrara, M. (2002). How people really detect lies. *Communication Monographs, 69,* 144–157.

Parkinson, B., Totterdell, P., Briner, R. B., & Reynolds, S. (1996). *Changing moods: The psychology of mood and mood regulation.* London: Longman.

Parks, M. R. (1994). Communicative competence and interpersonal control. In M. L. Knapp & G. R. Miller (Eds.), *Handbook of interpersonal communication* (2nd ed., pp. 589–620). Beverly Hills, CA: Sage.

Parks, M. R. (2007). *Personal relationships and personal networks.* Hillsdale, NJ: Erlbaum.

Parks, M. R., & Adelman, M. B. (1983). Communication networks and the development of romantic relationships: An expansion of uncertainty reduction theory. *Human Communication Research, 10,* 55–79.

Parks, M. R., & Floyd, K. (1996). Making friends in cyberspace. *Journal of Communication, 46,* 80–97.

Patterson, B. R. (2007). Relationship development revisited: A preliminary look at communication in friendship over the lifespan. *Communication Research Reports, 24*(1), 29–37.

Patterson, M. L. (1988). Functions of nonverbal behavior in close relationships. In S. W. Duck (Ed.), *Handbook of personal relationships* (pp. 41–56). New York: Wiley.

Patterson, M. L. (1995). A parallel process model of nonverbal communication. *Journal of Nonverbal Behavior, 19,* 3–29.

Payne, M. J., & Sabourin, T. C. (1990). Argumentative skill deficiency and its relationship to quality of marriage. *Communication Research Reports, 7,* 121–124.

Pennebaker, J. W. (1997). *Opening up: The healing power of expressing emotions.* New York: Guilford Press.

Pennington, N. (2009, November). *What it means to be a (Facebook) friend: Navigating friendship on social network sites.* Paper presented at the annual meeting of the National Communication Association, Chicago, IL.

Pennsylvania Dutch Country Welcome Center (n.d.). *The Amish: FAQs.* Retrieved from http://www.padutch.com/atafaq.shtml

Peplau, L. A., & Spalding, L. R. (2000). The close relationships of lesbians, gay men and bisexuals. In C. Hendrick & S. S. Hendrick (Eds.), *Close relationships: A sourcebook* (pp. 111–123). Thousand Oaks, CA: Sage.

Pervin, L. A. (1993). Affect and personality. In M. Lewis & J. M. Haviland (Eds.), *Handbook of emotions* (pp. 301–311). New York: Guilford Press.

Peterson, D. R. (2002). Conflict. In H. H. Kelley et al. (Eds.), *Close relationships* (2nd ed., pp. 360–396). Clinton Corners, NY: Percheron Press.

Petronio, S. (2000). The boundaries of privacy: Praxis of everyday life. In S. Petronio (Ed.), *Balancing the secrets of private disclosures* (pp. 37–49). Mahwah, NJ: Erlbaum.

Petronio, S., & Caughlin, J. P. (2006). Communication privacy management theory: Understanding families. In D. O. Braithwaite & L. A. Baxter (Eds.), *Engaging theories in family communication: Multiple perspectives* (pp. 35–49). Thousand Oaks, CA: Sage.

Philpott, T. (2004, October). Stop stop-loss. Retrieved from http://www.moaa.org/todaysofficer/columnists/Philpott/Stop.asp

Pierce, C. A., & Aguinis, H. (2009). Moving beyond a legal-centric approach to managing workplace romances: Organizationally sensible recommendations for HR leaders. *Human Resource Management, 48*(3), 447–464.

Planalp, S., & Honeycutt, J. M. (1985). Events that increase uncertainty in personal relationships. *Human Communication Research, 11*, 593–604.

Plutchik, R. (1980). *Emotions: A psycho-evolutionary synthesis.* New York: Harper & Row.

Plutchik, R. (1993). Emotions and their vicissitudes: Emotions and psychopathology. In M. Lewis & J. M. Haviland (Eds.), *Handbook of emotions* (pp. 53–66). New York: Guilford Press.

Pomerantz, A. (1990). On the validity and generalizability of conversation analytic methods: Conversation analytic claims. *Communication Monographs, 57*, 231–235.

Price, J. (1999). *Navigating differences: Friendships between gay and straight men.* Binghamton, NY: The Haworth Press.

Privitera, C., & Campbell, M. A. (2009). Cyberbullying: The new face of workplace bullying? *Cyberpsychology & Behavior, 12*(4), 395–400.

Pruitt, D. G., & Carnevale, P. J. (1993). *Negotiation in social conflict.* Monterey, CA: Brooks-Cole.

Pyszczynski, T., Greenberg, J., Solomon, S., Arndt, J., & Schimel, J. (2004). Why do people need self-esteem? A theoretical and empirical review. *Psychological Bulletin, 130*(3), 435–468.

Quan-Haase, A., Cothrel, J., & Wellman, B. (2005). Instant messaging for collaboration: A case study of a high-tech firm. *Journal of Computer-Mediated Communication, 10.* Retrieved from http://jcmc.indiana.edu/vol10/issue4/quan-haase.html

Quenqua, D. (2009). I love you, man (as a friend). *The New York Times.* Retrieved from http://www.nytimes.com

Rabby, M. K. (1997, November). *Maintaining relationships via electronic mail.* Paper presented at the annual meeting of the National Communication Association, Chicago, IL.

Rahim, M. A., & Mager, N. R. (1995). Confirmatory factor analysis of the styles of handling interpersonal conflict: First-order factor model and its invariance across groups. *Journal of Applied Psychology, 80*, 122–132.

Rainey, V. P. (2000, December). The potential for miscommunication using email as a source of communications. *Transactions of the Society for Design and Process Science, 4*, 21–43.

Ramasubramanian, S. (2010). Testing the cognitive-affective consistency model of intercultural attitudes: Do stereotypical perceptions influence prejudicial feelings? *Journal of Intercultural Communication Research, 39*(2), 105–121.

Ramirez-Sanchez, R. (2008). Marginalization from within: Expanding co-cultural theory through the experience of the Afro punk. *The Howard Journal of Communications, 19,* 89–104.

Randall, W. S. (1998). *George Washington: A life.* New York: Owl Books, Henry Holt.

Rawlins, W. K. (1992). *Friendship matters: Communication, dialectics, and the life course.* New York: Aldine de Gruyter.

Rawlins, W. K. (1994). Being there and growing apart: Sustaining friendships during adulthood. In D. J. Canary & L. Stafford (Eds.), *Communication and relational maintenance* (pp. 275–294). New York: Academic Press.

Ray, J. J. (1972). A new balanced F scale, and its relation to social class. *Australian Psychologist, 7*, 155–166.

Reeder, H. M. (2003). The effect of gender role orientation on same- and cross-sex friendship formation. *Sex Roles, 49*, 143–152.

Regan, P. C., Kocan, E. R., & Whitlock, T. (1998). Ain't love grand: A prototype analysis of the concept of romantic love. *Journal of Social and Personal Relationships, 15*, 411–420.

Regional vocabularies of American English. (n.d.). In *Wikipedia.* Retrieved from http://en.wikipedia.org/wiki/Regional_vocabularies_of_American_English

Reis, H. T., & Patrick, B. C. (1996). Attachment and intimacy: Component processes. In E. T. Higgins, & A. W. Kruglanski (Eds.), *Social psychology: Handbook of basic principles* (pp. 523–563). New York: Guilford Press.

Reis, H. T., & Shaver, P. (1988). Intimacy as an interpersonal process. In S. W. Duck (Ed.), *Handbook of personal relationships* (pp. 367–389). New York: Wiley.

Reuters. (2004, August 18). Army guardsman sues to get out. *The Washington Post.* Retrieved from http://www.washingtonpost.com/wp-dyn/articles/A9535-2004Aug17.html

Riach, K., & Wilson, F. (2007). Don't screw the crew: Exploring the rules of engagement in organizational romance. *British Journal of Management, 18*, 79–92.

Richards, J. M., Butler, E. A., & Gross, J. J. (2003). Emotion regulation in romantic relationships: The cognitive consequences of concealing feelings. *Journal of Social and Personal Relationships, 20,* 599–620.

Ridge, R. D., & Berscheid, E. (1989, May). *On loving and being in love: A necessary distinction.* Paper presented at the annual convention of the Midwestern Psychological Association, Chicago, IL.

Riedy, M. K., & Wen, J. H. (2010). Electronic surveillance of Internet access in the American workplace: Implications for management. *Information & Communications Technology Law, 19*(1), 87–99.

Riela, S., Rodriguez, G., Aron, A., Xu, X., & Acevedo, B. P. (2010). Experiences of falling in love: Investigating culture, ethnicity, gender, and speed. *Journal of Social and Personal Relationships, 27,* 473–493.

Rintel, E. S., & Pittam, J. (1997). Strangers in a strange land: Interaction management on Internet relay chat. *Human Communication Research, 23,* 507–534.

Ritchie, L. D., & Fitzpatrick, M. A. (1990). Family communication patterns: Measuring interpersonal perceptions of interpersonal relationships. *Communication Research, 17,* 523–544.

Rodrigues, L. N., & Kitzmann, K. M. (2007). Coping as a mediator between interparental conflict and adolescents' romantic attachment. *Journal of Social and Personal Relationships, 24*(3), 423–439.

Rohlfing, M. E. (1995). Doesn't anybody stay in one place anymore? An exploration of the under-studied phenomenon of long-distance relationships. In J. T. Wood & S. Duck (Eds.), *Under-studied relationships: Off the beaten track* (pp. 173–196). Thousand Oaks, CA: Sage.

Roloff, M. E., & Soule, K. P. (2002). Interpersonal conflict: A review. In M. L. Knapp & J. A. Daly (Eds.), *Handbook of interpersonal communication* (3rd ed., pp. 475–528). Thousand Oaks, CA: Sage.

Rosenburg, M. (1965). *Society and the adolescent self-image.* Princeton, NJ: Princeton University Press.

Rosenfeld, H. M. (1987). Conversational control functions of nonverbal behavior. In A.W. Siegman & S. Feldstein (Eds.), *Nonverbal behavior and communication* (2nd ed., pp. 563–602). Hillsdale, NJ: Erlbaum.

Rosenfeld, L. B., & Welsh, S. M. (1985). Differences in self-disclosure in dual-career and single-career marriages. *Communication Monographs, 52,* 253–263.

Rothbard, M. N. (1999). *Conceived in liberty* (Vol. 4). Auburn, AL: Mises Institute.

Rothbart, M. K., Ahadi, S. A., & Evans, D. E. (2000). Temperament and personality: Origins and outcomes. *Journal of Personality and Social Psychology, 78,* 122–135.

Rowatt, W. D., Cunningham, M. R., & Druen, P. B. (1998). Deception to get a date. *Personality and Social Psychology Bulletin, 24,* 1228–1242.

Rowling, J. K. (1997). *Harry Potter and the sorcerer's stone.* New York: Scholastic Inc.

Rowling, J. K. (1999). *Harry Potter and the chamber of secrets.* New York: Scholastic Inc.

Roy, R., Benenson, J. F., & Lilly, F. (2000). Beyond intimacy: Conceptualizing sex differences in same-sex friendships. *Journal of Psychology, 134,* 93–101.

Rubin, L. (1985). *Just friends.* New York: Harper & Row.

Rubin, L. B. (1996). Reflections on friendship. In K. M. Galvin & P. J. Cooper (Eds.), *Making connections: Readings in relational communication* (pp. 254–257). Los Angeles: Roxbury.

Rubin, Z. (1973). *Liking and loving: An invitation to social psychology.* New York: Holt, Rinehart & Winston.

Rubin, Z., Peplau, L. A., & Hill, C. T. (1981). Loving and leaving: Sex differences in romantic attachments. *Sex Roles, 7,* 821–835.

Rueter, M. A., & Koerner, A. F. (2008). The effect of family communication patterns on adopted adolescent adjustment. *Journal of Marriage and Family, 70,* 715–727.

Rusbult, C. E. (1987). Responses to dissatisfaction in close relationships: The exit-voice-loyalty-neglect model. In D. Perlman & S. Duck (Eds.), *Intimate relationships: Development, dynamics, and deterioration* (pp. 209–237). Newbury Park, CA: Sage.

Rusbult, C. E., Arriaga, X. B., & Agnew, C. R. (2001). Interdependence in close relationships. In G. J. O. Fletcher & M. S. Clark (Eds.), *Blackwell handbook of social psychology, vol. 2: Interpersonal processes* (pp. 359–387). Oxford: Blackwell.

Saarni, C. (1993). Socialization of emotion. In M. Lewis & J. M. Haviland (Eds.), *Handbook of emotions* (pp. 435–446). New York: Guilford Press.

Sabourin, T. C., Infante, D. A., & Rudd, J. E. (1993). Verbal aggression in marriages: A comparison of violent, distressed but nonviolent, and nondistressed couples. *Human Communication Research, 20,* 245–267.

Sahlstein, E. (2004). Relating at a distance: Negotiating being together and being apart in long-distance relationships. *Journal of Social and Personal Relationships, 21,* 689–702.

Salovey, P., & Rodin, J. (1988). Coping with envy and jealousy. *Journal of Social and Clinical Psychology, 7,* 15–33.

Savicki, V., Kelley, M., & Oesterreich, E. (1999). Judgments of gender in computer-mediated communication. *Computers in Human Behavior, 15,* 185–194.

Schaefer, C. M., & Tudor, T. R. (2001). Managing workplace romances. *SAM Advanced Management Journal, 66*(3), 4–10.

Schein, E. H. (1985). *Organizational culture and leadership*. San Francisco: Jossey-Bass.

Scherer, K. R. (1974). Acoustic concomitants of emotional dimensions: Judging affect from synthesized tone sequences. In S. Weitz (Ed.), *Nonverbal communication: Readings with commentary* (pp. 105–111). New York: Oxford University Press.

Scherer, K. R. (2001). Appraisal considered as a process of multilevel sequential checking. In K. R. Scherer, A. Schorr, & T. Johnstone (Eds.), *Appraisal processes in emotion* (pp. 92–120). Oxford, UK: Oxford University Press.

Schlaepfer, T. E., Harris, G. J., Tien, A. Y., Peng, L., Lee, S., & Pearlson, G. D. (1995). Structural differences in the cerebral cortex of healthy female and male subjects: A magnetic resonance imaging study. *Psychiatry Research, 61,* 129–135.

Schneider, C. S., & Kenny, D. A. (2000). Cross-sex friends who were once romantic partners: Are they platonic friends now? *Journal of Social and Personal Relationships, 17*(3), 451–466.

Schramm, W. (Ed.). (1954). *The process and effects of mass communication*. Urbana: University of Illinois Press.

Schrodt, P. (2006). Development and validation of the Stepfamily Life Index. *Journal of Social and Personal Relationships, 23*(3), 427–444.

Schrodt, P., & Afifi, T. D. (2007). Communication processes that predict young adults' feelings of being caught and their associations with mental health and family satisfaction. *Communication Monographs, 74*(2), 200–228.

Searle, J. (1965). What is a speech act? In M. Black (Ed.), *Philosophy in America* (pp. 221–239). Ithaca, NY: Cornell University Press.

Searle, J. A. (1969). *Speech acts*. Cambridge, UK: Cambridge University Press.

Searle, J. A. (1976). The classification of illocutionary acts. *Language in Society, 5,* 1–24.

Sebold, A. (2002). *The lovely bones*. New York: Little, Brown.

Seta, J. J., & Seta, C. E. (1993). Stereotypes and the generation of compensatory and noncompensatory expectancies of group members. *Personality and Social Psychology Bulletin, 19,* 722–731.

SFGate.com. (2005, February 6). Ad campaigns that go wrong. Retrieved from http://articles.sfgate.com/2005-02-06/opinion/17360611_1_parker-pens-latin-america-clairol

Shackelford, T. K., & Buss, D. M. (1997). Anticipation of marital dissolution as a consequence of spousal infidelity. *Journal of Social and Personal Relationships, 14,* 793–808.

Shah, M. B., King, S., & Patel, A. S. (2004). Intercultural disposition and communication competence of future pharmacists. *American Journal of Pharmaceutical Education, 69,* 1–11.

Shannon, C. E., & Weaver, W. (1949). *The mathematical theory of communication*. Urbana: University of Illinois Press.

Shaver, P. R., Wu, S., & Schwartz, J. C. (1992). Cross-cultural similarities and differences in emotion and its representation. In M. S. Clark (Ed.), *Emotion* (pp. 175–212). Newbury Park, CA: Sage.

Shedletsky, L. J., & Aitken, J. E. (2004). *Human communication on the Internet*. Boston: Pearson Education/Allyn and Bacon.

Shelton, J. N., Richeson, J. A., & Bergsieker, H. B. (2009). Interracial friendship development and attributional biases. *Journal of Social and Personal Relationships, 26*(2–3), 179–193.

Shelton, J. N., Trail, T. E., West, T. V., & Bergsieker, H. B. (2010). From strangers to friends: The interpersonal process model of intimacy in developing interracial friendships. *Journal of Social and Personal Relationships, 27*(1), 71–90.

Shoda, Y., Mischel, W., & Peake, P. K. (1990). Predicting adolescent cognitive and self-regulatory competencies from preschool delay of gratification: Identifying diagnostic conditions. *Developmental Psychology, 26*(6), 978–986.

Shweder, R. A. (1993). The cultural psychology of the emotions. In M. Lewis & J. M. Haviland (Eds.), *Handbook of emotions* (pp. 417–431). New York: Guilford Press.

Sias, P. M., & Cahill, D. J. (1998). From co-workers to friends: The development of peer friendships in the workplace. *Western Journal of Communication, 62,* 273–300.

Sias, P. M., Drzewiecka, J. A., Meares, M., Bent, R., Konomi, Y., Ortega, M., & White, C. (2008). Intercultural friendship development. *Communication Reports, 21*(1), 1–13.

Sias, P. M., Heath, R. G., Perry, T., Silva, D., & Fix, B. (2004). Narratives of workplace friendship deterioration. *Journal of Social and Personal Relationships, 21*(3), 321–340.

Sias, P. M., Krone, K. J., & Jablin, F. M. (2002). An ecological systems perspective on workplace relationships. In M. L. Knapp & J. A. Daly (Eds.), *Handbook of interpersonal communication* (pp. 615–642). Thousand Oaks, CA: Sage.

Sias, P. M., & Perry, T. (2004). Disengaging from workplace relationships: A research note. *Human Communication Research, 30,* 589–602.

Sillars, A., Roberts, L. J., Leonard, K. E., & Dun, T. (2000). Cognition during marital conflict: The relationship of thought and talk. *Journal of Social and Personal Relationships, 17,* 479–502.

Sillars, A., Smith, T., & Koerner, A. (2010). Misattributions contributing to empathic (in)accuracy during parent–adolescent conflict discussions. *Journal of Social and Personal Relationships, 27*(6), 727–747.

Sillars, A. L. (1980). Attributions and communication in roommate conflicts. *Communication Monographs, 47,* 180–200.

Sillars, A. L., & Wilmot, W. W. (1994). Communication strategies in conflict and mediation. In J. Wiemann & J. Daly (Eds.), *Communicating strategically: Strategies in interpersonal communication* (pp. 163–190). Hillsdale, NJ: Erlbaum.

Silvera, D. H., Krull, D. S., & Sassler, M. A. (2002). Typhoid Pollyanna: The effect of category valence on retrieval order of positive and negative category members. *European Journal of Cognitive Psychology, 14,* 227–236.

Silversides, B. V. (1994). *The face pullers: Photographing native Canadians, 1871–1939.* Saskatoon, Saskatchewan, Canada: Fifth House.

Silverstein, M., & Giarrusso, R. (2010). Aging and family life: A decade review. *Journal of Marriage and Family, 72,* 1039–1058.

Simonson, H. (2011). *Major Pettigrew's last stand.* New York: Random House.

Smith, C. A., & Kirby, L. D. (2004). Appraisal as a pervasive determinant of anger. *Emotion, 4,* 133–138.

Smith, G., & Anderson, K. J. (2005). Students' ratings of professors: The teaching style contingency for Latino/a professors. *Journal of Latinos and Education, 4,* 115–136.

Smith, L., Heaven, P. C. L., & Ciarrochi, J. (2008). Trait emotional intelligence, conflict communication patterns, and relationship satisfaction. *Personality and Individual Differences, 44,* 1314–1325.

Snyder, M. (1974). Self-monitoring of expressive behavior. *Journal of Personality and Social Psychology, 30,* 526–537.

Solomon, D. H., & Samp, J. A. (1998). Power and problem appraisal: Perceptual foundations of the chilling effect in dating relationships. *Journal of Social and Personal Relationships, 15,* 191–209.

Soto, J. A., Levenson, R. W., & Ebling, R. (2005). Cultures of moderation and expression: Emotional experience, behavior, and physiology in Chinese Americans and Mexican Americans. *Emotion, 5,* 154–165.

Spears, R., Postmes, T., Lea, M., & Watt, S. E. (2001). A SIDE view of social influence. In J. P. Forgas & K. D. Williams (Eds.), *Social influence: Direct and indirect processes* (pp. 331–350). Philadelphia: Psychology Press–Taylor and Francis Group.

Spender, D. (1984). Defining reality: A powerful tool. In C. Kramarae, M. Schultz, & W. O'Barr (Eds.), *Language and power* (pp. 195–205). Beverly Hills, CA: Sage.

Spender, D. (1990). *Man made language.* London: Pandora Press.

Spitzberg, B. (1997). A model of intercultural communication competence. In L. A. Samovar & R. E. Porter (Eds.), *Intercultural communication: A reader* (pp. 379–391). Belmont, CA: Wadsworth.

Spitzberg, B. H., & Cupach, W. R. (1984). *Interpersonal communication competence.* Beverly Hills, CA: Sage.

Spitzberg, B. H., & Cupach, W. R. (2002). Interpersonal skills. In M. L. Knapp & J. A. Daly (Eds.), *Handbook of interpersonal communication* (3rd ed., pp. 564–611). Thousand Oaks, CA: Sage.

Sprecher, S. (2001). A comparison of emotional consequences of and changes in equity over time using global and domain-specific measures of equity. *Journal of Social and Personal Relationships, 18,* 477–501.

Sprecher, S., & Metts, S. (1989). Development of the romantic beliefs scale and examination of the effects of gender and gender-role orientation. *Journal of Social and Personal Relationships, 6,* 387–411.

Sprecher, S., & Metts, S. (1999). Romantic beliefs: Their influence on relationships and patterns of change over time. *Journal of Social and Personal Relationships, 16*(6), 834–851.

Stafford, L. (2003). Maintaining romantic relationships: A summary and analysis of one research program. In D. J. Canary & M. Dainton (Eds.), *Maintaining relationships through communication: Relational, contextual, and cultural variations* (pp. 51–77). Mahwah, NJ: Erlbaum.

Stafford, L. (2005). *Maintaining long-distance and cross-residential relationships.* Mahwah, NJ: Erlbaum.

Stafford, L. (2010). Measuring relationship maintenance behaviors: Critique and development of the revised relationship maintenance behavior scale. *Journal of Social and Personal Relationships, 28,* 278–303.

Stafford, L., & Canary, D. J. (1991). Maintenance strategies and romantic relationship type, gender, and relational characteristics. *Journal of Social and Personal Relationships, 8,* 217–242.

Stafford, L., Dainton, M., & Haas, S. (2000). Measuring routine and strategic relational maintenance: Scale revision, sex versus gender roles, and the prediction of relational characteristics. *Communication Monographs, 67,* 306–323.

Stafford, L., & Merolla, A. J. (2007). Idealization, reunions, and stability in long-distance dating relationships. *Journal of Social and Personal Relationships, 24,* 37–54.

Stafford, L., Merolla, A. J., and Castle, J. (2006). When long-distance dating partners become geographically close. *Journal of Social and Personal Relationships, 23,* 901–919.

Stiff, J. B., Dillard, J. P., Somera, L., Kim, H., & Sleight, C. (1988). Empathy, communication, and prosocial behavior. *Communication Monographs, 55,* 198–213.

Stimson, E. (1998, March). The real Mister Rogers: This Presbyterian minister is as genuinely nice in person as he is on TV. Retrieved from http://www.adventistreview.org/thisweek/story5.htm

Stone, E. (2004). *Black sheep and kissing cousins: How our family stories shape us.* New Brunswick, NJ: Transaction.

Strauss, V. (2006, March 21). Putting parents in their place: Outside class. *The Washington Post,* p. A08.

Streek, J. (1980). Speech acts in interaction: A critique of Searle. *Discourse Processes, 3,* 133–154.

Streek, J. (1993). Gesture as communication I: Its coordination with gaze and speech. *Communication Monographs, 60,* 275–299.

Suitor, J. J., Sechrist, J., Plikuhn, M., Pardo, S. T., Gilligan, M., & Pillemer, K. (2009). The role of perceived maternal favoritism in sibling relations in midlife. *Journal of Marriage and Family, 71,* 1026–1038.

Suler, J. R. (2004). The online disinhibition effect. *CyberPsychology and Behavior, 7,* 321–326.

Surra, C., & Hughes, D. (1997). Commitment processes in accounts of the development of premarital relationships. *Journal of Marriage and the Family, 59,* 5–21.

Swain, S. O. (1992). Men's friendships with women: Intimacy, sexual boundaries, and the informant role. In P. M. Nardi (Ed.), *Men's friendships: Vol. 2. Research on men and masculinities* (pp. 153–172). Newbury Park, CA: Sage.

Talbot, N. (2008). Using body language to attract. Retrieved from http://www.allstardatingtips.com/body-language.html

Tannen, D. (1990). *You just don't understand: Women and men in conversation.* New York: Morrow.

Tardy, C. H. (2000). Self-disclosure and health: Revising Sidney Jourard's hypothesis. In S. Petronio (Ed.), *Balancing the secrets of private disclosures* (pp. 111–122). Mahwah, NJ: Erlbaum.

Tardy, C., & Dindia, K. (1997). Self-disclosure. In O. Hargie (Ed.), *The handbook of communication skills.* London: Routledge.

Tavernise, S. (2011, May 26). Married couples are no longer a majority, census finds. *The New York Times.* Retrieved from http://www.nytimes.com

Tavris, C. (1989). *Anger: The misunderstood emotion.* New York: Touchstone Press.

Thayer, R. E., Newman, J. R., & McClain, T. M. (1994). Self-regulation of mood: Strategies for changing a bad mood, raising energy, and reducing tension. *Journal of Personality and Social Psychology, 67,* 910–925.

The English language: Words borrowed from other languages. (n.d.). Retrieved from http://www.krysstal.com/borrow.html

The Global Development Research Center (2011, November 6). www.gdrc.org

The National Center for Victims of Crimes. (2008). *Dating violence fact sheet.* Retrieved from http://www.ncvc.org

Thomas, L. T., & Levine, T. R. (1994). Disentangling listening and verbal recall: Related but separate constructs? *Human Communication Research, 21,* 103–127.

Thompson, J. K., Heinberg, L. J., Altabe, M., & Tantleff-Dunn, S. (1999). *Exacting beauty: Theory, assessment, and treatment of body image disturbances.* Washington, DC: American Psychological Association.

Thorne, B. (1986). Boys and girls together . . . but mostly apart: Gender arrangements in elementary schools. In W. Hartup & Z. Rubin (Eds.), *Relationships and development* (pp. 167–184). Hillsdale, NJ: Erlbaum.

Tillema, T., Dijst, M., & Schwanen, T. (2010). Face-to-face and electronic communications in maintaining social networks: The influence of geographical and relational distance and of information content. *New Media & Society, 12*(6), 965–983.

Ting-Toomey, S. (1985). Toward a theory of conflict and culture. In W. B. Gudykunst, L. P. Stewart, & S. Ting-Toomey (Eds.), *Communication, culture, and organizational processes* (pp. 71–86). Beverly Hills, CA: Sage.

Ting-Toomey, S. (1997). Managing intercultural conflicts effectively. In L. A. Samovar & R. E. Porter (Eds.), *Intercultural communication: A reader* (pp. 392–403). Belmont, CA: Wadsworth.

Ting-Toomey, S. (1999). *Communicating across cultures.* New York: Guilford Press.

Ting-Toomey, S. (2005). The matrix of face: An updated face-negotiation theory. In W. B. Gudykunst (Ed.), Theorizing about intercultural communication (pp. 211–234). Thousand Oaks, CA: Sage.

Tippett, M. (1994). The face pullers [Review of the book *The face pullers,* by B. V. Silversides]. *Canadian Historical Review, 75,* 1–4.

Tjaden, P., & Thoennes, N. (2000). Full report of the prevalence, incidence, and consequences of violence against women: Findings from the national violence against women survey. *Research Report.* Washington, DC, and Atlanta, GA: U.S. Department of Justice, National Institute of Justice, and U.S. Department of Health and Human Services, Centers for Disease Control and Prevention.

Tovares, A. V. (2010). All in the family: Small stories and narrative construction of a shared family identity that includes pets. *Narrative Inquiry, 20*(1), 1–19.

Tracy, S. J., Lutgen-Sandvik, P., & Alberts, J. K. (2006). Nightmares, demons, and slaves: Exploring the painful metaphors of workplace bullying. *Management Communication Quarterly, 20*(2), 148–185.

Triandis, H. (1988). Collectivism v. individualism: A reconceptualisation of a basic concept in cross-cultural social psychology. In G. K. Verma & C. Bagley (Eds.), Cross-cultural studies of personality, attitudes and cognition (pp. 60–95). New York: St. Martin's Press.

Tsai, J. L., & Levenson, R. W. (1997). Cultural influences of emotional responding: Chinese American and European American dating couples during interpersonal conflict. *Journal of Cross-Cultural Psychology, 28,* 600–625.

Turkle, S. (1995). *Life on the screen: Identity in the age of the Internet.* New York: Simon & Schuster.

Turner, J. C., Hogg, M. A., Oakes, P. J., Reicher, S. D., & Wetherell, M. S. (1987). *Rediscovering the social group: A self-categorization theory.* Cambridge, MA: Basil Blackwell.

Tyner, L. J., & Clinton, M. S. (2010). Sexual harassment in the workplace: Are human resource professionals victims? *Journal of Organizational Culture, Communications and Conflict, 14*(1), 33–49.

U. S. Census Bureau (2012, May 17). Most children younger than age 1 are minorities, census bureau reports. Retrieved from http://www.census.gov/newsroom/releases/archives/population/cb12-90.html

U.S. Equal Employment Opportunity Commission. (1980). Guidelines on discrimination because of sex. *Federal Register, 45,* 74676–74677.

U.S. Equal Employment Opportunity Commission. (2011). *Sexual harassment charges: 1997–2011.* Retrieved from http://www.eeoc.gov/statistics/enforcement/sexual_harassment.cfm

Vallacher, R. R., Nowak, A., Froehlich, M., & Rockloff, M. (2002). The dynamics of self-evaluation. *Personality and Social Psychology Review, 6,* 370–379.

Vangelisti, A. L., Crumley, L. P., & Baker, J. L. (1999). Family portraits: Stories as standards for family relationships. *Journal of Social and Personal Relationships, 16*(3), 335–368.

Vazire, S., & Gosling, S. D. (2004). E-Perceptions: Personality impressions based on personal websites. *Journal of Personality and Social Psychology, 87,* 123–132.

Veale, D., Kinderman, P., Riley, S., & Lambrou, C. (2003). Self-discrepancy in body dysmorphic disorder. *British Journal of Clinical Psychology, 42,* 157–169.

Villaume, W. A., & Bodie, G. D. (2007). Discovering the listener within us: The impact of trait-like personality variables and communicator styles on preferences for listening style. *International Journal of Listening, 21,* 102–123.

Vogl-Bauer, S. (2003). Maintaining family relationships. In D. J. Canary & M. Dainton (Eds.), *Maintaining relationships through communication: Relational, contextual, and cultural variations* (pp. 31–50). Mahwah, NJ: Erlbaum.

Waldron, H. B., Turner, C. W., Alexander, J. F., & Barton, C. (1993). Coding defensive and supportive communications:

Discriminant validity and subcategory convergence. *Journal of Family Psychology, 7,* 197–203.

Waldvogel, J. (2007). Greetings and closings in workplace email. *Journal of Computer-Mediated Communication, 12,* 122–143.

Wallace, P. (1999). *The psychology of the Internet.* Cambridge, UK: Cambridge University Press.

Wallack, T. (2005, 24 January). Blogs: Beware if your blog is related to work. *The San Francisco Chronicle.* Retrieved from http://www.sfgate.com

Walther, J. B., & Parks, M. R. (2002). Cues filtered out, cues filtered in: Computer-mediated communication and relationships. In M. L. Knapp & J. A. Daly (Eds.), *Handbook of interpersonal communication* (3rd ed., pp. 529–563). Thousand Oaks, CA: Sage.

Walther, J. B., Van Der Heide, B., Hamel, L., & Schulman, H. (2008, May). *Self-generated* versus *other-generated statements and impressions in computer-mediated communication: A test of warranting theory using Facebook.* Paper presented at the annual meeting of the International Communication Association, Montreal, Canada.

Walther, J. B., Van Der Heide, B., Kim, S. Y., Westerman, D., & Tong, S. T. (2008). The role of friends' appearance and behavior on evaluations of individuals on Facebook: Are we known by the company we keep? *Human Communication Research, 34,* 28–49.

Wang, H., & Andersen, P. A. (2007, May). *Computer-mediated communication in relationship maintenance: An examination of self-disclosure in long-distance friendships.* Paper presented at the annual meeting of the International Communication Association, San Francisco, CA.

Warr, P. B., and Payne, R. (1982). Experiences of strain and pleasure among British adults. *Social Science & Medicine, 16*(19), 1691–1697.

Waterman, A. (1984). *The psychology of individualism.* New York: Praeger.

Watson, K. W., Barker, L. L., & Weaver, J. B., III. (1995). The listening styles profile (LSP-16): Development and validation of an instrument to assess four listening styles. *International Journal of Listening, 9,* 1–13.

Watzlawick, P., Beavin, J. H., & Jackson, D. D. (1967). *Pragmatics of human communication: A study of interactional patterns, pathologies, and paradoxes.* New York: Norton.

Weger, H., & Emmett, M. C. (2009). Romantic intent, relationship uncertainty, and relationship maintenance in young adults' cross-sex friendships. *Journal of Social and Personal Relationships, 26*(6–7), 964–988.

Weinberg, N., Schmale, J. D., Uken, J., & Wessel, K. (1995). Computer-mediated support groups. *Social Work with Groups, 17,* 43–55.

Weisz, C., & Wood, L. F. (2005). Social identity support and friendship outcomes: A longitudinal study predicting who will be friends and best friends 4 years later. *Journal of Social and Personal Relationships, 22*(3), 416–432.

Welch, R. D., & Houser, M. E. (2010). Extending the four-category model of adult attachment: An interpersonal model of friendship attachment. *Journal of Social and Personal Relationships, 27*(3), 351–366.

Wellman, B. (1992). Men in networks: Private communities, domestic friendships. In P. M. Nardi (Ed.), *Men's friendships: Vol. 2. Research on men and masculinities* (pp. 74–114). Newbury Park, CA: Sage.

Wells, G. L., Lindsay, R. C. L., & Tousignant, J. P. (1980). Effects of expert psychological advice on human performance in judging the validity of eyewitness testimony. *Law and Human Behavior, 4,* 275–285.

Wheeless, L. R. (1978). A follow-up study of the relationships among trust, disclosure, and interpersonal solidarity. *Human Communication Research, 4,* 143–145.

White, G. L. (1980). Physical attractiveness and courtship progress. *Journal of Personality and Social Psychology, 39,* 660–668.

Whorf, B. L. (1952). *Collected papers on metalinguistics.* Washington, DC: Department of State, Foreign Service Institute.

Widmer, E., Treas, J., & Newcomb, R. (1998). Attitudes toward nonmarital sex in 24 countries. *Journal of Sex Research, 35,* 349–358.

Wiederman, M. W., & Kendall, E. (1999). Evolution, sex, and jealousy: Investigation with a sample from Sweden. *Evolution and Human Behavior, 20,* 121–128.

Wiemann, J. M. (1977). Explication and test of a model of communicative competence. *Human Communication Research, 3,* 195–213.

Williams, W. L. (1992). The relationship between male-male friendship and male-female marriage: American Indian and Asian comparisons. In P. M. Nardi (Ed.), *Men's friendships: Vol. 2. Research on men and masculinities* (pp. 186–200). Newbury Park, CA: Sage.

Wilmot, W. W., & Hocker, J. L. (2010). *Interpersonal conflict* (8th ed.). Boston: McGraw-Hill.

Winstead, B. A., Derlaga, V. J., & Rose, S. (1997). *Gender and close relationships.* Thousand Oaks, CA: Sage.

Winterson, J. (1993). *Written on the body.* New York: Knopf.

Wolvin, A., & Coakley, C. G. (1996). *Listening.* Madison, WI: Brown & Benchmark.

Wolvin, A. D. (1987). *Culture as a listening variable.* Paper presented at the summer conference of the International Listening Association, Toronto, Canada.

Wood, J. T. (1998). *But I thought you meant . . . : Misunderstandings in human communication.* Mountain View, CA: Mayfield.

Wood, W., Rhodes, N., & Whelan, M. (1989). Sex differences in positive well-being: A consideration of emotional style and marital status. *Psychological Bulletin, 106,* 249–264.

Worthen, J. B., Garcia-Rivas, G., Green, C. R., & Vidos, R. A. (2000). Tests of a cognitive-resource-allocation account of the bizarreness effect. *Journal of General Psychology, 127,* 117–144.

Wu, C. (2011, September 21). Students vote to adopt gender-neutral constitution. The Student Life. Retrieved from http://tsl.pomona.edu/articles/2011/9/22/news/356-students-vote-to-adopt-gender-neutral-constitution

Wu, D. Y. H., & Tseng, W. (1985). Introduction: The characteristics of Chinese culture. In W. Tseng & D. Y. H. Wu (Eds.), *Chinese culture and mental health* (pp. 3–13). Orlando, FL: Academic Press.

YouTube Statistics. (n.d.). Retrieved from http://www.youtube.com/t/press_statistics

Zacchilli, T. L., Hendrick, C., & Hendrick, S. S. (2009). The romantic partner conflict scale: A new scale to measure relationship conflict. *Journal of Social and Personal Relationships, 26,* 1073–1096.

Zahn-Waxler, C. (2001). The development of empathy, guilt, and internalization of distress: Implications for gender differences in internalizing and externalizing problems. In R. Davidson (Ed.), *Anxiety, depression, and emotion: Wisconsin symposium on emotion, Vol. 1* (pp. 222–265). New York: Oxford University Press.

Znaniecki, F. (1934). *The method of sociology.* New York: Farrar & Rinehart.

Zorn, T. E. (1995). Bosses and buddies: Constructing and performing simultaneously hierarchical and close friendship relationships. In J. T. Wood & S. Duck (Eds.), *Under-studied relationships: Off the beaten track* (pp. 122–147). Thousand Oaks, CA: Sage.

Zuckerman, M., Hodgins, H., & Miyake, K. (1990). The vocal attractiveness paradigm: Replication and elaboration. *Journal of Nonverbal Behavior, 14,* 97–112.

Zuckerman, M., Miyake, K., & Hodgins, H. S. (1991). Cross-channel effects of vocal and physical attractiveness and their implications for interpersonal perception. *Journal of Personality and Social Psychology, 60,* 545–554.

INDEX

More Media in LaunchPad

}

bedfordstmartins.com/ipcandyou

Go online to find the **Key Terms Videos** that complement the book content. Here is a list of the videos and where their concepts appear in the text. Find even more videos in LaunchPad.